REFERENCE
LIBRARY
OF
BLACK
AMERICA

REFERENCE LIBRARY OF BLACK AMERICA

Volume IV

Edited by
Kenneth Estell

Distributed by Afro-American Press

Reference Library of Black America is based upon the sixth edition of *The African American Almanac*, published by Gale Research Inc. It has been published in this 5-volume set to facilitate wider usage among students.

While every effort has been made to ensure the reliability of the information presented in this publication, Gale Research Inc. does not guarantee the accuracy of the data contained herein. Gale accepts no payment for listing; and inclusion in the publication of any organization, agency, institution, publication, service, or individual does not imply endorsement of the publisher. Errors brought to the attention of the publisher and verified to the satisfaction of the publisher will be corrected in future editions.

The paper used in this publication meets the minimum requirements of American National Standard for Information Sciences—Permanence Paper for Printed Library Materials, ANSI Z 39.48-1984.

Printed in the United States of America
Printed in 1995

Advisory Board

Contributors

Stephen W. Angell
Associate Professor of Religion, Florida A&M University

Robin Armstrong
Adjunct Lecturer, University of Michigan, Dearborn

Claudette Bennett
Bureau of the Census, United States Department of Commerce

John Cohassey

Allen G. Harris
President, Air Force Association,
General Dainiel James Chapter

Hayward Derrick Horton
Assistant Professor of Sociology, Iowa State University

George Johnson
Professor of Law, Howard University School of Law

Faustine C. Jones-Wilson
Professor of Education, Howard University; Editor, *The Journal of Negro Education*

Donald Franklin Joyce
Director, Felix G. Woodward Library, Austin Peay State University

Kwame Kenyatta
Detroit Board of Education; New African People's Organization

Mark Kram
Sportswriter, *Philadelphia Daily News*

Marilyn Hortense Mackel
Associate Professor, Western State University College of Law, Judge Pro Tempore,
Los Angeles County Superior Court, Juvenile Department

Ionis Bracy Martin
Lecturer, Central Connecticut State University

Dan Morgenstern
Director, Institute for Jazz Studies, Rutgers University

Wilson J. Moses
Professor of History, Pennsylvania State University

Richard Prince
National Association of Black Journalists

Nancy Rampson

Michael D. Woodard
Director, Los Angeles Institute for Multicultural Training;
Visiting Scholar, UCLA Center for Afro-American Studies

Contents

Contents

Contents

Introduction

The Reference Library of Black America is based upon the sixth edition of *The African-American Almanac*, first published in 1967 as *The Negro Almanac* and since cited by *Library Journal* as an outstanding reference work.

New Features in This Edition

All material was extensively reviewed by the editor and a board of prominent advisors and, where appropriate, updated and/or expanded. For example, the expanded chapter on national organizations now includes a history of black organizations in the United States and provides biographical information on leaders of major associations, past and present. The chapter on fine art now includes coverage of the applied arts—architecture, industrial design, fashion design, and graphic art—and a directory of museums in the United States.

Some chapters which appeared in the fifth edition were totally rewritten to focus on issues facing contemporary African-Americans. In particular the chapters on law, employment and income, the family, and education, were rewritten to reflect new and changing concerns within the black community regarding such issues as racism in the criminal justice system, factors in employment and unemployment, family structure and stability, and African-centered education.

Several completely new topics were added to this edition, including: a chapter on Africans in America since the first arrival of Africans in the Western Hemisphere through the Civil War and Reconstruction; a chapter on black nationalism covering the history of cultural nationalism and Pan-Africanism in the United States; a chapter on popular music covering contemporary music forms, including rhythm and blues, soul, gospel, rap, and country music. In addition, an appendix listing African-American recipients of selected major awards is new to this edition.

While many chapters have been expanded, others which appeared in the fifth edition have been incorporated into new or existing sections of the book. For example, biographical profiles included in the chapters on women and on prominent African Americans have been absorbed into existing chapters.

Content and Arrangement

Information in this edition of *The Reference Library of Black America* appears in twenty-seven subject chapters. Many chapters open with an essay focusing on historical developments or the contributions of African Americans to the subject area, followed by concise biographical profiles of selected individuals.

Although the individuals featured in this edition represent only a small portion of the African-American community, they embody excellence and diversity in their respective fields of endeavor. Where an individual has made a significant contribution in more than one area, his or her biographical profile appears in the subject area for which he or she is best known, and cross references in other chapters lead the user to the profile.

In order to facilitate further research, a bibliography and list of publishers is provided. The bibliography has been divided into two major divisions: "Africana" and "African Americana." Within these two divisions titles are arranged alphabetically by author under categories indicative of their subject matter.

More than eight hundred maps and illustrations aid the reader in understanding the topics and people covered in the work. A name and keyword index provides access to the contents.

19

Media

19

Media

**Book Publishers ■ Newspaper and Magazine Publishers ■ Broadcasting
■ Editors, Journalists, and Media Executives ■ Publishers, Newspapers, Magazines
and Journals, Radio Networks, Radio Stations, Cable Television Networks, and
Television Stations**

**Essays by Donald Franklin Joyce
and Richard Prince**

Book Publishers

by Donald Joyce

Since black book publishing began in the United States in 1817, three types of publishers have emerged in this sector of the American book publishing industry: religious publishers; institutional publishers; and trade book publishers.

Religious Publishers

Religious publishing enterprises were established by black religious denominations in order to publish books and other literature to assist clergy and laity in recording denominational history and provide religious instruction. Some black religious publishers also published books on secular subjects which were generally related to celebrating some aspect of black culture or documenting black history.

Prior to the Civil War, two black religious publishing enterprises existed. The African Methodist Episcopal Church organized the AME Book Concern in Philadelphia in 1817—the first black-owned book publishing enterprise in the United States. Publishing its first book in that same year, *The Book of Discipline*, the AME Book Concern published a host of classic religious and secular books until its operations were suspended in 1952 by the General Conference of the African Methodist Episcopal Church. In 1841 the African Methodist Episcopal Zion Church formed the AME Zion Book Concern in New York City. This firm, which only published religious works, was moved to its present location in Charlotte, North Carolina, in 1894, where it continues to be an active book publisher.

In Jackson, Tennessee, the Colored Methodist Episcopal Church (CME), presently known as the Christian Methodist Episcopal Church, started the CME Publishing House in 1870. The CME Publishing House, which only publishes books on religious subjects, is currently located in Memphis, Tennessee.

Another book publishing enterprise owned by black Methodists is the AME Sunday School Union and Publishing House, which was established in Bloomington, Illinois, in 1882, but moved to Nashville, Tennessee, in 1886. Publishing secular and religious books, the AME Sunday School Union and Publishing House remains today as the oldest publishing unit owned by the African Methodist Episcopal Church.

One of the most successful black religious publishers to come into existence during the nineteenth century was the National Baptist Publishing Board. Under the leadership of Dr. Richard Henry Boyd and the auspices of the National Baptist Convention, U.S.A., the National Baptist Publishing Board was organized in Nashville in 1896. By 1913, this well-managed firm, publishing religious and secular books, grew to become one of the largest black-owned businesses in the United States. In 1915, however, a dispute arose between the National Baptist Convention, U.S.A. and Dr. Richard Henry Boyd over the ownership of the National Baptist Publishing Board. In a court suit, the Tennessee Supreme Court decided in favor of Dr. Boyd; today the National Publishing Board, owned by the Boyd family, is a thriving religious publishing enterprise.

In 1907 the Church of God in Christ established the Church of God in Christ Publishing House in Memphis. Restricting its publications to religious books and pamphlets, this publisher continues today to meet the ever expanding needs for religious literature for one of the fastest growing black religious denominations in the United States.

Faced with the loss of the National Baptist Publishing Board, the National Baptist Convention, U.S.A., Inc. established in 1916 the Sunday School Publishing Board of the National Baptist Convention, U.S.A., Inc., in Nashville. Over the years, this firm has developed into one of the largest black-owned publishing enterprises in the United States, publishing religious and secular books and pamphlets.

Like the Sunday School Publishing Board of the National Baptist Convention, U.S.A., Inc., Muhammad's Temple No. 2, Publications Department, which was founded in 1956 by the Nation of Islam, published religious as well as secular books. Between 1956 and 1974, several books were issued by this firm. However, since 1974, Muhammad's Temple No. 2, Publications Department has become inactive.

Institutional Publishers

During the last decades of the nineteenth century and the early decades of the twentieth century, educational, cultural, social, and political institutions were established to meet the specific needs of black Americans. Many of these institutions developed publishing programs, which included book publishing.

Colleges and Universities

Hampton Institute became the first black educational institution to published books when the Hampton Institute Press was established in 1871. An active publisher until 1940, the Hampton Institute Press published travel books, poetry, textbooks, songbooks, conference proceedings, and *The Southern Workman*, one of the leading national African-American periodicals published between 1871 and its demise in 1939.

In 1896 the Atlanta University Press entered the book publishing market with the release of *Atlanta University Publication Series*, which were monographs reporting on the findings of studies conducted by the university's department of sociology under the direction of Dr. W.E.B. DuBois. These works represented some of the earliest studies in urban sociology conducted in the South. The Atlanta University Press remained in operation until 1936.

Industrial Work of Tuskegee Graduates and Former Students During the Year 1910, compiled by Monroe N. Work (1911), was the first book released by the Tuskegee Institute Press. With the publication of this book and other works by the press, Booker T. Washington sought to publicize the success of Tuskegee's program to white philanthropists in the North. The Tuskegee Institute Press, which was active until 1958, published several other important works, including John Kenny's *The Negroes in Medicine* (1912) and *Lynching by States, 1882–1958* (1958), by Jessie Parkhurst Guzman.

In 1910 another book publishing enterprise was launched on the campus of Tuskegee Institute—the Negro Yearbook Publishing Company. A partnership consisting of Robert E. Park, the famed white sociologist, Emmett J. Scott, secretary to Booker T. Washington, and Monroe N. Work, a sociology professor, this firm published the first edition of *The Negro Yearbook* in 1912. The most comprehensive reference book to appear to date on African Americans, *The Negro Yearbook* was highly regarded as the definitive work on statistics and facts on blacks worldwide. However, the Negro Yearbook Publishing Company fell into financial trouble in 1929, and was taken over by Tuskegee Institute, which financed its operation until 1952. Between 1912 and 1952, *The Negro Yearbook* remained a classic model for most general reference works on blacks.

John W. Work's *The Negro and His Song* (1915) was the first book issued under the Fisk University Press imprint. During the 1930s and 1940s, when Charles Spurgeon Johnson chaired the university's department of sociology, several important studies were issued by the Fisk University Press, including E. Franklin Frazier's *The Free Negro Family* (1932); *The Economic Status of the Negro*, by Charles Spurgeon Johnson (1933); and *People versus Property*, by Herman Long and Charles Spurgeon Johnson (1947). The last publication released by the Fisk University Press was *Build a Future: Addresses Marking the Inauguration of Charles Spurgeon Johnson* (1949).

Although the board of trustees of Howard University approved the establishment of a university press on February 17, 1919, no university press was organized at the university until 1974. Nonetheless, between 1919 and 1974, several books bearing the "Howard University Press" imprint were published, including *The Founding of the School of Medicine of Howard University, 1868-1873*, by Walter Dyson (1929); and *The Housing of Negroes in Washington, DC: A Study in Human Ecology*, by William H. Jones (1929). On April 8, 1974, the Howard University Press was officially organized as a separate administrative unit within the university with a staff of twelve professionals experienced in book publishing. The Howard University Press' inaugural list of thirteen books included such titles as *A Poetic Equation: Conversations Between Nikki Giovanni and Margaret Walker* (1974) and *Saw the House in Half, a Novel*, by Oliver Jackman (1974). The Howard University Press continues to flourish as one of the most viable university presses in the country.

Cultural and Professional Organizations and Institutions

Black cultural and professional organizations and institutions have also developed publishing programs which included book publishing. The books published by these organizations documented areas of black history and depicted various aspects of African-American culture.

Founded in 1897 by the Reverend Alexander Crummell, nineteenth century black scholar, clergyman, and missionary, the American Negro Academy quickly organized a publishing program which embraced book publishing. The Academy, whose membership included many of the foremost black intellectuals of the day, released twenty-one occasional papers as pamphlets and monographs. The American Negro Academy went out of existence in 1928.

The Association for the Study of Negro Life and History (now the Association for the Study of Afro-American History and Literature) began its book publishing program in 1918. By 1940, the association had published twenty-eight books. After that year, the book publishing activities of the association declined until 1950, when its founder Carter G. Woodson died and provided in his will for the transfer of the Associated Publishers, Inc. to the association.

The Associates in Negro Folk Education, organized in Washington, DC by Howard University philosophy professor Alain Locke, with a grant from the American Adult Education Association, published a series of seven books, known as the Bronze Booklets, from 1935 to 1940. Written by black scholars on various aspects of black American life and edited by Dr. Locke, some of these titles included *A World View of Race*, by Ralph J. Bunche (1936), *The Negro and Economic Reconstruction*, by T. Arnold Hill (1937), and *Negro Poetry and Drama*, by Sterling Brown (1937).

Civil Rights, Social Welfare, and Political Organizations

In 1913, five years after its founding, the National Association for the Advancement of Colored People launched its book publishing program with the publication of three books: *A Child's Story of Dunbar*, by Julia L. Henderson (1919); *Norris Wright Cuney*, by Maude Cuney Hare (1913); and *Hazel*, by Mary White Ovington (1913). In 1914 George Williamson Crawford's *Prince Hall and His Followers* appeared and in 1919, *Thirty Years of Lynching in the United States, 1889–1918* was released. After 1919 few books were published by the NAACP, with the organization limiting its publishing to *Crisis* magazine, pamphlets, and its annual reports.

In contrast, the National Urban League has been a very active book publisher. The League first embarked on book publishing in 1927 when it published *Ebony and Topaz*, an anthology of Harlem Renaissance writers, poets, and artists edited by Charles Spurgeon Johnson. Through the years numerous sociological and economic studies on the plight of black Americans have been published by the Urban League, including *Negro Membership in Labor Unions* (1930), *Race, Fear and Housing in a Typical American Community* (1946), and *Power of the Ballot: A Handbook for Black Political Participation* (1973). In addition to these monograph studies, the organization began publishing *The State of Black America* in 1976.

Although the publishing program of the Universal Negro Improvement Association and African Communities League focused on the publication of its newspaper, *The Negro World*, this political organization also published books. Two volumes of *The Philosophy and Opinions of Marcus Garvey*, compiled and edited by Amy Jacques-Garvey, were published under the imprint of the

Press of the Universal Negro Improvement Association.

Commercial Publishers

Until the 1960s, most black commercial publishers engaged in book publishing enterprises were short-lived. However, in 1967 Haki Madhubuti founded Third World Press in Chicago. Third World Press is now the oldest continually operating black commercial book publisher in the United States.

Over the years, black publishers have come to find that a sizable black readship exists; since 1970 several major black publishers have emerged. In 1978 Black Classic Press was founded by librarian Paul Coates to publish obscure, but significant, works by and about people of African descent. In 1978 Dempsey Travis founded Urban Research Press. Open Hand Publishing Inc. was founded in 1981 by Anna Johnson.

In 1983 Kassahun Checole founded Africa World Press to publish material on the economic, political, and social development of Africa. Checole, a former African studies instructor at Rutgers University, found it difficult to attain books needed for his courses. Now African World Press publishes nearly sixty titles a year and its sister company, Red Sea Press, is now one of the largest distributors of material by and about Africans.

Just Us Books, Inc., founded by writer Wade Hudson and graphic artists Cheryl Willis Hudson, publishes books and educational material for children that focus on the African-American experience. The idea to start the children's book publisher first came to Cheryl in 1976, when she was unable to find black images to decorate her daughter's nursery. Just Us Books published its first book in 1988—an alphabet book featuring African-American children posed to create the letters. The company currently has sales of over $800,000.

Newspaper and Magazine Publishers

Newspapers

The black press in the United States is heir to a great, largely unheralded tradition. It began with the first black newspaper, *Freedom's Journal*, edited and published by Samuel Cornish and John B. Russwurm, on March 16, 1827. *The North Star*, the newspaper of abolitionist Frederick Douglass, was first published on December 3, 1847.

By the 1880s, African Americans' ability to establish a substantial cultural environment in many cities of the North led to the creation of a new wave of publications, including the *Washington Bee*, the *Indianapolis World*, the *Philadelphia Tribune*, the *Cleveland Gazette, Baltimore Afro-American* and the *New York Age*. By 1900, daily papers appeared in Norfolk, Kansas City, and Washington, DC.

Among famous black newspaper editors were William Monroe Trotter, editor of the *Boston Guardian*, a self-styled "radical" paper that showed no sympathy for the conciliatory stance of Booker T. Washington; Robert S. Abbott, whose *Chicago Defender* pioneered the use of headlines; and T. Thomas Fortune of the *New York Age*, who championed free public schools in an age when many opposed the idea.

In 1940 there were over 200 black newspapers, mostly weeklies with local readerships, and about 120 black magazines in the country. The *Pittsburgh Courier*, a weekly, had the largest circulation, about 140,000 per issue.

Haki Madhubuti

Headquarters for the *Baltimore Afro-American*, founded in 1892.

The National Negro Newspaper Publishers Association

The National Negro Newspaper Publishers Association, was founded in 1940 to represent black newspaper publishers. The organization scheduled workshops and trips abroad to acquaint editors and reporters with important news centers and news sources. A result was a trend to more progressive and interpretive reporting. In 1956 the association changed its name to the National Newspaper Publishers Association. Today it represents 148 publishers.

The Amsterdam News

Founded in 1909 by James H. Anderson, the *Amsterdam News*, has become one of the most well-known black newspaper in the nation. It was first published on Decem-ber 4, 1909 in Anderson's home on 132 W. 65th Street in New York City. At that time one of only fifty black "news sheets" in the country, the *Amsterdam News* had a staff of ten, consisted of six printed pages, and sold for 2 cents a copy. Since then, the paper has been printed at several Harlem addresses.

In 1935 the paper was sold to two black physicians, Clilan B. Powell and P.M.H. Savory. In 1971 the paper was again sold to a group of investors, headed by Clarence B. Jones and Percy E. Sutton.

Black Newspapers in the 1990s

A number of newspapers that began publishing in the 1960s, 70s, and 80s have gone out of business, mainly due to their inability to attract advertising, both locally and nationally, and because of general economic

857

decline. Today there are a reported 214 black newspapers in the United States. Of these, the papers with the largest paid circulations included, New York's *Black American*, the *Hartford Inquirer*, and the *Atlanta Voice*.

Magazines

As early as the 1830s, black magazines were being published in the United States. However, it was not until the 1900s that the first truly successful magazines appeared. In 1910 the National Association for the Advancement of Colored People began publishing *Crisis*. In November 1942 John H. Johnson launched the *Negro Digest* and in 1945 he published the first issue of *Ebony*. The idea for the new magazine came from two *Digest* writers, and the magazine's name

John Johnson with daughter, Linda Johnson.

was given to it by Johnson's wife, Enice Johnson. Its first print run of 25,000 copies sold out immediately. The success of *Ebony* led to the demise of the *Negro Digest*, and in 1951 the magazine ceased publication. However, *Ebony*, which has remained a success, has a circulation rate of almost 2 million.

In 1950 Johnson launched the magazine *Tan*, and in 1951 *Jet* magazine. Like *Ebony*, *Jet* was an instant success, selling over 300,000 copies in its first year. *Tan*, a woman's magazine, was later converted into a show business and personality monthly called *Black Stars*.

Since the founding of *Ebony*, several new and specialized black magazines have appeared. In 1967 *Black American Literature Review*, a journal presenting essays, interviews, poems, and book reviews, was founded. Also in 1967 Project Magazines, Inc. began publishing *Black Careers*. In 1969 the Black World Foundation published the first edition of *The Black Scholar*.

Earl G. Graves, a young businessman, in 1970 embarked on a concept to publish a monthly digest of news, commentary, and informative articles for blacks interested in business enterprise. Within a few short years his magazine, *Black Enterprise*, was accepted as the authority on African Americans in business and as an important advocate for an active, socially responsive, black middle class. Today *Black Enterprise* has a subscription rate of over 251,000. A second magazine directed at black women founded in 1970, *Essence*, has steadily gained in its circulation since its inception. Featuring health and beauty, fashion, and contemporary living sections, *Essence* is considered one of the top women's magazines. Since 1981 Susan Taylor has been the magazine's editor-in-chief.

In 1980 *Black Family*, a magazine promoting positive lifestyles for African Americans, was founded. In 1986 *American Vi-*

Earl Graves

sions: The Magazine of Afro-American Culture, the official magazine of the African American Museums Association was first published.

In 1993 there were a reported sixty-one black magazines being published in the United States. Of these, only *Ebony* had circulation rates of more than 1 million—*Jet* trailed with 968,545 and *Essence* followed with 850,116.

Broadcasting

by Richard Prince

There were black journalists before there was a broadcast industry, but in the Jim Crow America of the 1920s, there had to be black-oriented radio before there could be black broadcast journalists. That mission fell to a vaudevillian jack-of-all trades from Cincinnati, Jack L. Cooper (1888–1970).

Radio

While early radio shows featured black singing groups, they featured no blacks talking. To Cooper, this "was like taxation without representation," and so on Sunday, November 3, 1929, at 5 P.M., Chicago's white-owned WSBC premiered "The All-Negro Hour," starring Cooper and friends. Born was the concept of black radio, and Cooper went on to become the nation's first black radio station executive, the first black newscaster, the first black sportscaster, and the first to use radio as a service medium.

Cooper wore many hats. He played second base for a semi-pro baseball team; he had been a singer, a buck-and-wing dancer, and an end man in a minstrel show. He fought 160 amateur boxing bouts and he managed theaters. Between about 1910 and 1924, he worked as a journalist, writing for a number of black newspapers, including the *Freeman*, *Ledger* and *Recorder* in Indianapolis; and the *Bluff City News* and *Western World Reporter* in Memphis. In 1924, he became the assistant theatrical editor of the *Chicago Defender*.

"The All-Negro Hour" was like a vaudeville revue on the air, featuring music, comedy, and serials. While it ended its run in 1935, Cooper continued with WSBC, pioneering the black-radio format by producing several black-oriented shows. Crucial to that format was local news and public affairs of interest to African Americans.

The first example of public service programming aired December 9, 1938, when Cooper launched the "Search for Missing Persons" show. Aimed at reuniting people who had lost contact with friends and relatives through migration and over time, it reportedly had reunited 20,000 people by 1950. According to *Ebony* magazine, Cooper also remodeled a van into a mobile unit to relay "on-the-spot news events directly to four radio stations in the Chicago and suburban area," including news flashes from the *Pittsburgh Courier* and interviews of famous personalities who came to town, such as boxer Joe Louis. Cooper also did play-by-play sportscasts of black baseball games from the van.

"Listen Chicago," a news discussion show that ran from 1946 to 1952, provided African Americans with their first opportunity to use radio as a public forum. Following Cooper's lead, between 1946 and 1955 the number of black-oriented stations jumped from 24 to 600. News was a part of the explosion. "We have learned to do newscasts that answer the question, 'How is this news going to af-

fect me as a Negro?,'" Leonard Walk of WHOD Pittsburgh said in 1954. "We have learned that church and social news deserves a unique place of importance in our daily Negro programming." Yet by and large these broadcasters were not trained journalists. Black stations did not begin to broadcast news as we know it today until the 1960s.

In 1972, the Mutual Black Network was formed for news and sports syndication, under the auspices of the Mutual Broadcasting Network. By the end of the 1970s, the Mutual Black Network had just over 100 affiliates and 6.2 million listeners. The Sheridan Broadcasting Corporation, a black-owned broadcasting chain based in Pittsburgh, purchased the Mutual Black Network in the late 1970s, renaming it the Sheridan Broadcasting Network. A second African-American radio network, the National Black Network, was formed in 1973. Among its regular features was commentary by journalist Roy Wood, which he named "One Black Man's Opinion." In January 1992 the American-Urban Radio Network was formed, and the National Black Network has since gone out of business.

The networks were a mixed blessing. They provided their affiliates with broadcast-quality programs produced from an African-American perspective. But this relatively inexpensive access to news, sports, and public affairs features discouraged the local stations that subscribed from producing their own shows. News and public affairs staffs at the black-oriented stations remained minimal. There were some notable exceptions. New York's WLIB-AM had a black format that included a highly acclaimed news and public affairs department. A series of shows produced by the station on disadvantaged youth in the city won two Peabody Awards in 1970. After the station was purchased in 1972 by African-American civic leader Percy Sutton, the station became "Your Total Black News and Information Station," offering more news and public affairs programming than any other black-formatted radio outlet in the country.

In Washington, DC, *The Washington Post* donated its commercial FM radio license to Howard University in 1971. The new station, WHUR-FM, inaugurated "The Daily Drum," a full hour-long evening newscast that featured special coverage of the local black community, as well as news from Africa and the diaspora.

Television

Until the late 1960s, most serious black journalists were in print journalism—chiefly the black press—not in broadcasting. An exception was Lionel Monagas, who died at age seventy on April 5, 1992, and who worked in the early 1950s as a director of CBS-TV network programs such as "Person to Person" and "Face the Nation." He had started out as a traffic typist with the CBS affiliate in Washington, DC.

In 1956 Monagas became the first black professional at public station Channel 35 in Philadelphia, later known as WHYY-TV. He produced several children's programs there, including a ten-part series on "The History of the Negro," narrated by Ossie Davis.

Mal Goode became the first African American network TV reporter in 1962, at ABC-TV. Baseball great Jackie Robinson complained to James Hagerty, the former press secretary to President Eisenhower who was hired as an ABC vice president to set up a competitive news department. Robinson told Hagerty that the only two Negroes he had seen at ABC were "a lady with a white uniform in the lobby dusting and a Negro doorman. [Hagerty's] face got red, and he

said we intend to do something about that," Goode said. Goode was a reporter at *The Pittsburgh Courier* at the time, but in 1949 Pittsburgh's KQV Radio had given the newspaper two 15-minute slots to fill on Tuesday and Wednesday nights. Goode read the news on the program. According to Goode, ABC chose him for the job after spending half a year interviewing thirty-eight black male candidates. One reason he was chosen, he said, was because he was considered dark enough so blacks would know he was black, but light enough so that whites wouldn't feel threatened. Goode went on to work for ABC for eleven years. He was its United Nations correspondent, and covered the Cuban missile crisis, the aftermath of Martin Luther King Jr.'s assassination and the Poor People's March on Washington.

Jobs like Goode's were hard to come by. In his memoir *Black Is the Color of My TV*

Mal Goode

Tube, Emmy-winner Gil Noble of New York's WABC-TV recalls being at WLIB-AM radio during this era. "We would sit in the newsroom and fantasize about earning $300 a week, but few of our number worked at that level. Pat Connell, a former disc jockey at Newark's WNJR, known as 'Pat the Cat,' was anchoring the CBS morning newscast. Mal Goode was reporting for ABC-TV news, as well as for the local station WABC. NBC didn't have any blacks at that time, as far as I can recall, and in the mid-'60s, WNEW-TV had none, nor did WPIX-TV or WOR-TV have any." When Noble went downtown to audition for a major radio station job, he recalled, he would intone in the ultimate radio voice—"a [Walter] Cronkite delivery that outdid the original"—only to get the familiar brushoff, "Thanks very much. You're fine, but we already have a Negro on staff."

However, a few blacks were allowed on the white-controlled airwaves. William C. Matney, Jr., who had been managing editor of the *Michigan Chronicle*, a black community paper, and a reporter for the *Detroit News*, in 1963 became a TV and radio reporter for WMAQ-TV, the NBC-owned station in Chicago. He joined NBC-TV news in 1966. Veteran Norma Quarles, now at CNN, was hired as a trainee at NBC News in 1966, moving a year later to the NBC station in Cleveland as a reporter and anchor. Lem Tucker, who died in March 1991, joined NBC News as a copy boy in 1965 and moved up to assistant bureau chief in Vietnam.

In 1967, a self-described "teacher moonlighting as a jazz disc jockey" who also called play-by-play for basketball games and read the news, applied for a job at soon-to-be all-news WCBS radio in New York. Ed Bradley, who would later co-host CBS-TV's most successful news show, "60 Minutes," impressed a news director by refusing to write some copy and record it because, he explained, "You won't learn enough about

Ed Bradley

me that way." Instead, he borrowed a tape recorder, went out on the street, did an update of a story about an anti-poverty program, and got the job. But in Portsmouth, Virginia, an audacious twenty-five-year-old newscaster named Max Robinson was fired from a UHF station after he broke the rules by showing his face on camera. It was 1964, and only the word "News" was to appear on the screen. White viewers were enraged to see that one of "those" people was allowed to work in the studio. According to his news director, James Snyder, in 1971 Robinson became the first black anchor in a major market, at WTOP-TV in Washington, DC. Later, at ABC-TV, Robinson would be the networks' first black regular co-anchor. But that wouldn't happen until 1978.

It took the riots of the 1960s and a stern warning from a federal commission for the broadcast industry to undertake any concentrated hiring of African Americans. When American cities began to burn, blacks held about 3.6 percent of TV news jobs. White news directors had to scramble to find black journalists to cover the story. In 1968, the National Advisory Commission on Civil Disorders, known as the Kerner Commission, concluded that "the world that television and newspapers offer to their black audience is almost totally white, in both appearance and attitude." "Within a year," wrote Noble, "many of us found ourselves working downtown at major radio and TV stations."

In June 1969 the Federal Communications Commission adopted rules prohibiting discrimination in broadcast industry employment and required stations to file annual reports showing the racial makeup of their workforce by job category. Black public-affairs shows were aired, such as Noble's "Like It Is," public broadcasting's "Black Journal" hosted by Tony Brown, Philadelphia's "Black Perspectives on the News," in nearly every city with a substantial black population. Still, by the time Mal Goode retired in 1973, there were only seven black reporters at the three networks.

By the 1990s, African Americans were breaking into broadcast management and ownership, although the numbers were still small. TV general managers included Charlotte Moore English of KSHB-TV Kansas City; Marcellus Alexander of WJZ-TV in Baltimore; Eugene Lothery of WCAU-TV in Philadelphia; Clarence McKee, CEO and chairman of WTVT-TV in Tampa, Florida; and Dorothy Brunson, owner of a small UHF station, WGTW-TV, in Philadelphia.

Ronald Townsend, president of the Gannett Television Group, comprising ten stations, chaired the National Association of Broadcasters' TV board. Jonathan Rodgers became president of the CBS Television Sta-

tions Division in August 1990, making him network television's highest-ranking African-American news executive. Bryant Gumbel, co-host of the NBC-TV "Today" show, CBS News correspondent Ed Bradley, and talk-show host Oprah Winfrey became three of the highest paid and most-recognized faces on television, and Bradley among the most respected. ABC-TV's Carole Simpson became a substitute and weekend network TV anchor. African Americans were anchoring local newscasts in markets around the country.

Still, African Americans, while 12 percent of the population in the 1990 census, represented only 9.8 percent of the television news workforce and 5 percent of the radio workforce. They were four percent of the news directors at commercial TV stations and about five percent at commercial radio stations. Those heading news operations included Gary Wordlaw at WJLA-TV Washington, DC and Will Wright at WWOR-TV New York. And, according to an annual survey by the Center for Media and Public Affairs, most of the news on nightly network television shows continued to be presented by white males. Blacks accounted for only five percent of all field reports and anchor stories combined, its 1991 survey found. The most visible African American correspondent was George Strait, ABC-TV health reporter, who tied for fifty-seventh in the number of stories filed. Simpson was in sixth place, based on the number of brief news reports read.

Public Television

For most of its short history, public television, begun in the early 1950s, failed to realize the hopes of many African Americans. Tony Brown's "Black Journal," later "Tony

NBC "Today Show" host Bryant Gumbel interviews former President Richard Nixon, 1990.

Tony Brown

Brown's Journal," was well-received by black viewers as the only national black public affairs series on television. It was constantly threatened with cancellation, however, after conservatives complained about its anti-administration attitude. The show was rescued after it secured underwriting from Pepsi Cola.

In 1975, the only black FCC commissioner, Benjamin Hooks, joined the critics, accusing public broadcasters of "arrogance" and of concentrating their efforts on the cultured, white cosmopolitans. A United States House of Representatives subcommittee held hearings. A 1975 review of public broadcasting stations' top three job categories (officials, managers, and professionals) showed that 59 percent (or 108) of the 184 public radio licensees and 33 percent (52) of the 160 public television licensees had no minority staff at these levels.

In the early 1990s, the highest-ranking African Americans in public television were Jennifer Lawson, who joined PBS in November 1989 as its first executive vice president for national programming and promotion services; Donald L. Marbury, director of the Television Program Fund of the Corporation for Public Broadcasting; and George L. Miles, Jr., executive vice president and chief operating officer of WNET-TV New York. Lawson was responsible for obtaining and commissioning the programs PBS provides to its member stations as well as the promotion of those programs. Marbury was charged with managing the $45 million television program fund, which provides funding support for major series in public television, such as "Frontline."

The most visible African American journalist on public television has been "MacNeil-Lehrer News Hour" correspondent Charlayne Hunter-Gault, a former *New York Times* reporter noted for her in-depth reporting. Other black journalists with the show include Kwame Holman, Washington correspondent, and producer Jackie Farmer. PBS' most acclaimed piece of African American journalism was "Eyes on the Prize," a history of the civil rights movement produced by Henry Hampton, which aired in 1987, with a sequel in 1990. Its most controversial was a one-hour film on black homosexual men, "Tongues Untied," by filmmaker Marlon Riggs in 1991.

In 1980, Howard University launched WHMM-TV, becoming the first licensee of a public TV station on a black campus and the only black-owned public television station in the nation. On August 31, 1991, San Francisco's Minority Television Project went on the air with KMTP-TV, which became the nation's second black-owned public television station. One of the principals was Adam Clayton Powell, III, son of the late Harlem congressman.

Public Radio

Before 1967, there were only two black educational outlets in the country; by 1990 there were 40 black public radio stations. Many of them were community radio stations, owned and operated by nonprofit foundations, controlled by a local board of directors, and relying on listener donations. Others were on college campuses. One of the most successful was WPFW-FM, a 50,000-watt outlet controlled by African Americans, launched in 1977 by the Pacifica Foundation.

Stations such as WCLK-FM at Clark College in Atlanta, WBVA-FM in Harrodsburg, Kentucky, and WVAS-FM at Alabama State University in Montgomery, tailored news and public affairs programming to their local, African-American audiences. WVAS was used as a broadcast journalism lab by students majoring in the field. On National Public Radio, African American journalists Phyllis Crockett, Vertamae Grosvenor, Cheryl Duvall, and Brenda Wilson have won awards for reports on South Africa and issues involving African Americans.

Cable Television

The 1980s saw the explosion of cable television and the decline of the television networks. Black Entertainment Television, founded by former congressional aide Robert L. Johnson, made its debut in 1980 and established a news division by the end of the decade. That division produced a weekly news show, "BET News" and "Lead Story," a talk show featuring black pundits.

The biggest development in cable journalism, however, was the spectacular growth of Ted Turner's Cable News Network, which went on line in June 1980. By the 1991 Persian Gulf war, CNN had established itself as the station to watch in a crisis. Transmitted across the globe, it became a medium for world leaders to communicate among one another.

Veteran journalist Bernard Shaw, principal Washington anchor, was one of three CNN reporters who captivated the world's audiences with their continuous coverage of the first night of bombing on Baghdad during Operation Desert Storm on January 16, 1991. Other African Americans at CNN include Jay Suber, vice president and executive producer, news features, CNN Newsroom; Graylian Young, Southeast bureau chief; CNN anchors Andrea Arceneaux, Leon Harris and Joe Oliver; Cassandra Henderson, anchor for CNN Newsroom, Lyn Vaughn and Gordon Graham, Headline News anchors; sports anchor Fred Hickman, and correspondent Norma Quarles.

Robert Johnson

■ EDITORS, JOURNALISTS, AND MEDIA EXECUTIVES

Robert S. Abbott (1870–1940)
Chicago Defender *Founder*

A native of St. Simon Island, Georgia, Abbott studied at Beach Institute in Savannah, and later completed his undergraduate work at Claflin College in Orangeburg, South Carolina. Migrating to Chicago, he attended Kent Law School and took a job in a printing house until he completed his law studies in 1899.

Abbott returned to Chicago and published the first edition of the *Defender* on May 5, 1905, which he initially sold on a door-to-door basis. Abbott died in 1940, whereupon the *Defender* was handed over to his nephew, John H. Sengstacke, who introduced a daily edition of the paper in 1956.

Ida B. Wells Barnett (1864–1931)
Editor, Anti-lynching Crusader

Ida B. Wells Barnett was born in Mississippi and educated at Rusk University. She served as editor of the black newspaper, the *Memphis Free Speech*, and in 1892 became part-owner. Through the paper she engaged in a vigorous campaign against the practice of lynching. On May 27, 1882 the paper's offices were destroyed by a mob.

In 1895 she married *Chicago Conservator* editor Ferdinand Lee Barnett. That same year Barnett published her first pamphlet against lynching, *A Red Record*. Over the years Barnett wrote numerous other pamphlets and articles and conducted speaking tours throughout the United States and Europe.

Ed Bradley

Ed Bradley (1941–)
Television News Correspondent

A native of Philadelphia, Pennsylvania, Edward R. Bradley received a B.S. degree in education from Cheyney State College in Cheyney, Pennsylvania. From 1963 to 1967 Bradley worked as a disc jockey and news reporter for WDAS radio in Philadelphia. From there he moved on to WCBS radio in New York. He joined CBS as a stringer in the Paris bureau in 1971. Within a few months he was transferred to the Saigon bureau, where he remained until he was assigned to the Washington bureau in June 1974.

Until 1981 Bradley served as anchor for "CBS Sunday Night News" and as principal correspondent for "CBS Reports." In 1981 he replaced Dan Rather as a correspondent for the weekly news program, "60 Minutes." In 1992 Bradley was made host of the CBS news program, "Street Stories."

Bradley has won seven Emmy Awards for broadcast journalism, two Alfred I. duPont-Columbia University Awards for broadcast journalism, a George Foster Peabody Broadcasting Award, a George Polk Award, and an NCAA Anniversary Award.

Tony Brown (1933–)
Commentator, Columnist, Producer

William Anthony Brown, born in Charleston, West Virginia, is probably best known as the producer and host of the longest-running minority affairs program in history, "Tony Brown's Journal."

He received his bachelor of arts degree in 1959 and his master's degree in social work in 1961 from Wayne State University in Detroit. Brown took a job with the *Detroit Courier* as drama critic. It was during this time that he began to be active in the civil rights movement, helping to organize the 1963 "March to Freedom" with Dr. Martin Luther King in Detroit. After leaving the paper, where he had worked up to the position of city editor, Brown landed a job with the local PBS station, WTVS, where he became involved in television programming and production. At WTVS he produced the station's first series aimed at a black audience, "C.P.T." (Colored People's Time). He joined the New York staff of the PBS program "Black Journal" in 1970, as the show's executive producer and host—in 1977 the show's name was changed to "Tony Brown's Journal" and can still be seen on PBS.

In 1971 Brown founded and became the first dean of Howard University's School of Communications. He continued in that post until 1974.

Brown has been an advocate of community and self-help programs. In 1980 he organized a "Black College Day," designed to emphasize the importance of historically black colleges and universities. In 1985 Brown organized the Council for the Economic Development of Black Americans and

launched the "Buy Freedom" campaign (now known as the "Buy Freedom Network"), which encourages black consumers nationwide to patronize black-owned businesses.

Brown has written, produced, and directed a film, *The White Girl*, and has appeared as a commentator for National Public Radio and has a syndicated newspaper columnist. He is a member of the National Association of Black Television and Film Producers, the National Association of Black Media Producers, the National Communications Council, and the National Black United Fund. Brown is the recipient of a Black Emmy Award and the NAACP Image Award. He is currently president of Tony Brown Productions in New York City.

Edward J. Castleberry (1928–)
Broadcast Journalist

Born July 28, 1928 in Birmingham, Alabama Castleberry spent two years at Miles College in that city. His career has been in radio broadcasting at many stations in the United States. He started as a disc jockey at WEDR and WJLD in Birmingham, Alabama (1950–1955), and has worked in the various capacities of disc jockey, program director and newsman at WMBM in Miami, Florida (1955–1958), WCIN in Cincinnati, Ohio (1958–1961), WABQ in Cleveland, Ohio (1961–1964), WVKD in Columbus, Ohio (1964–1967), WHAT in Philadelphia, Pennsylvania (1967–1968) and WEBB in Baltimore, Maryland. He then became an anchorman and entertainment editor at the Mutual and National black networks.

Castleberry has been twice named Newsman of the Year in 1980 and received the Outstanding Citizen award from the Alabama House of Representatives in 1983. In 1985 he was honored by the Smithsonian Institution in Washington DC. Castleberry was awarded the World War II Victory Medal for his service in the United States Navy 1945–1947.

Spencer Christian (1947–   )
Television Weatherperson

Born in Richmond, Virginia, Spencer Christian received his B.A. degree in English from Hampton University. Upon graduation he went to work as a teacher in New York.

In 1971 Christian went to work for WWBT–TV in Richmond as a news reporter; from 1972 to 1975 he served as the station's weatherperson. In 1975 he moved to WBAL–TV in Baltimore and to New York's WABC–TV in 1977. Christian joined the "Good Morning American" team on ABC in 1986, where he is currently weatherperson and co-

Spencer Christian

host. He has recently published *Spencer Christian's Weather Book*, with Tom Biracree.

Xerona Clayton (1930–   )
Broadcast Executive

Clayton was born Xerona Brewster on August 30, 1930 in Muskogee, Oklahoma. She received a B.S. from Tennessee State University in 1952. She also attended the Ru-Jac School of Modeling in Chicago.

Clayton was the first African-American woman to have her own television show in the south when she became hostess of the "Xerona Clayton Show" at WAGA–TV in Atlanta. She has also been a newspaper columnist for the *Atlanta Voice*, taught public school in Chicago and Los Angeles and has dabbled in photography and fashion modeling.

Clayton has also been active in the civil rights movement. Her first husband, now deceased, was the public relations director for Martin Luther King. Clayton came to the attention of Atlanta officials and was appointed to the position of community relations director of the Model Cities Program. She has also raised funds for sickle cell anemia research and the Martin Luther King Jr. Birthplace Memorial Restoration Committee.

In 1968 Clayton won the Outstanding Leadership award given by the National Association of Market Developers and a year later the Bronze Woman of the Year in Human Relations award given by Phi Delta Kappa sorority. She is also the recipient of the Georgia Associated Press award for Superior Television Programming 1969–1971.

Clayton is the founder of the Atlanta chapter of Media Women and a member of the National Academy of Television Arts and Sciences. She has co-starred in a major mo-

Xerona Clayton

tion picture, *House on Skull Mountain*. Clayton has re-married and is currently the corporate vice-president for urban affairs at the Turner Broadcasting System in Atlanta, Georgia.

T. Thomas Fortune (1856–1928)
New York Age *Founder*

T. Thomas Fortune was one of the most prominent black journalists involved in the flourishing black press of the post-Civil War era.

Born in Florida, the son of a Reconstruction politician, Fortune was particularly productive before his thirtieth year, completing such works as *Black and White: Land, Labor and Politics in the South* and *The Negro in Politics* while in his twenties.

Fortune attended Howard University for two years, leaving to marry Carrie Smiley of Jacksonville, Florida. The couple went to New York in 1878, with Fortune taking a job as a printer for the *New York Sun*. In time, Fortune caught the attention of *Sun* editor Charles A. Dana, who eventually promoted him to the editorial staff of the paper.

Fortune also edited *The Globe*, a black daily, and was later chief editorial writer for the *The Negro World*. In 1900 Fortune joined Booker T. Washington in helping to organize the successful National Negro Business League. His later activity with Washington gained him more notoriety than his earlier writing, although the latter is clearly more vital in affording him an important niche in the history of black protest.

In 1883 Fortune founded the *New York Age*, the paper with which he sought to "champion the cause" of his race. In time, the *Age* became the leading black journal of opinion in the United States. One of Fortune's early crusades was against the practice of separate schools for the races in the New York educational system.

Fortune was later responsible for coining the term "Afro-American" as a substitute for Negro in New York newspapers. He also set up the Afro-American Council, an organization which he regarded as the precursor of the Niagara Movement. In 1907 Fortune sold the *Age*, although he remained active in journalism as an editorial writer for several black newspapers.

Mal Goode (1908–)
Television News Correspondent

Malvin Russell Goode had been with the *Pittsburgh Courier* 14 years when in 1962 he joined ABC to cover the United Nations. His first test was the Cuban missile crisis, just two months later, during which Goode distinguished himself with incisive TV and radio reports during the long hours of UN debate.

Goode was born in White Plains, Virginia; educated in the public schools of Homestead, Pennsylvania; and graduated from the University of Pittsburgh. He was employed for twelve years as a laborer in the steel mills while in high school and college and for five years after graduation. In 1936, he was appointed to a post in Juvenile Court and became boys work director of the Centre Avenue YMCA, where he led the fight to eliminate discrimination in Pittsburgh branches of the YMCA.

Goode served with the Pittsburgh Housing Authority for six years and in 1948 joined the *Pittsburgh Courier*. The following year he started a career in radio with station KQV, doing a 15-minute news show two nights each week. In 1950, he started a five minute daily news program on WHOD.

Goode was named news director at WHOD in 1952. He and his sister, the late Mary Dee, had the only brother-sister team in radio for six years. He was the first black to hold membership in the National Association of Radio and TV News Directors.

For two months, in 1963, he joined with three colleagues to conduct courses in journalism for 104 African students in seminars at Lagos, Nigeria; Addis Ababa, Ethiopia; and Dar es Salaam, Tanzania.

Earl G. Graves (1935–)
Publisher and Media Executive

In the 1970s, Earl Graves emerged as one of America's leading publishers and exponents of black entrepreneurship. Within a few short years his magazine, *Black Enterprise*, was accepted as the authority on African Americans in business and as an important advocate for an active, socially responsive, black middle class.

Earl Graves

Born in Brooklyn, Graves graduated from Morgan State College. In 1965, he was hired to a position on the staff of Robert Kennedy, then senator from New York. In 1968, he organized Earl Graves Associates, a firm which serves as a consultant on urban affairs, black economic development and publishes *Black Enterprise*.

Graves also has interests in radio as president of EGG Dallas Broadcasting, Inc., which operates KNOK–AM and KNOK–FM in Fort Worth, Texas.

Bryant Gumbel (1948–)
Television Anchor

In January 1981 Bryant Gumbel was named co-anchor (with Jane Pauley) of the "Today" show on NBC. Prior to that time, Gumbel had made regular sports reports on

Bryant Gumbel

"Today," although his primary responsibilities were with NBC Sports as host of pregame programming during coverage of the National Football League, Major League Baseball, and other sports broadcasts.

He began his broadcasting career in October 1972 when he was named a weekend sportscaster for KNBC, the NBC station in Los Angeles. Within a year, he became weekday sportscaster and was appointed the station's sports director in 1976. He remained in that post until July 1980.

Before embarking on his career in television, Gumbel was a sports writer. After submitting his first piece to *Black Sports* magazine in 1971, he was given additional freelance assignments and was soon hired as a staff writer. Within eight months he was elevated to editor-in-chief.

A native of New Orleans, Gumbel grew up in Chicago. He received a liberal arts degree from Bates College in Lewiston, Maine in 1970.

Ragan A. Henry (1934–)
Broadcast and Newspaper Executive

Ragan A. Henry is president of Broadcast Enterprises National Inc. and former publisher of *The National Leader*, a black national newspaper launched in May 1982, both headquartered in Philadelphia. Henry is also president of radio stations in several states and is a partner in the Philadelphia law firm of Wolf, Black, Schorr, and Solis-Cohen.

Henry was born in Sadiesville, Kentucky on February 2, 1934. He received his A.B. from Harvard College in 1956 and his L.L.B. from Harvard Law School in 1961. He also attended Temple University Graduate School in 1963. Prior to joining his current law firm, he had been a partner in the Philadelphia firm of Goodis, Greenfield, Henry and Edelstein from 1964 to 1977.

Henry has been a visiting professor at Syracuse University's S.I. Newhouse School of Communications since 1979 and was a lecturer at LaSalle College from 1971–1973. He serves on the boards of directors of Continental Bank, Abt Associates, Inc., National Association of Black Owned Broadcasters (president of the board), LaSalle College, and the Hospital of the University of Pennsylvania. He has been chairman of the John McKee Scholarship Committee Fellowships, Noyes and Whitney Foundation.

Cheryl Willis Hudson (1948–)
Wade Hudson (1948–)
Publishing Executives

Cheryl Willis Hudson, publisher, and Wade Hudson, president and chief executive officer, founded Just Us Books, Inc. in 1988 to publish children's books and learning material that focus on the African-American experience.

A native of Portsmouth, Virginia, Cheryl Willis Hudson graduated (cum laude) from Oberlin College, and has studied at Northeastern University and Parsons School of Design. Prior to founding Just Us Books, she worked as an art editor and designer for several publishers, including Houghton Mifflin, MacMillan Publishing, and Arete Publishing.

Wade Hudson, a native of Mansfield, Louisiana, attended Southern University and has worked with numerous civil rights organizations, including CORE, the Southern Christian Leadership Conference, and the Society for Opportunity, Unity and Leadership, which he co-founded. He has worked as a public relations specialist for Essex County and Kean colleges in New Jersey.

Eugene D. Jackson (1943–)
Broadcast Executive

Eugene D. Jackson is president of Unity Broadcasting Network in New York City, parent company of the National Black Network, and of four radio stations of which Jackson is also president—WDAS–AM and –FM in Philadelphia and KATZ–AM and WZEN–FM in St. Louis.

Jackson was born in Wauhomis, Oklahoma on September 5, 1943. He received a B.S. degree from the University of Missouri at Rolla in 1967 and an M.S. from Columbia University in 1971.

Jackson serves on the boards of directors of the National Association of Broadcasters, the Council of Concerned Black Executives, Freedom National Bank, and Trans Africa (1977). He was a member of the Council on Foreign Relations in 1978 and on the board

of governors of the International Radio and TV Society from 1974 to 1976.

From 1969 to 1971, Jackson directed major industry programs for the Interracial Council for Business Opportunity in New York City. He was a production and project engineer for the Black Economic Union in New York City from 1968 to 1969 and an industrial engineer for Colgate-Palmolive from 1967 to 1968.

John H. Johnson (1918–)
Publisher, Media Executive

One of America's foremost businessmen, John H. Johnson sits at the head of the most prosperous and powerful black publishing company in the United States. Beginning with *Negro Digest* in 1942, and following with *Ebony* in 1945, Johnson built a chain of journalistic successes that now also includes *Jet*, *Ebony Jr.*, and *EM: Ebony Man*.

Born in Arkansas City, Arkansas, Johnson, at age six, lost his father, a mill worker, and was raised by his mother and stepfather. His segregated schooling was obtained locally until the family moved to Chicago. Johnson attended DuSable High School in Chicago, excelling academically and in extracurricular activities, writing for the yearbook and school paper.

After graduation, an insurance executive heard a speech delivered by Johnson, and was so impressed he offered him a partial scholarship at the University of Chicago. After two years, however, Johnson quit classes, although he entered the Northwestern School of Commerce in 1938, studying for an additional two years before joining the Supreme Liberty Life Insurance Company. While running the company's house organ, it occurred to Johnson that a digest of weekly or monthly gathered news items of special interest and importance to the black

John H. Johnson

community might achieve a wide black readership. The idea resulted in the creation of *Negro Digest*, a periodical containing both news reprints and feature articles. Of the latter, perhaps the most beneficial to circulation was Eleanor Roosevelt's contribution, "If I Were a Negro."

Buoyed by success, Johnson decided to approach the market with yet another offering, a pictorial magazine patterned after *Life*. The first issue of *Ebony* sold out its press run of 25,000 copies and soon became a permanent staple in the world of journalism as large companies began to advertise regularly in it.

In addition to serving as president and publisher of Johnson Publishing Company, Inc., Johnson is chairman and chief executive officer of Supreme Life Insurance Company, chairman of WJPC–AM in Chicago, and president of Fashion Fair Cosmetics. He has served on the boards of directors of the Greyhound Corporation, Verex Corporation, Marina Bank, Supreme Life Insurance Company, and Zenith Radio Corporation. John-

son also serves as a trustee for the Art Institute of Chicago and United Negro College Fund; on the advisory council of the Harvard Graduate School of Business; as a director for the Chamber of Commerce of the United States; on the advertising council of Junior Achievement, and Chicago USO. He has received honorary doctoral degrees from numerous colleges and universities, and many honors and awards from civil and professional organizations.

Robert L. Johnson (1946–   )
Cable Television Executive

Robert Johnson worked for the Washington, DC Urban League, the Corporation for Public Broadcasting, and as a press secretary, before joining the National Cable Television Association in 1976. While serving as vice president of government relations for the association, Johnson came up with the idea of creating a cable channel aimed at black viewers. In 1989 he took out a $15,000 personal loan to start Black Entertainment Television (BET).

In addition to running BET, Johnson functions as the publisher of the magazines *Emerge* and *YSB: Young Sisters and Brothers* and operates a radio network. He serves as a board member of the Cable Television Advertising Bureau and has been awarded the Pioneer award by the Capitol Press Club (1984) and the Business of the Year award by the Washington, DC Chamber of Commerce.

Clarence B. Jones (1931–   )
Publishing Executive

Born in Philadelphia, Jones graduated from Columbia University and Boston University Law School and then practiced as an attorney, specializing in civil rights and copyright cases for a New York City law firm. During this period, he was counsel for Dr. Martin Luther King Jr. and the Southern Christian Leadership Conference. In 1968 and again in 1972, he served as a delegate from New York State to the Democratic Convention. Jones was also an observer at Attica prison during the uprising there in 1971.

In 1971, Jones, as head of Inner City Broadcasting, led a group of investors in the purchase of the New York *Amsterdam News*, the nation's largest black newspaper. Inner City Broadcasting also owned radio station WLIB and has full ownership of WBLS–FM.

Haki R. Madhubuti (1942–)
Publisher, Poet, Writer

Born Don L. Lee in Little Rock, Arkansas, Madhubuti has studied at Wilson Junior College, Roosevelt University, and the University of Illinois, and received a master of fine arts degree from the University of Iowa. His published works include *Think Black*; *Black Pride*; *For Black People (and Negroes Too)*; *Don't Cry, Scream*; *Enemies: The Clash of Races*; *Killing Memory: Seeking Ancestors*; and *Black Men: Obsolete, Single, Dangerous?*. He has taught and served as writer-in-residence at numerous universities, including Chicago State University, Cornell, Howard, Morgan State, and the University of Illinois.

Madhubuti was one of the founding members of the Organization of Black American Culture, Writers' Workshop, and has served as vice chairperson of the African Liberation Day Support Committee and on the executive council of the Congress of African People.

Currently Madhubuti is director of the Institute of Positive Education in Chicago,

publisher and editor of Third World Press, president of the African-American Publishers and Booksellers, and Writers' Association, and the operator of a chain of book stores.

The Third World Press, founded by Madhubuti in 1967, has published numerous titles by African-American writers, including Frances Cress-Welsing's *The Isis Papers: The Keys to the Colors*, and Chancellor Williams' *The Destruction of Black Civilization*.

John Henry Murphy (1840–1922)
Publisher

John Henry Murphy was born a slave in Baltimore, Maryland. He became superintendent of Bethel African Methodist Episcopal Church and founded the Sunday school newspaper, the *Sunday School Helper*. In 1892 he purchased the *Baltimore Afro-American* for $200. By 1922 the *Afro-American* had reached a circulation of 14,000, be-

John Henry Murphy

coming the largest black newspaper in the Northeast.

At first, Murphy set the paper's type himself, having acquired this skill during his forties. Throughout, he insisted that his paper maintain political and editorial independence. Murphy died April 5, 1922. The paper grew and is now under the helm of Murphy's great-nephew, John H. Murphy III.

Norma Quarles (1936–)
Television News Correspondent

Born in New York City, Norma Quarles is an alumna of Hunter College and City College of New York. She first worked as a buyer for a New York specialty shop before moving to Chicago where she became a licensed real estate broker.

In 1965 she began her broadcast career in Chicago at WSDM Radio, working as a news reporter and disk jockey. She later returned to New York where she joined NBC in 1966 for a one-year training program. After three years with WKYC–TV in Cleveland, she was transferred to WNBC–TV. In 1978 Quarles moved to NBC News as a correspondent based in Chicago. She had been producing and reporting the "Urban Journal" series for WMAQ–TV for a year at that time. Before joining WMAQ, Quarles was an award-winning reporter for WNBC–TV in New York, where she also anchored the early local news broadcasts during the "Today" show. In 1988 Quarles left NBC, after twenty-one years, to join Cable News Network's New York bureau.

Quarles is a member of the National Academy of Television Arts and Sciences, Sigma Delta Chi, and a board member of the Governor's National Academy of Television Arts and Sciences.

Norma Quarles

Dudley Randall (1914–)
Publisher, Poet, Librarian

Dudley Randall was born in Washington DC on January 14, 1914 and was living in Detroit by the time he was nine years old. An early harbinger of Randall's poetic talent was the appearance of one of his poems in the *Detroit Free Press* at the early age of thirteen. After serving in the United States Army Signal Corp. (1942–1946) Randall worked in the foundry at the Ford Motor Company and as a postal carrier and clerk while attending Wayne State University in Detroit. He received his B.A. in 1949 and a Master of Arts in Library Science from the University of Michigan in 1951. He has also done graduate work at the University of Ghana.

Randall worked in progressively responsible librarian positions at Lincoln University in Jefferson City, Missouri (1951–1954), Morgan State College in Baltimore, Maryland (1954–1956) and the Wayne County Federated Library System in Wayne, Michigan (1956–1969). From 1969 to 1975 he was a reference librarian and poet-in-residence at the University of Detroit. In 1969 he also served as a visiting lecturer at the University of Michigan.

Randall's love of poetry led to his founding of the *Broadside Press* and in 1980 he founded the Broadside Poets Theater and the Broadside Poetry Workshop.

Randall has been active in many Detroit cultural organizations and institutions including the Detroit Council for the Arts and the International Afro-American Museum in Detroit. In 1981 Randall received the Creative Artist Award in Literature from the Michigan Council for the Arts and in 1986 he was named the first poet laureate of Detroit.

regarded as an independent thinker beholder to no particular orthodoxy. His 1991 book *Looking Backward at Us*, like much of his other writings, deals with the African-American experience and social conditions and race relations in the United States.

Raspberry has taught journalism at Howard University and the University of Maryland School of Journalism. He is also a member of the Poynter Institute for Media Studies board of advisors and the Pulitzer Prize Board.

Max Robinson (1939–1988)
Television News Correspondent

Born in Richmond, Virginia, Max Robinson attended Oberlin College, Virginia Union University, and Indiana University. He began his career as a newsreader at

William J. Raspberry (1935–   )
Commentator, Journalist

Born in Okolona, Mississippi, on October 12, 1935, Raspberry received his B.S. degree in history from Indiana Central College in 1958. While a student there he worked at the *Indianapolis Recorder* as a reporter, photographer and editorial writer from 1956 through 1960. In 1960 Raspberry was drafted by the Army and he served as a Public Information Officer until his discharge in 1962. He began working for the *Washington Post* as a teletypist but soon worked his way up to reporter, assistant city editor and finally a columnist in 1966. He continues writing today as a nationally syndicated columnist.

Raspberry has also appeared as a television panelist and commentator and in 1965 was named Journalist of the Year by the Capital Press Club for his coverage of the Los Angeles Watts riot. He is generally

William Raspberry

Max Robinson

WTOV–TV in Portsmouth, Virginia. In 1965 he worked as a studio floor director at WTOP–TV (now WUSA) in Washington, DC, before moving on to WRC–TV, to work as a news reporter, and to WTOP–TV, where he worked as anchor.

In 1978 Robinson joined ABC "World News Tonight," becoming the first black network anchor. Almost immediately, Robinson took it upon himself to fight racism at whatever cost necessary. ABC management became frustrated with Robinson and moved him to the post of weekend anchor. In 1983 Robinson left ABC for WMAQ–TV in Chicago, where he remained until 1985.

Robinson died of complications from acquired immune deficiency syndrome (AIDS) on December 20, 1988, in Washington, DC. He was the recipient of three Emmy awards, the Capital Press Club Journalist of the Year

Award, and the Ohio State Award, as well as an award from the National Education Association. He also taught at Federal City College, in Washington, DC, and the College of William and Mary, in Williamsburg, Virginia.

Carl Thomas Rowan (1925–)
Commentator, Journalist

Carl Rowan was born August 11, 1925, in Ravenscroft, Tennessee. He attended Tennessee A&I (now Tennessee State University) in Nashville and Washburn University in Topeka, Kansas. He received his bachelor of arts degree from Oberlin College in 1947; in 1948 he received a master of arts degree from the University of Minnesota.

In 1948 he was hired as a copywriter, then later as a staff writer, by the *Minneapolis Tribune*, where he worked until 1961. In 1961 he was hired by the United States Department of State as deputy assistant secretary for public affairs. After three years with the Department of State, Rowan was

Carl Rowan

appointed United States ambassador to Finland by President Lyndon Johnson in 1963, and in 1964 he was appointed director of the United States Information Agency, which operates overseas educational and cultural programs, including the worldwide radio service "Voice of America." In 1965 Rowan resigned from the USIA.

He has authored several books, including *South of Freedom, Wait Till Next Year, Between Us Blacks*, and a memoir entitled *Breaking Barriers*. He is a syndicated columnist and is work appears in numerous newspapers across the country.

Rowan has served as a political commentator for the Post-Newsweek Broadcasting Company, and has been a frequent panelist on the NBC program "Meet the Press" and the syndicated programs "Agronsky & Co." and "Inside Washington."

John B. Russwurm (1799–1851)
Freedom's Journal *Co-Founder*

Born in Port Antonio, Jamaica, Russwurm graduated from Bowdoin College, in Brunswick, Maine, in 1826. From Brunswick, Russwurm moved to New York, where on March 16, 1827 he and Samuel E. Cornish published the first edition of *Freedom's Journal*—the nation's first African-American newspaper.

In 1829 Russwurm decided to immgrate to Monrovia, Liberia. From 1830 to 1835 he published the *Liberia Herald*. Cornish, who had left the paper in late 1827, resumed his role as editor in 1830, publishing the paper under the name *Rights of All*.

Russwurm went on to serve as superintendent of education in Monrovia, and later as governor of a settlement. Russwurm died June 9, 1851.

John Herman Henry Sengstacke (1912–)
Publishing Executive

A nephew of the great publisher Robert Abbott, John Sengstacke was born in Savannah, Georgia. He received a B.A. from Hampton Institute in 1933. Upon graduation, he went to work with Robert Abbott, attended school to learn printing, and wrote editorials and articles for three Abbott papers. In 1934, he became vice president and general manager of the company.

During World War II, Sengstacke was an advisor to the United States Office of War Information, during a period of severe tension between the government and black press. He also presided over the Chicago rationing board.

In 1940, after the death of his uncle, Sengstacke became president of the Robert S. Abbott Publishing Company. In 1905, his uncle had founded the weekly *Defender*. In 1956, Sengstacke founded the *Daily Defender*, one of only three black dailies in the country. In 1940 he founded the Negro Newspaper Publishers Association, now known as the National Newspaper Publishers Association, and served six terms as president. Today he is president of *Tri-State Defender*, Inc., *Florida Courier* Publishing Company, New *Pittsburgh Courier* Publishing Company, and Amalgamated Publishers, Inc., and chairman of *Michigan Chronicle* Publishing Company and Sengstacke Enterprises, Inc., and treasurer of Chicago Defender Charities, Inc.

Sengstacke has served in leadership positions with many professional, educational, and civic organizations, received a number of presidential appointments, and is the recipient of several academic awards. He has been trustee of Bethune-Cookman College, chairman of the board of Provident Hospital and Training School Association, member of the board of directors of the American Society of Newspaper Editors, on the advisory board of the Boy Scouts of America, and a principal in Chicago United.

Bernard Shaw (1940–)
Television News Anchor

Bernard Shaw is the Washington anchor for the Cable News Network (CNN). Shaw was on board as anchor from the Washington desk at CNN when that cable network went on the air on June 1, 1980. Shaw has often reported first-hand on major international news stories. He was present when the Chinese government's tanks rolled into Tiananmen Square in May 1989, crushing the student-led pro-democracy movement. In January of 1991, Shaw, along with two other colleagues from CNN, were stranded in

Bernard Shaw

Baghdad when allied bombing attacks launched Operation Desert Storm. From their hotel room, Shaw and the others provided first-hand accounts of the bombing raid on the city.

Shaw's first job as a television journalist came in 1971 with CBS News at their Washington bureau. He conducted an exclusive interview with Attorney General John Mitchell at the height of the Watergate scandal. Shaw left CBS in 1977 to join ABC News as Miami bureau chief and Latin American correspondent. Shaw was one of the first reporters to file from location on the Jonestown massacre story in Guyana and he and his team provided the only aerial photos of the mass suicide-murder site. ABC sent Shaw to Iran to report on the 1979 hostage crisis in at the American Embassy in Teheran. He then returned to Washington as ABC's senior Capitol Hill correspondent.

Prior to joining CBS News, Shaw was a reporter for Group W, Westinghouse Broadcasting Company, based first in Chicago and then in Washington (1966–1971). Shaw served as Group W's White House correspondent during the last year of the Johnson Administration (1968). His other assignments included local and national urban affairs, the struggles of the Mexican Americans and Puerto Ricans, and the plight of the American Indians in Billings, Montana. In 1966, he reported on the aftermath of the assassination of Dr. Martin Luther King Jr. in Memphis and his funeral in Atlanta.

Carole Simpson (1940–)
Television News Anchor

Carole Simpson, a native of Chicago, graduated from the University of Michigan with a bachelor of arts degree in journalism and did graduate work in journalism at the University of Iowa. She first entered broadcasting in 1965 as a reporter for a local radio

Carole Simpson

station, WCFL in Morris, Illinois. In 1968 she moved to radio station WBBM in Chicago and in 1970 she went to work as a reporter for the Chicago television station WMAQ.

Simpson made her first network appearance as a substitute anchor for NBC "Nightly News" and as anchor on NBC's "Newsbreak" on weekends. In 1982 Simpson joined ABC in Washington as a general assignment correspondent. She is currently an ABC News correspondent and weekend anchor.

Simpson has served as president of the Radio and Television Correspondents Association, as chairperson of the ABC Women's Advisory Board, as a member of the board of directors of the Washington Chapter of the Society of Professional Journalists, and is a member of Theta Sigma Phi. She has been awarded the Media Journalism Award, the

Milestone Award in Broadcast Journalism from the National Commission of Working Women, and the Silver Bell Award from the Ad Council.

Barbara Smith (1946–)
Publisher, Editor, Writer

Barbara Smith has co-authored and co-edited numerous books, including *Yours in Struggle, Three Feminist Perspectives on Anti-Semitism and Racism, Home Girls, A Black Feminist Anthology, But Some of Us Are Brave,* and *Black Women's Studies.* Smith, together with Myrna Bain, Cherrie Moraga, Mariana Romo-Carmona, operate Kitchen Table: Women of Color Press, the first publisher in the United States committed to publishing and distributing the work of third world women.

Pierre Montea Sutton (1947–)
Broadcast Executive

Pierre Sutton is president of Inner City Broadcasting Corporation in New York City and president of its radio stations in New York and California. He is the son of Percy E. Sutton, chairman of the board of Inner City Broadcasting and former borough president of Manhattan.

Pierre Sutton was born in New York City on February 1, 1947. He received a B.A. degree from the University of Toledo in 1968 and attended New York University in 1972.

He began his career in 1971 as vice president of Inner City Research and Analysis Corporation, was executive editor of the *New York Courier* newspaper in 1971–1972, served a public affairs director for WLIB radio from 1972 to 1975, was vice president of Inner City Broadcasting from 1975 to 1977, and became president in 1977. He has served as a board member of the Minority Investment Fund, first vice president of the National Association of Black Owned Broadcasters, chairman of the Harlem Boy Scouts, member of the board and executive committee of the New York City Marathon, trustee of the Alvin Ailey Dance Foundation, board member of the Better Business Bureau of Harlem, and member of the board of the Hayden Planetarium.

Susan Taylor (1946–)
Editor

Since 1981, Susan Taylor has been editor-in-chief of *Essence*, a magazine established in 1970 for black women.

A former actress, cosmetologist, and founder of her own cosmetics company, Nequai Cosmetics, Taylor began her relationship with *Essence* magazine as a freelance writer. In 1971 she became the magazine's beauty editor; from 1971 to 1980 she served as fashion and beauty editor. Taylor, now as editor-in-chief, is also executive coordinator of Essence Communications.

Lem Tucker (1938–1991)
Television News Correspondent

A native of Saginaw, Michigan, Lemuel Tucker was a graduate of Central Michigan University. Tucker worked as a Washington bureau correspondent for CBS news from 1977 until 1988. Prior to that he was with ABC News as New York City correspondent, from 1972 until 1977. From 1965 through 1972, Tucker was with NBC News where he served for some of that time as assistant bureau chief in Vietnam. He was awarded an Emmy for his reporting on hunger in the

Susan Taylor

Lem Tucker

United States, a series of seven reports broadcast during 1968 and 1969. He died in March of 1991 in Washington, DC.

PUBLISHERS

Afram Press
PO Box 2262
Philadelphia, PA 19101
(609)871-6992

Africa Fund
198 Broadway, 4th Fl.
New York, NY 10036
(212)962-1210

Africa World Press, Inc.
PO Box 1892
Trenton, NJ 08607
(609)771-1666

African-American Institute
833 United Nations Plaza
New York, NY 10017
(212)949-5666

**African & Caribbean Imprint Library
  Services**
236 Main St.
Falmouth, MA 02540
(508)540-5378

**African Studies Association/Crossroads
  Press**
Emory University
Atlanta, GA 30032
(404)329-6410

Africana Publishing Co.
30 Irving Pl.
New York, NY 10003
(212)254-4100

Afro-Am Publishing/Distributing Co., Inc.
407 E. 25th St., Ste. 600
Chicago, IL 60616
(312)791-1611

Akili Books of America
PO Box 1291
South Gate, CA 90280
(213)635-7191

Amen-Ra Publishing Co.
PO Box 328642
Columbus, OH 43232
(614)863-5189

Ankn Enterprises
PO Box 46085
Los Angeles, CA 90046
(213)850-7203

Arts & Communications Network Inc.
PO Box 435
Rosendale, NY 12440
(914)687-0767

Asante Publications
218 Main St., No. 425
Kirkland, WA 98033-6199
(619)287-7926

Associated Publishers, Inc.
1407 14th St. NW
Washington, DC 20005-3704
(202)265-1441

**Association of Caribbean Universities
and Research Institutes**
PO Box 11532
Caparra Heights Sta.
San Juan, Puerto Rico 00922
(809)764-0000

Aye-Aye Press
31 Queen St.
PO Box 1122
St. Croix, VI 00821
(809)778-8465

Balamp Publishing
4205 Fullerton
Detroit, MI 48238
(313)491-1950

Beckham House Publishers, Inc.
PO Box 177
Hampton, VA 23669
(804)851-9598

Benin Press Ltd.
5225 S. Blackstone Ave.
Chicago, IL 60615
(312)643-2363

Benin Publishing Co.
803 Columbus Dr.
Teaneck, NJ 07666
(201)837-8641

Black Classic Press
PO Box 13414
Baltimore, MD 21203
(410)602-0980

Black Economic Research Team Inc.
PO Box 13513
Baltimore, MD 21203

Black Entrepreneurs Press
4502 S. Congress Ave., Ste. 254
Austin, TX 78745

Black Graphics International
PO Box 732, Linwood Sta.
Detroit, MI 48206
(313)890-1128

Black Resource Guide, Inc.
501 Oneida Pl. NW
Washington, DC 20011
(202)291–4373

Blacklight Fellowship
2859 W. Wilcox St.
Chicago, IL 60612
(312)722–1441

Broadside Press
PO Box 04257
Detroit, MI 48204
(313)934–1231

Calaloux Publications
PO Box 812028
Wellesley, MA 02181–0012
(617)237–2230

Carib House (USA)
11305 Goleta St.
Los Angeles, CA 91342
(818)890–1056

Carver Publishing, Inc.
PO Box 9353
Hampton, VA 23670–0353
(804)838–1244

Charill Publishers
4468 San Francisco Ave.
St. Louis, MO 63115
(314)382–4998

Communicators Press
221 Sheridan St. NW
Washington, DC 20011
(202)726–8618

Detroit Black Writers' Guild, Inc.
5601 W. Warren
Detroit, MI 48210
(313)897–2551

Duncan & Duncan, Inc.
2809 Pulaski Hwy.
Edgewood, MD 21040
(410)538–5579

Essai Seay Publications
PO Box 55
East St. Louis, IL 62202–0055
(618)271–7890

Freeland Publications
PO Box 18941
Philadelphia, PA 19119
(215)226–2507

Gumbs & Thomas Publishers, Inc.
142 W. 72nd St., Ste. 9
New York, NY 10023
(212)769–8022

Heritage Press
PO Box 18625
Baltimore, MD 21216
(301)728–8521

Holloway House Publishing Co.
8060 Melrose Ave.
Los Angeles, CA 90046
(213)653–8060

Institute for Liberian Studies
4719 Chester Ave.
Philadelphia, PA 19143

Institute for Southern Studies
2009 Chapel Hill Rd.
Durham, NC 27707
(919)419–8311

Joint Center for Political and Economic Studies
1090 Vermont Ave. NW, Ste. 1100
Washington, DC 20005–4961
(202)789–3500

Just Us Books, Inc.
301 Main St., Ste. No. 22–24
Orange, NJ 07050
(201)672–7701

Kitchen Table: Women of Color Press
PO Box 908
Latham, NY 12110

M.L. Williams Publishing Co., Inc.
PO Box 53552
1315 Walnut St., Ste. 1624
Philadelphia, PA 19105
(215)735–1121

Majority Press
PO Box 538
Dover, MA 02030
(508)655–1631

National Center for Urban Ethnic Affairs
PO Box 20
Washington, DC 20064
(202)232–3600

New Day Press, Inc.
Karamu House
2355 E. 89th St.
Cleveland, OH 44106
(216)795–7070

Omenana
116 Howland St.
Roxbury, MA 02121
(617)445–0161

Open Hand Publishing Inc.
PO Box 22048
Seattle, WA 98122
(206)447–0597

Path Press, Inc.
53 W. Jackson Blvd., Ste. 724
Chicago, IL 60604
(312)663–0167

Raw Ink Press
Southwest Sta., PO Box 70417
Washington, DC 20024–0417
(202)686–4686

Red Sea Press, Inc.
15 Industry Ct.
Trenton, NJ 08638
(609)771–1666

Sabayt Publications, Inc.
PO Box 64898
Chicago, IL 60664
(312)667-2227

Shamal Books, Inc.
GPO Box 16
New York, NY 10116

Third World Press
7524 S. Cottage Grove Ave.
Chicago, IL 60619
(312)651-0700

Universal Black Writer Press
PO Box 5, Radio City Sta.
New York, NY 10101-0005

Urban Research Press, Inc.
840 E. 87th St.
Chicago, IL 60619
(312)994-7200

WREE (Women for Racial and Economic Equality)
198 Broadway, Rm. 606
New York, NY 10038
(212)385-1103

NEWSPAPERS

Alabama

Birmingham Times
The Birmingham Times Publishing Co.
115 3rd Ave. W
PO Box 10503
Birmingham, AL 35202
(205)251-5158

Circulation: 10,350

Birmingham World
407 15th St. N
Birmingham, AL 35203-1877
(205)251-6523

Circulation: 12,600

Campus Digest
Tuskegee University
Tuskegee, AL 36083
(205)727-8263

Greene County Democrat
Greene County Newspaper Co.
PO Box 598
Eutaw, AL 35462

Circulation: 3,500

Inner City News
Inner City Enterprises, Inc.
PO Box 1545
Mobile, AL 36633-1545
(205)452-9329

Circulation: 8,000

Mobile Beacon
2311 Costarides St.
PO Box 1407
Mobile, AL 36633
(205)479-0629

Circulation: 4,952

Montgomery-Tuskegee Times
3900 University Hwy.
Montgomery, AL 36108

Circulation: 10,000

The New Times
The New Times Group, Inc.
156 S. Broad St.
Mobile, AL 36602–0356
(205)432–0356

Circulation: 5,150

Shoals News Leader
PO Box 427
Florence, AL 35631
(205)766–5542

Circulation: 10,000

Speakin' Out News
2006 Poole Ave. NW
PO Box 2826
Huntsville, AL 35804
(205)852–9449

Circulation: 16,500

Arizona

Arizona Informant
1746 E. Madison, No. 2
Phoenix, AZ 85034
(602)257–9300

Circulation: 10,000

Arkansas

Arkansas State Press
PO Box 164037
Little Rock, AR 72216
(501)371–9991

Circulation: 5,000

California

Bakersfield News Observer
1219 20th St.
Bakersfield, CA 93301
(805)324–9446

Berkeley Tri City Post
The Alameda Publishing Corp.
PO Box 1350
Oakland, CA 94604
(510)763–1120

Circulation: 20,000

Black Voice News
PO Box 1581
Riverside, CA 92502
(714)682–6070

Circulation: 7,500

California Advocate
452 Fresno St.
PO Box 11826
Fresno, CA 93775
(209)268–0941

Circulation: 22,500

California Voice
2956 Sacramento St., Ste. C
Berkeley, CA 94702
(510)644–2446

Circulation: 37,325

Carson Bulletin
Rapid Publishing
PO Box 4248
Compton, CA 90224
(213)774–0018

Circulation: 17,l000

Central Star/Journal Wave
Central News-Wave Publications
2621 W. 54th St.
Los Angeles, CA 90043
(213)290–3000

    Circulation: 39,900

Compton/Carson Wave
Central News-Wave Publications
2621 W. 54th St.
Los Angeles, CA 90043
(213)290–3000

    Circulation: 38,200

Compton Bulletin
Rapid Publishing
PO Box 4248
Compton, CA 90224
(213)774–0018

    Circulation: 22,000

Compton Metropolitan Gazette
First–Line Publishers
17939 Chatsworth St., Ste. 429
Granada Hills, CA 91344
(818)782–8695

    Circulation: 60,000

Culver City/Westchester Star
Central News-Wave Publications
2621 W. 54th St.
Los Angeles, CA 90043
(213)290–3000

    Circulation: 33,750

Firestone Park News/Southeast News Press
PO Box 19027A
Los Angeles, CA 90019
(213)291–9486

    Circulation: 24,000

Herald Dispatch
3860 Crenshaw Blvd., Ste. 110
PO Box 19027A
Los Angeles, CA 90008
(213)291–9486

    Circulation: 35,000

Inglewood/Hawthorne Wave
Central News-Wave Publications
2621 W. 54th St.
Los Angeles, CA 90043
(213)290–3000

    Circulation: 44,075

Inglewood Tribune
Rapid Publishing
349 W. Compton
PO Box 4248
Compton, CA 90244
(213)774–0018

    Circulation: 10,000

L.A. Metropolitan Gazette
First-Line Publishers/L.A. Metro Group
14621 Titus St., Ste. 228
Van Nuys, CA 91402
(818)782–8695

    Circulation: 60,000

Long Beach Express
First-Line Publishers/L.A. Metro Group
14621 Titus St., Ste. 228
Van Nuys, CA 91402
(818)782–8695

    Circulation: 60,000

Los Angeles Sentinel
1112 E. 43rd St.
PO Box 11456
Los Angeles, CA 90011
(213)232–3261

Circulation: 28,000

Lynwood Journal
Rapid Publishing
349 W. Compton
PO Box 4248
Compton, CA 90224
(213)774–0018

Lynwood Wave
Central News-Wave Publications
2621 W. 54th St.
Los Angeles, CA 90043
(213)290–3000

Circulation: 24,020

Mesa Tribune Wave
Central News-Wave Publications
2621 W. 54th St.
Los Angeles, CA 90043
(213)290–3000

Circulation: 30,100

Metro Reporter
1366 Turk St.
San Francisco, CA 94115
(415)931–5778

Circulation: 108,895

Metro Star
42353 47th St. W.
Quartz Hill, CA 93534

New Bayview
Double Rock Press
1624 Oakdale Ave.
PO Box 24477
San Francisco, CA 94124–0477
(310)282–7894

Circulation: 12,000

Oakland Post
The Alameda Publishing Corp.
PO Box 1350
Oakland, CA 94604
(415)763–1120

Circulation: 62,496

Pasadena Gazette
First-Line Publishers/L.A. Metro Group
14621 Titus St., Ste. 228
Van Nuys, CA 91402
(818)782–8695

Circulation: 60,000

Precinct Reporter
1677 W. Baseline St.
San Bernardino, CA 92411
(714)889–0597

Circulation: 55,000

Richmond Post
The Alameda Publishing Corp.
PO Box 1350
Oakland, CA 94604–1350
(415)763–1120

Circulation: 13,661

Sacramento Observer
The Observer Newspapers
PO Box 209
Sacramento, CA 95801
(916)452-4781

Circulation: 49,090

The San Bernardino American News
1583 W. Baseline St.
San Bernardino, CA 92411-1756
(714)889-7677

Circulation: 5,000

The San Diego Voice and Viewpoint
1729 N. Euclid Ave.
San Diego, CA 92105
(619)266-2233

Circulation: 13,000

San Fernando Gazette Express
First-Line Publishers/L.A. Metro Group
14621 Titus St., Ste. 228
Van Nuys, CA 91402
(818)782-8695

Circulation: 60,000

San Francisco Post
The Alameda Publishing Corp.
PO Box 1350
Oakland, CA 94604
(415)763-1120

Circulation: 18,289

Seaside Post News-Sentinel
The Alameda Publishing Corp.
1244A Broadway Ave.
PO Box 670
Seaside, CA 93955
(408)394-6632

Circulation: 10,120

Southwest News Wave
Central News-Wave Publications, Inc.
2621 W. 54th St.
Los Angeles, CA 90043
(213)290-3000

Circulation: 40,450

Southwest Topics/Sun Wave
Central News-Wave Publications
2621 W. 54th St.
Los Angeles, CA 90043
(213)290-3000

Circulation: 30,000

Sun-Reporter
Reporter Publications
1366 Turk St.
San Francisco, CA 94115
(415)931-5778

Circulation: 11,249

Watts Star Review
PO Box 19027A
Los Angeles, CA 90019
(213)291-9486

Circulation: 30,000

Wilmington Beacon
Rapid Publishing
349 W. Compton
PO Box 4248
Compton, CA 90224
(213)774-0018

Colorado

Denver Weekly News
PO Box 38939
Denver, CO 80238-0939
(303)839-5800

Circulation: 17,500

Media

Connecticut

Hartford Inquirer
PO Box 1260
Hartford, CT 06143
(203)522-1462

Circulation: 125,000

Inner-City
2 Eld St.
New Haven, CT 06511
(203)773-0688

Circulation: 25,000

Delaware

The Defender
1702 Locust St.
Wilmington, DE 19802
(302)656-3252

Circulation: 15,300

District of Columbia

Metro Chronicle
529 14th St., Ste. 1143
Washington, DC 20045
(202)347-1114

New Observer
811 Florida Ave. NW
Washington, DC 20001
(202)232-3060

The Washington Capital Spotlight
  Newspaper
1264 National Press Bldg.
Washington, DC 20045
(202)628-0700

Circulation: 60,000

The Washington Informer
3117 Martin Luther King Jr. Ave. SE
Washington, DC 20032
(202)561-4100

Circulation: 27,000

The Washington New Observer
811 Florida Ave. NW
Washington, DC 20001
(202)232-3060

Circulation: 20,000

Florida

Black Miami Weekly
PO Box F
Miami, FL 33147

The Bulletin
2490 Dr. M.L. King, Jr. Way
PO Box 2560
Sarasota, FL 34230-2560
(813)953-3990

Circulation: 19,000

Capital Outlook
1501 E. Park
Tallahassee, FL 32301
(904)878-3895

Circulation: 11,333

Daytona Times
Daytona Times, Inc.
429 S. Dr. M.L. King Blvd.
PO Box 1110
Daytona Beach, FL 32115
(904)253-0321

Circulation: 20,150

The Famuan
Florida A&M University
Tallahassee, FL 32307
(904)599-3159

Circulation: 4,000

Florida Sentinel-Bulletin
2207-21st Ave.
PO Box 3363
Tampa, FL 33601
(813)248-1921

Circulation: 23,345

Florida Star Times
PO Box 40629
Jacksonville, FL 32203
(904)354-8880

Florida Sun Review
LMH Publications
702 18th St.
PO Box 2348
Orlando, FL 32802
(407)423-1156

Circulation: 16,500

Ft. Pierce Chronicle
1527 Avenue D
Fort Pierce, FL 34950
(407)461-7093

Circulation: 10,500

The Miami Times
900 NW 54th St.
Miami, FL 33127
(305)757-1147

Circulation: 28,250

News Reporter
1610 N. Howard Ave.
Tampa, FL 33607
(813)254-2608

Circulation: 9,694

The Orlando Times
PO Box 555339
Orlando, FL 32855-5339
(407)841-3710

Circulation: 5,710

Pensacola Voice
213 E. Yonge St.
Pensacola, FL 32503
(904)434-6963

Circulation: 35,896

Voice of the Wildcats
Bethune-Cookman College
640 2nd Ave.
Daytona Beach, FL 32115
(904)255-1401

Circulation: 3,000

The Weekly Challenger
2500 9th St. S.
Saint Petersburg, FL 33705
(813)896-2922

Circulation: 32,000

Westside Gazette
PO Box 5304
Fort Lauderdale, FL 33310
(305)523-5115

Circulation: 21,500

Georgia

Atlanta Daily World
145 Auburn Ave. NE
Atlanta, GA 30335–1201
(404)659–1110

Circulation: 20,000

Fort Valley Herald
Atlantic Communications of Georgia, Inc.
315 N. Camellia Blvd.
PO Box 899
Fort Valley, GA 31030
(912)825–7000

Circulation: 6,000

Metro County Courier
PO Box 2385
Augusta, GA 30903
(404)724–6556

Circulation: 19,040

Southeastern News
PO Box 489
Cordele, GA 31015
(912)278–67114

The Atlanta Inquirer
947 Martin Luther King Jr. Dr. NW
Atlanta, GA 30314
(404)523–6086

Circulation: 55,041

The Atlanta Voice
633 Pryor St. SW
Atlanta, GA 30312
(404)524–6426

Circulation: 103,000

The Columbus Times
2230 Buena Vista Rd.
PO Box 2845
Columbus, GA 31993–2999
(404)324–2404

Circulation: 20,000

The Herald
1803 Barnard St.
PO Box 486
Savannah, GA 31402
(912)232–4505

Circulation: 8,000

The Savannah Tribune
Savannah Tribune, Inc.
916 Montgomery St.
PO Box 2066
Savannah, GA 31402
(912)233–6128

Circulation: 16,000

Illinois

Chatham-Southeast Citizen
Citizen Newspapers
412 E. 87th St.
Chicago, IL 60619
(312)487–7700

Circulation: 26,630

Chicago Crusader
Crusader Newspapers
6429 S. Martin Luther King Dr.
Chicago, IL 60637
(312)752–2500

Circulation: 48,000

Chicago South Shore Scene
7426 S. Constance
Chicago, IL 60649
(312)363–0441

Circulation: 20,000

Chicago Citizen
Citizen Newspapers
412 E. 87th St.
Chicago, IL 60619
(312)487–7700

Chicago Independent Bulletin
2037 W. 95th St.
Chicago, IL 60643
(312)783–1040

Circulation: 64,000

Chicago Metro News
3437 S. Indiana Ave.
Chicago, IL 60616–3840
(312)842–5950

Circulation: 84,500

Chicago Shoreland News
AJA Enterprise
11740 S. Elizabeth
Chicago, IL 60643
(312)568–7091

Circulation: 380,000

Chicago Standard News
Standard Newspapers
615 S. Halsted
Chicago Heights, IL 60411
(708)755–5021

Circulation: 15,000

Chicago Weekend
Citizen Newspapers
412 E. 87th St.
Chicago, IL 60619
(312)487–7700

Circulation: 21,300

Decatur Voice
625 E. Wood St.
Decatur, IL 62523
(217)423–2231

Circulation: 19,000

East St. Louis Crusader
10th and State St.
East Saint Louis, IL 62205
(618)271–2000

East St. Louis Monitor
East St. Louis Monitor Publishing, Inc.
1501 State St.
Box 2137
East Saint Louis, IL 62205
(618)271–0468

Circulation: 22,500

Hyde Park Citizen
Citizen Newspapers
412 E. 87th St.
Chicago, IL 60619
(312)487–7700

Circulation: 15,000

Muslim Journal
Muslim Journal Enterprises, Inc.
910 W. Van Buren St., No. 100
Chicago, IL 60607–3523
(312)243–7600

Circulation: 16,000

Observer
6040 S. Harper St.
Chicago, IL 60637
(312)288–5840

  Circulation: 30,000

South End Citizen
Citizen Newspapers
412 E. 87th St.
Chicago, IL 60619
(312)487–7700

  Circulation: 17,087

South Suburban Citizen
Citizen Newspapers
412 E. 87th St.
Chicago, IL 60619
(312)487–7700

  Circulation: 18,500

South Suburban Standard
615 S. Halsted
Chicago Heights, IL 60411
(708)755–5021

  Circulation: 25,000

The Final Call
734 W. 79th St.
Chicago, IL 60620
(312)602–1230

  Circulation: 105,000

The Mississippi Enterprise
540 1/2 N. Farish St.
PO Box 87236
Chicago, IL 60680–0236

  Circulation: 2,800

Tri-City Journal
8 S. Michigan Ave., Ste. 1111
Chicago, IL 60603
(312)346–8123

  Circulation: 50,000

Indiana

Frost Illustrated
Frost, Inc.
3121 S. Calhoun
Fort Wayne, IN 46807–1901
(219)745–0552

  Circulation: 1,375

Gary American
2268 Broadway
Gary, IN 46407
(219)883–4903

  Circulation: 11,000

Gary New Crusader
1549 Broadway
Gary, IN 46407
(219)885–4357

  Circulation: 27,000

Info
Info Printing & Publishing, Inc.
1953 Broadway
Gary, IN 46407
(219)882–5591

  Circulation: 21,055

The Indianapolis Recorder
The George P. Stewart Printing, Inc.
2901 N. Tacoma Ave.
PO Box 18267
Indianapolis, IN 46218
(317)924–5143

Circulation: 10,281

Iowa

The New Iowa Bystander
PO Box 762
Des Moines, IA 50303

Kansas

The Kansas City Voice
2727 N. 13th St.
Kansas City, KS 66104
(913)371-0303

Kentucky

Louisville Defender
PO Box 2557
Louisville, KY 40201
(502)772-2591

Circulation: 2,270

The Suspension Press
PO Box 2064
Covington, KY 41012
(606)581-6589

Circulation: 40,200

Louisiana

Baton Rouge Community Leader
1010 North Blvd.
Baton Rouge, LA 70802
(504)343-0544

Circulation: 21,700

Community Leader
1210 North Blvd.
Baton Rouge, LA 70802

Louisiana Weekly
616 Baronne St.
New Orleans, LA 70150
(504)524-5563

Circulation: 4,156

New Orleans Data News Weekly
Data Enterprises, Inc.
1001 Howard Ave., Ste. 2309
PO Box 51933
New Orleans, LA 70151
(504)522-1418

Circulation: 21,000

The Alexandria News Weekly
1746 Mason
Alexandria, LA 71301
(318)443-7664

Circulation: 13,750

The Shreveport Sun
The Shreveport Sun, Inc.
PO Box 9328
Shreveport, LA 71139-9328
(318)631-6222

Circulation: 5,000

Maryland

Baltimore Afro-American
The Afro-American Co.
628 N. Eutaw St.
Baltimore, MD 21201
(301)728-8200

Circulation: 13,385

Every Wednesday
Afro-American Newspapers
628 N. Eutaw St.
Baltimore, MD 21201
(301)728–8200

Circulation: 42,777

Richmond Afro-American
The Afro-American Co.
628 N. Eutaw St.
Baltimore, MD 21201
(301)728–8200

Circulation: 13,385

Washington Afro-American
The Afro-American Co.
628 N. Eutaw St.
Baltimore, MD 21201
(301)728–8200

Circulation: 5,500

Massachusetts

Bay State Banner
925 Washington St.
Dorchester, MA 02124
(617)288–4900

Circulation: 11,500

Boston Greater News
PO Box 497
Roxbury, MA 02119–0004
(617)445–7063

Circulation: 12,300

Michigan

Ecorse Telegram
4122 10th St.
PO Box 4585
Ecorse, MI 48229
(313)928–2955

Circulation: 12,000

Jackson Blazer
PO Box 806
Jackson, MI 49204
(517)787–0450

Circulation: 6,100

Michigan Chronicle
Sengstacke Newspaper Corp.
479 Ledyard St.
Detroit, MI 48201
(313)963–5522

Circulation: 35,000

Michigan Citizen
New Day Publishing Enterprises
12541 2nd St.
Highland Park, MI 48203
(313)869–0033

Circulation: 41,520

The Detroit Times
B&Y Publications
11000 W. McNichols
Detroit, MI 48221
(313)342–1717

Circulation: 20,000

The Grand Rapids Times
PO Box 7258
Grand Rapids, MI 49510
(616)245–8737

The Michigan Sentinel
28440 Southfield Rd.
Lathrup Village, MI 48076
(313)559–1010

Circulation: 18,000

Minnesota

Minneapolis Spokesman
3744 4th Ave. S.
Minneapolis, MN 55409
(612)827–4021

Circulation: 1,300

St. Paul Recorder
3744 4th Ave. S.
Minneapolis, MN 55409
(612)827–4021

Twin Cities Courier
84 S. 6th St., Ste. 501
Minneapolis, MN 55402
(612)332–3211

Mississippi

Jackson Advocate
PO Box 3708
Jackson, MS 39207–3708
(601)948–4122

Circulation: 23,000

Mississippi Memo Digest
2511 5th St.
Box 5782
Meridian, MS 39301
(601)693–2372

Circulation: 3,050

Missouri

Call
Kansas City Call Inc.
PO Box 410–477
Kansas City, MO 64141
(816)842–3804

Kansas City Globe
Jordan Communications Co., Inc.
615 E. 29th St.
PO Box 090410
Kansas City, MO 64109
(816)531–5253

Circulation: 30,000

The Evening Whirl
PO Box 5088 Nagel Sta.
Saint Louis, MO 63115
(314)383–3875

Circulation: 40,000

The St. Louis American
American Publishing Co.
4144 Lindell Blvd.
Saint Louis, MO 63108
(314)533–8000

St. Louis Argus
4595 Martin Luther King Dr.
Saint Louis, MO 63113
(314)531–1323

Circulation: 15,000

St. Louis Crusader
4371 Finney Ave.
Saint Louis, MO 63113
(314)531–5860

St. Louis Sentinel Newspaper
Woods Publications
2900 N. Market
Saint Louis, MO 63106
(314)531-2691

Circulation: 20,200

Nevada

Las Vegas Sentinel-Voice
1201 S. Eastern Ave.
Las Vegas, NV 89104
(702)383-4030

Circulation: 5,000

New Jersey

Afro-American
429 Central Ave.
East Orange, NJ 07108
(201)672-9102

Black Voice/Carta Boricua
Rutgers University
Student Activities Center
Box 28
George St.
New Brunswick, NJ 08903
(908)828-9554

Circulation: 4,000

New Jersey Afro-American
PO Box 22162
Newark, NJ 07103
(201)242-5364

Circulation: 20,000

New York

Afro-American Times
1360 Fulton St.
Brooklyn, NY 11216
(718)636-9500

Afro-Americans in New York Life and History
Afro-American Historical Association of the Niagara Frontier, Inc.
PO Box 1663, Hertle Sta.
Buffalo, NY 14216
(716)878-5412

Circulation: 600

Amsterdam News
2340 Frederick Douglass Blvd.
New York, NY 10027
(212)932-7400

Circulation: 32,701

Big Red News
Smith Haj Enterprises
155 Water St., 4th Fl.
Brooklyn, NY 11201
(718)852-6001

Circulation: 53,766

Black American
Cool Magazine, Inc.
310 Lenox Ave., No. 304
New York, NY 10027-4411
(212)564-5110

Circulation: 352,640

Brooklyn New York Recorder
86 Bainbridge St.
Brooklyn, NY 11233
(718)493-4616

Buffalo Criterion
623 William St.
Buffalo, NY 14206
(716)882-9570

Buffalo Fine Print News
806 Fillmore Ave.
Buffalo, NY 14205
(716)855-3810

Circulation: 10,000

Communicade
Okang Communications Corp.
104 Magnolia St.
PO Box 60739
Rochester, NY 14606
(716)235-6695

Circulation: 3,000

Daily Challenge
1360 Fulton St.
Brooklyn, NY 11216
(718)636-9500

Hudson Valley Black Press
PO Box 2160
Newburgh, NY 12550
(914)562-1313

Circulation: 42,500

Jamaica Shopping & Entertainment Guide
North American Publications
164-11 89th Ave., Ste. 190
Jamaica, NY 11432
(718)591-7777

Circulation: 30,000

NY Carib News
28 W. 39th St.
New York, NY 10018
(212)944-1991

Circulation: 71,500

The Challenger
1303 Fillmore Ave.
Buffalo, NY 14211
(716)897-0442

Circulation: 10,000

The City Sun
The City Sun Publishing Co., Inc.
GPO 560
Brooklyn, NY 11202
(718)624-5959

Circulation: 20,000

The New York Voice-Harlem U.S.A.
75-43 Parsons Blvd.
Flushing, NY 11366
(718)591-6600

Circulation: 1,624

Westchester County Press
PO Box 1631
White Plains, NY 10602
(914)684-0006

Circulation: 20,000

Westchester Observer
542 E. 3rd St.
Mount Vernon, NY 10553

North Carolina

Carolina Peacemaker
400 Summit Ave.
Greensboro, NC 27405
(919)274-6210

    Circulation: 5,490

Iredell County News
PO Box 407
Statesville, NC 28687
(704)873-1054

    Circulation: 5,000

Star of Zion
A.M.E. Zion Publishing House
PO Box 31005
Charlotte, NC 28231-1005
(704)377-4329

    Circulation: 7,700

The 'M' Voice Newspaper
PO Box 8361
Greenville, NC 27834
(919)757-0365

The Carolina Times
PO Box 3825
Durham, NC 27702
(919)682-2913

    Circulation: 5,300

The Carolinian
518 E. Martin St.
PO Box 25308
Raleigh, NC 27601
(919)834-5558

    Circulation: 9,200

The Charlotte Post
1531 Camden Rd.
PO Box 30144
Charlotte, NC 28230
(704)376-0496

    Circulation: 11,500

The Fayetteville Black Times
The Black Press, Inc.
108 Webb St.
PO Box 863
Fayetteville, NC 28302

The Public Post
PO Box 1951
Laurinburg, NC 28352
(919)875-8938

The Wilmington Journal
412 S. 7th St.
Wilmington, NC 28401
(919)762-5502

    Circulation: 8,600

Winston-Salem Chronicle
617 N. Liberty St.
PO Box 1636
Winston-Salem, NC 27102
(919)722-8624

    Circulation: 7,500

Ohio

Call and Post
1949 E. 105 St.
PO Box 6237
Cleveland, OH 44101
(216)791–7600

    Circulation: 43,283

Cincinnati Herald
Porter Publishing
836 Lincoln Ave.
Cincinnati, OH 45206

    Circulation: 24,500

South East Times
3249 E. 137th St.
Cleveland, OH 44120
(216)921–2788

The Akron Reporter
1134 S. Main St.
PO Box 2042
Akron, OH 44309
(216)253–0007

    Circulation: 17,000

The Buckeye Review
William Publishing Co.
620 Belmont Ave.
Youngstown, OH 44502
(216)743–2250

    Circulation: 5,100

The Toledo Journal
3021 Douglas Rd.
PO Box 2536
Toledo, OH 43606
(419)472–4521

    Circulation: 17,000

Oklahoma

The Black Chronicle
PO Box 17498
Oklahoma City, OK 73136
(405)424–4695

    Circulation: 28,927

The Oklahoma Eagle
PO Box 3267
Tulsa, OK 74101
(918)582–71124

    Circulation: 12,800

Oregon

Portland Observer
PO Box 3137
Portland, OR 97211
(503)288–0015

    Circulation: 10,000

The Portland Skanner
PO Box 5455
Portland, OR 97228–5455
(503)287–3562

    Circulation: 20,000

Pennsylvania

New Pittsburgh Courier
315 E. Carson St.
Pittsburgh, PA 15219
(412)481–8302

    Circulation: 30,000

Philadelphia New Observer
1930 Chestnut St., Ste. 900
PO Box 30092
Philadelphia, PA 19103
(215)665–8400

    Circulation: 18,400

The Leader
Intercounty Publishing Co.
2923 W. Cheltenham Ave.
Philadelphia, PA 19150
(215)885–4111
    Circulation: 29,000

The Lincolnian
Lincoln University
English Dept
Lincoln University, PA 19352
(215)932–8300
    Circulation: 1,300

The Philadelphia Tribune
524–526 S. 16th St.
Philadelphia, PA 19146
(215)893–4050
    Circulation: 33,890

Rhode Island

Ocean State Grapevine
PO Box 16333
Providence, RI 02916–0693

South Carolina

Charleston Black Times
South Carolina Black Media Group
1310 Harden
Columbia, SC 29204
(803)799–5252
    Circulation: 6,883

Columbia Black News
South Carolina Black Media Group
PO Box 11128
Columbia, SC 29211
(803)799–5252

    Circulation: 22,834

Florence Black Sun
1310 Harden
Columbia, SC 29204
(803)799–5252
    Circulation: 5,734

Greenville Black Star
1310 Harden
Columbia, SC 29204
(803)799–5252
    Circulation: 6,849

Orangeburg Black Voice
1310 Harden
Columbia, SC 29204
(803)799–5252
    Circulation: 5,365

Rock Kill Black View
South Carolina Black Media Group
1310 Harden
Columbia, SC 29204
(803)799–5252
    Circulation: 4,882

Sumter Black Post
1310 Harden
Columbia, SC 29211
(803)799–5252
    Circulation: 5,355

The Charleston Chronicle
Chronicle Communications Corp.
534 King St.
PO Box 20548
Charleston, SC 29413–0548
(803)723–2785

Circulation: 8.000

The Coastal Times
701 E. Bay St.
BTC Box 1407
Charleston, SC 29403
(803)723-5318

Circulation: 4,580

View South News
PO Box 1849
Orangeburg, SC 29116
(803)531-1662

Circulation: 5,000

Tennessee

The Catholic Mentor
Winston Derek Publishers, Inc.
PO Box 90883
Nashville, TN 37209
(615)321-0535

Fisk News
Fisk University
1000 17th Ave. N.
Nashville, TN 37203
(615)329-8710

Circulation: 1,000

Memphis Silver Star News
3144 Park Ave.
Memphis, TN 38111

Tri-State Defender
PO Box 2065
Memphis, TN 38101-2065
(901)523-1818

Circulation: 15,000

Texas

Dallas Examiner
424 Centre St.
Dallas, TX 75208
(214)948-9175

Circulation: 50,000

Dallas Post Tribune
2726 S. Beckley
Dallas, TX 75224
(214)946-7678

Circulation: 30,000

Houston Forward Times
Forward Times Publishing Co.
4411 Almeda Rd.
PO Box 8346
Houston, TX 77288-8346
(713)526-4727

Circulation: 52,260

Houston Informer
PO Box 3086
Houston, TX 77253
(713)527-8261

Circulation: 23,000

Houston Defender
PO Box 8005
Houston, TX 77288
(713)663-7716

Circulation: 15,000

Houston Sun
2322 Blodgett St.
PO Box 600603
Houston, TX 77260-5218
(713)524-4474

Circulation: 80,000

Lubbock Southwest Digest
510 E. 23rd St.
Lubbock, TX 79404
(806)762–3612

   Circulation: 3,000

The Dallas Weekly Newspaper
Ad-Mast Publishing, Inc.
Anthony T. Davis Bldg.
3101 Martin Luther King, Jr. Blvd.
Dallas, TX 75215
(214)428–8958

   Circulation: 50,000

The Villager
1223–A Rosewood Ave.
Austin, TX 78702
(512)476–0082

   Circulation: 6,000

The Waco Messenger
Smith Printing Co.
PO Box 2087
Waco, TX 76703
(817)799–6911

   Circulation: 3,000

Virginia

Journal & Guide
362 Campostella Rd.
Norfolk, VA 23523–2204
(804)625–3686

   Circulation: 25,000

Roanoke Tribune
PO Box 6021
Roanoke, VA 24017
(703)343–0326

   Circulation: 5,200

Washington

Facts News
2765 E. Cherry St.
PO Box 22015
Seattle, WA 98122
(206)324–0552

   Circulation: 40,270

The Northwest Dispatch
PO Box 5637
Tacoma, WA 98405
(206)272–7587

   Circulation: 11,600

Seattle Medium
2600 S. Jackson
Seattle, WA 98144
(206)323–3070

   Circulation: 37,000

Tacoma True Citizen
2600 S. Jackson St.
Seattle, WA 98144
(206)627–1103

   Circulation: 13,500

West Virginia

West Virginia Beacon Digest
PO Box 981
Charleston, WV 25324
(304)342–4600

   Circulation: 35,861

Wisconsin

Milwaukee Community Journal
Community Journal, Inc.
3612 N. Martin Luther King Dr.
Milwaukee, WI 53212
(414)265-5300

Circulation: 39,430

Milwaukee Courier
2431 W. Hopkins St.
Milwaukee, WI 53206
(414)449-4866

Circulation: 15,000

Milwaukee Star
3815 N. Teutonia Ave.
Milwaukee, WI 53206
(414)449-4870

Circulation: 25,000

Milwaukee Times
2183 N. Sherman Blvd.
PO Box 16489
Milwaukee, WI 53216-0489
(414)444-8611

MAGAZINES AND JOURNALS

A&T Register
North Carolina Agricultural & Technical
  University
Box E25
Greensboro, NC 27411
(919)334-7700

About . . . Time
About . . . Time Magazine, Inc.
283 Genesee St.
Rochester, NY 14611
(716)235-7150

Circulation: 27,700

Alternative Press Index
PO Box 33109
Baltimore, MD 21218
(410)243-2471

Circulation: 650

American Visions: The Magazine of Afro-American Culture
Warwick Communications
Carter G. Woodson House
Smithsonian Institution
Washington, DC 20560
(202)462-1779

Circulation: 100,000

The Atlanta Tribune
L & L Communications, Inc.
875 Old Roswell Rd., Ste. C-100
Roswell, GA 30076
(404)587-0501

Circulation: 32,000

AUC Digest
Atlanta University Center
PO Box 3191
Atlanta, GA 30302
(404)523-6136

Circulation: 10,100

Black American Literature Forum
Indiana State University
Dept. of English
Terre Haute, IN 47809
(812)237-2968

Circulation: 1,240

Black Careers
Project Magazine, Inc.
PO Box 8214
Philadelphia, PA 19101-8214
(215)387-1600

Circulation: 400,000

Black College Sports Review
Winston-Salem Chronicle
617 N. Liberty St.
Winston-Salem, NC 27102
(919)723-9026

The Black Collegian
Black Collegiate Services, Inc.
1240 S. Broad St.
New Orleans, LA 70125-2091
(504)821-5694

    Circulation: 114,400

Black Employment and Education
   Magazine
Hamdani Communications Inc.
2625 Piedmont Rd.
Bldg. 56, Ste. 282
Atlanta, GA 30324
(404)469-5891

    Circulation: 175,000

Black Enterprise
Earl Graves Publishing
130 5th Ave.
New York, NY 10011
(212)242-8000

    Circulation: 251,983

Black Family
Kent Enterprises, Inc.
Box 1046
Herndon, VA 22070-1046

    Circulation: 225,000

Black Health
Altier & Maynard Communications, Inc.
6 Farmingville Rd.
Ridgefield, CT 06877
(203)431-3454

    Circulation: 26,000

Black News Digest
U.S. Dept. of Labor
Office of Information & Public Affairs
200 Constitution Ave. NW
Washington, DC 20210
(202)523-7323

The Black Scholar
Black World Foundation
PO Box 2869
Oakland, CA 94609
(415)547-6633

    Circulation: 70,000

Black Tennis Magazine
PO Box 210767
Dallas, TX 75211
(214)339-7370

    Circulation: 5,000

The Black Writer
Terrell Associates
PO Box 1030
Chicago, IL 60690
(312)995-5195

    Circulation: 600

Botswana Review
PO Box 278
Ivoryton, CT 06442

Callaloo
The Johns Hopkins University Press
701 W. 40th St., Ste. 275
Baltimore, MD 21211
(410)516-6982

    Circulation: 1,650

Career Focus
Communications Publishing Group, Inc.
106 W. 11th St., Ste. 250
Kansas City, MO 64105–1806
(816)756–3039

    Circulation: 260,000

Chocolate Singles
Chocolate Singles Enterprises, Inc.
PO Box 333
Jamaica, NY 11413
(212)624–6247

The Christian Index
The Christian Methodist Episcopal Church
PO Box 665
Memphis, TN 38101
(901)345–1173

    Circulation: 6,000

Class Magazine
900 Broadway
New York, NY 10003
(212)677–3055

    Circulation: 204,845

Clubdate Magazine
1826 E. 93rd St.
Cleveland, OH 44106–2052
(216)752–8410

    Circulation: 15,897

Confrontation/Change Review
3955 Denlinger Rd.
Dayton, OH 45426
(513)837–0498

    Circulation: 3,200

Corporate Headquarters
HQ Publications
516 North Ave. E
Westfield, NJ 07090
(201)233–8837

    Circulation: 10,760

The Crisis
NAACP/Crisis Publishing
260 5th Ave., 6th Fl.
New York, NY 10001–6408
(212)481–4100

    Circulation: 350,000

Dollars & Sense Magazine
1610 E. 79th St.
Chicago, IL 60649
(312)375–6800

    Circulation: 286,000

Ebony
820 S. Michigan Ave.
Chicago, IL 60605
(312)322–9200

    Circulation: 1,887,595

EM: Ebony Man
Johnson Publishing Co.
820 S. Michigan Ave.
Chicago, IL 60605
(312)322–9200

    Circulation: 200,000

Emerge
Emerge Communications Inc.
170 Varick St., 12th Fl.
New York, NY 10013
(212)627–4151

    Circulation: 150,000

Essence
Essence Communications, Inc.
1500 Broadway 6th Fl.
New York, NY 10036
(212)642–0600

  Circulation: 850,116

Feelin' Good
Ware Publishing, Inc.
400 Corporate Pointe, No. 580
Culver City, CA 90230
(213)649–3320

  Circulation: 250,000

Gladiator
135 W. 50th St.
New York, NY 10020
(212)307–8000

  Circulation: 30,000

In a Word
Society of the Divine Word
Bay Saint Louis, MS 39520
(601)467–1097

  Circulation: 38,500

**The International Review of African
  American Art**
Museum of African American Art
4005 Crenshaw Blvd., 3rd Fl.
Los Angeles, CA 90008–2534
(213)294–7071

Ivy Leaf
Alpha Kappa Alpha Sorority, Inc.
5656 W. Stony Island Ave.
Chicago, IL 60637
(312)684–1282

  Circulation: 37,000

Jet
Johnson Publishing Co., Inc.
820 S. Michigan Ave.
Chicago, IL 60605
(312)322–9200

  Circulation: 968,545

Journal of Black Studies
Sage Periodicals Press
2455 Teller Rd.
Newbury Park, CA 91320
(805)499–0721

  Circulation: 1,460

The Journal of Negro Education
Howard University
PO Box 311
Washington, DC 20059
(202)806–8120

  Circulation: 2,000

Journal of Negro History
Assn. for the Study of Afro-American Life
  and History
Morehouse College
Box 721
Atlanta, GA 30314
(404)681–2650

  Circulation: 4,000

**Journal of the National Medical
  Association**
Slack, Inc.
6900 Grove Rd.
Thorofare, NJ 08086–9447
(609)898–1000

  Circulation: 24,500

Journal of the National Technical Association
Black Collegiate Services, Inc.
1240 S. Broad St.
New Orleans, LA 70125–2091
(504)821–5694

Circulation: 18,820

Lincoln Review
The Lincoln Institute for Research and
  Education, Inc.
1001 Connecticut Ave. NW, Ste. 1135
Washington, DC 20036
(202)223–5112

Circulation: 7,000

Living Blues
Center for the Study of Southern Culture
University of Mississippi
University, MS 38677
(601)232–5518

Circulation: 16,000

Message Magazine
Review and Herald Publishing Assoc.
55 W. Oak Ridge Dr.
Hagerstown, MD 21740
(301)791–7000

Circulation: 78,330

Minorities and Women in Business
Venture X, Inc.
PO Drawer 210
Burlington, NC 27216
(919)229–1462

Circulation: 85,000

Minority Business Entrepreneur
924 N. Market St.
Inglewood, CA 90302
(310)673–9398

Circulation: 26,851

Minority Business Social and Cultural Directory
PO Box 10112
Augusta, GA 30903
(404)722–7327

Circulation: 18,000

National Scene Magazine
22 E. 41st St.
New York, NY 10017
(212)862–3700

The Negro Educational Review
The Negro Educational Review, Inc.
Box 2895, General Mail Center
Jacksonville, FL 32203
(904)646–2860

Circulation: 5,000

Negro History Bulletin
The Assn. for the Study of Afro-American
  Life & History, Inc.
1407 14th St. NW
Washington, DC 20005–3704
(202)667–2822

Circulation: 10,000

The New Research Traveler & Conventioneer
11717 S. Vincennes Ave.
Chicago, IL 60643
(312)881–3712

Circulation: 88,550

New Visions
16360 Broadway
Maple Heights, OH 44137
(216)581–7070

Nightmoves
Nightmoves Publishing Co.
105 W. Madison, Ste. 1100
Chicago, IL 60602

Circulation: 100,000

NSBE Magazine
NSBE Publications
1454 Duke St.
Alexandria, VA 22314
(703)549–2207

Circulation: 20,934

Players
Players International Publications
8060 Melrose Ave.
Los Angeles, CA 90046
(213)653–8060

Circulation: 175,000

Right On!
Lexington Library, Inc.
355 Lexington Ave.
New York, NY 10017
(212)973–3200

Circulation: 350,000

SENGA
Megasin Publications
7501 Morrison Rd.
New Orleans, LA 70126
(504)242–6022

Shooting Star Review
Shooting Star Productions Inc.
7123 Race St.
Pittsburgh, PA 15208–1424
(412)731–7039

SISTERS
National Council of Negro Women, Inc.
1667 K. St. NW, Ste. 700
Washington, DC 20006
(202)659–0006

Circulation: 100,000

**Sophisticate's Black Hairstyles and
    Care Guide**
Associated Publications Inc.
1165 N. Clark St., No. 607
Chicago, IL 60610
(312)266–8680

Circulation: 182,250

Upscale
Upscale Communications
594 Fielding Ln.
Atlanta, GA 30311
(404)758–7467

Circulation: 200,000

US Black Engineer
Career Communications Group, Inc.
729 E. Pratt St., Ste. 504
Baltimore, MD 21202
(410)244–7101

Circulation: 15,636

Voice of Missions
475 Riverside Dr., Rm. 1926
New York, NY 10115
(212)870–2258

Washington View
Viewcomm, Inc.
1101 14th St. NW
Washington, DC 20005
(202)371-1313

   Circulation: 40,000

The Western Journal of Black Studies
Cooper Publication
Pullman, WA 99164-5910
(509)335-8681

   Circulation: 430

Word Up!
Word Up! Publications, Inc.
63 Grand Ave.
River Edge, NJ 07661
(201)487-6124

RADIO NETWORKS

American-Urban Radio Network
463 7th Ave.
New York, NY 10018
(212)714-1000

Black Radio Network
166 Madison Ave., 6th Fl.
New York, NY 10016
(212)686-6850

Sheridan Broadcasting Network
411 7th Ave., Ste. 1500
Pittsburgh, PA 15219
(412)456-4000

RADIO STATIONS

Alabama

WBIL-FM
PO Box 666
Tuskegee, AL 36083
(205)727-2100

WBLX-AM
1204 Dauphin St.
Mobile, AL 36604
(205)432-7609

WBLX-FM
1204 Dauphin St.
Mobile, AL 36604
(205)432-7609

WENN-FM
424 16th St. N.
Birmingham, AL 35203
(205)254-1820

WGOK-AM
Box 1425
Mobile, AL 36633
(205)432-8661

WHBB-AM
505 Lauderdale St.
PO Box 1055
Selma, AL 36701
(205)875-3350

WJLD-AM
1449 Spaulding Ishkooda Rd.
Birmingham, AL 35211
(205)942-1776

WLAY-FM
620 E. 2nd St.
Muscle Shoals, AL 35660
(205)381-1450

WMML-FM
1050 Government St.
Mobile, AL 36604-2404
(205)433-9577

WMMV-FM
PO Box 9091
Spanish Fort, AL 36527-0901
(205)433-9577

WQGL-FM
PO Box 566
Butler, AL 36904
(205)459-3222

WRAG-AM
Hwy. 17 S.
PO Box 71
Carrollton, AL 35447
(205)367-8136

WSBM-AM
624 S. Chestnut St.
PO Box 932
Florence, AL 35631
(205)764-8121

WSLY-FM
11474 U.S. Hwy. 11
York, AL 36925
(205)392-5234

WTUG-FM
142 Skyland Blvd.
Tuscaloosa, AL 35405
(205)345-7200

WZMG-AM
915 Saugahatchee Lake Rd.
PO Box 2329
Opelika, AL 36803

WZTN-AM
PO Box 9133
Montgomery, AL 36108-0133
(205)262-8211

WZZA-AM
1570 Woodmont Dr.
Tuscumbia, AL 35674
(205)381-1862

Arizona

KISP-AM
4745 N. 7th St., Ste. 135
Phoenix, AZ 85014
(602)234-1015

Arkansas

KCAT-AM
PO Box 8808
Pine Bluff, AR 71611-8808
(501)534-5000

KELD-AM
2525 Northwest Ave.
El Dorado, AR 71730
(501)863-6162

KJWH–AM
214 Van Buren
Camden, AR 71701
(501)836–9393

KMZX–FM
314 N. Main St., Ste. 106
North Little Rock, AR 72114
(501)376–1063

KXAR–FM
Hwy 29 at I–30
Hope, AR 71801
(501)777–3601

California

KACE–FM
161 N. LaBrea Ave.
Inglewood, CA 90301
(213)330–3100

KDAY–AM
1700 N. Alvarado St.
Los Angeles, CA 90026–1777
(213)665–1105

KDIA–AM
100 Swan Way
Oakland, CA 94621
(510)633–2548

KDLA–AM
1700 N. Alvarado St.
Los Angeles, CA 90026
(213)781580

KFSR–FM
California State University Fresno
Shaw & Maple Sts.
Fresno, CA 93740–0046
(209)278–4500

KGFJ–AM
1100 S. LaBrea Ave.
Los Angeles, CA 90019
(213)930–9090

KJLH–FM
3847 Crenshaw Blvd.
Los Angeles, CA 90008
(213)299–5960

KKBT–FM
6735 Yucca St.
Hollywood, CA 90028
(213)466–9566

KMJC–AM
4875 N. Harbor Dr.
San Diego, CA 92106–2304
(619)224–1556

KSRH–FM
185 Mission Ave.
San Rafael, CA 94901
(415)457–5774

WILD–FM
55 Green St., 2nd Fl.
San Francisco, CA 94111
(415)391–1077

Colorado

KDKO–AM
2559 Welton St.
Denver, CO 80205
(303)295–1255

KEPC–FM
5675 S. Academy Blvd.
Colorado Springs, CO 80904
(719)540–7489

KKMG–FM
411 Lakewood Circle
Colorado Springs, CO 80910–2617
(719)576–1100

Connecticut

WKND–AM
544 Windsor Ave.
PO Box 1480
Windsor, CT 06095
(203)688–6221

WNHC–AM
112 Washington Ave.
North Haven, CT 06473
(203)234–1340

WQTQ–FM
Weaver High School
415 Granby St.
Hartford, CT 06112
(203)722–8661

WYBC–FM
165 Elm St.
PO Box WYBC
New Haven, CT 06520
(203)432–4118

District of Columbia

WHUR–FM
529 Bryant St. NW
Washington, DC 20059
(202)806–3500

WMMJ–FM
400 H St. NE
Washington, DC 20002
(202)675–4800

WOL–AM
400 H St. NE
Washington, DC 20002
(202)675–4800

Florida

WAMF–FM
Florida A&M University
314 Tucker Hall
Tallahassee, FL 32307
(904)599–3083

WANM–AM
300 W. Tennessee
Tallahassee, FL 32301
(904)222–1070

WAVS–AM
4124 SW 64th Ave.
Davie, FL 33314
(305)584–1170

WEDR–FM
Box 551748
Opa–Locka, FL 33054
(305)623–7711

WEXY–AM
412 W. Oakland Park Blvd
Fort Lauderdale, FL 33311–1712
(305)561–1520

WHJX–FM
10592 E. Balmoral Circle, Ste. 1
Jacksonville, FL 32218
(904)696–1015

WHQT–FM
3200 Ponce de Leon Blvd.
Miami, FL 33134
(305)445–5411

WJHM–FM
434 Sanlando Center, No. 124
Longwood, FL 32779–4299
(407)788–1400

WLIT–AM
3033 Riviera Dr., No. 200
Naples, FL 33940–4134
(803)248–9040

WMBM–AM
814 1st St.
Miami Beach, FL 33139
(305)672–1100

WPOM–AM
6667 42nd Terrace N.
West Palm Beach, FL 33407
(407)844–6200

WPUL–AM
2598 S. Nova Rd.
South Daytona, FL 32021
(904)767–1131

WRBD–AM
4431 Rock Island Rd.
Fort Lauderdale, FL 33319
(305)731–4800

WRTO–FM
2960 Coral Way
Miami, FL 33145
(305)445–4040

WRXB–AM
3000 34th St. S., Ste. 206B
Saint Petersburg, FL 33711
(813)864–1515

WSRX–FM
2634 E. Tamiami Trail
Naples, FL 33962
(813)775–1999

WSWN–AM
2001 State Road 715
PO Box 1505
Belle Glade, FL 33430
(407)996–2063

WTCL–AM
Box 157
Chattahoochee, FL 32324
(904)663–2323

WTMP–AM
PO Box 1101
Tampa, FL 33601
(813)626–4108

WTOT–AM
140 W. Lafayette St., Ste. A
PO Box 569
Marianna, FL 32446
(904)482–3046

WWAB–AM
1203 W. Chase St.
Lakeland, FL 33801
(813)646–2151

WWKO–AM
200 Burnett Rd.
Cocoa, FL 32926
(407)636–8600

WYFX–AM
400 Gulfstream Blvd.
Delray Beach, FL 33444
(407)737–1040

WZAZ–AM
2611 WERD Radio Dr.
Jacksonville, FL 32204
(904)389–1111

WZAZ–FM
PO Box 5635
Jacksonville, FL 32247
(904)389–1111

Georgia

WAKB–FM
PO Box 769
Wrens, GA 30833–0769
(404)547–0967

WBKZ–AM
4005 Atlanta Hwy., Ste. 100
PO Box 88
Athens, GA 30603
(404)548–8800

WFXM–FM
369 2nd St.
PO Box 4527
Macon, GA 31208
(912)742–2505

WGOV–AM
Hwy. 84 W.
PO Box 1207
Valdosta, GA 31603
(912)242–4513

WHGH–AM
PO Box 2218
Thomasville, GA 31799
(912)228–4124

WIGO–AM
1532 Howell Mill Rd.
Atlanta, GA 30318
(404)352–3943

WJGA–FM
PO Box 3878
Jackson, GA 30233
(404)775–3151

WPGA–FM
PO Drawer 980
Perry, GA 31069
(912)987–2980

WQVE–FM
Box 434
Camilla, GA 31730
(912)294–0010

WRDW–AM
11480 Eisenhower Dr.
Augusta, GA 30907
(803)278–1212

WSNT–AM
PO Box 150
Sandersville, GA 31082
(912)552–5182

WSNT–FM
PO Box 150
Sandersville, GA 31082
(912)552–5182

WVEE–FM
120 Ralph McGill Blvd., Ste. 1000
Atlanta, GA 30365–6901
(404)898–8900

WVVS–FM
Box 142
Valdosta, GA 31698
(912)333–5661

WXAG–AM
2145 S. Milledge Ave.
Athens, GA 30605
(404)549–1470

WXGC–FM
Box 3124
Milledgeville, GA 31061–1000
(912)453–4102

WXRS–AM
Box 1590
Swainsboro, GA 30401
(912)237–1590

Hawaii

KINE–FM
741 Bishop St./Kilohana
Honolulu, HI 96813–4812
(808)524–7100

Illinois

WBCP–AM
PO Box 1023
Champion, IL 61820
(217)359–1580

WCFJ–AM
1000 Lincoln Hwy.
Ford Heights, IL 60411
(708)758–8600

WDKT–AM
PO Box 067607
Chicago, IL 60661
(205)772–7300

WEMG–AM
12844 S. Halsted St.
Chicago, IL 37921
(312)468–1060

WGCI–FM
332 S. Michigan Ave., Ste. 600
Chicago, IL 60604
(312)984–1400

WKRO–AM
Rte, 1, US–51
Cairo, IL 62914
(618)734–1490

WLUV–FM
2272 Elmwood
Rockford, IL 61103
(815)877–9588

WOUI–FM
3300 S. Federal St.
Chicago, IL 60616
(312)567–3087

WVAZ–FM
408 S. Oak Park Ave.
Oak Park, IL 60302
(708)524–3200

Indiana

WPZZ–FM
645 Industrial Dr.
Franklin, IN 46131
(317)736–4040

WSYW–AM
8203 Indy Ct.
Indianapolis, IN 46214–2300
(317)271–9799

WTLC–FM
2126 N. Meridan St.
Indianapolis, IN 46202
(317)923–1456

WUEV–FM
1800 Lincoln Ave.
Evansville, IN 47722
(812)479–2022

Iowa

KALA–FM
518 W. Locust St.
Davenport, IA 52803–2898
(319)383–8911

KIGC–FM
William Penn College
N. Market & Trueblood Aves.
Oskaloosa, IA 52577
(515)673–1095

KRUI–FM
897 South Quad
Iowa City, IA 52242
(319)335–9525

KUNI–FM
University of Northern Iowa
Cedar Falls, IA 50614–0359
(319)273–6400

Kansas

KSWC–FM
Southwestern College
Winfield, KS 67156
(316)221–1070

Kentucky

WCKU–FM
651 Perimeter Dr., Ste. 102
Lexington, KY 40517
(606)269–9540

WLBN–AM
Box 680
Lebanon, KY 40033
(502)692–3126

WLOU–AM
2549 S. 3rd St.
Louisville, KY 40208
(502)636–3535

WQKS–AM
905 S. Main St.
Hopkinsville, KY 42240
(502)886–1480

Louisiana

KBCE–FM
Box 69
Boyce, LA 71409
(318)793–4003

KFXZ–FM
3225 Ambassador Caffery Pkwy.
Lafayette, LA 70506–7214
(318)898–1112

KGRM–FM
Drawer K
Grambling, LA 71245
(318)247–3245

KJCB–AM
413 Jefferson St.
Lafayette, LA
(318)233–4262

KNEK–FM
PO Box 598
Washington, LA 70589
(318)826–3921

KNWD–FM
Northwestern State University
PO Box 3038
Natchitoches, LA 71497
(318)357–5693

KRUS–AM
Box 430
500 N. Monroe St.
Ruston, LA 71270
(318)255–2530

KSCL–FM
2911 Centenary Blvd.
Shreveport, LA 71104
(318)869–5296

KTRY–AM
Box 1075
Bastrop, LA 71220
(318)281–3656

KXZZ–AM
311 Alamo St.
Lake Charles, LA 70601
(318)436–7277

KYEA–FM
516 Martin St.
West Monroe, LA 71292
(318)322–1491

WABL–AM
Bankston Rd.
PO Box 787
Amite, LA 70422
(504)748–8385

WQUE–AM
1440 Canal St., Ste. 800
New Orleans, LA 70112
(504)581–1280

WQUE–FM
1440 Canal St.
New Orleans, LA 70112
(504)581–1280

WXOK–AM
7707 Waco Dr.
Baton Rouge, LA 70806
(504)927–7060

WYLD–AM
2228 Gravier
New Orleans, LA 70119
(504)822–1945

Maine

WMHB–FM
10 Mayflower Hill Dr.
Waterville, ME 04901
(207)872–8037

Maryland

WANN–AM
PO Box 631
Annapolis, MD 21404
(410)269–0700

WESM–FM
University of Maryland, Eastern Shore
Backbone Rd.
Princess Anne, MD 21853
(301)651–2816

WJDY–AM
1633 N. Division St.
Salisbury, MD 21801
(301)742–5191

WPGC–FM
6301 Ivy Ln., Ste. 800
Greenbelt, MD 20770
(301)441–3500

WWIN–FM
200 S. President St., 6th Fl.
Baltimore, MD 21202
(410)332–8200

WXYV–FM
1829 Reistertown Rd.
Baltimore, MD 21208
(301)653–2200

Massachusetts

WAIC–FM
1000 State St.
Springfield, MA 01109
(413)736–7662

WILD–AM
90 Warren St.
Boston, MA 02119
(617)427–2222

WJJW–FM
N. Adams State College
Campus Center
North Adams, MA 01247
(413)663–9136

WKKL–FM
Cape Cod Community College
Rte. 132
West Barnstable, MA 02668
(508)362–4941

WLVG–AM
670 Cummins Way
Boston, MA 02126–3243
(617)576–2895

Michigan

WDZZ–FM
1830 Genessee Tower
Flint, MI 48503
(313)767–0130

WGPR–FM
3146 E. Jefferson Ave.
Detroit, MI 48207
(313)259–8862

WILS–AM
PO Box 25008
Lansing, MI 48909–5008
(517)393–1320

WJLB–FM
645 Griswold St., Ste. 633
Detroit, MI 48226–4177
(313)965–2000

WKWM–AM
PO Box 828
Kentwood, MI 49518–0828
(616)676–1237

WLLJ–AM
Box 393
206 E. State
Cassopolis, MI 49031–0393
(616)445–2543

WMXD–FM
15600 W. 12 Mile Rd.
Southfield, MI 48076
(313)569–8000

WNMC–FM
1701 E. Front St.
Traverse City, MI 49684
(616)922–1091

WQBH–AM
Penobscot Bldg.
Detroit, MI 48226
(313)965–4500

WTLZ–FM
126 N. Franklin St., Ste. 514
Saginaw, MI 48607
(517)754–1071

Minnesota

KMOJ–FM
501 Bryant Ave. N
Minneapolis, MN 55405
(612)377–0594

Mississippi

WACR–AM
1910 14th Ave. N
PO Box 1078
Columbus, MS 39703
(601)328–1050

WALT–AM
3436 Hwy. 45 N
PO Box 5797
Meridian, MS 39302
(601)693–2661

WBAD–FM
PO Box 4426
Greenville, MS 38704–4426
(601)335–9265

WCLD–FM
Drawer 780
Cleveland, MS 38732
(601)843–4091

WESY–AM
7 Oaks Rd.
PO Box 5804
Greenville, MS 38704–5804
(601)378–9405

WJMG–FM
1204 Gravel Line St.
Hattiesburg, MS 39401
(601)544–1941

WKKY–FM
PO Box 1919
McComb, MS 39648–1919
(601)475–4108

WKXG–AM
Browning Rd.
PO Box 1686
Greenwood, MS 38930
(601)453–2174

WLTD–FM
224 Shiloh Dr.
Jackson, MS 39212–3048

WMIS–AM
20 E. Franklin
Natchez, MS 39120
(601)442–2522

WMPG–AM
PO Box 5353
Meridian, MS 39302
(601)693–4851

WNBN–AM
1290 Hawkins Crossing Rd.
Meridian, MS 39301
(601)483–7930

WORV–AM
1204 Graveline
Hattiesburg, MS 39401
(601)544–1941

WQAZ–FM
PO Box 119
Cleveland, MS 38730

WQFX–FM
Security Bldg., Penthouse Ste.
PO Box 789
Gulfport, MS 39502
(601)863–3626

WQIS–AM
PO Box 1229
Laurel, MS 39440
(601)425–1491

WRDC–AM
114 T.M. Jones Hwy.
Boyle, MS 38730
(601)843–8225

WTYJ–FM
20 E. Franklin
Natchez, MS 39120
(601)442–2522

Missouri

KATZ–AM
1139 Olive St., Ste. 303
St. Louis, MO 63101
(314)241–6000

KCOU–FM
University of Missouri
101–F Pershing Hall
Columbia, MO 65201
(314)882–7820

KCXL–AM
810 E. 63rd St.
Liberty, MO 64110
(816)333–2583

KIRL–AM
3713 Hwy. 94 N
St. Charles, MO 63301
(314)946–6600

KMJM–FM
PO Box 4888
St. Louis,MO 63108
(314)361–1108

KPRS–FM
3 Crown Ctr., Ste. 118
Kansas City, MO 64108
(816)471–2100

KWUR–FM
Washington University
Box 1182
Saint Louis, MO 63130
(314)935–5952

Montana

KNMC–FM
10 Cowan Dr.
Havre, MT 59501
(406)265–3221

Nebraska

KIOS–FM
3230 Burt St.
Omaha, NE 68131
(402)554–6444

KZUM–FM
941 O St., Ste. 1025
Lincoln, NE 68508–3608
(402)474–5086

Nevada

KCEP–FM
330 W. Washington St.
Las Vegas, NV 89106
(702)648–4218

New Hampshire

WPCR–FM
Plymouth State College
Plymouth, NY 03264
(603)535–2242

New Jersey

WNJR–AM
600 N. Union Ave.
Hillside, NJ 07205
(908)688–5000

WRRC–FM
2083 Lawrenceville Rd.
Lawrenceville, NJ 08648
(609)896–5211

WUSS–AM
1507 Atlantic Ave.
Atlantic City, NJ
(609)345–7134

New York

WBLK–FM
712 Main St., Ste. 112
Buffalo, NY 14202
(716)852–5955

WBLS–FM
801 2nd Ave.
New York, NY 10017
(212)661–3344

WDKX–FM
683 E. Main St.
Rochester, NY 14605
(716)262–2050

WHCR–FM
City College of New York
138th & Convent Ave.
New York, NY 10031
(212)690–5499

WJPZ–FM
316 Waverly Ave.
PO Box 239
Syracuse, NY 13210
(315)443–4689

WOLF–AM
Box 1490
Syracuse, NY 13201
(315)472–0222

WRKS–FM
1440 Broadway
New York, NY 10018
(212)642–4300

WUFO–AM
89 LaSalle Ave.
Buffalo, NY 14214
(716)834–1080

North Carolina

WAAA–AM
4950 Indiana Ave.
Box 11197
Winston–Salem, NC 27106
(919)767–0430

WBCG–FM
PO Box 38
Murfreesboro, NC 27855
(919)398–4111

WBMS–AM
PO Box 718
Wilmington, NC 28402
(919)763–4633

WDUR–AM
2515 Apex Hwy.
Durham, NC 27713
(919)596–2000

WIKS–FM
207 Glenburnie Dr.
PO Box 12684
New Bern, NC 28561
(919)633–1500

WISP–AM
Box 668
Kingston, NC 28502–0668
(919)523–9797

WJMH–FM
4002 E. Spring Garden
Greensboro, NC 27407
(919)855–6500

WLWL–AM
PO Box 1536
Rockingham, NC 28379
(919)997–2526

WNAA–FM
NC A&T State University
Price Hall, Ste. 200
Greensboro, NC 27411
(919)334–7936

WOKN–FM
PO Box 804
Goldsboro, NC 27530
(919)734–4213

WPEG–FM
520 Hwy. 29 N
PO Box 128
Concord, NC 28025
(704)786–9111

WQOK–FM
8601 Six Forks Rd., Ste. 609
Raleigh, NC 27615
(919)848–9736

WRRZ–AM
701 Bus. S.
Clinton, NC 28328
(919)592–2165

WRSV–FM
600 N. Grace St.
PO Box 2666
Rocky Mount, NC 27802
(919)442–9776

WRVS–FM
1704 Weeksville Rd.
Box 800
Elizabeth City, NC
(919)335–3517

WSMY–AM
PO Box 910
Roanoke Rapids, NC 27870
(919)536–3115

WSNC–FM
Winston–Salem State University
601 MLK Junior Dr.
Winston–Salem, NC 27110
(919)750–2320

WZFX–FM
225 Green St., Ste. 900
Fayetteville, NC 28302
(919)486–4991

Ohio

WCKX–FM
510 E. Mound St.
Columbus, OH 43215–5539
(614)464–0020

WIZF–FM
7030 Reading Rd., No. 316
Cincinnati, OH 45237
(513)351–5900

WJMO–AM
11821 Euclid Ave.
Cleveland, OH 44106
(216)795–1212

WJTB–AM
105 Lake Ave.
Elyria, OH 44035
(216)327–1844

WNRB–AM
PO Box 625
Niles, OH 44446
(216)652–0106

WOKG–AM
PO Box 727
Warren, OH 44482
(216)394–1501

WVKO–AM
4401 Carriage Hill Ln.
Columbus, OH 43220
(614)451–2191

WVOI–AM
PO Box 5408
Toledo, OH 43613
(419)243–7052

WZAK–FM
1729 Superior Ave.
Cleveland, OH 44114
(216)621–9300

WZIP–FM
302 E. Buchtel Ave.
Akron, OH 44325–1004
(216)972–7105

Oklahoma

KHIB–FM
Southeastern State University
Box 4129, Sta. A
Durant, OK 74701
(405)924–0138

KTLV–AM
3336 SE 67th St.
Oklahoma City, OK 73135
(405)672–1220

KTOW–FM
8886 W. 21st St.
Sand Springs, OK 74063
(918)245–0254

KWSH–AM
Old Hwy. 270
PO Box 1260
Wewoka, OK 74884
(405)257–5441

KXOJ–AM
Box 1250
Sapulpa, OK 74067
(918)224–2620

Pennsylvania

WAMO–FM
411 7th Ave., Ste. 1500
Pittsburgh, PA 15219
(412)471–2181

WCXJ–AM
7138 Kelly St.
Pittsburgh, PA 15208
(412)243–3050

WDAS–FM
Belmont Ave. at Edgely Rd.
Philadelphia, PA 19131
(215)878–2000

WDNR–FM
Widener University
PO Box 1000
700 E. 14th St.
Chester, PA 19013
(215)499–4439

WHAT–AM
2471 N. 54th St.
Philadelphia, PA 19131
(215)581–5161

WIXQ–FM
Millersville University
SMC Basement
Millersville, PA 17551
(717)872–3333

WKDU–FM
3210 Chestnut St.
Philadelphia, PA 19104
(215)895–5920

WLIU–FM
Office of Student Activities
Lincoln University, PA 19352
(215)932–8300

WUSL–FM
440 Domino Ln.
Philadelphia, PA 19128
(215)483–8900

Rhode Island

WRBU–FM
88 Benevolent St.
Providence, RI 02906
(401)272–9550

South Carolina

WASC–AM
840 Wofford
Spartanburg, SC
(803)585–1530

WCIG–FM
U.S. Hwy. 76
Mullins, SC 29574
(803)423–1140

WDOG–FM
PO Box 442
Allendale, SC 29810
(803)584–3500

WDXZ–FM
PO Box 1364
Mount Pleasant, SC 29465
(803)881–1400

WELP–AM
PO Box 19104
Greenville, SC 29602–9104
(803)235–4600

WFXA–FM
104 Bennett Ln.
North Augusta, SC 29841
(803)279–2330

WGCD–AM
165 Harris St.
PO Box 746
Chester, SC 29706
(803)581–1490

WHYZ–AM
PO Box 4309
Greenville, SC 29608
(803)246–1970

WLBG–AM
Box 1289
Laurens, SC 29360
(803)984–3544

WLGI–FM
Rte. 2, PO Box 69
Hemingway, SC 29554
(803)558–2977

WLWZ–FM
PO Box 19104
Greenville, SC 29602–9104
(803)235–4600

WMNY–FM
Rte. 1, Box 189
Santee, SC 29142–9718
(803)854–2671

WMTY–AM
370 Burnett
Greenwood, SC 29646
(803)223–4300

WMTY-FM
370 Burnett
Greenwood, SC 29646
(803)223-4300

WORG-AM
Rte. 1, Box 189
Santee, SC 29142-9718
(803)854-2671

WQKI-AM
Riley Road
St. Matthews, SC 29135
(803)874-2777

WUJM-AM
PO Box 1165
Goose Creek, SC 29445-1165
(919)763-6611

WUJM-FM
PO Box 1165
Goose Creek, SC 29445-1165

WWDM-FM
PO Box 38
Sumter SC 29150
(803)495-2558

WWWZ-FM
Fairfield Office Park, Ste. 304
1064 Gardner Rd.
Charleston, SC 29407
(803)556-9132

WYNN-FM
170 E. Palmetto St.
PO Box 100531
Florence, SC 29501-0531

(803)662-6364

Tennessee

KHUL-FM
80 N. Tillman
Memphis, TN 38111
(901)323-0101

WABD-AM
150 Stateline Rd.
Clarksville, TN 37040
(615)431-5555

WBOL-AM
PO Box 191
Bolivar, TN 38008
(901)658-3690

WFKX-FM
425 E. Chester
Jackson, TN 38301
(901)427-9616

WHRK-FM
112 Union Ave.
Memphis, TN 38103
(901)529-4397

WJTT-FM
409 Chestnut St., Ste. A154
Chattanooga, TN 37402
(615)265-9494

WQQK-FM
1320 Brick Church Pike
PO Box 70085
Nashville, TN 37207
(615)227-1470

Media

WQZZ–AM
609 W. 7th St.
Columbia, TN 38401
(615)381–7100

WRVU–FM
PO Box 9100, Sta. B
Nashville, TN 37235
(615)322–3691

WVOL–AM
1320 Brick Church Pike
PO Box 70085
Nashville, TN 37207
(615)227–1470

Texas

KALO–AM
7700 Gulfway
Port Arthur, TX 77642
(409)963–1276

KBWC–FM
711 Wiley Ave.
Marshall, TX 75670
(903)938–8341 X266

KCOH–AM
5011 Almeda
Houston, TX 77004
(713)522–1001

KGBC–AM
Box 1138
Galveston, TX 77553
(713)744–4567

KHRN–FM
Hwy. 6 S., Box 1075
Hearne, TX 77859
(409)279–9211

KIIZ–AM
Box 2469
Harker Heights, TX 76543
(817)699–5000

KJBX–AM
6602 Quirt
Lubbock, TX 79408
(806)745–5800

KJMZ–FM
545 E. John Carpenter Fwy., 17th Fl.
Irving, TX 75062
(214)556–8100

KKDA–FM
PO Box 530860
Grand Prairie, TX 75053
(214)556–8100

KMHT–FM
PO Box 330
Huntsville, TX 77342-0330
(214)938–6789

KMJQ–FM
24 Greenway Plaza
Houston, TX 77046
(713)623–0102

KMXO–AM
221 N. Leggett
Abilene, TX 79603
(915)672–5700

932

KSFA–AM
PO Box 631408
Nacogdoches, TX 75963
(409)560–6677

KYOK–AM
24 Greenway, No. 1590
Houston, TX 77046
(713)621–1590

KZEY–AM
PO Box 4248
Tyler, TX 75712
(903)593–1744

Utah

KWCR–FM
Weber State University
3750 Harrison Blvd., Ste. 1906
Ogden, UT 84408–1906
(801)626–6000

Virginia

WANT–AM
PO Box 6747
Richmond, VA 23230
(804)353–9113

WARR–AM
553 Michigan Dr.
Hampton, VA 23669–3899
(919)257–2121

WBSK–AM
645 Church St., Ste. 201
Norfolk, VA 23510
(804)627–5800

WCDX–FM
PO Box 9373
Norfolk, VA 23510
(804)627–5800

WILA–AM
865 Industrial Ave.
PO Box 3444
Danville, VA 24543
(804)792–2133

WJJS–AM
1105 Main St.
Madison Heights, VA 24551
(804)847–1266

WKBY–AM
Rte. 2, Box 105A
Chatham, VA 24531
(804)432–8108

WMYK–FM
645 Church St., Ste. 400
Norfolk,VA 23510
(804)622–4600

WOWI–FM
645 Church St., Ste. 201
Norfolk, VA 23510–2809
(804)627–5800

WPAK–AM
800 Old Plank Rd.
Farmville, VA 23901
(804)392–8114

WPLZ–FM
3267 S. Crater Rd.
PO Box 1510
Petersburg, VA 23805
(804)733–4567

WTOY–AM
709 Bowman Ave.
Salem, VA 24153
(703)387–1480

WWHS–FM
Box 606
Hampden–Sydney College
Hampden–Sydney, VA 23943
(804)223–8882

Washington

KASB–FM
601–108th Ave. SE
Bellevue, WA 98004–6698
(206)455–6154

KKFX–AM
101 Nickerson St., Ste. 260
Seattle, WA 98109–1620
(206)728–1250

KRIZ–AM
2600 S. Jackson St.
Seattle, WA 98144
(206)329–7880

KTPS–FM
1101 S. Yakima Ave.
Tacoma, WA 98405
(206)596–1600

KZIZ–AM
c/o KRIZ–AM
2600 S. Jackson St.
Seattle, WA 98144
(206)627–1103

Wisconsin

KUWS–FM
1800 Grand Ave.
Superior, WI 54880–2898
(715)394–8530

WBZN–AM
2400 S. 102nd St.
West Allis, WI 53227
(414)321–1007

WMVP–AM
4222 W. Capitol Dr., Ste. 1290
Milwaukee, WI 53216
(414)444–1290

West Virginia

WITB–FM
Box 278
Salem College
Salem, WV 26426
(304)782–5229

CABLE TELEVISION NETWORKS

BET (Black Entertainment Television)
1232 31st St. NW
Washington, DC 20007
(202)337–5260

TELEVISON STATIONS

California

KMTP–TV
1311 Sutter St., Ste. 200
San Francisco, CA 94109
(415)882–5566

KNTV–TV
645 Park Ave.
San Jose, CA 95110
(408)286–1111

District of Columbia

WHMM–TV
222 4th St. NW
Washington, DC 20059
(202)806–3200

Florida

WTVT–TV
3213 W. Kennedy Blvd.
Tampa, FL 33609
(813)876–1313

Georgia

WGXA–TV
PO Box 5008
Macon, GA 31497
(912)745–2424

Illinois

WEEK–TV
2907 Springfield Rd.
Peoria, IL 61611
(309)698–2525

Indiana

WPTA–TV
3401 Butler Rd.
Box 2121
Ft. Wayne, IN 46801
(219)483–0584

WRTV–TV
1330 N. Meridian St.
Indianapolis, IN 46206
(317)635–9788

Louisiana

WNOL–TV
1661 Canal St.
New Orleans, LA 70112
(504)525–3838

Maine

WVII–TV
371 Target Industrial Circle
Bangor, ME 04401
(207)945–6457

Michigan

WGPR–TV
3146 E. Jefferson, Ave.
Detroit, MI 48207
(313)259–8862

Minnesota

KBJR–TV
KBJR Bldg.
Duluth, MN 55802
(218)727–8484

Mississippi

WLBM–TV
4608 Skyland Dr.
PO Box 5840
Meridian, MS 39302
(601)485–3030

WLBT–TV
715 S. Jeffereson St.
Jackson, MS 39205
(601)948–3333

New York

WHEC–TV
191 East Ave.
Rochester, NY 14604
(716)546–5670

WKBW–TV
7 Broadcast Plaza
Buffalo, NY 14202
(716)845–6100

Oregon

KBSP–TV
4923 Indian School Rd. NE
Salem, OR 97305
(503)390–2202

Texas

KTXS–TV
PO Box 2997
Abilene, TX 79604
(915)677–2281

Virginia

WJCB–TV
1930 Pembroke Ave.
Hampton, VA 23669
(804)627–7500

Wisconsin

WJFW–TV
S. Oneida Ave.
Rhinelander, WI 54501
(715)369–4700

20
Performing Arts

⓴

Performing Arts

The Origins of African-American Performance Art ■ Reclaiming the Black Image: 1890 to 1920 ■ The African-American Performance Artist: 1920 to 1960 ■ The African-American Performance Artist since 1960 ■ African-American Performance Artists

Essay by Donald Franklin Joyce

For more than two hundred years, African-American performers have appeared on the American stage, often in the face of prejudice and bigotry. Showcasing their talents, they have made unique contributions to American performance art. The artistic heritage of today's African-American actors, dancers and comedians can be traced back to the last decades of the eighteenth century.

plays from the period that depicted blacks in demoralizing roles were *Robinson Crusoe, Harlequin* (1792), and *The Triumph of Love* (1795) by John Randolph, which included the native black character named Sambo. Thus, the earliest appearances of blacks on the American stage were as characters void of intellectual and moral sensibilities.

■ THE ORIGINS OF AFRICAN-AMERICAN PERFORMANCE ART

The Earliest Plays with African-American Actors

The first performances by African-American actors on the American stage were in plays authored by white playwrights who portrayed blacks as buffoons or intellectually inept characters. In 1769, for example, Lewis Hallam's comedy *The Padlock* was staged with a West Indian slave character named Mongo, who was a clown to be played by a black. Other white-authored

The African Grove Theatre

New York City's free African-American community founded the first African-American theater in 1821—the African Grove Theatre, located at Mercer and Bleecker streets "in the rear of the one-mile stone on Broadway." A group of amateur African-American actors organized by Henry Brown presented *Richard III* at the theater on October 1, 1821. The African Grove Theatre subsequently produced *Othello, Hamlet,* and such lighter works as *Tom and Jerry* and *The Poor Soldier, Obi.*

939

One of the principal actors at the African Grove Theatre was James Hewlet, a West Indian-born black who distinguished himself in roles of *Othello* and *Richard III*. Hewlet later toured England and billed himself as "The New York and London Colored Comedian." Ira Aldridge, who later distinguished himself as one of the great Shakespearean tragic actors, was also a member of the permanent group that performed at the African Grove Theatre. Aldridge was cast in comic and singing roles as well as in Shakespearean tragedies.

It was at the African Grove Theatre that the first play written and produced by an African American was performed on the American stage. The play was Henry Brown's *The Drama of King Shotaway*, which was presented in June 1823.

Because of disturbances created by whites in the audience, the local police raided the African Grove Theatre on several occasions. The theater evidently was wrecked by police and hoodlums during one of these raids, which forced its closing in late 1823. The group of black actors attached to the African Grove Theatre, determined to preserve their company, continued for several years to present plays at different rented locations throughout New York City.

■ MINSTRELSY

Talented slaves were among the earliest black entertainers in colonial and antebellum America. On plantations throughout the South, slave performers—using clappers, jawbones, and blacksmith rasps—danced, sang and told jokes for the entertainment of their fellow slaves as well as their masters, who often showcased their talents at local gatherings. Some masters hired out talented slaves to perform in traveling troupes.

During the late 1820s and early 1830s, white entertainers, observing the artistry of black performers, began to imitate blacks in their routines. Blackening their faces with cork, these white entertainers performed jigs, songs, and jokes with topical allusions to blacks in their lyrics. Thus, the art of minstrelsy as theatrical material was born.

White minstrel troupes in blackface became very popular on the American stage in the 1830s. Among some of the more famous white minstrel performers were Thomas Dartmouth Rice, "Daddy Rice," the original "Jim Crow," Edwin Forrest and Dan Emmett, and the Christy Minstrels.

Some traveling white minstrel troupes used African-American performers to enhance the authenticity of their productions. One such troupe was the Ethiopian Minstrels, whose star performer was William Henry Lane, an African-American dancer who used the stage name "Master Juba." Lane was one of the greatest dancers of his generation. Throughout the United States and England, "Master Juba" was enthusiastically praised by audiences and critics alike. One anonymous English critic, quoted by dance historian Marian Hannah Winter, wrote the following critique of one of Lane's performances:

> Juba exceeded anything ever witnessed in Europe. The style as well as the execution is unlike anything seen in this country. The manner in which he beats time with feet, and the extraordinary command he possesses over them, can only be believed by those who have been present at the exhibition. (1948. "Juba and American Minstrelsy." *Chronicles of the American Dance*, edited by Paul Magriel).

Although black minstrel troupes began to appear in the 1850s, it was not until after the Civil War that they became established on the American stage. Although black minstrels inherited the negative stereotypes of

Poster advertising a minstrel performance.

blacks that white minstrels had established, the African-American performer won a permanent place on the American stage, providing a training ground for the many black dancers, comedians, singers and composers to come. Notable among these stage personalities were dancer-comedians Billy Kersands, Bert Williams, Bob Height, Dewey "Pigmeat" Martin, and Ernest Hogan; singers like Gertrude "Ma" Rainey and Bessie Smith; and composers James Bland and William Christopher Handy. To a great extent, black minstrelsy created a national appreciation for the talent of black stage entertainers, drawing audiences to black shows and other forms of black entertainment for generations to come.

■ RECLAIMING THE BLACK IMAGE: 1890 TO 1920

By the 1890s, black producers, writers and stage performers sought to reform the demeaning images of blacks that were prevalent on the American stage. *The Creole Show*, cast by black producer Sam Jack, in 1891, was the first all-black musical to depart from minstrelsy. Featuring an all-black chorus line, *The Creole Show* premiered in Boston in 1891 and later played at the Chicago World's Fair for the entire season. In 1895 black producer John W. Ishaw presented *The Octoroon*, another all-black musical that moved away from the minstrel tradition. *Oriental America*, which Ishaw also produced, broke further from minstrel conventions by not closing with the traditional walkaround, but with an operatic medley.

Trip to Coontown, written and directed by Bob Cole in 1898, completely broke away from the minstrel tradition. The plot of this all-black musical was presented completely through music and dance. The first musical produced, written and performed by African

Americans on Broadway, it ushered in a new era for blacks on the American stage.

Between 1898 and 1911, thirteen all-black musicals opened on Broadway, showcasing the talents of black musicians, lyricists, directors, producer and writers.

The highly popular *Clorinda: The Origin of the Cakewalk*, with music by composer Will Marion Cook and lyrics by poet Paul Laurence Dunbar, opened in 1898 at the Casino Roof Garden and featured comedian-singer Ernest Hogan. The comic-dance duo of Bert Williams and George Walker premiered their first Broadway musical, *The Policy Players*, in 1899. This success was followed by Williams and Walker's *Sons of Ham*, which played on Broadway for two seasons beginning in September 1900. Their *In Dahomey*, premiered on Broadway in 1903 and, after a long run, toured successfully in England. *The Southerners*, with music by Will Marion Cook, opened on Broadway in 1904 with an interracial cast starring Abbie Mitchell. The Williams and Walker team returned to Broadway in 1906 with a new musical, *Abyssinia*, which consistently played to a full house.

In the same year the versatile Ernest Hogan appeared on Broadway in *Rufus Rastus*, and in 1902 Hogan starred in *Oyster Man*, which enjoyed a successful run on Broadway. Bob Cole, J. Rosamond Johnson, and James Weldon Johnson wrote and performed in *The Shoo-Fly Regiment*, another musical that opened on Broadway in 1902. Williams and Walker appeared in their last Broadway production together, *Bandanna Land*, in 1908. George Walker fell into ill health after the show closed, and died in 1911. Bert Williams went on to appear in *Mr. Lord of Koal* on Broadway in 1909, and later was the star comedian performer in the *Ziegfield Follies*. The last black musical to open on Broadway before the 1920s was *His*

Bert Williams and George Walker

Honor the Barber in 1911, with S. H. Dudley in the lead.

Black actors on the dramatic stage, like the performers in all-black musicals, were attempting to shed the demeaning image of the African American projected by most white-produced minstrelsy and drama. The presentation of three plays—*The Rider of Dreams, Granny Maumee,* and *Simon the Cyrenian*—by white playwright Ridgely Torrence at the Garden Theatre in Madison Square Garden on April 5, 1917 was an exceptional and highly successful effort to objectively portray the African American on the dramatic stage.

■ THE AFRICAN-AMERICAN ACTOR, DANCER AND COMEDIAN, 1920 TO 1950

Black Musicals

On May 23, 1921, *Shuffle Along* opened on Broadway, signaling the return of black musicals to "The Great Whiteway" and the ar-

rival of the Harlem Renaissance on the American stage. Featuring the talented singer-dancer Florence Mills, *Shuffle Along* was written by Noble Sissle, Eubie Blake, Flournoy Miller and Aubrey Lyles. Florence Mills quickly became a sought-after performer, appearing in *The Plantation Revue,* which opened on Broadway on July 17, 1922, and touring England. In 1926, Mills returned to Harlem and played the lead in *Black Birds* at the Alhambra Theatre, for a six-week run. Subsequently, Mills performed in Paris for six months.

Noble Sissle and Eubie Blake returned to Broadway on September 24, 1924, with their new musical *Chocolate Dandies.* Two years later, in 1926, Flournoy Miller and Aubrey Lyles opened on Broadway in *Runnin' Wild* which introduced the Charleston to the country. Bill "Bojangles" Robinson, starring in *Blackbirds of 1928,* dazzled Broadway audiences with his exciting tap dancing style. Several other black musicals opened on Broadway during the 1920s, including *Rang Tang* (1927), *Keep Shuffling* (1928), and *Hot Chocolates* (1929).

943

Bill "Bojangles" Robinson performing with Shirley Temple in the movie "The Little Colonel," 1935.

Porgy and Bess, opening on Broadway in 1935, became the major all-black musical production of the 1930s. With music by George Gershwin, this adaptation of the novel and play by DuBose and Dorothy Heyward was an immediate success as a folk opera. Todd Duncan was cast as Porgy, with Ann Brown as Bess, and comedian-dancer John Bubbles as the character Sportin' Life.

In the 1940s, black musicals were scarce on Broadway. *Cabin in the Sky*, starring Ethel Waters, Dooley Wilson, Todd Duncan, Rex Ingram, J. Rosamond Johnson, and Katherine Dunham and her dancers ran for 165 performances after it opened on October 25, 1940. *Carmen Jones*, perhaps the most successful all-black musical of the decade, opened in 1943 with Luther Saxon, Napoleon Reed, Carlotta Franzel and Cozy Cove; it had a run of 231 performances and

was taken on tour. In 1946 *St. Louis Woman*, featuring Rex Ingram, Pearl Bailey, Juanita Hall and June Hawkins, played a short run to mixed reviews.

The Dramatic Theater

During the Harlem Renaissance years, the African-American dramatic actor remained less active than the black performer in musicals, and the image of the African American projected by white playwrights was generally inadequate. For example, when Charles Gilpin starred in Eugene O'Neill's *Emperor Jones* at the Provincetown Theatre in 1920, critic Loften Mitchell noted that:

> This play, while offering one of the most magnificent roles for a Negro in the American theatre, is the first in a long line to deal with the Negro on this level. O'Neill obviously saw in the Negro rich subject matter, but he was either incapable or unwilling to deal directly with the matter. (1967. *Black Drama, the Story of the American Negro in the Theatre*).

Nonetheless, African-American actors and actresses had to accept the roles in which they were cast by white playwrights. In 1924, the O'Neill play *All God's Chillun' Got Wings* opened at the Provincetown Theatre, with Paul Robeson and Mary Blair to mixed reviews because of its interracial theme. Rose McClendon starred in Paul Green's Pulitzer Prize-winning *In Abraham's Bosom* in 1926, and was ably supported by Abbie Mitchell and Jules Bledsoe. Marc Connelly's *Green Pastures* opened on Broadway on February 26, 1930; with Richard B. Harrison playing "De Lawd" it ran for 557 performances and was taken on an extensive road tour.

Three plays by Langston Hughes that did treat the African American objectively were produced successfully on Broadway in the 1930s. *Mulatto*, which opened in 1935 and starred Rose McClendon and Morris McKenney, had the longest Broadway run of any play written by an African American in the history of the American theater, with 373 consecutive performances. It was followed by *Little Ham* (1935) and *Troubled Island* (1936).

The Federal Theater Project

In the mid-1930s the Works Progress Administration (WPA) sponsored one of the greatest organized efforts to assist and encourage American actors, especially African-American actors. The Federal Theater Project employed a total of 851 black actors to work in sixteen segregated units of the project in Chicago, New York, and other cities from 1935 until 1939, when Congress ended the project. While the project was in operation, black actors appeared in seventy-five plays, including classics, vaudeville contemporary comedy, children's shows, circuses and "living newspaper" performances. Notable among the black actors who worked in the project, and later became stars on Broadway and in the film, were Butterfly McQueen, Canada Lee, Rex Ingram, Katherine Dunham, Edna Thomas, Thomas Anderson and Arthur Dooley Wilson.

In the wake of the Federal Theater Project, The American Negro Theater was established in Harlem by Abram Hill, Austin Briggs-Hall, Frederick O'Neal, and Hattie King-Reeves. Its objective was to authentically portray black life and give black actors and playwrights a forum for their talents. Some of their productions eventually made it to Broadway. In 1944, the theater produced *Anna Lucasta* in the basement of the 135th Street Library in Harlem. It was successful enough to move to Broadway, and featured Hilda Simms, Frederick O'Neal,

Alice Childress, Alvin Childress, Earle Hyman and Herbert Henry. Abram Hill's *Walk Hard* opened in Harlem in 1946, and became a Broadway production with Maxwell Glanville in the lead. The American Negro Theater provided a training ground for many black actors who later became stars on Broadway and in Hollywood, including Ruby Dee, Ossie Davis, Harry Belafonte, and Sidney Poitier.

Dramatic Theater in the 1950s

The rise of television in the 1950s generally had an adverse affect on the American theater. Employment for all actors fell sharply, especially for black actors. Ethel Waters did, however, open on Broadway in 1950 as the lead in *Member of the Wedding*, which was well-received. Louis Peterson's *Take a Giant Step* opened on Broadway in September 1953 to critical praise; in the cast were Frederick O'Neal, Helen Martin, Maxwell Glanville, Pauline Myers, Estelle Evans, and Louis Gossett, Jr.

One of the most successful all-black plays to appear on Broadway opened in March 1959: Lorraine Hansberry's *Raisin in the Sun*, which won the New York Drama Critics Circle Award. Its cast included Sidney Poitier, Ruby Dee, Diana Sands, Claudia McNeil, Louis Gossett, Jr., Ivan Dixon, Lonnie Elder, III, and Douglas Turner Ward. *Raisin in the Sun* indicated the future of blacks in the American theater.

Black Dance

Black dance, like other forms of black entertainment, had its beginnings in Africa and on the plantations of early America, where slaves performed to entertain themselves and their masters. White minstrels in blackface incorporated many of these black dance inventions into their shows, while black minstrel dancers, such as "Master Juba" (William Henry Lane) thrilled audiences with their artistry.

Many performers in the early black musicals that appeared on Broadway from 1898 and 1910 were expert show dancers, such as George Walker and Bert Williams. Similarly, in the all-black musicals of the 1920s, performers like Florence Mills and Bill "Bojangles" Robinson captivated audiences with their show dancing. The musical *Runnin' Wild* (1926) was responsible for creating the Charleston dance craze of the "Roaring Twenties."

By the early 1930s, black pioneers of modern dance were appearing on the dance stage. Four of these black innovators were Hemsley Winfield, Asadata Dafore, Katherine Dunham and Pearl Primus.

Hemsley Winfield presented what was billed as "The First Negro Concert in America" in Manhattan's Chanin Building on April 31, 1931. Two suites on African themes were performed, along with solos by Edna Guy and Winfield himself. In 1933, Winfield became the first black to dance for the Metropolitan Opera, performing the role of the Witch Doctor in *Emperor Jones*.

Austin Asadata Dafore Horton, a native of Sierra Leone, electrified audiences in New York with his 1934 production of *Kykunkor*. Dance historian Lynne Fauley Emery concludes that *Kykunkor* "was the first performance by black dancers on the concert stage which was entirely successful. It revealed the potential of ethnic material to black dancers, and herein lay Dafore's value as a great influence on black concert dance." (1988. *Black Dance from 1619 to Today*, 2nd rev. ed.).

Katherine Dunham had her first lead dance role in Ruth Page's West Indian ballet *La Guiablesse* in 1933. In 1936, Dunham re-

Katherine Dunham, a pioneer of modern dance, 1992.

ceived a master's degree in anthropology from the University of Chicago; her thesis was on "*The Dances of Haiti*," the result of her on-site study of native dances in the West Indies. For the next thirty years, Dunham and her dance company toured the United States and Europe, dazzling audiences with her choreography. During the 1963–64 season, Dunham choreographed the Metropolitan Opera's production of *Aida*, becoming the first black American to do so.

Pearl Primus, like Katherine Dunham, was trained in anthropology. Her research in primitive African dance inspired her first composition performed as a professional dancer, *African Ceremonial*, which she presented on February 14, 1943. On October 4, 1944, Primus made her Broadway debut at the Belasco Theater in New York. Her performance included dances of West Indian, African and African-American origin; the concert was widely acclaimed and launched her career as a dancer. Primus has traveled to Africa many times to research African dances; in 1959. she was named director of

Liberia's Performing Arts Center. She later opened the Primus-Borde School of Primal Dance with her husband, dancer Percival Borde, and is currently involved in Pearl Primus Dance Language Institute in New Rochelle, New York.

By late 1950s, several black dancers and dance companies were distinguishing themselves on the concert stage. Janet Collins was the "premiere danseuse" of the Metropolitan Opera Ballet from 1951 until 1954. Arthur Mitchell made his debut as a principal dancer with the New York City Ballet in 1955. Alvin Ailey established his company in 1958. And Geoffrey Holder, who made his Broadway debut in 1954 in *House of Flowers*, became a leading choreographer.

The Black Comedian

The earliest black comedians in America, like other early black entertainers, were slaves who in their free time entertained themselves and their masters. In the early minstrel shows, white comedians in blackface created comic caricatures of blacks, whom they referred to as "coons". When African-Americans began appearing in minstrel shows shortly after the Civil War, they found themselves burdened with the "coon" comic caricatures created by white performers. The dance-comedy team of Bert Williams and George Walker were the most famous of the early black comedians, appearing in numerous all-black musicals between 1899 and 1909.

In the all-black musicals of the 1920s, a new comic movement emerged: the comedy of style, which emphasized such antics as rolling the eyes or shaking the hips. The venom and bite of black folk humor was replaced by a comedy of style that was more acceptable to the white audiences of these all-black musicals.

The Apollo Theater, a popular venue for black entertainment.

Real black folk humor, however, did survive and thrive in black nightclubs and black theaters such as the Apollo, in Harlem and the Regal in Chicago in the 1930s, 1940s, and 1950s. In these settings, known as the "Chitterling Circuit," such black comedians as Tim Moore, Dusty Fletcher, Butterbeans and Susie, Stepin Fetchit, Jackie "Moms" Mabley, Redd Foxx, and Slappy White performed without restrictions.

■ THE AFRICAN-AMERICAN ACTOR, DANCER AND COMEDIAN SINCE 1960

As the black civil rights movement challenged the national conscience in the 1960s, every facet of African-American life changed, including black performing arts. More plays about African-Americans by both black and white playwrights were produced, providing increased employment for black actors. On the dance stage, more opportunities were opened to blacks as composers, choreographers and dancers. And many black comedians, by invitation, moved from the "Chitterling Circuit" to posh white-clientele nightclubs and, in some instance, to theaters.

The Dramatic Theater

Three events in the 1960s signaled trends that would affect African-American dramatic actors for the next thirty years: the production of Jean Genet's play, *The Blacks*; the staging of the Leroi Jones (Imamu Amiri Baraka) play, *The Dutchman*; and the founding of the Negro Ensemble Company.

On May 4, 1961 *The Blacks*, by French playwright/author Jean Genet, opened off-Broadway at the St. Mark's Theater. A play

about African-Americans written for white audiences, *The Blacks* provided employment for a host of black actors, including Roscoe Lee Browne, James Earl Jones, Louis Gossett, Jr., Helen Martin, Cicely Tyson, Godfrey Cambridge, Raymond St. Jacques, Maya Angelou, Charles Gordone and many others who appeared in its road tours. Subsequently, black dramatic actors appeared on and off-Broadway in several major plays by white playwrights. Notable among them were *In White America* by Judith Rutherford Marechal (1968), with Gloria Foster and Moses Gunn; *The Great White Hope* by William Sackler (1968), starring James Earl Jones; and *So Nice, They Named It Twice* by Neil Harris (1975), featuring Bill Jay and Veronica Redd.

On May 23, 1961, when the Leroi Jones (Imamu Amiri Baraka) play *Dutchman*

James Earl Jones performing in the play *Fences*, 1987.

948

opened at the Cherry Lane Theatre, the black revolutionary play was introduced to theater audiences. Black actors were provided with the opportunity to perform in roles that not only affirmed blackness, but portrayed black political militancy. Several black revolutionary plays followed that afforded opportunities for black actors, including James Baldwin's *Blues for Mister Charlie* (1964), with Al Freeman, Jr. and Diana Sands; and *The Toilet/The Slave*, (1964) by Leroi Jones (Imamu Amiri Baraka), starring James Spruill, Walter Jones, Nan Martin and Al Freeman, Jr. In 1991, black revolutionary plays such as *General Hag's Skeezag* continued to provide important roles for black actors.

Perhaps, most beneficial to black actors was the founding of the Negro Ensemble Company in New York in 1967. This theatrical production company, initially financed by a three-year grant of $1,200,000 from the Ford Foundation, was the brainchild of playwright/actor Douglas Turner Ward. Housed originally at the St. Mark's Theater and currently at Theater Four, the Negro Ensemble is headed by actor Robert Hooks as executive director, Gerald Krone as administrative director, and Douglas Turner Ward as artistic director. The Negro Ensemble's objective is to develop African-American managers, playwrights, actors, and technicians.

The Negro Ensemble has staged more than one hundred productions, including the work of forty black playwrights, and provided work for countless aspiring and seasoned black actors. Several plays produced by the Negro Ensemble have eventually gone to Broadway, including Douglas Turner Ward's *The River Niger* (1973), which won a Tony Award and an Obie Award, and Charles Fuller's Pulitzer Prize-winning *The Soldier's Play* (1981). A plethora of outstanding black actors and ac-

tresses have appeared in Ensemble productions, including Marshall Williams, Denise Nichols, Esther Rolle, Roxie Roker, Adolph Ceasar, Denzel Washington, Moses Gunn, and Barbara Montgomery.

Several black playwrights had plays successfully produced on Broadway independently of the Negro Ensemble Company. Ntozake Shange's widely-acclaimed *For Colored Girls Who Have Considered Suicide When the Rainbow Is Enuf* (1972) had a cast of seven black women actresses. August Wilson's *Fences*, which opened on March 26, 1987 and featured James Earl Jones, won the 1987 Pulitzer Prize in drama. Wilson's *Two Trains Running*, which opened April 13, 1992 and starred Roscoe Lee Browne and Laurence Fishburne, received the New York Drama Critic's Award for 1992.

Black Musicals

The years from 1961 to the mid-1980s constituted one of the most active periods for African-American performers in musical theater. Many of the black musicals produced during these years, both on and off-Broadway, enjoyed substantial runs and extended road tours.

Langston Hughes' musical *Black Nativity* opened on Broadway on December 11, 1961. Directed by Vinette Carroll, the cast was headed by gospel singers Marion Williams and the Stars of Faith, and also featured Alex Bradford, Clive Thompson, Cleo Quitman and Carl Ford. Although it ran for only fifty-seven performances on Broadway, it went on to tour extensively throughout the United States and abroad.

In 1964, Sammy Davis, Jr. dazzled Broadway in Clifford Odets' *Golden Boy*. Davis was supported by a brilliant cast which included Robert Guillaume, Louis Gossett, Jr.,

Ossie Davis, with co-star Ruby Dee, in the play
Purlie Victorious, 1961.

Lola Falana and Billy Daniels. *Golden Boy*
ran for 586 performances.

Leslie Uggams and Robert Hooks appeared in *Hallelujah Baby*, which opened in
New York's Martin Beck Theater on April 26,
1967. *Hallelujah Baby*, a musical look at five
decades of black history, received a Tony
Award and ran for 293 performances.

Purlie, based on Ossie Davis' 1961 play
Purlie Victorious, opened on May 9, 1970,
with Melba Moore and Robert Guillaume in
lead roles. *Purlie* received good reviews and
enjoyed a run of 688 performances.

Micki Grant's *Don't Bother Me, I Can't
Cope*, starring Micki Grant and Alex Bradford, opened on April 19, 1972 to rave reviews. For this musical, which ran for 1,065
performances, Micki Grant received a
Drama Desk Award and an Obie award.

Virginia Capers, Joe Morton and Helen
Martin opened *Raisin*, based on Lorraine
Hansberry's play *Raisin in the Sun*, on Oc-
tober 13, 1973. *Raisin* received the Tony
Award for the best musical in 1974 and had a
run of 847 performances.

Despite initially poor reviews, *The Wiz*, a
black musical version of *The Wizard of Oz*,
became a highly successful show. Opening
on Broadway on January 5, 1975, *The Wiz*
featured an array of talented performers, including Stephanie Mills, Hinton Battle, Ted
Ross, Andre DeShields, Dee Dee Bridgewa-
ter, and Mabel King. *The Wiz* swept the Tony
Award ceremonies in 1975 and became the
longest-running black musical in the history
of Broadway, with 1,672 performances.

Ain't Misbehavin', another popular black
musical of the 1970s, opened on May 8, 1978.
Based on a cavalcade of songs composed by
Thomas "Fats" Waller, *Ain't Misbehavin'*
starred Nell Carter, Andre DeShields,
Armelia McQueen, Ken Page, and Charlene
Woodard. It played to Broadway audiences
for 1,604 performances and Nell Carter received a Tony Award as "best featured actress."

Two spectacular black musicals premiered on Broadway in the 1980s. *Dream
Girls*, which opened at the Imperial Theater
on December 20, 1981, captivated Broadway
audiences with a cast that included Jennifer
Holiday, Cleavant Derricks, Loretta Devine
and Cheryl Alexander. *Dream Girls* ran for
1,522 performances on Broadway and had
an extensive road tour. Jennifer Holiday
won a Tony Award for her role as Effie Melody White. On April 27, 1986, Debbie Allen
opened in the lead role of *Sweet Charity*.
Reviews were favorable and the musical enjoyed a run of 386 performances, establishing Debbie Allen as a musical theater actress.

A few new all-black musicals have
opened in the early 1990s, including *Five*

Guys Name Moe, a tribute to musician Louis Jordan with Clarke Peters and Charles Augin, and *Jelly's Last Jam*, featuring Gregory Hines.

Black Dance

Since the early 1960s, two of the leading dance companies in the United States have been headed by black males and composed largely of black dancers. They are the Alvin Ailey American Dance Theater and the Dance Theater of Harlem.

The Alvin Ailey American Dance Theater

The Alvin Ailey American Dance Theater, since its founding in 1958, has performed before more people throughout the world than

Alvin Ailey

any other American dance company. With a touring circuit that has included forty-eight states and forty-five countries on all continents, the Alvin Ailey American Dance Theater has been seen by more than 15,000,000 people. Today, the Alvin Ailey organization consists of three components: the Alvin Ailey American Dance Theater, the Alvin Ailey Repertory Ensemble, and the Alvin Ailey American Dance Center.

Between 1958 and 1988, the Alvin Ailey Dance Theater performed 150 works by forty-five choreographers, most of whom were black. Notable among these black choreographers have been Tally Beatty, Donald McKayle, Louis Johnson, Eleo Romare, Billy Wilson, George Faison, Pearl Primus, Judith Jamison, Katherine Dunham, Ulysses Dove, Milton Myers, Kelvin Rotardier, and Gary DeLoatch. More than 250 dancers, again mostly black, have performed with the dance theater. Among its star performers have been Judith Jamison, Clive Thompson, Dudley Wilson, Donna Wood, Gary DeLoatch, George Faison and Sara Yaraborough. A prolific choreographer, Alvin Ailey has created numerous works for his dance theater and other dance companies, including *Revelations* (1958); *Reflections in D*, with music by Duke Ellington (1962); *Quintet* (1968); *Cry* (1971); *Memoria* (1974); and *Three Black Kings* (1976). Alvin Ailey choreographed *Carmen* for the Metropolitan Opera in 1973 and *Precipice* for the Paris Opera in 1983.

The Alvin Ailey Repertory Ensemble was established in 1974 as a training and performing company. Many of its graduates advance to the dance theater or perform with other dance companies. In 1988, the AARE had more than 100 members.

The Alvin Ailey American Dance Center is the official school of the Ailey organization. It attracts students from across the United States and abroad and offers a certificate in

Judith Jamison, a dancer in the Alvin Ailey Dance Theater, performing in 1977.

dance. The center's curriculum includes training in ballet, the Dunham Technique, jazz and modern dance.

The Dance Theater of Harlem

In 1969, Arthur Mitchell, who had established himself as one of the leading ballet dancers in the United States, and Karel Shook, a white ballet teacher, founded the Dance Theater of Harlem. The Dance Theater of Harlem made its formal debut in 1971 at the Guggenheim Museum in New York City. Three of Mitchell's works were premiered at this concert: *Rhythmetron, Tones,* and *Fete Noire.*

Today, the dance theater's repertory is wide-ranging. It includes works in the Balanchine tradition such as *Serenade,* as well as black-inspired works like *Dougla.* Among the most spectacular works performed by theater are *Firebird, Giselle, Scheherazade,* and *Swan Lake.* Some of the dancers who have had long associations with the theater are Lowell Smith, Virginia Johnson, Shelia Rohan and Troy Game. Many of theater's graduates have gone on to perform with other dance companies in the United States and Europe. The Dance Theater of Harlem's school currently has about 1,000 students.

Other Black Dancers

Between 1960 and 1990, several other black dancers have led distinguished careers in concert dance and show dancing. Among them have been Eleo Pomare, Debbie Allen, Rod Rogers, Fred Benjamin, Pepsi Bethel, Eleanor Hampton, Charles Moore, Garth Fagan, Carmen de Lavallade, and Mary Hinkson. Foremost among black choreographers have been Geoffrey Holder, Louis Johnson and Donald McKayle. Prominent among the black dancers who are reviving the tap dance tradition are Chuck Green, Buster Brown, Honi Coles, Hinton Battle, Maurice and Gregory Hines, Lavaughn Robinson, and Nita Feldman.

The Black Comedian

Black comedians enjoyed greater exposure during the 1960s. No longer confined to the "Chitterling Circuit", comedians such as

Arthur Mitchell

Gregory Hines (right), dancing with his brother Maurice, 1982.

Jackie "Moms" Mabley, Redd Foxx, and Slappy White began to perform to audiences in exclusive white clubs as well as to audiences within the black community. They used black folk humor to comment on politics, civil rights, work, sex, and a variety of other subjects. Jackie "Moms" Mabley made two popular recordings: *Moms Mabley at the UN* and *Moms Mabley at the Geneva Conference*. In January 1972, Redd Foxx premiered on television as Fred Sanford in "Sanford and Son," which remains one of the most popular syndicated shows.

Several younger black comedians came into prominence in the early 1960s. Dick Gregory used black folk humor to make political commentary. Bill Cosby specialized in amusing chronicles about boyhood in America. Godfrey Cambridge, although successful, did not rely on black folk humor. During

the late 1960s and the early 1970s, Flip Wilson, who parodied historical and social experience by creating black characters who lived in a black world, became extremely popular on television. His cast of characters, which included "Freddy the Playboy," "Sammy the White House Janitor," and "Geraldine," were the epitome of black folk humor as commentary on an array of issues.

Another pivotal black comedian who began his career in the 1960s was Richard Pryor. His well-timed, risque, sharp folk humor quickly won him a large group of faithful fans. Pryor, who has recorded extensively, has starred successfully in several films, including *Lady Sings the Blues*, *Car Wash*, and *Stir Crazy*.

During the 1980s and 1990s, numerous black comedians have become successful in the various entertainment media. Eddie

954

Murphy made his first appearance on the television show "Saturday Night Live" on November 15, 1980. From television, Murphy went on to Hollywood, making his movie debut in the film *48 Hours* in 1982. Starring roles followed in such films as *Beverly Hills Cop*, which was the highest-grossing comedy film in history, and *Coming to America*. Murphy has established his own company, Eddie Murphy Productions, to create and produce television and film projects. Arsenio Hall came to prominence in 1987 as a successful interim guest host on the now defunct "The Late Show," which won him a lucrative movie contract with Paramount Pictures. In 1988, Hall was featured with Eddie Murphy in the film *Coming to America*. Arsenio Hall now hosts his own highly successful late-night talk show.

Eddie Murphy

■ AFRICAN-AMERICAN PERFORMANCE ARTISTS

Alvin Ailey (1931–1991)
Dancer, Choreographer

Alvin Ailey, founder of the Alvin Ailey American Dance Theater, won international fame as both dancer and choreographer. Ailey studied dancing after graduating from high school, where he was a star athlete. After briefly attending college, Ailey joined the stage crew of the Lester Horton Theater in Los Angeles, for which Ailey eventually performed as a dancer. In 1953, after Horton's death, Ailey became the company choreographer. In 1954, Ailey performed on Broadway as the lead dancer in *House of Flowers*.

Ailey formed his own dance group in 1958 and began giving four performances annually. In 1962, the Ailey troupe made an official State Department tour of Australia, receiving accolades throughout the country. One critic called Ailey's work "the most

Bill Cosby, 1992.

stark and devastating theatre ever presented in Australia."

After numerous appearances as a featured dancer with Harry Belafonte and others, Ailey performed in a straight dramatic role with Claudia McNeil in Broadway's *Tiger, Tiger Burning Bright*. Other Broadway appearances included *Ding Dong Bell, Dark of the Moon*, and *African Holiday*. Ailey also choreographed or staged several operas, including Barber's *Anthony and Cleopatra* (1966), Bernstein's *Mass* (1971), and Bizet's *Carmen*. In addition, Ailey created works for various international ballet stars and companies.

In 1965, Ailey took his group on one of the most successful European tours ever made by an American dance company. In London, it was held over six weeks to accommodate the demand for tickets, and in Hamburg it received an unprecedented 61 curtain calls. A German critic called this performance "a triumph of sweeping, violent beauty, a furious spectacle. The stage vibrates. One has never seen anything like it." In 1970, Ailey's company became the first American modern dance group to tour the Soviet Union.

During the mid-seventies Ailey, among his other professional commitments, devoted much time to creating special jazz dance sequences for America's Bicentennial celebration. Among numerous honors, including several honorary degrees, Ailey was awarded the NAACP's Spingarn Medal in 1976.

Ira Aldridge (c.1807–1867)
Actor

Ira Aldridge was one of the leading Shakespearean actors of the nineteenth century. Although he was denied the opportunity to perform before the American public in his prime, the fame that he won abroad estab-

lished him as one of the prominent figures of international theater.

Aldridge's origins are obscure. Some accounts give his birthplace as Africa; others name Bel-Air, Maryland; still others list New York City. The year of his birth is also uncertain, reported dates range from 1804 to 1807. It seems clear that he attended the African Free School in New York until he was about sixteen years old, at which time he left home.

Aldridge's early dramatic training centered around the African Grove Theatre in New York in 1821. His first role was in *Pizarro*, and he subsequently played a variety of small roles in classical productions before accepting employment as a steward on a ship bound for England.

After studying briefly at the University of Glasgow in Scotland, Aldridge went to London in 1825 and appeared in the melodrama *Surinam, or a Slave's Revenge*. In 1833, he appeared in London's Theatre Royal in the title role of *Othello*, earning wide acclaim. For the next three decades, he toured the continent with great success, often appearing before European royalty.

Aldridge died in Lodz, Poland, on August 7, 1867. He is honored by a commemorative tablet in the New Memorial Theatre in Stratford-upon-Avon, England.

Debbie Allen (1950–)
Actress, Singer, Dancer, Director

A cum laude graduate of Howard University, the Houston-born Debbie Allen began her career on the Broadway stage in the chorus line of the hit musical *Purlie* (1972). She then portrayed Beneatha in the Tony and Grammy award winning musical *Raisin* (1973). Other early stage roles were in the national touring company of *Guys and Dolls* and the drama *Anna Lucasta*, performed for the New Federal Theatre at the Henry Street Settlement in New York.

Allen was subsequently selected to star in an NBC pilot, "3 Girls 3," and then appeared on other television hits such as "Good Times" and "The Love Boat". At this time, her talent as a choreographer recognized, she worked on such television projects as "Midnight Special" as well as two films, *The Fish that Saved Pittsburgh* (1979) and *Under Fire* (1981).

The year of 1982 was pivotal for Allen. She appeared in the film *Ragtime* and the television series, "Fame" as well as the Joseph Papp television special, "Alice at the Palace." Allen also starred in a dance performance for the Academy Awards ceremonies.

Allen's career continued with roles in the television special, *Ben Vereen . . . His Roots* and the miniseries "Roots: The Next Generation" (1979). She also appeared on stage again in *Ain't Misbehavin* (1979) and a revival of *West Side Story* (1980), which earned her a Tony Award nomination and a Drama Desk Award.

As each season passed on "Fame," Allen became more involved as choreographer and was soon regularly directing episodes of the series. In 1988, she was selected by the producers to become director of the television sitcom, "A Different World." In another acknowledgment of her stature as a performer and creative talent, she starred in her own television special during the 1988–89 season.

Eddie "Rochester" Anderson (1906–1977)
Comedian

For many years, Eddie Anderson was the only black performing regularly on a network radio show. As the character Rochester on the Jack Benny program, he became one of the best-known black American entertainers.

Anderson was born in Oakland, California in 1906, the son of "Big Ed" Anderson, a minstrel performer, and Ella Mae, a tight-wire walker. During the 1920s and early 1930s, Anderson traveled throughout the Middle and Far West singing, dancing, and performing as a clown in small clubs. On Easter Sunday 1937, he was featured on Jack Benny's radio show, in what was supposed to be a single appearance; Anderson was such a hit that he quickly became a regular on the program.

Anderson is best known for his work with Benny (in television as well as on radio), but he also appeared in a number of movies, including *What Price Hollywood?* (1932),

Debbie Allen

957

Performing Arts

Eddie Anderson

Cabin in the Sky (1943), and *It's a Mad, Mad, Mad, Mad World* (1963).

Anderson died on February 28, 1977 at the age of seventy-one.

Pearl Bailey (1918–1990)
Singer, Actress

Born March 29, 1918 in Newport News, Virginia, Pearl Bailey moved to Philadelphia with her family in 1933. She sang at small clubs in Scranton, Pennsylvania and in Washington, DC before becoming the vocalist for the band of Cootie Williams and later for Count Basie. In the early 1940s, Baily had her first successful New York engagements at the Village Vanguard and the Blue Angel. During World War II, she toured with the USO. Bailey made her New York stage debut in 1946 in *St. Louis Woman*, for which she

won a Donaldson Award as the year's most promising new performer. She also appeared in the films *Variety Girl* (1947) and *Isn't it Romantic?* (1948).

During the 1950s Bailey appeared in the movies *Carmen Jones*, *That Certain Feeling*, and *Porgy and Bess*, and on Broadway in *House of Flowers*. In the 1950s and 1960s, she worked as a recording artist, nightclub headliner, and television performer. In 1967, she received a special Tony Award for her starring role on Broadway in *Hello, Dolly*. In 1969, she published an autobiography, *The Raw Pearl*. Her other books include *Talking to Myself* (1971), *Pearl's Kitchen* (1973), *Duey Tale* (1975), and *Hurry Up, America, and Spit* (1976).

In 1975, Bailey was named a special adviser to the United States Mission to the United Nations. In 1976, she appeared in the film *Norman, Is That You?* with Redd Foxx, and on stage in Washington, DC in *Something To Do*, a musical saluting the American worker. She also received an award in 1976 from the Screen Actors Guild for Outstanding Achievement in Fostering the Finest Ideals of the Acting Profession. Georgetown University made her an honorary doctor of Human Letters in 1977.

In January 1980, Bailey gave a one-night concert at Radio City Music Hall in New York. In 1981, she performed as the voice of the cartoon character "Owl" in the Disney movie *The Fox and the Hound*.

Bailey married the jazz drummer Louis Bellson in 1952. She died August 17, 1990, in Philadelphia.

Josephine Baker (1906–1975)
Dancer, Singer

Born in St. Louis on June 3, 1906, Josephine Baker received little formal education; she left school at the age of eight to

Josephine Baker

ant eccentricities as walking pet leopards down the Champs-Elysèes.

In 1930, after completing a world tour, Baker made her debut as a singing and dancing comedienne at the Casino de Paris. Critics called her a "complete artist, the perfect master of her tools." In time, she ventured into films, starring alongside French idol Jean Gabin in *Zouzou* (1934), and into light opera, performing in *La Créole* (1934), an operetta about a Jamaican girl.

During World War II, Baker served first as a Red Cross volunteer, and later did underground intelligence work through an Italian Embassy attaché. After the war, the French government decorated her with the Legion of Honor. She returned to the entertainment world, regularly starring at the Folies Bergère, appearing on French television, and going on another extended international tour. In 1951, in the course of a successful American tour, Baker made headlines by speaking out against discrimination and refusing to perform in segregated venues.

Beginning in 1954, Baker earned another reputation—not as a lavish and provocative entertainer, but as a progressive humanitarian. She used her fortune to begin adopting and tutoring a group of orphaned babies of all races, retiring from the stage in 1956 to devote all her time to her "rainbow family." Within three years, however, her "experiment in brotherhood" had taken such a toll on her finances that she was forced to return to the stage, starring in *Paris, Mes Amours*, a musical based in part on her own fabled career.

Baker privately, and without voicing discouragement, survived numerous financial crises. Illness hardly managed to dampen her indomitable spirit. Through her long life, she retained her most noteworthy stage attributes—an intimate, subdued voice, coupled with an infectiously energetic and vivacious manner.

supplement the family income by working as a kitchen helper and baby-sitter. While still in elementary school, she took a part-time job as a chorus girl. At seventeen, she performed as a chorus girl in Noble Sissle's musical comedy *Shuffle Along*, which played in Radio City Music Hall in 1923. Her next show was *Chocolate Dandies*, followed by a major dancing part in *La Revue Nègre*, an American production that introduced *le jazz hot* to Paris in 1925.

In Paris, Baker left the show to create her most sensational role, that of the "Dark Star" of the Folies Bergère. In her act, she appeared topless on a mirror, clad only in a protective waist shield of rubber bananas. The spectacular dance made her an overnight star and a public figure with a loyal following. In true "star" tradition, she catered to her fans by adopting such flamboy-

Baker died in Paris on April 12, 1975, after opening a gala to celebrate her fiftieth year in show business.

Harry Belafonte (1927–   )
Singer, Actor

Born in New York City, Harry Belafonte moved to the West Indies at the age of eight. At thirteen, Belafonte returned to New York, where he attended high school. Belafonte joined the Navy in 1944; after his discharge, while working as a janitor in New York, he became interested in drama. He studied acting at Stanley Kubrick's Dramatic Workshop and with Erwin Piscator at the New School for Social Research, where his classmates included Marlon Brando and Walter Matthau. A successful singing engagement at The Royal Roost, a New York jazz club, led to other engagements around the country. But Belafonte, dissatisfied with the music he was performing, returned to New York, opened a restaurant in Greenwich Village, and studied folk singing. His first appearances as a folk singer in the 1950s "helped give folk music a period of mass appeal," according to John S. Wilson in a 1981 *New York Times* article. During his performances at the Palace Theater in New York, Belafonte had audiences calypsoing in the aisles.

Belafonte produced the first integrated musical shows on television, which both won him two Emmy awards and resulted in his being fired by the sponsor. The famous incident in which white British singer Petula Clark touched his arm while singing a song caused a national furor in pre-civil rights America. When Dr. Martin Luther King marched on Montgomery, Alabama, and Washington, DC, Harry Belafonte joined him and brought along a large contingent of performers. Touring in the stage musical *Three for Tonight* in which he had appeared on Broadway in 1955, Belafonte was forced to flee in the middle of a performance in Spartanburg, South Carolina and be rushed to the airport in the mayor's car. Word had come that the Ku Klux Klan was marching on the theater.

Belafonte also appeared on Broadway in John Murray Anderson's *Almanac* (1953), and his movies include *Carmen Jones* (1954), *Island in the Sun* (1957), *The World, the Flesh, and the Devil* (1958), *Odds against Tomorrow* (1959), *The Angel Levine* (1969), *Buck and the Preacher* (1972), and *Uptown Saturday Night* (1974).

In the 1980s, Belafonte appeared in his first dramatic role on television in the NBC presentation of "Grambling's White Tiger," and in 1981, Columbia Records released his first album in seven years, *Loving You Is Where I Belong*, consisting of mostly ballads. He has received numerous awards and honors, including the 1982 Martin Luther King, Jr. Nonviolent Peace Prize and three honorary doctorates.

James Hubert "Eubie" Blake (1883–1983)
Musician, Composer

Eubie Blake was born in Baltimore on February 7, 1883. The son of former slaves, Blake was the last of ten children and the only one to survive beyond two months. His mother worked as a laundress, his father as a stevedore.

At the age of six, Blake started taking piano lessons. He studied under the renowned teacher Margaret Marshall and subsequently was taught musical composition by Llewelyn Wilson, who at one time conducted an all-black symphony orchestra sponsored by the city of Baltimore. At the age of seventeen, Blake was playing for a Baltimore night club.

In 1915, Blake joined Nobel Sissle. That year, Blake and Sissle sold their first song, "It's All Your Fault," to Sophie Tucker, and her introduction of the song started them on their way. Blake and Sissle moved to New York and, together with Flournoy Miller and Aubrey Lyles, created one of the pioneer black shows, *Shuffle Along*, in 1921; the show was produced again on Broadway in 1952. *Chocolate Dandies* and *Elsie* followed in 1924.

During the early 1930s, Blake collaborated with Andy Razaf and wrote the musical score for Lew Leslie's *Blackbirds*. Out of this association came the hit *Memories of You*. During World War II, Blake was appointed musical conductor for the United Services Organizations (USO) Hospital Unit. In 1946 he announced his retirement and enrolled in New York University.

For many years, Blake's most requested song was "Charleston Rag," which he composed in 1899 and which was written down by someone else because Blake could not then read music. Among his most famous songs were "How Ya' Gonna Keep 'Em Down on the Farm," "Love Will Find a Way," and "You're Lucky to Me." Some of his other works include "I'm Just Wild About Harry," "Serenade Blues," "It's All Your Fault," and "Floradora Girls," with lyrics by Sissle.

Though known as the master of ragtime, Blake always most loved the music of the classical masters. In the intimacy of his Brooklyn studio, Blake rarely played the music for which the world reveres him. In 1978, Blake's life and career were celebrated in the Broadway musical *Eubie!*. Several thousand people attended concerts at the Shubert Theatre and St. Peters Lutheran Church celebrating Blake's 100th birthday on February 8, 1983. Blake also received honorary doctorates from numerous colleges and universities. He died on February 12, 1983.

John Bubbles (1902–1986)
Dancer, Singer

John Bubbles, inventor of rhythm tap dancing, was born John William Sublett in 1902 in Louisville, Kentucky. At the age of seven, he teamed with a fellow bowling-alley pinboy, Ford "Buck" Washington, to form what became one of the top vaudeville acts in show business. Throughout the 1920s and 1930s, Buck and Bubbles played the top theaters in the country at fees of up to $1,750 a week. The two appeared in several films, including *Cabin in the Sky* (1943). Bubbles captured additional fame as "Sportin' Life" in the 1935 version of *Porgy and Bess*. After Buck's death in 1955, Bubbles virtually disappeared from show business until 1964, when he teamed up with Anna Maria Alberghetti in a successful nightclub act.

In 1979, at the age of 77 and partially crippled from an earlier stroke, Bubbles recreated his characterization of "Sportin' Life" for a one-night show entitled *Black Broadway* at New York's Lincoln Center. The show was repeated in 1980 for a limited engagement at the Town Hall in New York. In the fall of 1980, Bubbles received a Lifetime Achievement Award from the American Guild of Variety Artists and a Certificate of Appreciation from the city of New York.

Bubbles died on May 19, 1986, at the age of eighty-four.

Anita Bush (1883–1974)
Actress, Singer

Anita Bush was involved with the theater from early childhood. Her father was the tailor for the Bijou, a large neighborhood theater in Brooklyn, and Anita would carry the costumes to the theater for him, giving her a backstage view of performers and productions. Her singing/acting career took off in her early twenties, when she was in the chorus of the Williams and Walker Company. With Williams and Walker, she performed in such Broadway hits as *Abyssinia* and *In Dahomey*, which also had a successful European tour. When the group split up in 1909, she went on to form the Anita Bush Stock Company, which included her own show of chorus girls and such greats as Charles Gilpin and Dooley Wilson, with whom she also founded the Lafayette Players.

Bush died on February 16, 1974.

Godfrey Cambridge (1933–1976)
Actor, Comedian

Born in New York, Godfrey Cambridge's parents had emigrated from British Guiana. He attended grammar school in Nova Scotia, while living with his grandparents. After finishing his schooling in New York at Flushing High School and Hofstra College, he went on to study acting.

Cambridge made his Broadway debut in *Nature's Way* (1956), and was featured in *Purlie Victorious* both on stage in 1961, and later on screen. He also appeared off-Broadway in *Lost in the Stars* (1958), *Take a Giant Step*, and *The Detective Story* (1960). Cambridge won the Obie award for the 1960–1961 season's most distinguished off-Broadway performance for his role in *The Blacks*. In 1965, he starred in a stock version of *A Funny Thing Happened on the Way to the Forum*.

As a comedian, Cambridge appeared on "The Tonight Show" and many other variety hours. His material, drawn from the contemporary racial situation, was often presented in the style associated with the contemporary wave of black comedians. One of Cambridge's most memorable roles was as the star of a seriocomic Hollywood film, *The Watermelon Man* (1970), in which the comedian played a white man who changes color

Godfrey Cambridge

overnight. Cambridge has also performed dramatic roles on many television series.

During the mid-seventies, Cambridge remained in semi-retirement, making few public appearances. Cambridge died at the age of forty-three in California on November 29, 1976. His death occurred on a Warner Brothers set, where he was playing the role of Ugandan dictator Idi Amin for the television film "Victory at Entebbe."

Diahann Carroll (1935–   )
Actress, Singer

Diahann Carroll was born in the Bronx, the daughter of a subway conductor and a nurse. As a child, she was a member of the Abyssinian Baptist Church choir; at the age of ten, Carroll won a Metropolitan Opera scholarship. Singing lessons held little appeal for her, however, so she continued her schooling at the High School of Music and Art. As a concession to her parents, Carroll enrolled at New York University, where she was to be a sociology student, but stage fever led her to an appearance on a television talent show, which netted her $1,000. A subsequent appearance at the Latin Quarter club launched her professional career.

In 1954, Carroll appeared in *House of Flowers*, winning favorable press notices. In that year, she also appeared in a film version of *Carmen Jones*, in the role of Myrt.

Movie and television appearances kept Carroll busy until 1958, the year she was slated to appear as an Asian in Richard Rodgers' *Flower Drum Song*. The part did not materialize. Three years later, Rodgers cast her in *No Strings* as a high-fashion model, a role for which she earned a Tony award in 1962.

In the late 1960s, Carroll was cast as lead in the television series "Julia," in which she played a nurse and war widow. She also appeared in the films *Porgy and Bess* (1959), *Goodbye Again* (1961), *Paris Blues* (1961), *Claudine*, with James Earl Jones) (1974), *Sister, Sister* (1982), and *The Five Heartbeats* (1991). She has been featured in the television series "Dynasty" and "A Different World" and has written an autobiography.

Bill Cosby (1937–)
Actor, Comedian

Bill Cosby is one of the most successful performers and businessmen in the United States.

A native of Philadelphia, Cosby dropped out of high school to become a medic in the Navy, obtaining his diploma while in the service. On becoming a civilian, he entered Temple University, where he played football and worked evenings as a bartender.

While doing this work, Cosby began to entertain the customers with his comedy routines and, encouraged by his success, left Temple in 1962 to pursue a career in show business. He began by playing small clubs around Philadelphia and in New York's Greenwich Village. Within two years, he was playing the top nightclubs around the country and making television appearances on the Johnny Carson (also acting as guest host), Jack Paar, and Andy Williams shows. Cosby became the first black to star in a prime time television series. "I Spy" ran from 1965 to 1968 and won Cosby three Emmy Awards.

In the 1970s, Cosby appeared regularly in nightclubs in Las Vegas, Tahoe, and Reno, and did commercials for such sponsors as Jell-O, Del Monte and Ford. From 1969 until 1972, he had his own television series, *The Bill Cosby Show*. During the early 1970s he

Bill Cosby, with cast members of "The Cosby Show," 1987.

developed and contributed vocals to the Saturday morning children's show "Fat Albert and the Cosby Kids." He appeared in such films as *Uptown Saturday Night* (1974), *Let's Do It Again* (1975), *A Piece of the Action* (1977), and the award-winning television movie "To All My Friends on Shore."

In 1975, Random House published his book, *Bill Cosby's Personal Guide to Tennis: or, Don't Lower the Lob, Raise the Net.* For several years, he was involved in educational television with the Children's Television Workshop. He returned to college, spending five years at the University of Massachusetts earning a master's degree and then in 1977, a doctorate in education.

He was star and creator of the consistently top-rated "The Cosby Show," from 1985 to 1992, author of two best-selling books, *Fatherhood* (1986) and *Time Flies* (1987), and a performer at the top venues in Las Vegas, where he earned $500,000 a week. He also won top fees as a commercial spokesman for Jell-O, Kodak, and Coca Cola. He has recorded more than 27 albums and has received five Grammy Awards. Cosby is currently interested in hosting a new version of the old Groucho Marx game show, "You Bet Your Life."

Cosby and his wife, Camille, live in rural New England with their five children. The Cosbys made headlines when they donated $20 million to Spelman College in Atlanta.

Rupert Crosse (1928–1973)
Actor

Born in Nevis, British West Indies, Rupert Crosse moved to Harlem at an early age. Crosse returned to Nevis at the age of seven, after the death of his father. Reared by his grandparents and strongly influenced by his grandfather, a schoolmaster, Crosse received a solid education before returning to

New York, where he attended Benjamin Franklin High School. Crosse also later worked at odd jobs before interrupting high school to spend two years in military service in Germany and Japan. Once out of service, Crosse finished high school and entered Bloomfield College and Seminary in New Jersey. Though he intended to become a minister, it was obvious from the jobs he had held—machinist, construction worker, and recreation counselor—that his career plans were not yet definite.

Crosse subsequently enrolled at the Daykarhanora School, studying acting and appearing in the Equity Library Theatre off-Broadway production *Climate of Eden.* He then transferred to John Cassavetes' workshop, where he helped to create *Shadows* (1961), winner of a Venice Film Festival Award. Crosse's first Hollywood role was in a Cassavetes movie, *Too Late Blues* (1962). His most important film role was as Ned McCaslin in the screen adaptation of William Faulkner's Pulitzer Prize-winning novel, *The Reivers* (1969). Crosse was nominated for an Academy Award as best supporting actor for this outstanding performance. His other film credits include *The Wild Seed* and *Ride in the Whirlwind.*

Crosse's stage credits are also numerous, including appearances in *Sweet Bird of Youth, The Blood Knot,* and *Hatful of Rain.* Television viewers saw Crosse in "Dr. Kildare," "I Spy," and "The Man from U.N.C.L.E.," as well as several other series.

Rupert Crosse died of cancer on March 5, 1973 at the age of forty-five at his sister's home in Nevis.

Dorothy Dandridge (1922–1965)
Actress

Dorothy Dandridge was born on November 9, 1922, in Cleveland, Ohio; her mother was the actress Ruby Dandridge. As children, Dorothy and her sister, Vivian, performed as "The Wonder Kids," touring the United States. In 1934, they were joined by a third performer, Etta Jones, and the trio became the Dandridge Sisters. The Dandridge Sisters were a popular act, performing at the Cotton Club in Harlem and in the motion picture *A Day at the Races* (1937). By the 1940s, Dorothy Dandridge had struck out on her own, appearing in the "soundies" (musical shorts) *Easy Street*; *Yes, Indeed*; *Cow Cow Boogie*; *Jungle Jig*; *Paper Doll*; and *Sing for My Supper*.

Dandridge married Harold Nicholas (of the famed Nicholas Brothers dance team) in 1942, and had a daughter, Harolyn, in 1943. Harolyn was diagnosed as having a severe developmental disability, and was sent to an institution; shortly thereafter, Dandridge divorced Nicholas. She carried on a fairly suc-

cessful career as a nightclub singer during the 1940s and 1950s. Her greatest triumph, however, came as a film actress, particularly in the all-black musical *Carmen Jones* (1954), for which she received an Oscar nomination for Best Actress, becoming the first African-American woman to receive this nomination. Another important role was in *Island in the Sun* (1957), where she was paired romantically with a white man, John Justin—a breakthrough in desegregating the screen. In 1959, Dandridge played Bess opposite Sidney Poitier's Porgy in the movie version of *Porgy and Bess*. Ultimately, she appeared in over twenty-five films.

Dandridge married the white Las Vegas restaurateur Jack Dennison in 1959, but three years later divorced and declared personal bankruptcy. She died of an overdose of a prescription antidepressant on September 8, 1965.

Dorothy Dandridge, 1956.

Ossie Davis (1917–   )
Actor

Ossie Davis grew up in Waycross, Georgia, and attended Howard University in Washington, DC, where Dr. Alain Locke suggested he pursue an acting career in New York. After completing service in the Army, Davis landed his first role in 1946 in the play *Jeb*, where he met Ruby Dee, whom he married two years later.

After appearing in the movie *No Way Out* (1950), Davis won Broadway roles in *No Time for Sergeants*, *Raisin in the Sun*, and *Jamaica*. In 1961, he and Dee starred in *Purlie Victorious*, which Davis himself had written. Two years later, they repeated their roles in the movie version, *Gone Are the Days*.

Davis' other movie credits from this period include *The Cardinal* (1963), *Shock Treatment* (1964), *The Hill* (1965), *A Man*

Ossie Davis with Ruby Dee, 1987.

Called Adam (1966), and *The Scalphunter* (1968).

Davis then directed such films as *Cotton Comes to Harlem* (1970) and *Black Girl* (1972). His play *Escape to Freedom: A Play about Young Frederick Douglass* had its debut at Town Hall in New York and later was published by Viking Junior Books. Davis has also been involved with television scripts and educational programming. "The Ruby Dee/Ossie Davis Story Hour" was produced for television in 1974. The arts education television series "With Ossie and Ruby" appeared in 1981. Davis and Ruby Dee also founded the Institute of New Cinema Artists and the Recording Industry Training Program.

Davis's continued movie appearances include roles in *Let's Do It Again* (1975), *Hot Stuff* (1979), and *Nothing Personal* (1979). Recent film credits include *Harry and Son*

(1984) and Spike Lee's *School Daze* (1988) and *Do the Right Thing* (1989). In addition, Davis has appeared on such television series as "The Defenders," "The Nurses," "East Side, West Side," and "Evening Shade."

Sammy Davis, Jr. (1925–1990)
Actor, Comedian, Dancer, Singer

Sammy Davis Jr. was often called "the world's greatest entertainer," a title that attested to his remarkable versatility as singer, dancer, actor, mimic, and musician.

Davis was born in New York City on December 8, 1925. Four years later he was appearing in vaudeville with his father and "uncle" in the Will Mastin Trio. In 1931, Davis made his movie debut with Ethel Waters in *Rufus Jones for President*; this was followed by an appearance in *Season's Greetings*.

Throughout the 1930s, the Will Mastin Trio continued to play vaudeville, burlesque, and cabarets. In 1943, Davis entered the Army and served for two years by writing, directing, and producing camp shows. After his discharge, he rejoined the trio, which in 1946 cracked the major club circuit with a successful Hollywood engagement.

Davis recorded a string of hits ("Hey There," "Mr. Wonderful," "Too Close for Comfort") during his steady rise to the top of show business. In November 1954, he lost an eye in an automobile accident, which fortunately did not interfere with his career. He scored a hit in his first Broadway show *Mr. Wonderful* (1956), and later repeated this success in *Golden Boy* (1964).

In 1959, Davis played Sportin' Life in the movie version of *Porgy and Bess*. Other Davis movies from this period include

Sammy Davis, Jr.

Oceans 11 (1960) and *Robin and the Seven Hoods* (1964). His 1966 autobiography *Yes, I Can* became a best seller, and he starred in his own network television series.

In 1968, the NAACP awarded Davis its Spingarn Medal. In the 1970s, Davis appeared in films, television, and nightclubs. In 1972, he was involved in a controversy over his support of Richard Nixon which was publicized by a famous photograph of Nixon hugging Davis at the 1972 Republican Convention. In 1974, Davis renounced his support of Nixon and Nixon's programs. In the same year, his television commercials for Japan's Suntory Whiskey won the grand prize at the Cannes Film Festival, and the National Academy of TV Arts and Sciences honored him for his unique contributions to television.

In 1975, Davis became host of an evening talk and entertainment show. In 1980, he marked his fiftieth anniversary as an entertainer and the Friars Club honored him with its Annual Life Achievement Award. In 1989, he appeared in the film *Tap* with Gregory Hines and Harold Nicholas.

Davis married three times. His first marriage was in 1959 to singer Loray White. He married his second wife, actress Mai Britt, in 1961; she is the mother of his three children. In 1970, he married dancer Altovise Gore.

Ruby Dee (1923–   )
Actress

Ruby Dee was born in Cleveland but grew up in Harlem, attending Hunter College in New York. In 1942, she appeared in *South Pacific* with Canada Lee. Five years later, she met Ossie Davis while they were both playing in *Jeb*. They were married two years later.

Ruby Dee's movies roles from this period include parts in *No Way Out* (1950), *Edge of* the City (1957), *Raisin in the Sun* (1961), Genet's *The Balcony* (1963, and *Purlie Victorious* (1963), written by Davis. Since 1960, she has appeared often on network television.

In 1965, Ruby Dee became the first black actress to appear in major roles at the American Shakespeare Festival in Stratford, Connecticut. Appearances in movies including *The Incident* (1967), *Uptight* (1968), *Buck and the Preacher* (1972), *Black Girl* (directed by Davis) (1972), and *Countdown at Kusini* (1976) followed. Her musical satire *Take It from the Top*, in which she appeared with her husband in a showcase run at the Henry Street Settlement Theatre in New York premiered in 1979.

As a team, Ruby Dee and Ossie Davis have recorded several talking story albums for Caedmon. In 1974, they produced "The Ruby Dee/Ossie Davis Story Hour," which was sponsored by Kraft Foods and carried by more than 60 stations of the National Black Network. Together they founded the Institute of New Cinema Artists to train young people for jobs in films and television, and then the Recording Industry Training Program to develop jobs in the music industry for disadvantaged youths. In 1981, Alcoa funded a television series on the Public Broadcasting System titled "With Ossie and Ruby," which used guests to provide an anthology of the arts. Recent film credits include *Cat People* (1982) and, with Ossie Davis, Spike Lee's *Do the Right Thing* (1989).

Katherine Dunham (1910–   )
Choreographer, Dancer

Katherine Dunham has for many years been one of the leading exponents of primitive dance in the world of modern choreography.

Born in Joliet, Illinois on June 22, 1910, Dunham attended Joliet Township Junior College and the University of Chicago, where she majored in anthropology. With funding from a Rosenwald Fellowship, she was able to conduct anthropological studies in the Caribbean and Brazil. She later attended Northwestern University, where she earned her Ph.D., MacMurray College, where she received a L.H.D in 1972, and Atlanta University, where she received a Ph.D.L. in 1977.

In the 1930s, she founded the Dunham Dance Company whose repertory drew on techniques Dunham learned while studying in the Caribbean. She has used her training in anthropology and her study of primitive rituals from tropical cultures to create unique dance forms that blend primitive qualities with sophisticated Broadway stage settings. In 1940, she appeared in the musical *Cabin in the Sky*, which she had choreographed with George Balanchine. She later toured the United States with her dance group; after the war, she played to enthusiastic audiences in Europe.

Among Dunham's choreographic pieces are *Le Jazz Hot* (1938) *Bhahiana* (1939), *Plantation Dances* (1940), *Haitian Suite (II)* (1941), *Tropical Revue* (1943), *Havana 1910/1919* (1944), *Carib Song* (1945), *Bal Negre* (1946), *Rhumba Trio* (1947), *Macumba* (1948), *Adeus Terras* (1949), *Spirituals* (1951), *Afrique du Nord* (1953), *Jazz Finale* (1955), *Ti 'Cocomaque* (1957), and *Anabacoa* (1963). Under the pseudonym Kaye Dunn, Dunham has written several articles and books on primitive dance. She has been referred to as "the mother of Afro-American dance."

On January 15, 1979, at Carnegie Hall in New York, Dunham received the 1979 Albert Schweitzer Music Award, and selections from her dance repertory from 1938 to 1975 were staged.

Dunham has founded schools of dance in Chicago, New York, Haiti, Stockholm, and Paris. She has also lectured at colleges and universities across the country.

Stepin Fetchit (1902–1985)
Actor

Stepin Fetchit's place in movie history is a controversial one. Praised by some critics as an actor who opened doors for other African Americans in Hollywood, he has been berated by others for catering to racist stereotypes and doing little to raise the status of black actors. His characters—lazy, inarticulate, slow-witted, and always in the service of whites—have become so uncomfortable to watch that his scenes are sometimes cut when films in which he appeared are shown on television. Even at the height of his career, civil rights groups protested his roles, which they considered demeaning caricatures.

Born Lincoln Theodore Monroe Andrew Perry in Key West, Florida in 1902, Stepin Fetchit's early career was in the Royal American Shows plantation revues. He and his partner, Ed Lee, took the names "Step 'n' Fetchit: Two Dancing Fools from Dixie." When the duo broke up, Fetchit appropriated "Stepin Fetchit" for himself.

Fetchit appeared in numerous motion pictures in the 1920s and 1930s, including *In Old Kentucky* (1927), *Salute* (1929), *Hearts in Dixie* (1929), *Show Boat* (1929), *Swing High* (1930), *Stand Up and Cheer* (1934), *David Harum* (1934), *One More Spring* (1936), and *Zenobia* (1939). Fetchit earned a great deal of income from these films, and spent it wildly. His extravagant lifestyle ended when he filed for bankruptcy in the 1930s.

Fetchit made sporadic appearances in films later in his life, among them *Miracle in Harlem* (1949), *Bend of the River* (1952), *Amazing Grace* (1974), and *Won Ton Ton, The Dog Who Saved Hollywood* (1976).

Redd Foxx (1922–1991)
Actor, Comedian

Redd Foxx's most famous role was Fred Sanford, the junkman on the popular NBC series "Sanford and Son," which began in 1972. It was the second most popular role on television (after Archie Bunker in "All in the Family"). As a result, Foxx became one of the highest paid actors in show business. In 1976, it was reported that he was earning $25,000 per half-hour episode, plus 25 percent of the producer's net profit.

Sanford is actually Foxx's family name. He was born John Elroy Sanford in St. Louis, and both his father and his brother were named Fred. As a boy, he concocted a washtub band with two friends and played for tips on street corners, earning as much as $60 a night. At 14, Foxx and the band moved to Chicago; the group broke up during World War II.

Redd Foxx, 1977.

969

Foxx then moved to New York, where he worked as a rack pusher in the garment district as he sought for work in night clubs and on the black vaudeville circuit. While in New York, he played pool with a hustler named Malcolm Little, who was to change his name to Malcolm X.

In the early 1950s, Foxx tried to find work in Hollywood. He had a brief stint with *The Dinah Washington Show*, but mostly survived by performing a vaudeville act and working as a sign painter. This comedy act was adult entertainment, which limited his bookings.

Foxx's first real success came in 1955, when he began to record party records. He ultimately made more than 50 records, which sold over 20 million copies. His television career was launched in the 1960s with guest appearances on "The Today Show," "The Tonight Show," and other variety programs. He also began to appear in Las Vegas nightclubs.

Throughout the long run of "Sanford and Son," Foxx disputed with his producers over money. Originally, he was not receiving a percentage of the show's profits, which led him to sit out several episodes; a breach of contract suit filed by the producers resulted. There were racial undertones to these disputes, with Foxx referring to himself as a "tuxedo slave" and pointing to white stars who owned a percentage of their shows. Eventually, Foxx broke with the show and with NBC.

Foxx then signed a multimillion dollar, multiyear contract with ABC, which resulted in a disastrous comedy variety hour that he quit on the air in October 1977. The ABC situation comedy "My Buddy," which he wrote, starred in, and produced followed. In 1978, however, ABC filed a breach of contract suit. In 1979, Foxx was back at NBC planning a sequel to "Sanford and Son." He also made a deal with CBS, which in 1981

was suing him for a second time, allegedly to recover advances not paid back.

In 1976, Foxx performed in the MGM movie *Norman, Is That You?* He continued his appearances in nightclubs in Las Vegas and New York. In 1979, the book *Redd Foxx, B.S.* was published, comprised of chapters written by his friends.

In 1973, Foxx received the Entertainer of the Year Award from the NAACP. In 1974, he was named police chief of Taft, Oklahoma, an all-black village of 600 people. He also ran a Los Angeles nightclub to showcase aspiring young comedians, both black and white. In addition, Foxx did numerous prison shows, probably more than any other famous entertainer, which he paid for out of his own pocket.

Al Freeman, Jr. (1934–)
Actor

Al Freeman Jr. has won recognition for his many roles in the theater and motion pictures. His title role in the television film "My Sweet Charlie" (1970) earned him an Emmy Award nomination.

Albert Cornelius Freeman, Jr. was born in San Antonio, Texas, son of the pianist Al Freeman Sr. and Lottie Coleman Freeman. After attending schools in San Antonio and then Ohio, Freeman moved to the West Coast to study law at Los Angeles City College. Following a tour of duty with the Army in Germany, Freeman returned to college and decided to change his major to theater arts after being encouraged by fellow students to audition for a campus production.

Freeman did radio shows and appeared in little theater productions in the Los Angeles area before performing in his first Broadway play, *The Long Dream* (1960). Other Broadway credits include *Kicks and Company* (1961), *Tiger, Tiger Burning Bright* (1962),

Blues for Mr. Charley (1964), *Conversations at Midnight* (1964), *The Dozens* (1969), *Look to the Lilies* (1970), and *Medea* (1973).

Off-Broadway, Freeman worked in *The Living Premise* (1963), *Trumpets of the Lord* (1963), *The Slave* (1964) and *Great MacDaddy* (1974). He also appeared in *Troilus and Cressida* (1965) and *Measure for Measure* (1966) for the New York Shakespeare Festival. He has also done more than a dozen feature films, including *Dutchman* (1967), *Finian's Rainbow* (1968), *The Detective* (1968), *The Lost Man* (1969), and *Castle Keep* (1969).

Freeman has appeared in such television series as "The Defenders," "The FBI," and "Naked City," and was featured as Lieutenant Ed Hall in ABC's daytime drama "One Life to Live." He also appeared on television in Norman Lear's "Hot l Baltimore" (1975).

Morgan Freeman, 1992.

Morgan Freeman (1937–)
Actor

Born in Memphis, Tennessee on June 1, 1937, Morgan Freeman grew up in Greenwood, Mississippi. He joined the U.S. Air Force in 1955, but left a few years later to pursue an acting career in Hollywood, taking classes at Los Angeles City College. He moved to New York City in the 1960s.

Freeman's first important role was in the short-running off-Broadway play *The Nigger-Lovers* in 1967. Soon thereafter, he appeared in the all-black version of the musical *Hello, Dolly!*.

Americans who grew up in the 1970s remember Freeman fondly as a regular on the public television program "The Electric Company," in which he appeared from 1971–76; his most notable character was the hip Easy Reader. More theater roles followed in productions of *The Mighty Gents*

(1978), *Othello* (1982), *The Gospel at Colonus* (1983), and *The Taming of the Shrew* (1990).

In 1987, Freeman was cast in the Broadway play *Driving Miss Daisy*. He won an Obie award for his portrayal of Hoke, the chauffeur for a wealthy white woman in the American south. Freeman recreated his Broadway role for the 1989 movie version of the play, receiving an Academy Award nomination for Best Actor. In the same year, Freedman appeared in the highly-successful movie *Glory*, about an all-black Union regiment in the Civil War.

Charles Gilpin (1878–1930)
Actor

Charles Gilpin was born in Virginia in 1878. After a brief period in school, he took up work as a printer's devil. In 1890, he began to travel intermittently with vaudeville troupes, a practice he continued for two decades, working as a printer, elevator operator, prizefight trainer, and porter during long interludes of theatrical unemployment.

From 1911 to 1914, Gilpin toured with a group called the Pan-American Octette. In 1914 he had a bit part in a New York production, *Old Ann's Boy*. Two years later he founded the Lafayette Theatre Company, one of the earliest black stock companies in New York.

After Eugene O'Neill saw Gilpin in *Abraham Lincoln*, he was chosen to play the lead in *Emperor Jones*, the role in which he starred from 1920 to 1924. In 1921, Gilpin was awarded the NAACP Spingarn Award for his theatrical accomplishment.

Gilpin lost his voice in 1926 and was forced to earn his living once again as an elevator operator. He died in 1930.

Danny Glover (1947–)
Actor

A native of San Francisco, Danny Glover attended San Francisco State University and trained at the Black Actors Workshop of the American Conservatory Theatre.

Glover went on to appear in many stage productions, including *Island*, *Macbeth*, *Sizwe Banzi is Dead*, and New York productions of *Suicide in B Flat*, *The Blood Knot*, and *Master Harold . . . and the Boys*, which won him a Theatre World Award.

Glover's film credits include *Escape from Alcatraz* (1979), *Chu Chu and the Philly Flash* (1984), *Iceman* (1984), *Witness* (1985), *Places in the Heart* (1985), *The Color Purple* (1985), *Lethal Weapon* (1987) and its sequels, and *Bat 21* (1988).

On television, Glover appeared in the hit series "Hill Street Blues," the miniseries

Danny Glover, 1992.

"Chiefs," "Lonesome Dove," and other projects including "Many Mansions," "Face of Rage," "A Place at the Table," "Mandela," and "A Raisin in the Sun."

Whoopi Goldberg (1949–   )
Actress, Comedienne

Born Caryn E. Johnson in Manhattan's Chelsea district on November 13, 1949, Whoopi Goldberg began performing at the age of eight at the children's program at Hudson Guild and Helen Rubeinstein Children's Theatre. After trying her hand at theater, improvisation and chorus parts on Broadway, she moved to San Diego in 1974 and appeared in repertory productions of *Mother Courage* and *Getting Out.*

Goldberg joined the Black St. Hawkeyes Theatre in Berkeley as a partner with David

Whoopi Goldberg, 1992.

Schein, and then went solo to create *The Spook Show*, performing in San Francisco and later touring the United States and Europe.

In 1983, Goldberg's work caught the attention of Mike Nichols, who created and directed her Broadway show a year later. She made her film debut in *The Color Purple* (1985), winning an NAACP Image Award as well as a Golden Globe Award.

Goldberg's other film credits include *Jumpin' Jack Flash, Burglar, Fatal Beauty, The Telephone, Homer and Eddie, Clara's Heart, Beverly Hills Brats, Ghost*, for which she won an Academy Award as best supporting actress, *Sister Act, The Player*, and *Made in America.*

On television, she starred in "Whoopi Goldberg on Broadway," "Carol, Carl, Whoopi and Robin," "Funny, You Don't Look 200," and hosted "Comedy Tonight." She received an Emmy nomination in 1985 for her guest appearance on "Moonlighting," has had a recurring role on "Star Trek: The Next Generation," and was a founding member of the Comic Relief benefit shows.

Louis Gossett, Jr. (1936–   )
Actor

Born in Brooklyn on May 27, 1936, Louis Gossett began acting at the age of seventeen when a leg injury prevented him from pursuing his first love—basketball. In 1953, he won out over 445 contenders for the role of a black youngster in *Take A Giant Step*, for which he received a Donaldson Award as Best Newcomer of the Year.

While performing in *The Desk Set* in 1958, Gossett was drafted by the professional basketball team the New York Knicks, but decided to remain in theater. Ultimately, he would appear in more than sixty stage productions, including such plays as *Lost in the*

Louis Gossett, Jr., 1993.

Stars, A Raisin in the Sun, The Blacks and *Murderous Angels.*

On television, Gossett played characters roles in such series as "The Nurses," "The Defenders" and "East Side, West Side." In 1977, he won an Emmy for his performance in the acclaimed mini-series, "Roots." He also starred in such films as *Skin Game* (1971), *The Deep* (1977), *Officer and a Gentleman* (1983), *Iron Eagle* (1986), and *Iron Eagle II* (1988).

In 1989, Gossett starred in his own television series, "Gideon Oliver."

Arsenio Hall (1960–　)
Actor, Comedian, Talk Show Host

A Cleveland native, Arsenio Hall started his professional career as a standup comic, making the rounds of clubs and honing his presentation. Soon, he was appearing on television specials as well as touring with noted musical performers.

Hall was selected as a guest-host of Fox Television's "Joan Rivers Show" when Rivers left, and soon won over both studio and television audiences. When this show concluded, he went on to star with Eddie Murphy in the movie *Coming To America* (1988).

Paramount then hired Arsenio Hall to be the host of his own show. Within weeks after the show's premiere in 1989, Hall had again built a solid audience following, particularly with young viewers, and provided the most substantial competition established evening talk shows had ever faced.

Juanita Hall (1902–1968)
Singer

Born on November 6, 1902 in Keyport, New Jersey, Hall studied at the Juilliard School of Music after singing in Catholic Church choirs as a child. Hall devoted her life to music as a singer in stage and movie productions and choirs.

Her first major stage appearance was in Ziegfield's *Showboat* in 1927. Her lengthy stage career culminated in her role as "Bloody Mary" in Rodgers and Hammerstein's *South Pacific* in 1949. Hall went on to appear in *Flower Drum Song* and the movie version of both shows. She served as a soloist and assistant director of the Hall Johnson Choir (1931–1936), conducted the Works Progress Administration chorus in New York City (1936–1941) and organized the Juanita Hall Choir in 1942.

Hall performed at the Palladium in London and was a guest on the Ed Sullivan and Perry Como television shows. She was the recipient of the Donaldson, Antoinette Perry

Arsenio Hall, on the set of his popular talk show "The Arsenio Hall Show," 1990.

and Bill Bojangles awards. Hall died February 28, 1968 in Bay Shore, New York.

Richard B. Harrison (1864–1935)
Actor

Richard B. Harrison was one of the few actors to gain national prominence on the basis of one role, his characterization of "De Lawd" in *Green Pastures.*

Harrison was born in Canada in 1864, and moved to Detroit as a young boy. There he worked as a waiter, porter, and handyman, saving whatever money he could to attend the theatrical offerings playing in town. After studying drama in Detroit, he made his professional debut in Canada in a program of readings and recitations.

For three decades, Harrison entertained black audiences with one-man performances of *Macbeth*, *Julius Caesar*, and *Damon and Pythias*, as well as with poems by Shakespeare, Poe, Kipling, and Paul Laurence Dunbar. In 1929, while serving on the faculty of North Carolina A&T as drama instructor, he was chosen for the part in *Green Pastures.*

When he died in 1935, Harrison had performed as "De Lawd" 1,656 times. His work earned him the 1930 Spingarn Medal and numerous honorary degrees.

Gregory Hines (1946–   )
Actor, Dancer

After a distinguished career as a tap dancer, Gregory Hines made an unusual transition to dramatic actor.

Born in New York City, Hines began dancing with his brother Maurice under the instruction of tap dancer Henry LeTang. When Gregory was five, the brothers began performing professionally as the Hines Kids. Appearing in nightclubs and theaters around the country, they were able to benefit from contact with dance legends such as "Honi" Coles, Sandman Sims, the Nicholas Brothers and Teddy Hale.

Gregory Hines, 1988.

On television, Hines appeared in the series "Amazing Stories" and the special "Motown Returns to the Apollo," which earned him an Emmy nomination. When not appearing in films or television, he toured internationally with a solo club act. *Gregory Hines*, his first solo album, was released by CBS/Epic in 1988. The album was produced by Luther Vandross, who teamed with Gregory for a single, *There's Nothing Better Than Love*, which reached number one on the R&B charts in 1987.

Hines has received numerous awards, including the Dance Educators Award and the Theater World Award. Hines has been nominated for several Tony awards, and in 1992 received the award for best actor in a musical for his role in *Jelly's Last Jam*.

As teenagers, the two performed as the Hines Brothers. When Gregory reached age eighteen, the two were joined by their father, Maurice Sr., on drums, and the trio became known as Hines, Hines and Dad. They performed internationally and appeared on "The Tonight Show." Eventually, Gregory tired of the touring and settled in California, where he formed the jazz-rock band Severance.

Gregory Hines subsequently moved back to New York and landed a role in *The Minstrel Show* (1978). He would later appear in such Broadway musicals as *Eubie!* (1978), *Sophisticated Ladies* (1981), and *Comin' Uptown* (1990) as well as feature films including *The Cotton Club* (1985), *White Nights* (1985), *Running Scared* (1985), and *Off Limits* (1988). Hines starred in the 1989 Tri-Star film *Tap* with Sammy Davis Jr., not only acting and dancing, but singing as well.

Geoffrey Holder (1930–)
Actor, Dancer, Choreographer, Costume Designer, Director

Geoffrey Holder has succeeded as an artist in many areas. Holder was born on August 1, 1930, in Port-of-Spain, Trinidad. At an early age, he left school to become the costume designer for his brother's dance troupe, which he took over in 1948. Holder led the dancers, singers, and steel band musicians through a series of successful small revues to the Caribbean Festival in Puerto Rico, where they represented Trinidad and Tobago. His appearances with his troupe in the mid-1950s were so popular that he is credited with launching the calypso vogue.

Early in his career, Holder he appeared in New York as a featured dancer in *House of Flowers* (1954). He later performed with the Metropolitan Opera and as a guest star on many television shows. Film credits include *Live and Let Die* (1973), the James Bond adventure, and *Dr. Doolittle* (1967), the children's classic starring Rex Harrison.

Holder received two Tony Awards in 1976, as director and costume designer for the Broadway show *The Wiz*, the all-black adaptation of *The Wizard of Oz*. In 1978, he directed and choreographed the successful Broadway musical *Timbuktu*. In 1982, Holder appeared in the film *Annie* based on the hit Broadway musical, playing Punjab, a character from the original comic strip.

Holder received a Guggenheim Fellowship to pursue his painting, and his impressionist paintings have been shown in galleries such as the Corcoran in Washington, DC. Holder also has written two books. *Black Gods, Green Islands* is a retelling of West Indian legends; his *Caribbean Cookbook* is a collection of recipes that Holder also illustrated.

Holder is married to the ballet dancer Carmen de Lavallade.

Lena Horne

Lena Horne (1917–   )
Actress, Singer

Lena Horne has been called the most beautiful woman in the world, and her beauty has been no small factor in the continued success of her stage, screen, and nightclub career.

Horne was born on June 30, 1917, in Brooklyn, New York. She joined the chorus line at the Cotton Club in 1933, and then left to tour as a dancer with Noble Sissle's orchestra. She was given a leading role in *Blackbirds of 1939*, but the show folded quickly, whereupon she left to join Charlie Barnett's band as a singer. She made her first records (including the popular "Haunted Town") with Barnett. In the early 1940s she also worked at New York's Cafe Society Downtown.

Horne then went to Hollywood, where she became the first black woman to sign a term contract with a film studio. Her films included *Panama Hattie* (1942), *Cabin in the Sky* (1943), *Stormy Weather* (1943), and *Meet Me in Las Vegas* (1956). In 1957, she took a break from her film and nightclub schedule to star in her first Broadway musical, *Jamaica*. Her popular recordings included "Stormy Weather," "Blues in the Night," "The Lady Is a Tramp," and "Mad about the Boy."

Throughout the 1960s and 1970s, Horne appeared in nightclubs and concerts. Her greatest recent success, however, was on Broadway. On May 12, 1981 she opened a one-woman show called *Lena Horne: The Lady and Her Music* to critical and box-office success. Although it opened too late to qualify for the Tony Award nominations, the show was awarded a special Tony at the June ceremonies. In December of that year, she received New York City's highest cultural award, the Handel Medallion.

Horne was married for 23 years to Lennie Hayton, a white composer, arranger, and conductor who died April 24, 1971. She had been married previously to Louis Jones. A generous and gracious woman, Horne has quietly devoted much time to humane causes.

Eddie Hunter (1888–1974)
Comedian

Eddie Hunter got his start when working as an elevator operator in a building frequented by the great tenor Enrico Caruso. Hunter had been writing vaudeville comedy parts on the side, and Caruso encouraged and helped him. In 1923, Hunter's show *How Come?*, a musical revue, reached Broadway.

Hunter performed in his own persona in the majority of the shows he wrote. *Going to the Races*, produced at the Lafayette Theatre in Harlem, had Hunter and his partner live on stage, interacting with a movie of themselves playing on the screen. Hunter considered this show one of his best. As one of the principal performers in *Blackbirds*, he toured Europe during the late twenties. His show *Good Gracious* also toured Europe.

Depicting himself as "the fighting comedian," Hunter developed a reputation for speaking out against racial discrimination in the performing arts. He frequently told the story about Phoenix, Arizona, where the male members of the show were forced to sleep in the theater where they were performing; accommodations for blacks simply did not exist at the time. Hunter characterized his European reception as being relatively free of prejudice, and felt that he only received the respect and recognition due to him when abroad.

By 1923, Hunter had a full recording contract with Victor Records. His recordings included "It's Human Nature to Complain," "I Got," and "My Wife Mamie." Shortly thereafter, he suspended his singing career to begin traveling with a new show he had developed. But when "talking" movies came into being, vaudeville fell out of favor. Eddie Hunter thus retired from show business and entered the real estate business in the 1930s.

He died in 1974, at the age of eighty-six.

Earle Hyman (1926–   )
Actor

Earl Hyman was born in Rocky Mount, North Carolina on October 11, 1926. He began his acting career with the American Negro Theatre in New York City.

In 1963, Hyman made his foreign-language acting debut in Eugene O'Neill's *Emperor Jones* in Oslo, Norway, becoming the first American to perform a title role in a Scandinavian language. Hyman had originally become acquainted with Norway during a European trip made in 1957. He had planned to spend only two weeks in the Scandinavian country, but found himself so enchanted with Norway that he all but forgot the rest of Europe. When Hyman returned to New York, he resolved at once to learn Norwegian, and for practice, began to study the role of Othello (which he was performing for the Great Lakes Shakespeare Festival of 1962) in that language. By sheer coincidence, the director of *Den Nationale Scene* of Bergen, Norway, invited him to play Othello there in the spring of the following year, a performance which marked Hyman's first success in the Norwegian theater.

In 1965, Hyman returned to Norway to play *Emperor Jones* for a different theater company, and received high critical acclaim for his portrayal: Hyman remained in Norway, intermittently, for six years. Due to the interest in his life, Hyman has been the subject of several Norwegian radio broadcasts

Earle Hyman, performing with Frances Sternhagen in *Driving Miss Daisy*.

and television interviews. He still spends six months each year in Scandinavia playing "Othello" and other classical roles. A bronze bust of the actor as Othello has been erected in the Norwegian theater where Hyman performed, and he has also been presented with an honorary membership in the Norwegian Society of Artists, the third foreigner and first American to be so honored.

Hyman's many on and off-Broadway credits include *No Time for Sergeants* (1955), *St. Joan* (with Diana Sands at Lincoln Center) (1956), *Mister Johnson* (1956), *Waiting for Godot* (1957), Lorraine Hansberry's *Les Blancs* (1970), Edward Albee's *Lady from Dubuque*, and the black version of Eugene O'Neill's *Long Day's Journey into Night* (at the Public Theatre) (1981). Among other film and television work, Hyman has appeared on the daytime drama "Love of Life" and "The Cosby Show."

Rex Ingram (1895–1969)
Actor

A major movie and radio personality during the 1930s and 1940s, Rex Ingram was born in 1895 aboard the *Robert E. Lee*, a Mississippi riverboat on which his father was a stoker.

Ingram attended military schools, where he displayed an interest in acting. After working briefly as a cook for the Union Pacific Railroad and as head of his own small window-washing business, Ingram gravitated to Hollywood, where in 1919 he appeared in the original Tarzan film. Roles in such classics as *Lord Jim*, *Beau Geste* (1926), *King Kong* (1933), *The Green Pastures* (1936), and *Huckleberry Finn* (1939) followed. During the late twenties and early thirties, Ingram also appeared prominently in theater in San Francisco. During the late thirties, he starred in daytime radio soap op-

979

Rex Ingram, 1939.

Theater, performing a wide gamut of black roles, especially choreographed for her by Ailey. She has made guest appearances with many other dance companies, including the American Ballet Theatre, and with such opera companies as the Vienna State Opera and the Munich State Opera. In the 1980s, Jamison scored a great success on Broadway in *Sophisticated Ladies*, a musical featuring the music of Duke Ellington. In 1988, she formed the Jamison Project, of which she is currently director.

James Earl Jones (1931–   )
Actor

Jones (whose father Robert Earl Jones was featured in the movie *One Potato, Two Potato*) was born in Tate County, Mississippi, and raised by his grandparents on a

eras and in Works Progress Administration theater projects.

Ingram continued with a distinguished career on the New York stage, and in film and television. In 1957, he played Pozzo in *Waiting for Godot*. Later film credits include *Elmer Gantry* (1960), *Your Cheating Heart* (1964), *Hurry Sundown* (1967), and *Journey to Shiloh* (1968).

Judith Jamison (1944–   )
Choreographer

Born in Philadelphia, Judith Jamison started to study dance at the age of six. She was discovered in her early twenties by the choreographer Agnes De Mille, who admired her spontaneous style.

From 1965 to 1980, Jamison was a principal dancer for Alvin Ailey's American Dance

Judith Jamison, 1989.

farm near Jackson, Michigan. He turned to acting after a brief period as a premedical student at the University of Michigan (from which he graduated cum laude in 1953) and upon completion of military service with the Army's Cold Weather Mountain Training Command in Colorado.

After moving to New York, Jones studied at the American Theatre Wing, making his off-Broadway debut in 1957 in *Wedding in Japan.* Since then, he has appeared in numerous plays, on and off-Broadway, including *Sunrise at Campobello* (1958), *The Cool World* (1960), *The Blacks* (1961), *The Blood Knot* (1964), and *Anyone, Anyone.*

Jones' career as an actor progressed slowly until he portrayed Jack Jefferson in the Broadway smash hit *The Great White Hope.* The play was based on the life of Jack Johnson, the first black heavyweight champion. For this performance, Jones received the 1969 Tony Award for the best dramatic actor in a Broadway play, and a Drama Desk Award for one of the best performances of the 1968–1969 New York season.

By the 1970s, Jones was appearing in roles traditionally performed by white actors, including the title role in *King Lear* and an award-winning performance as Lenny in Steinbeck's *Of Mice and Men.*

In 1978, Jones appeared in the highly controversial *Paul Robeson*, a one-man show on Broadway. Many leading blacks advocated a boycott of the show because they felt it did not measure up to the man himself. However, many critics gave the show high praise.

In 1980, Jones starred in Athol Fugard's *A Lesson from Aloes*, a top contender for a Tony Award that year. He also appeared in the Yale Repertory Theater Production of *Hedda Gabler.* In the spring of 1982, he costarred with Christopher Plummer on Broadway in *Othello*, a production acclaimed as among the best ever done. In

James Earl Jones, 1991.

1987, Jones received a Tony award for his performance in August Wilson's Pulitzer Prize-winning play, *Fences.*

Jones' early film credits include *Dr. Strangelove* (1964) and *River Niger* (1976). He was the screen voice of Darth Vader in *Star Wars* (1977) and its sequel *The Empire Strikes Back* (1980). Jones has also appeared in the horror movie *Red Tide*, the adventure film *Conan the Barbarian* (1982), *Matewan* (1987), and *Field of Dreams* (1989).

Among numerous television appearances, Jones portrayed author Alex Haley in "Roots: The Next Generation" (1979) and has narrated documentaries for the Public Broadcasting System.

In 1976, Jones was elected to the Board of Governors of the Academy of Motion Picture Arts and Sciences. In 1979, New York

Canada Lee, 1951.

Britton and Vince Dundee. In 1933, a detached retina brought an end to his ring career. He had acquired the name Canada Lee when a ring announcer could not pronounce his real name.

In 1934, Lee successfully auditioned at the Harlem YMCA for his first acting role which was in a Works Progress Administration production of *Brother Moses*. In 1941, Orson Welles, who had met Lee in the Federal Theatre's all-black production of *Macbeth*, chose him to play Bigger Thomas in the stage version of Richard Wright's famed novel, *Native Son*.

In 1944, Lee served as narrator of a radio series called "New World Comin,'" the first such series devoted to racial issues. That same year, he also appeared in Alfred Hitchcock's film *Lifeboat*, and in the Broadway play *Anna Lucasta*.

City presented him with the "Mayor's Award of Honor for Arts and Culture." He received an honorary Doctorate of Humane Letters from the University of Michigan in 1971 and the New York Man of the Year Award in 1976. In 1985, he was inducted into the Theater Hall of Fame.

Canada Lee (1907–1951)
Actor

Canada Lee was born Leonard Corneliou Canagata in Manhattan on May 3, 1907. After studying violin as a young boy, he ran off to Saratoga to become a jockey. Failing in this, he returned to New York and began a boxing career. In 1926, after winning 90 out of 100 fights, including the national amateur lightweight title, he turned professional. Over the next few years, he won 175 out of some 200 fights against such top opponents as Jack

Spike Lee (1957–   )
Filmmaker

Lee was born March 20, 1957 in Atlanta, Georgia. His family moved briefly to Chicago

Spike Lee

Spike Lee, in a scene from the movie *She's Gotta Have It*, 1986.

before settling in New York in 1959. Lee received a B.A. in Mass Communication in 1979 from Morehouse College. After a summer internship at Columbia Pictures in Burbank, California, Lee enrolled in New York University's prestigious Institute of Film and Television. He received an M.A. in filmmaking in 1983. While at New York University he wrote and directed *Joe's Bed-Sty Barbershop: We Cut Heads* for which he won the 1982 Student Academy award given by the Academy of Motion Picture Arts and Sciences. The movie was later shown on public television's Independent Focus Series.

Notable films by Lee include *She's Gotta Have It* (1986), *School Daze* (1988), *Do The Right Thing* (1989), *Mo' Better Blues* (1990), *Jungle Fever* (1991) and *Malcolm X* (1992). *She's Gotta Have It* won the LA Film Critics

New Generation award and the Prix de Juenesse at the Cannes Film Festival.

Lee has also written two books: *Spike Lee's Gotta Have It: Inside Guerilla Filmmaking* (1987) and *Uplift the Race* (1988). He has established a fellowship for minority filmmakers at New York University and is a trustee of Morehouse College. Lee's production company, Forty Acres and a Mule Filmworks is located in Brooklyn, New York.

Jackie "Moms" Mabley (1897–1975)
Comedienne

Mabley was born Loretta Mary Aiken in North Carolina, and entered show business as a teenager when the team of Buck and Bubbles gave her a bit part in a vaudeville skit called "Rich Aunt from Utah."

With the help of comedienne Bonnie Bell Drew, Mabley developed a monologue, and was soon being booked on the black vaudeville circuit. Influenced by such acts as Butterbeans and Susie, she developed her own comic character, a world-weary old woman in a funny hat and droopy stockings, delivering her gags with a mixture of sassy folk wisdom and sly insights.

Her first big success came in 1923 at Connie's Inn in New York. Engagements at the Cotton Club in Harlem and Club Harlem in Atlantic City followed.

Moms Mabley was discovered by white audiences in the early 1960s. Her record album *Moms Mabley at the U.N.* became a commercial success, and was followed by *Moms Mabley at the Geneva Conference*. In 1962, she made her Carnegie Hall debut on a program with Cannonball Adderley and Nancy Wilson. Her subsequent Broadway, film, television, and record successes made her the favorite of a new generation.

Moms Mabley died on May 23, 1975 at the age of seventy-eight in the White Plains, New York hospital.

Hattie McDaniel (1898–1952)
Actress

Hattie McDaniel was born on June 10, 1898 in Wichita, Kansas, and moved to Denver, Colorado as a child. After a period of singing for Denver radio as an amateur, she entered vaudeville professionally, and by 1924 was a headliner on the Pantages circuit.

By 1931, McDaniel had made her way to Hollywood. After a slow start, during which she supported herself as a maid and washer woman, she gradually began to get more movie roles. Her early film credits included *Judge Priest* (1934), *The Little Colonel* (1935), *Showboat* (1936), *Saratoga* (1937)

and *Nothing Sacred*. Her portrayal of a "mammy" figure in *Gone with the Wind*, a role for which she received an Oscar award in 1940 as best supporting actress, is still regarded as a definitive interpretation. McDaniel was the first African-American to receive an Oscar award.

McDaniel subsequently appeared in films such as *The Great Lie* (1941), *In This Our Life* (1942), *Johnny Come Lately* (1943), *Since You Went Away* (1944), *Margie* (1946), *Never Say Goodbye* (1946), *Song of the South* (1946), *Mr. Blandings Builds His Dream House* (1948), *Family Honeymoon* (1948), and *The Big Wheel* (1949).

In addition to her movie roles, McDaniel enjoyed success in radio, in the 1930s, as Hi-Hat Hattie and in the 1940s in the title role of the very successful "Beulah" series.

McDaniel died on October 26, 1952.

Hattie McDaniel

Butterfly McQueen

Butterfly McQueen (1911–)
Actress

Butterfly McQueen's portrayal of Prissy in *Gone With the Wind* (1939) rivals Hattie Mc-Daniel's Oscar-winning role as the "mammy," and is certainly as popular with audiences as Vivien Leigh's Scarlett O'Hara or Clark Gable's Rhett Butler.

Born Thelma McQueen on January 8, 1911 in Tampa, Florida, McQueen began her career in the 1930s performing as a radio actress in "The Goldbergs," "The Danny Kaye Show," "The Jack Benny Show," and "The Beulah Show." She also appeared on stage in *Brown Sugar* (1937), *Brother Rat* (1937), and *What a Life* (1938).

After her role in *Gone with the Wind* in 1939, McQueen was cast in other motion pictures such as *I Dood It* (1943), *Cabin in the Sky* (1943), *Mildred Pierce* (1945), and

Duel in the Sun (1947). She appeared as Oriole on the television series "Beulah" from 1950–1952.

Given her outspokenness against racism and discrimination, and refusal to play stereotyped servant roles, McQueen's appearances after this period were sporadic. In 1968, she won accolades for her performance in the off-Broadway play, *Curley McDimple*. She was cast in the television program "The Seven Wishes of Joanna Peabody" in 1978, and the film *Mosquito Coast* in 1986.

McQueen received a B.A. in Spanish from New York City College in 1975.

Oscar Deveraux Micheaux (1884–1951)
Filmmaker, Author

Micheaux was born in 1884 at Metropolis, Illinois. Little is known about his early years other than he left home at 17 and worked briefly as a pullman porter. In 1904 he began homesteading in Gregory County, South Dakota.

Micheaux was a hard working farmer who loved to read and had a flair for writing. In 1913 he wrote, published and promoted *The Conquest: Story of a Negro Pioneer*. This novel was followed by *Forged Note: Romance of the Darker Races* in 1915 and *The Homesteader* in 1917. Much of his writing was melodramatic and probably autobiographical.

In 1918 the Lincoln Picture Co., an independent African-American film production company, tried to buy the film rights to *The Homesteader*. When Micheaux insisted that he direct the planned movie, the deal fell through. Micheaux went to New York where he formed the Oscar Micheaux Corp. Between 1919 and 1937 Micheaux made about thirty films, including *Body and Soul*, a 1924 movie in which Paul Robeson made his first cinematic appearance.

Although Micheaux was an excellent self-promoter of his books and films, his company went into bankruptcy in 1928. By 1931 however, Micheaux was back in the film business producing and directing *The Exile* (1931), and *Veiled Aristocrats* (1932). Between 1941 and 1943 he wrote four more

A poster from Oscar Micheaux's film *Within Our Gates*, 1920.

books, *Wind From Nowhere, Case of Mrs. Wingate, Masquerade* and *Story of Dorothy Stansfield*. In 1948 he made his last film *The Betrayal*. While none of Micheaux's films achieved critical acclaim they were quite popular with African-American audiences and attracted a limited white following. While his characters broke with the black stereotypes of the day, the themes of his movies ignored racial injustice and the day-to-day problems of African Americans.

Micheaux was known as a hard worker and a natty dresser who consumed neither alcohol or tobacco. Although he made a great deal of money, all of it was squandered away. Micheaux died penniless in Charlotte, North Carolina. Conflicting dates are given for his death—March 26, 1951 and April 1, 1951.

Florence Mills (1895–1927)
Singer, Dancer

Florence Mills was born in Washington, DC on January 25, 1895. She made her debut there at the age of five in *Sons of Ham*. In 1903, the family moved to Harlem, and in 1910 she joined her sisters in an act called the Mills Trio. She later appeared with a group called the Panama Four, which included Ada "Bricktop" Smith.

In 1921, Mills appeared in *Shuffle Along*, a prototype for African-American musicals, and her success led to a long engagement at the Plantation, a New York night spot. After a successful appearance in London, she returned to the United States in 1924 to star in *From Dixie to Broadway*, in which she performed her trademark song, "I'm Just a Little Blackbird Lookin' for a Bluebird." Later, her own *Blackbirds* revue was a great success in London and Paris.

Mills returned to the United States in 1927. Exhausted by her work abroad, she entered the hospital on October 25 for a routine appendectomy, and died suddenly a few days later.

Abbie Mitchell (1884–1960)
Singer, Actress

Most celebrated as a concert artist, Abbie Mitchell also performed on the stage and in light musical comedy. At the age of thirteen, she came to New York City from Baltimore, joining Will Marion Cook's Clorindy Company, and later achieving her first real success with the Williams and Walker Company.

By 1923, having performed in almost every European country, Mitchell returned home to give the first of her many voice concerts in the United States. Mitchell also performed with many opera companies and acted in several plays, including *Coquette* (with Helen Hayes) (1927), *Stevedore* (1934) and Langston Hughes' *Mulatto* (1937). She also headed the voice department at Tuskegee Institute for three years.

Mitchell died in 1960 after a long illness.

Arthur Mitchell (1934–)
Dancer, Choreographer

Mitchell was born in Harlem on March 27, 1934, and attended New York's famed High School of the Performing Arts. Mitchell was the first African-American male to receive the high school's dance award in 1951.

Upon graduation in 1952, Mitchell enrolled on a scholarship in the School of American Ballet, run by the eminent choreographer George Balanchine, who also directed the New York City Ballet. In 1955, Mitchell was invited by Balanchine to join the New York City Ballet. Before long, he was a principal dancer in the company, performing in such works as *Agon* and *A Midsummer Night's Dream*.

Mitchell left the New York City Ballet in 1969 to establish the Dance Theater of Harlem, which he founded to give young African Americans an opportunity to get out of the ghetto through the arts. Mitchell and the studio have received numerous awards and citations, including the Changers award given by *Mademoiselle* magazine in 1970 and the Capezio Dance Award in 1971. Surviving a financial crisis in 1990, the school and company are now back on their feet, though treading carefully due to the precarious state of the arts in the United States.

Eddie Murphy (1961–)
Actor, Comedian

Eddie Murphy was born on April 3, 1961 in the Bushwick section of Brooklyn, the son of a New York City policeman and amateur comedian. As a youngster, he did imitations of cartoon characters and, as he grew older, began preparing comic routines with impressions of Elvis Presley, Jackie Wilson, Al Green and the Beatles.

Murphy attended Roosevelt Junior-Senior High School on Long Island and hosted a talent show at the Roosevelt Youth Center before beginning to call local talent agents to secure bookings at Long Island nightclubs. He was a little-known stand-up comedian when he made his first appearance on the late-night television show "Saturday Night Live" in 1980. He made a memorable impression, and within three years was hailed as a major new star based on his work in the hit films *48 Hours* (1982) and *Trading Places* (1983).

After his success with the first two Paramount films, Murphy starred in *Beverly Hills Cop* (1985) and its sequel *Beverly Hills Cop II* (1987), which were two of the major box office hits of the decade. The concert film *Raw* followed, as well as an effort at light-hearted fantasy, *The Golden Child*. Murphy's more recent film appearances include *Coming to America, Harlem Nights, Boomerang*, and *The Distinguished Gentleman*.

Clarence Muse (1889–1979)
Actor, Director

Perhaps best known for his film acting, Clarence Muse was also successful as a director, playwright, and actor on the stage.

Born in Baltimore, Muse's parents came from Virginia and North Carolina, and his grandfather from Martinique. After studying law at Dickinson University in Pennsylvania, Muse sang as part of a hotel quartet in Palm Beach, Florida. A subsequent job with a stock company took him on tour through the South with his wife and son. Coming to New York, he barely scraped a living together, mostly performing as a vaudevillian.

After several plays with the now-famous Lincoln Theatre group and the Lafayette Players in Harlem, and a Broadway stint in *Dr. Jekyll and Mr. Hyde*, where having white roles played by blacks in white-face created quite a controversy, Muse had established himself as an actor and singer.

Muse's first movie role was in *Hearts in Dixie* (1929), produced at the William Fox Studio, in which Muse played a ninety-year-old man. Later, he returned to the stage for the role of a butler in the show that was to be called *Under the Virgin Moon*. After Muse wrote the theme song, the title was changed to his *When It's Sleepy Time Down South*. Both the song and the show were hits.

When the Federal Theatre Project in Los Angeles presented Hall Johnson's *Run Little Chillun*, Muse directed the show. After its successful two-year run, Muse made the screen adaption *Way Down South* (1939).

During Muse's career, he appeared in 219 films, and was at one time one of the highest paid black actors, often portraying faithful servant "Uncle Tom" characters. His movie credits include *Huckleberry Finn* (1931), *Cabin in the Cotton* (1932), *Count of Monte Cristo* (1934), *So Red the Rose* (1935), *Showboat* (1936), *The Toy Wife* (1938), *The Flame of New Orleans* (1941), *Tales of Manhattan* (1942), *Heaven Can Wait* (1943), *Night and Day* (1946), *An Act of Murder* (1948), *Porgy and Bess* (1959), *Buck and the Preacher* (1971), and *Car Wash* (1976). His last film was *Black Stallion* in 1979. He also appeared over the years in concerts and on radio.

Muse died October 13, 1979, the day before his ninetieth birthday. He had lived in Perris, California on his Muse-a-While Ranch.

Fayard Nicholas (1917–)
Harold Nicholas (1924–)
Dancers

The Nicholas Brothers were one of the great tap dance teams of the first half of the 20th century, whose acrobatics and precision were admired by the likes of Fred Astaire and George Balanchine, and whose appearances in motion pictures provide a record of their astounding abilities.

Fayard Nicholas was born in 1917; Harold in 1924. Their professional debut was, ironically, on the radio program "The Horn and Hardart Kiddie Hour" in 1931. In 1932, they became a featured act at Harlem's Cotton Club. They made their first Broadway appearance in the *Ziegfeld Follies* of 1936; this was followed by *Babes in Arms* in 1937.

The Nicholas Brothers' film debut was in *Pie Pie Blackbird* in 1932, and they appeared in several other movies in the 1930s and 1940s, including *Sun Valley Serenade* (1941) and *Stormy Weather* (1943). The latter is particularly memorable for the sequence in which they are featured.

Harold Nicholas married actress Dorothy Dandridge in 1942, but the couple later divorced. The two brothers continue to be active in the world of dance: Harold co-starred with Gregory Hines in the movie *Tap* in 1989, and Fayard won a Tony Award for Best Choreographer for the Broadway musical *Black and Blue* in the same year. In 1992, the Nicholas Brothers were honored by the Kennedy Center.

Frederick O'Neal (1905–)
Actor

Frederick O'Neal is the first black to hold the position of president of Actor's Equity, a fitting tribute to his long years of service to the American theater as both actor and teacher.

O'Neal was born August 27, 1905 in Brookville, Mississippi. After his father's death in 1919, he moved with his family to St. Louis, finishing high school there and appearing in several Urban League dramatic productions.

In 1927, with the help of some friends in St. Louis, O'Neal founded the Ira Aldridge Players, the second African-American acting troupe in America. For the next ten years, he played in thirty of its productions. In 1937, he came to New York, and three years later helped found the American Negro Theater. Today, its alumni include such established stars as Sidney Poitier, Earle Hyman, Harry Belafonte, Ruby Dee, Ossie Davis, and Hilda Simms.

O'Neal himself starred in *Anna Lucasta* (1944), for which he won the Clarence Derwent Award and the Drama Critics Award for the best supporting performance by an actor on Broadway. He was later featured in *Take a Giant Step*, *The Winner*, and several other stage productions. His films include *Pinky* (1949) and *The Man with the Golden Arm* (1956). He has also appeared on several television dramatic and comedy shows.

In 1964, O'Neal became the first black president of Actor's Equity. After devoting himself full-time to Actor's Equity, O'Neal was in 1970 elected international president of the Associated Actors and Artists of America, the parent union of all show business performers' unions. He became president and chairman of the board of the Schomburg Center for Research in Black Culture to raise money to conserve and preserve materials in the center, to solicit material, and toward construction of a new building. He has been a member of the New York State Council on the Arts, President of the Catholic Interracial Council, chairman of the AFL-CIO Civil Rights Committee, and vice president of the A. Philip Randolph Institute. In 1980, he received the National Urban Coalition's Distinguished Trade Unionist Award. In 1990, he received a special tribute from the Black Filmmakers Hall of Fame.

Sidney Poitier (1927–)
Actor

Sidney Poitier was born on February 20, 1927 in Miami, but moved to the Bahamas with his family at a very early age. At age fifteen, he returned to Miami; he later rode freight trains to New York City, where he found employment as a dishwasher. After Pearl Harbor, he enlisted in the Army and served on active duty for four years.

Back in New York, Poitier auditioned for the American Negro Theater, but was turned down by director Frederick O'Neal. After

989

Sidney Poitier, 1990.

the Field. Seven years earlier, Poitier had been the first black actor nominated for the award for his portrayal of an escaped convict in *The Defiant Ones.*

Subsequent notable film appearances include performances in *To Sir with Love* (1967), *Heat of the Night* (1967), *Guess Who's Coming to Dinner* (with Spencer Tracy and Katharine Hepburn) (1968), *Buck and the Preacher* (1972) and *A Warm December* (1973), in both of which he acted and directed, *Uptown Saturday Night* (1974), and *A Piece of the Action* (1977). After years of inactivity, Poitier performed in two additional films, *Little Nikita* and *Shoot To Kill*, both released in 1988. His directing ventures include *Stir Crazy* (with Richard Pryor and Gene Wilder) (1980), *Hanky Panky* (with Gilda Radner) (1982), and the musical *Fast Forward* (1985).

Poitier spent two years writing his memoirs, *This Life*, published by Knopf in 1980. In 1981, Citadel Press published *The Films of Sidney Poitier*, by Alvin H. Marill.

working diligently to improve his diction, Poitier was accepted in the theater group, receiving acting lessons in exchange for doing backstage chores.

In 1950, Poitier made his Hollywood debut in *No Way Out*, followed by successful appearances in *Cry the Beloved Country* (1952), *Red Ball Express* (1952), *Go, Man, Go* (1954), *Blackboard Jungle* (1956), *Goodbye, My Lady* (1956), *Edge of the City* (1957), *Band of Angels* (1957), *Something of Value* (1957), and *Porgy and Bess* (1959), among others. Poitier starred on Broadway in 1959 in Lorraine Hansberry's award-winning *Raisin in the Sun*, and repeated this success in the movie version of the play in 1961.

In 1965, Poitier became the first black to win an Oscar for a starring role, receiving this award for his performance in *Lilies of*

Pearl Primus (1919–)
Dancer, Choreographer

Pearl Primus's anthropological approach to dance makes her one of the most purposeful figures in that medium: for her, dance is education, not merely entertainment. Her aim is to show audiences and dancers alike the African roots of dance and to bring the African-American experience alive.

Primus was born in Trinidad on November 29, 1919. Originally intending to pursue a career in medicine, she received a bachelor of arts degree in pre-medical sciences and biology from Hunter College, with graduate work in medical education and psychology. But 1940s America did not welcome blacks or women in medicine, and after seeking employment in vain, Primus sought assistance from the government's National Youth Administration. She was put into a youth administration dance group, and by 1941 was accepted into New York City's New Dance Group. Her professional debut was at the Young Men's Hebrew Association in New York City on February 14, 1943. In April of that year, she began appearing at Café Society Downtown, the famed New York City nightclub, but left after ten months for an appearance on Broadway at the Belasco Theater. By this time she had her own dance company, Pearl Primus, Percival Borde, and Company. She toured Africa and the southern United States, and incorporated what she learned into her choreography.

Primus is best known for the dances *African Ceremonial* and *Strange Fruit*, which were incorporated into her *Solos for Performance at the Café Society* (ca. 1944), and *Hard Times Blues* (1945).

Richard Pryor (1940–)
Comedian, Actor

Comedian Richard Pryor has had great success as a stand-up comedian, writer, actor, and recording star. He has often used elements of his unconventional upbringing and adult life as material in his comedy routines.

Born Richard Franklin Lennox Thomas Pryor III on December 1, 1940, he was raised by his grandmother in the Peoria, Illinois brothel she ran. His mother worked there as a prostitute. His parents married when he was three years old, but the union did not last. His grandmother was a strict disciplinarian and young Richard was often beaten.

In school Pryor was often in trouble with the authorities. Pryor was expelled from high school for striking a teacher. In 1958 he joined the army and spent two years in Germany. He returned to Peoria after his military service and during the early 1960s began his work as a stand-up comic on a local circuit. He moved to New York City's Greenwich Village in 1963 where he honed his stand-up routine. A 1964 appearance on "The Ed Sullivan Show" led to his first movie role in *The Busy Body* (1966), followed by bit parts in *The Green Berets* and *Wild in the Streets*. During this time Pryor continued to play to live audiences.

In 1972, Pryor played Piano Man in *Lady Sings the Blues* and earned an Academy Award nomination for his performance. Throughout the 1970s, Pryor continued his work as a stand-up comic and also contributed his writing talents to television's "The Flip Wilson Show" and "Sanford and Son," Mel Brooks' film *Blazing Saddles*, and Lily Tomlin's television special, "Lily," for which he won an Emmy Award. He won two of

Richard Pryor

his five Grammy Awards for his comedy albums *That Nigger's Crazy* (1974) and *Bicentennial Nigger* (1976).

Pryor wrote and starred in *Bingo Long and the Traveling All Stars and Motor Kings* (1976) and received raves for his work in *Silver Streak* (also 1976). In 1979, the comedian's film *Richard Pryor Live in Concert* brought his stand-up act to millions.

In 1978, Pryor suffered a major heart attack, and in 1980, while freebasing cocaine, he set himself ablaze and suffered severe injuries. He addresses these incidents in his second concert movie, *Live on Sunset Strip* (1982). In 1985 Pryor co-wrote, directed and starred in *Jo Jo Dancer, Your Life Is Calling*, a semi-autobiographical tale of a comedian who relives his life immediately following a near fatal accident. Pryor's later films include *The Toy, Some Kind of Hero, Brewster's Millions, Critical Condition, Stir Crazy, Bustin' Loose, Moving*, and *See No Evil, Hear No Evil*. In 1989 Pryor co-starred with Eddie Murphy in *Harlem Nights*.

Pryor has been in failing health in recent years. He was diagnosed with multiple sclerosis in 1986 and has had triple bypass heart surgery. He is reportedly often wheelchair bound and lives a reclusive life in his Bel Air, California, home.

Phylicia Rashad (1948–)
Actress

Known to millions as Claire Huxtable, "America's Favorite Mom" from "The Cosby Show," Phylicia Rashad has led a distinguished acting career on television and the stage. She was born on June 19, 1948, in Houston, Texas, and until 1985 was known as Phylicia Ayers-Allen. Her sister is the famous Debbie Allen; both sisters received early instruction in music, acting, and dance. Phylicia graduated magna cum laude from

Howard University in 1970 with a B.F.A. in theater.

Early in her career, Rashad played the character Courtney Wright in the soap opera "One Life to Live." Her big break came with "The Cosby Show," in which she and Bill Cosby presided over the Huxtable family for seven years, from 1985 to 1992. Rashad has also appeared in Broadway and off-Broadway productions of *The Cherry Orchard, The Wiz, Zora, Dreamgirls, A Raisin in the Sun,* and *Into the Woods.*

Rashad has received two honorary doctorates, one from Providence College in Rhode Island and one from Barber-Scotia College in North Carolina. She and her husband Ahmad Rashad, a sportscaster for NBC, live in Westchester County, New York.

Bill "Bojangles" Robinson (1878–1949)
Dancer

Bill Robinson was born on May 25, 1878 in Richmond, Virginia. Having been orphaned early, he was raised by his grandmother, a former slave. By the time he was eight, he was earning his own way by dancing in the street for pennies and working as a stable boy.

In 1887, Robinson toured the South in a show called *The South Before the War*. The following year, he moved to Washington, DC where he again worked as a stable boy. By 1896, he had teamed up with George Cooper. This act was successful on the Keith circuit until the slump of 1907 caused it to fold. Robinson returned to Richmond and worked as a waiter until a year later when he was taken up by a theatrical manager and became a cabaret and vaudeville headliner.

In 1927, Robinson starred on Broadway in *Blackbirds*, and in 1932 he had top billing in *Harlem's Heaven*, the first all-black motion picture with sound. Later, he scored a Hollywood success by teaching his famous stair dance to Shirley Temple in *The Little Colonel* (1936). Robinson made fourteen movies, including *The Littlest Rebel* (1935), *In Old Kentucky* (1936), *Rebecca of Sunnybrook Farm* (1938), *Stormy Weather* (1943), and *One Mile from Heaven* (1938).

Throughout his long career on stage and in movies, Robinson was known as the "King of Tap Dancers." Robinson died on November 25, 1949.

Richard Roundtree (1942–)
Actor

Richard Roundtree is best known as John Shaft, the tough, renegade detective from the movie *Shaft* (1971). Born in New Rochelle, New York, on July 9, 1942, Roundtree graduated from New Rochelle High School, and attended Southern Illinois University on a football scholarship. After brief stints as a suit salesman and a model, he began a stage career with the Negro Ensemble Company. With *Shaft* (1971) and its sequels *Shaft's Big*

Richard Roundtree

Score (1972) and *Shaft in Africa* (1973), Roundtree reached the peak of his career and became a pop icon.

Roundtree's subsequently appeared in the films *Embassy* (1972), *Charley One Eye* (1973), *Earthquake* (1974), *Diamonds* (1975), and *Man Friday* (1976). He appeared in the television miniseries "Roots" (1977), and continues to be cast in various television programs and motion pictures.

Sinbad (1956–)
Comedian, Actor

The 6'5", red-haired Sinbad has delighted audiences with his comedy, which combines street parlance—noticeably free of obscenities—with tales of American life. Born David Adkins on November 10, 1956 in Benton Harbor, Michigan, Sinbad aspired to be a basketball star, winning a basketball scholarship to the University of Denver. A serious knee injury caused him to give up basketball, and he left college in 1978. Shortly thereafter, he renamed himself Sinbad, after the heroic character in *The Arabian Nights*, to boost his spirits. He spent three and a half years in the U.S. Air Force, hating every minute until his 1983 discharge.

By that time, Sinbad had decided to try his hand at stand-up comedy. A series of low-paying engagements throughout the United States followed, and his break came when he appeared on the television talent contest "Star Search" seven times in the mid-1980s. He later worked as a warm-up comedian for "The Cosby Show," and in 1989 was cast as dorm director Walter Oakes on "A Different World"—a role that was broadened in 1991 when Oakes became a counselor. In 1993, Sinbad starred in his own situation comedy about a single foster parent.

John Singleton (1968–)
Filmmaker

Singleton was born in Los Angeles in 1968. After graduating from high school in 1986 he enrolled in the University of Southern California's prestigious Film Writing Program which is part of their School of Cinema-Television. While there he formed an African-American Film Association and did a six month director's internship for the "Arsenio Hall Show." He twice won the school's Jack Nicholson Award for Best Feature Length Screenplays. Before graduating in 1990, he signed with the well known Creative Artists Agency.

Singleton was soon approached by Columbia Pictures to sell the film rights to *Boyz N the Hood* his original screenplay and college thesis. Singleton agreed, but only if he would be the movie's director. The movie

John Singleton

was released in July of 1991 to mixed critical reviews. Although its first showings were marred by moviehouse violence it garnered Singleton an Academy Award nomination for best director. He became the first African-American and the youngest person to be so honored.

Since *Boyz N the Hood* Singleton has done a short cable television film for Michael Jackson entitled *Remember the Time*. His second film, *Poetic Justice* was released in the summer of 1993.

Noble Sissle (1889–1975)
Lyricist, Singer

Noble Sissle was born in Indianapolis, Indiana. He reaped his early successes teamed up with the great Eubie Blake. Sissle wrote the lyrics and sang them in performance; Blake composed and played the music. Together the two created such songs as "I'm Just Wild about Harry," "It's All Your Fault," "Serenade Blues," and "Love Will Find a Way."

The 1921 *Shuffle Along*, the first black musical with a love theme, made Sissle and Blake famous. Joining forces with the writing and comedy team of Flournoy Miller and Aubrey Lyles, Sissle and Blake wrote the words and music to over a dozen songs for the show. *Shuffle Along* became a huge success in the United States and Europe, where it had a prolonged tour. As with most black performers in the early 1900s, Sissle and his troupe would have to travel as far as twenty or thirty miles out of their way to find a place to eat and sleep, since blacks were not welcome in the white hotels of the towns where they played.

Other Sissle and Blake shows included *Chocolate Dandies* (1924) and *Keep Shufflin* (1928). Noble Sissle died December 17, 1975 at his home in Tampa, Florida.

Wesley Snipes

Wesley Snipes (1962–)
Actor

Born in Orlando, Florida, Wesley Snipes spent his childhood in the Bronx, New York. At the age of twelve, he appeared in his first off-Broadway production, a minor role in the play *The Me Nobody Knows*. His interest in dance led him to enroll in New York's High School for the Performing Arts. However, before completing the curriculum, his mother sent him back to Orlando to finish school, where he continued to study drama.

Upon high school graduation, Snipes was awarded a scholarship to study theater at the State University of New York at Purchase. Snipes subsequently appeared in on and off-Broadway productions, including Wole Soyinka's *Death and the King's Horsemen*, Emily Mann's *Execution of Justice*, and John Pielmeier's *The Boys of Winter*. He has also appeared in Michael Jackson's video "Bad" and in the HBO production *Vietnam War Story*, for which he received cable television's best actor award.

Snipe's film appearances include roles in *Wildcats* (1986), *Streets of Gold* (1986),

Major League (1989), and *King of New York* (1990). In 1990 Snipes appeared in Spike Lee's *Mo' Better Blues*, with Denzel Washington. This was followed by a role in Mario Van Peebles' *New Jack City* (1991) and in Spike Lee's *Jungle Fever* (1991). His most recent films include *White Men Can't Jump*, *Passenger 57*, and *Rising Sun*.

Billie "Buckwheat" Thomas (1931–1980)
Actor

Familiar to generations of Americans, Billie "Buckwheat" Thomas, better known simply as "Buckwheat," was one of the principal characters in the "Our Gang" film shorts of the 1930s and 1940s. Buckwheat succeeded the character Farina, and like Farina, his gender was ambiguous: he was in most respects a boy, but wore dress-like gingham smocks, and in some episodes sported pigtails.

Billie Thomas was born in 1931, and joined the "Our Gang" cast in 1934, appearing in ninety-three episodes, the last in 1944. The film historian David Bogle described the character of Buckwheat as "a quiet, odd-ball type, the perfect little dum-dum tag-along." The comedian Eddie Murphy's parodies of Buckwheat in the 1980s were enormously popular; Buckwheat's generally unintelligible speech, blank expression, and untidy hair provided a wealth of material for Murphy's routine.

Billie Thomas himself had an uneventful life after the "Our Gang" series ended. He died in 1980 at the age of 49.

Cicely Tyson (1933–)
Actress

During the early 1970s, Cicely Tyson emerged as America's leading black dramatic star. She achieved this through two sterling performances—as Rebecca, the wife of a southern sharecropper in the film *Sounder*, and as the lead in a television special, "The Autobiography of Miss Jane Pittman," the story of an ex-slave who, past her hundredth year, challenges racist authority by deliberately drinking from a "white only" water fountain as a white deputy sheriff looks on.

Cicely Tyson was born in New York City and raised by a very religious, strict mother, who associated movies with sin and forbade Cicely to go to movie theaters. Blessed with poise and natural grace, Tyson became a model, and appeared on the cover of America's two foremost fashion magazines, *Vogue* and *Harper's Bazaar*, in 1956. Interested in acting, she began to study drama, and in 1959 appeared on a CBS culture series, "Camera Three," with what is believed to be the first natural African hair style worn on television.

Tyson won a role in an off-Broadway production of Jean Genet's *The Blacks* (1961), for which she received the 1962 Vernon Rice Award. She then played a lead part in the CBS series "East Side, West Side." Tyson subsequently moved into film parts, appearing in *The Comedians* (1967) and *The Heart Is a Lonely Hunter* (1968). Critical acclaim led to her role as Rebecca in *Sounder* (1972), for which she was nominated for an Academy award and named best actress by the National Society of Film Critics. She won an Emmy television acting trophy for "Jane Pittman" (1974).

Tyson's other film appearances include *The Blue Bird* (1976) and *The River Niger* (1976). On television, she has appeared in "Roots" (1977), "King" (1978), and "Wilma" (1978). She portrayed Harriet Tubman in "A Woman Called Moses," and Chicago schoolteacher Marva Collins in a made-for-television movie in 1981. Recent television appearances include "Cry Freedom" (1987) and "The Women of Brewster Place" (1989).

In 1979, Marymount College presented Tyson with an honorary Doctor of Fine Arts. Tyson owns a house on Malibu Beach in California. In November 1981, she married jazz trumpeter Miles Davis but the couple divorced before Davis' death.

Leslie Uggams (1943–   )
Singer, Actress

Born in the Washington Heights section of New York City on May 25, 1943, Leslie Uggams enjoyed a comfortable childhood. She made her singing debut at the age of six, performing with the choir of St. James Presbyterian Church in New York, and followed shortly thereafter with her acting debut in the television series "Beulah." Uggams developed her poise and stage presence early in life, attending the Professional Children's School, where she was chosen student body president in her senior year.

Uggams subsequently won $25,000 on the popular television quiz show, "Name That Tune," which renewed her interest in a singing career. In 1961, Uggams became a regular on "The Mitch Miller Show," a variety show featuring old favorites. She was at the time the only black performer appearing regularly on network television.

Throughout the 1960s, Uggams appeared in numerous nightclubs and had several supperclub and television engagements. Her big break came when she was signed as a replacement for Lena Horne in *Hallelujah Baby*, a show that presented a musical chronicle of the civil rights movement. Uggams won instant stardom and received a Tony award for her performance.

In 1977, Uggams appeared as Kizzy in the television adaption of Alex Haley's novel, *Roots*. In May 1982, she performed in a new Broadway show, *Blues in the Night*, at the Rialto Theater in New York City. She has also appeared on television in "Backstairs at

Leslie Uggams

Tony Award. He was also nominated for a Tony for his co-starring role in *Jesus Christ Superstar* (1971). His film appearances include roles in *Funny Lady* (1975), *All That Jazz* (1979), and *The Zoo Gang*.

Vereen has starred in the ABC comedy series "Tenspeed and Brown Shoe" and is known for his television specials; the highly-acclaimed "Ben Vereen—His Roots" (1978) won seven Emmy awards. He also portrayed Louis "Satchmo" Armstrong and received wide acclaim for his role of Chicken George in television's adaption of Alex Haley's *Roots* (1977) and for his performance in *Jubilee*.

Denzel Washington (1954–   )
Actor

Born in December 1954 in Mt. Vernon, New York, Denzel Washington attended an upstate private high school, the Oakland Academy, and then entered Fordham Uni-

the White House," a miniseries, and "The Book of Lists," in the film *Skyjacked*, and in the musicals *Jerry's Girls*, *The Great Gershwin*, and *Anything Goes*.

Ben Augustus Vereen (1946–   )
Dancer, Actor

Ben Vereen was born October 10, 1946, in the Bedford-Stuyvesant section of Brooklyn, New York and attended the High School of Performing Arts in Manhattan. His dancing ability had been discovered almost accidentally after he had been sent to dance school by his mother. Vereen has since been called America's premier song and dance man.

Ben Vereen made his stage debut in 1965 in *The Prodigal Son*. He went on to appear in *Sweet Charity* (1966), *Golden Boy* (1968), *Hair* (1968), and *No Place to Be Somebody* (1970). Vereen is best known for his Broadway role in *Pippin* (1972), which won him a

Denzel Washington

Denzel Washington as Malcolm X in Spike Lee's film *Malcolm X*.

versity as a pre-med major. Washington did not originally intend to become an actor, but when he auditioned for the lead role in a student production of Eugene O'Neill's *The Emperor Jones*, he won the part over theater majors. His performance in that play, and later in a production of *Othello*, led his drama instructor to encourage Washington to pursue an acting career.

Washington's first major role was in the off-Broadway drama *A Soldier's Story*; Washington recreated his role when the play was adapted into a motion picture in 1984. He played Dr. Phillip Chandler on the television series "St. Elsewhere," and appeared in a string of films, including *Carbon Copy* (1980), *Cry Freedom* (in which he portrayed South African activist Steven Biko) (1987), *The Mighty Quinn* (1989), *Glory* (which won him an Academy Award for Best Sup-

porting Actor) (1989), *Mo' Better Blues* (1990), *Mississippi Masala* (1992), and *Malcolm X* (1992).

Washington is married to the actress Pauletta Pearson.

Ethel Waters (1900–1977)
Actress, Singer

The distinguished career of Ethel Waters spanned half a century, and made its mark in virtually every entertainment medium—stage, screen, television, and recordings.

Ethel Waters was born on October 31, 1900, and spent most of her childhood in Chester, Pennsylvania. By the age of seventeen, she was singing professionally at the Lincoln Theatre in Baltimore. During this early phase of her career, she became the

Keenan Ivory Wayans

first woman to perform W.C. Handy's "St. Louis Blues" on stage.

After several years in nightclubs and vaudeville, Waters made her Broadway debut in the 1927 review *Africana*. In 1930, she appeared in *Blackbirds*, and in 1931 and 1932 she starred in *Rhapsody in Black*. The following year she was featured with Clifton Webb and Marilyn Miller in Irving Berlin's *As Thousands Cheer*. In 1935, she co-starred with Bea Lillie in *At Home Abroad*, and three years later she played the lead in *Mamba's Daughters*.

In 1940, Waters appeared in the stage version of *Cabin in the Sky*, a triumph which she repeated in the 1943 movie version. Her other film appearances include *Rufus Jones for President* (1931), *Tales of Manhattan* (1941), *Cairo* (1942), *Stage Door Canteen* (1943), and *Pinky* (1949).

Her autobiography, *His Eye Is on the Sparrow*, was a 1951 Book-of-the-Month Club selection. The title is taken from a song that she sang in her 1950 stage success, *Member of the Wedding*.

Keenan Ivory Wayans (1958–)
Comedian

Keenan Ivory Wayans was born in New York City in 1958. He began his career as a stand-up comic at the Improv clubs in New York City and Los Angeles. After appearances on such television series as "Benson," "Cheers," "Chips," and in the movies *Star 80* (1983) and *Hollywood Shuffle* (1987), Wayans struck fame with *I'm Gonna Git You, Sucka* (1989)—a hilarious sendup of 1970s "blaxploitation" films—which he wrote and produced. His greatest success has been the hit television series "In Living Color," a lively and irreverent show in which celebrities are often outrageously parodied. "In Living Color" won an Emmy award in 1990.

Wayans is the oldest of a family of ten; three of his siblings—Damon, Shawn, and Kim—are regulars on "In Living Color."

Bert Williams (1876–1922)
Comedian, Dancer

The legendary Bert Williams is considered by many to be the greatest black vaudeville performer in the history of the American stage.

Born in 1876 in the Bahamas, Williams moved to New York with his family, and then on to California, where he graduated from high school. After studying civil engineering for a time, he decided to try his hand at show business.

In 1895, Williams teamed with George Walker to form a successful vaudeville team.

Bert Williams

Five years later, they opened in New York in *The Sons of Ham* and were acclaimed for the characterizations that became their stock-in-trade—Walker as a dandy, and Williams in blackface, complete with outlandish costumes and black dialect. The show ran for two years.

In 1902, their show *In Dahomey* was so popular that they took it to England, where it met with equal success. The partners continued to produce such shows as *The Policy Players*, *Bandanna Land*, and *Abyssinia* until Walker's death in 1909.

Thereafter, Williams worked as a featured single in the *Ziegfeld Follies*, touring America for ten years in several versions of the show. His most famous songs were "Woodman, Spare That Tree"; "O, Death, Where is Thy Sting"; and "Nobody", his own composition and trademark.

Williams died of pneumonia on March 4, 1922.

Billy Dee Williams (1937–   )
Actor

A screen, television and stage actor with impressive credits, Billy Dee Williams has starred in some of the most commercially popular films ever released.

Born William December Williams in Harlem on April 6, 1937, Williams was a withdrawn, overweight youngster who initially planned to become a fashion illustrator. While studying on scholarship at the School of Fine Arts in the National Academy of Design, a CBS casting director helped him secure bit parts in several television shows, including "Lamp Unto My Feet" and "Look Up And Live."

Billy Dee Williams

Williams then began to study acting under Sidney Poitier and Paul Mann at the Actors Workshop in Harlem. He made his film debut in *The Last Angry Man* (1959), and then appeared on stage in *The Cool World* (1960), *A Taste of Honey* (1960), and *The Blacks* (1962). He later appeared briefly on Broadway in *Hallelujah Baby* (1967) and in several off-Broadway shows, including *Ceremonies in Dark Old Men* (1970).

Williams' next major role was in the acclaimed television movie, "Brian's Song" (1970), a performance for which he received an Emmy nomination. Motown's Berry Gordy then signed Williams to a seven-year contract after which he starred in *Lady Sings the Blues* (1972) and *Mahogany* (1976) with Diana Ross. His last movie for Gordy was *The Bingo Long Traveling All-Stars and Motor Kings* (1976).

In the early 1980s, Williams appeared in two of George Lucas' *Star Wars* adventures, *The Empire Strikes Back* and *Return of the Jedi*. He has appeared in numerous television movies, including "Scott Joplin," "Christmas Lilies of the Field," and the mini-series "Chiefs." When he was cast opposite Diahann Carroll in the prime time drama "Dynasty," his reputation as a romantic lead was secured. At the end of the decade, he starred in action films such as *Oceans of Fire* and *Number One With a Bullet*.

Flip Wilson (1933–   )
Comedian, Actor

Flip Wilson reached the pinnacle of the entertainment world with a series of original routines and ethnic characters rivaled only by those of Bill Cosby. Wilson's hilarious monologues, seen on a number of network television shows, made him the most visible black comedian of the early 1970s.

Flip Wilson

Born Clerow Wilson on December 8, 1933, Wilson was the tenth in a family of twenty-four children, eighteen of whom survived. The family was destitute, and Wilson was a troublesome child during his youth in Jersey City; he ran away from reform school several times, and was ultimately raised in foster homes.

Wilson's comic talents first surfaced while he was serving in the Air Force. Sent overseas to the Pacific, Wilson entertained his buddies with preposterous routines. Back in civilian life, he worked as a bellhop and part-time showman. Opportunity struck in 1959 when a Miami businessman sponsored him for one year at $50 a week, thus enabling Wilson to concentrate on the evolution of his routine. For the next five years or so, Wilson appeared regularly at the Apollo Theatre in Harlem. In 1965, he began a series of nationwide appearances on "The Tonight

Show." Long-term contracts and several hit records followed in quick sequence, and Wilson became firmly established as one of the truly innovative talents in the comedy profession.

With "The Flip Wilson Show" in the early 1970s, Wilson became the first black to have a weekly prime time television show under his own name. He became famous for his original character creations such as "Geraldine." On January 31, 1972 he appeared on the cover of *Time* magazine. In 1976, he made his dramatic debut on television in the ABC series "The Six Million Dollar Man."

During the early 1980s, Wilson appeared in numerous nightclubs and television specials. He has also made comedy albums, including *The Devil Made Me Buy This Dress*, for which he received a Grammy award.

Paul Winfield (1941–   )
Actor

Born in Los Angeles on May 22, 1941, Paul Winfield grew up in a poor family. Excelling in school, he attended a number of colleges—the University of Portland, Stanford University, Los Angeles City College, and the University of California, Los Angeles—but left UCLA before graduation to pursue his acting career.

Winfield appeared on television shows in the late 1960s and early 1970s—most notably as one of Diahann Carroll's boyfriends in the series "Julia." His great success in that period was in the film *Sounder* (1972), in which he played a sharecropper father in the nineteenth-century American South. For this role, he received an Academy Award nomination for best actor.

Winfield subsequently appeared in the motion pictures *Gordon's War* (1973), *Conrack* (1974), *Huckleberry Finn* (1974), and *A Hero Ain't Nothing But a Sandwich*

(1978). He received accolades for his portrayal of Dr. Martin Luther King, Jr. in the NBC movie "King" (1978), for which he received an Emmy nomination. His second Emmy nomination came with his role in the television miniseries "Roots: The Next Generation" (1979).

In the 1980s, Winfield kept busy with appearances on television in "The Charmings," "The Women of Brewster Place," "Wiseguy," and "227"; on film in *Star Trek II: The Wrath of Khan* (1982), *Damnation Alley* (1983), and *The Terminator* (1984); and on the stage in *A Midsummer Night's Dream*, *Othello*, and *The Seagull*. In 1990, he played the sarcastic Judge Larren Lyttle in the movie *Presumed Innocent*, and in 1992 appeared on Broadway in the cast of *A Few Good Men*.

Winfield has won several major awards, including an NAACP Image Award and election to the Black Filmmakers Hall of Fame.

Oprah Winfrey (1954–   )
Talk Show Host, Actress, Broadcasting Executive

Oprah Winfrey's rise to fame is a tale at once tragic and inspiring. She was born on January 29, 1954, in Kosciusko, Mississippi. Her name was supposed to have been "Orpah," after a biblical figure in the book of Ruth; sources vary as to the origin of the misspelling.

Winfrey was a precocious child who asked her kindergarten teacher to advance her to the first grade; Winfrey also skipped the second grade. Her parents, who were not married, separated when she was very young and sent her to live with her grandparents. At the age of six, Winfrey moved to Milwaukee to live with her mother. From the time she was nine, she was abused sexually by male family members and acquaintances;

Oprah Winfrey

and it was there that her life was put back on track. Her father insisted on hard work and discipline as a means of self-improvement, and Winfrey complied, winning a college scholarship that allowed her to attend Tennessee State University. In 1971, she began working part-time as a radio announcer for WVOL in Nashville. Two years later, after receiving a B.A. from Tennessee State, she became a reporter at WTVF-TV in Nashville. From 1976 to 1983, she lived in Baltimore, working for the ABC affiliate WJZ-TV, progressing from news anchor to cohost of the popular show, "People Are Talking." In 1984, she moved to Chicago and took over the ailing morning show, "A.M. Chicago." By September of the next year, the show was so successful that it was expanded to an hour format and renamed "The Oprah Winfrey Show." Now in syndication across the country, "The Oprah Winfrey Show" is one of the most popular television programs in history. In 1986, Winfrey founded Harpo, Inc., her own production company ("Harpo" is "Oprah" spelled backwards).

these events, which she did not discuss publicly until the 1980s, have had a profound effect on her life.

When she was fourteen, Winfrey went to live with her father in Nashville, Tennessee,

A talented actress, Winfrey has appeared in the motion picture *The Color Purple* (1985) and in the television movie "The Women of Brewster Place" (1989).

21
Classical Music

21

Classical Music

Black Musicians in Early America ■ Classical Music in the Twentieth Century ■ The Future for the Black Classical Musician ■ Composers, Conductors, Instrumentalists, and Singers

by Robin Armstrong

When the first Africans arrived in 1619 on the eastern coast of what is now the United States, they brought with them a rich musical heritage. In the culture from which these slaves were torn, music and dance accompanied almost every public activity. Each community had professional musicians, and everyone, from the youngest to the oldest, played, sang, and danced. Because theirs was an oral tradition, they did not need sheet music to bring their songs and dances with them—they carried it all in their heads. They brought to the new world not only their songs and dances, but their love of, and need for music as an integral part of daily life, and they participated in the music of their new world from the very beginning.

■ BLACK MUSICIANS IN EARLY AMERICA

Slave Music

As slaves, the Africans assumed the lives and culture of their owners; they learned the Europeans' language, religion, and music. They sang English psalms and hymns in church as they converted to Christianity. They heard folk and popular tunes in the taverns and homes. Some slaves in the South studied with itinerant music teachers. The most talented musicians gained professional-level skills which were quickly put to use by the whites. Both bonded servants and slave musicians, playing instruments such as the violin, flute, and piano, provided much of the recreational music for their masters. They accompanied dance balls and played at dancing schools. On the self-sufficient plantation in the south, the most musical of the domestic slaves provided evening "entertainments." Once public concerts became possible and popular in the new world, a few talented slaves publicly concertized. The pianist Thomas "Blind Tom" Green Bethune (1849–1909) began public concertizing while still a slave, and continued to perform after emancipation.

Art Music in the Nineteenth Century

As a free, black middle class arose in the nineteenth century and the popularity of

Matilda Sisieretta Jones

public concerts increased, black musicians began to provide "art music" for both black and white audiences. As in white middle- and upper-class communities, genteel songs and piano pieces could be heard in the parlors of the comfortable and well-off members of the black communities; music also accompanied most public celebrations and ceremonies. As these communities grew, they could support more professional musicians and music educators. Singing schools and private lessons on instruments were available to anyone interested. During much of the nineteenth century, the best black artists toured throughout the United States and Europe, performing for black and white audiences alike.

In the nineteenth century, a typical "art music" concert showcased a variety of musical pieces. Songs, arias, and ensemble vocal pieces were performed in the same show as chamber, band, and orchestral numbers. The most popular singers tended to be women such as Elizabeth Taylor Greenfield (c. 1824–1876), called the "Black Swan," and

Matilda Sisieretta Jones (1869–1933), also know as the "Black Patti" after the contemporary reigning white diva, Adelina Patti. African-American singers Anna Madah Hyers (1853–1920), Emma Louise Hyers (1855–1890), Sidney Woodward (1860–1924), Nellie Brown Mitchell (1845–1924), Marie Selida (1849–1937), Flora Baston Bergon (1864–1906), Rachel Walker (1873–1940), Thomas Bowers (1823–1885) all graced the concert stage during the nineteenth century.

Men tended to dominate the realm of instrumental music. Pianists included John William Boone (1864–1927), and Samuel Jamieson (1855–1930) in addition to Blind Tom. John Thomas Douglas (1847–1886), Walter F. Craig (1854–1920), and Edmond Dede (1877–1903) played the violin. Morris Brown, Jr. (1812–1890), Robert Jones, Jacob Stans, William Appo, James Hermenway (1800–1849), Francis Johnson (1792–1844), and Aaron J.R. Connor conducted all-Black orchestras, bands, and choruses. Most composed music as well. The Original Colored American Opera Troupe of Washington, DC, and the Theodore Drury Colored Opera Company, both established in the second half of the nineteenth century, were the earliest long-lasting black opera companies.

■ CLASSICAL MUSIC IN THE TWENTIETH CENTURY

Racism and Sexism in Performance Organizations

During most of the nineteenth century, African-American musicians performed for both black and white audiences. Towards the end of the century, however, white audiences began to favor European performers over any American performer, and white musicians over black. Despite their obvious success in classical music, by the beginning

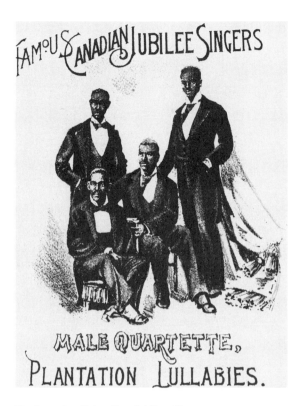

Poster advertising the Jubilee Singers.

of the twentieth century, African Americans were not considered suitable as classical musicians, and white audiences accepted them only on the vaudeville and minstrel stage. Whites considered blacks to be unable to contribute to art music as either performer or composer. For example, in response to composer Scott Joplin's attempt to produce his opera *Treemonisha* in New York, the *New York Age* stated on March 5, 1908, "Since ragtime has been in vogue, many Negro writers have gained considerable fame as composers of that style of music. From the white man's standpoint of view . . . after writing ragtime, the Negro does not figure." This was the prevailing attitude for some time.

Flutist Dorothy Antoinette Handy (b. 1930) wrote in the preface of her book *Black Women in American Bands and Orchestras*

that her book "originated in the mind of a fourteen-year-old black American female who decided that she wanted to be a symphonic orchestral flutist . . . she went to a New Orleans Philharmonic concert, and shortly before the end proceeded backstage from the reserved for colored section to the orchestra's first flutist. Question: "Are you accepting any pupils?" Answer: "Do you mean that you, a Negro, want to study flute?" Unfortunately, this attitude has continued to reign in the second half of the century as well. In 1975, San Francisco Symphony Orchestra timpanist Elayne Jones, the only black "first chair" player in a major American orchestra, filed a suit claiming contract violation on grounds of racism and sexism because she was denied tenure. She lost her case.

Despite this opposition, African Americans have never been absent from the world of classical music. While the merits of compositions by African-American composers have been undeniable, they have been ignored. Although for much of this century they have been denied entrance to this country's major metropolitan (white) symphonies they have constantly worked towards inclusion. William Grant Still's *Afro-American Symphony* was the first symphonic work written by a black composer to be performed by a major symphony orchestra when in 1931 it was performed by the Rochester Philharmonic Symphony. In 1933, Florence Price became the first black female to have a symphony played by a major orchestra, when the Chicago Symphony Orchestra performed her Symphony in E Minor at the Chicago World's Fair. In 1934, Price conducted her Concerto in F Minor in Chicago. William Grant Still became the first African American to conduct a major orchestra in the deep south when in 1955, he conducted the New Orleans Symphony Orchestra.

Conductor James DePreist rehearses with the New Philharmonic Orchestra, 1984.

The Musical Styles of Black Classical Composers

Black symphonic music falls into two categories: black-stream music, synonymous with Gunther Schuller's *Third Stream*, which is serious music influenced by the ethnic background of the composer; and traditional European music created by black composers. At the end of the nineteenth century, black composers became the first group of American composers to write nationalistic pieces by incorporating black traditional folk idioms into their vocal and instrumental pieces.

Until a few years ago, compositions of either style were largely unknown, but the public relations efforts and researches of Paul Freeman, Domique de Lerma, C. Edward Thomas, and Eileen Southern have

Composer Margaret Bonds

brought to light a great many first-rate symphonic compositions both old and new. Among the best black-stream pieces are Florence Price's Symphony in E Minor (1933), William Grant Still's *Afro-American Symphony* (1931), Margaret Bond's *Credo*, and Ornette Coleman's *Skies of America*. Examples of black symphonic music in which there is no obvious contribution from the black heritage include Chevalier de Saint-Georges' *Symphonic Concertante* (1782), Julia Perry's *Stabat Mater* (1951), and Ulysses Kay's *Markings* (1966).

Research and Recording of Music by Classical Composers

After years of neglect, the role of the African American in the history of music is fi-nally being given serious attention. Rediscoveries of excellent classical pieces by African-American composers, both contemporary and older, have begun to ventilate the stereotype of black music as a limited program of spirituals, jazz, and the blues. Studies of comprehensive musicology (the study of music in relation to the culture and society in which it exists) are beginning to focus on the unique, non-European nature of African-American music.

Several new organizations have devoted time, energy and finances to promoting African-American creations and performances in the arts. The African-American Music Opportunities Association (AAMOA), in existence since 1969, was formed out of the need for more acknowledgment of black music and musicians. Since its formation, C. Edward Thomas has developed the organi-

Director Walter Trumbull rehearses with the Boys Choir of Harlem.

zation's concepts into viable and dynamic programs which have already substantially changed American musical sociology. The AAMOA has put out its own record label for nonsymphonic repertoires with the release of David Baker's Sonata for Piano and String Quartet in a performance which features Brazilian virtuoso Helena Freire. On March 18, 1974, the first four records of the Black Composers Series were formally released by Columbia Records. These discs featured works by Chevalier de Saint-Georges, Samuel Coleridge-Taylor, William Grant Still, George Walker, Ulysses Kay, and Roque Cordero under the artistic direction of Paul Freeman. This Black Composer's Series grew out of an agreement between CBS and the AAMOA for at least twelve recordings of some twenty black composers.

The Center for Black Music Research, established in 1982 at Chicago's Columbia College, has actively contributed to the research publications and performances of contemporary and historic compositions that they have sponsored. They have an ever-growing library and computer database of resources used by scholars all over the country. African-American classical and popular music has received more and more attention in the mainstream academic world as musicologists and ethnomusicologists have begun to focus more attention in that direction.

Grace Bumbry in Verdi's *Don Carlos*.

Black and Integrated Performance Organizations

The Symphony of the New World (1965–1976) was established by timpanist Elayne Jones and conductor Benjamin Steinberg as the first racially integrated orchestra in the country. Other founding members include the cellist Kermit Moore and the bassist Lucille Dixon. This orchestra served as a stepping stone for many musicians, and many of the leading black artists in the nation have performed with them. The group has premiered many works by black composers.

In the 1970s two national black opera companies were formed. Opera/South was founded in 1970 by Sister Elise of the Catholic order of the Sisters of the Blessed Sacrament and members of the Mississippi Inter-Collegiate Opera Guild (Jackson State University, Utica Junior College, and Tougaloo College). In addition to staging grand opera, the company performed operas by black composers including *Highway No. 1 USA* and *A Bayou Legend*, both by William Grant Still, and *Jubilee* and *The Juggler of Our Lady* both by Ulysses Kay. In 1973, Sister Elise with Margaret Harris, Benjamin Matthews, and Wayne Sanders, organized Opera Ebony. Performers with these two companies have included conductors Leonard de Paur, Margaret Harris, and Everett Lee; pianist Way Sanders; and singers Donnie Ray Albert, William Brown, Alpha Floyed, Ester Hinds, Robert Mosely, Wilma Shakesnider, and Walter Turnbull. These companies, as well as the production by the Houston Opera Company in 1975 of Scott Joplin's *Treemonisha*, have served as a showcase for black talent, and have sent some of the singers to major opera companies.

Black Representation in Major American Orchestras and Opera Companies

As in other areas of American life, the civil rights struggle continues. Programs begun as a response to the civil rights movements in the 1960s to support young black artists died as a result of the economic recession of the 1970s. A 1981 survey by the National Urban League disclosed that of the nearly 5,000 musicians playing regularly in fifty-six leading orchestras, only seventy were black. Only six of the 538 members of the "Big Five" orchestras—New York, Boston, Chicago, Cleveland and Philadelphia—were black. Few employ black conductors. The American Symphony Orchestra League published a report in 1992 with similar findings. The 146 orchestras that participated in the survey reported that of a total 8326 positions, only 133 were filled by black musicians.

In the early 1980s, The Metropolitan Opera had fifteen black artists on its roster, and the New York City Opera had eleven singers in principal roles with two conductors and one stage director. Prior to World War II, there were no black singers in any opera house in the United States, but now they are accepted almost anywhere.

■ THE FUTURE FOR THE BLACK CLASSICAL MUSICIAN

It is impossible to know what lies in the future for African-American classical composers, conductors, and other performing artists. Gains made by blacks in orchestras during the 1970s were lost in the 1980s; the conservative court and political systems of this country in the late 1980s and the 1990s has led to a feeling of backlash. Yet as the music of African Americans has been increasingly accepted and celebrated by both the musical and academic worlds, formation of the companies mentioned above have provided an avenue for blacks to accept classical music and be accepted into it. Optimistically, the black musician of the 1990s will be appreciated more as an integral part of the long and varied musical heritage of America.

■ COMPOSERS, CONDUCTORS, INSTRUMENTALISTS, AND SINGERS

Adele Addison (1925–   )
Singer

Adele Addison received her musical training at Westminster Choir College in 1946 and the University of Massachusetts in 1963. After making her recital debut at Town Hall, New York City, in 1952, she went on to perform recital tours throughout the United States and Canada. In 1963, she made a tour of the Soviet Union under the cultural exchange program.

Addison has appeared with the New England, New York City, and Washington opera companies. Her premiere performances included John La Montaine's *Fragments from the Song of Songs* with the New Haven Symphony (1959) and Poulenc's *Gloria* with the Boston Symphony (1961). She performed the soloist opening concert at Philharmonic Hall, Lincoln Center in 1962.

Roberta Alexander (1949–   )
Singer

Opera magazine said of Roberta Alexander "... a soprano who, with a range of over two octaves, rich low notes and crystalline, brilliant top notes, excellent diction and clear execution of coloratura passages,

Roberta Alexander

should make a name for herself;" and so she has.

She was born in Lynchburg, Virginia, grew up in Yellow Springs, Ohio and currently makes her home in Amsterdam, the Netherlands. She has a B.S. degree in music education from Central State University in Ohio and a master's degree in voice from the University of Michigan at Ann Arbor.

Her premier with the Metropolitan Opera came in 1983's fall season as Zerlina in *Don Giovanni*. Other Met successes were as Bess in *Porgy and Bess* and in the title role of *Jenufa*.

In the summer of 1984, she made her debut at the Aix-en Provence Festival in France in Mozart's *La Finta Giardiniera*, and in 1985, in Vienna she performed as Cleopatra in Handel's *Giulio Cesare*. She has also performed as Ilia in *Idomeneo* and in *La Boheme* in Berlin. She has also performed extensively at the Netherlands Opera, the London Opera, and in America at the Santa Fe Opera in New Mexico and at the Houston Grand Opera in Texas. In 1987, she returned to the Met where she once again performed the role of Mimi in *La Boheme*.

Betty Lou Allen (1930–   )
Educator, Singer

Born in Campbell, Ohio, Betty Lou Allen studied at Wilberforce University and toured with Leontyne Price as the Wilberforce Sisters. She continued her musical studies at the Hartford School of Music (1950) and the Berkshire Music Center (1951), and studied voice with Sarah Peck Moore, Paul Ulanowsky, and Zinka Milanov.

Allen's New York debut was in Virgil Thompson's *Four Saints in Three Acts* with the New York City Opera Company (1953) and her formal opera debut was at the Teatro Colon, Buenos Aires (1964). She has appeared as a soloist with leading orchestras and conductors, including Bernstein, Dorate, and Maazel.

Allen has served as a faculty member of such schools as the North Carolina School of the Arts, The Curtis Institute of Music in Philadelphia, and The Manhattan School of Music in New York City. She is currently the executive director and chair of the voice department at the Harlem School of the Arts in New York.

Marian Anderson (1902–1993)
Singer

At the peak of her career, Marian Anderson was regarded as the world's greatest contralto. When she made her Town Hall debut in New York on December 31, 1935, Howard Taubman, the *New York Times* reviewer, described it as "music-making that probed too deep for words."

Marian Anderson was born on February 27, 1902 in Philadelphia. As a young choir girl, she demonstrated her vocal talents by singing parts from soprano, alto, tenor and bass. At the age of nineteen she began studying with Giuseppe Boghetti, and four years later she appeared as soloist with the New York Philharmonic. After a short engagement with the Philadelphia Symphony Orchestra, she traveled to Europe on a scholarship granted by the National Association of Negro Musicians.

On Easter Sunday in 1939 Anderson gave what is perhaps her most memorable concert—singing on the steps of the Lincoln Memorial after having been barred from making an appearance at Constitution Hall by the Daughters of the American Revolution.

In 1955, after years of successful concert work, she made her Metropolitan Opera debut in Verdi's *Un Ballo in Maschera*. Two

Marian Anderson

years later, a State Department tour took her around the world. In September of 1958, she was named to the United States delegation to the United Nations.

In 1982, when Marian Anderson celebrated her eightieth birthday, Grace Bumbry and Shirley Verrett sang at New York City's Carnegie Hall in tribute to Anderson.

Thomas Jefferson Anderson (1928–   )
Composer, Educator

Thomas Jefferson Anderson was born in Coatesville, Pennsylvania. His mother was a musician, and as a teenager he toured with a jazz orchestra. He received a bachelor's in music from West Virginia State College in 1950 and a master's degree in education from Pennsylvania State University in 1951. Anderson went on to study at the Aspen

School of Music, and in 1958 received a Ph.D. from the University of Iowa.

Anderson was composer-in-residence with the Atlanta Symphony Orchestra on a grant from the Rockefeller Foundation during the 1969–1971 seasons. His most widely performed works have been *Chamber Symphony* (1968); *Squares* (1965), an essay for orchestra; and *Personals* (1966), a cantata for narrator, chorus, and brass ensemble. He has also written music for bands *(In Memoriam Zach Walker)*, works for piano *(Watermelon)* and various compositions for solo voice and for chorus.

Dr. Anderson has taught music in public school and served as a faculty member at West Virginia State College, Langston University in Oklahoma, Tennessee State University in Maine.

Martina Arroyo (1939–   )
Singer

Martina Arroyo, a New York native, made her debut at the Metropolitan Opera in February 1965 in the title role of *Aida* and has since sung engagements with opera houses in Vienna, Berlin, Buenos Aires, London, and Hamburg. In addition to operatic appearances, she has also been a frequent guest soloist with many of the world's major orchestras.

In addition to *Aida*, Arroyo's Metropolitan repertoire includes Donna Anna in *Don Giovanni*, Liu in *Turandot*, Leonora in *Il Trovatore*, Elsa in *Lohengrin*, and the title role of *Madame Butterfly*. These performances have developed since 1958, the year she made her debut in Carnegie Hall in the American premiere of Pizzetti's *Murder in the Cathedral*. That same year she made her Metropolitan debut as the celestial voice in *Don Carlo*.

Arroyo sang at the White House in 1977, sharing the stage with Andre Previn and Isaac Stern at a dinner for twenty-six heads of state marking the signing of the Panama Canal treaty. In April 1987, she was guest artist for the New Mexico Symphony Orchestra, where she sang the overture of Verdi's *La Forza del Destino* as well as several other pieces. In 1988, she performed once again with New York's Met production of *Turandot, Cavalleria Rusticana* and *Aida*.

Over the past several years, Arroyo has taught as well as performed in various summer song festivals.

David Nathaniel Baker, Jr. (1931–   )
Composer, Educator

David Nathaniel Baker, Jr. was born in Indianapolis and obtained his bachelor's and master's in music education from Indiana University. He taught music in the public schools of Indianapolis, and Indiana Central College and Lincoln University (Missouri) before returning to his alma mater as a faculty member. Baker has logged considerable experience with both jazz bands and college and municipal symphony orchestras. He was a member of Quincy Jones' All-Star Jazz Orchestra, which toured Europe in 1961, and has performed with Stan Kenton, Lionel Hampton, and Wes Montgomery.

Baker is currently chairman of the jazz department at the Indiana University School of Music.

Kathleen Battle (1948–   )
Singer

Soprano Kathleen Battle was born in Portsmouth, Ohio, and is a graduate of the University of Cincinnati's College of Conser-

Kathleen Battle

In recent years, Battle has recorded such works as *Ariadne auf Naxos* and Mahler's Symphony No. 4. She has also recorded various Schubert Lieder and Handel Arias. Battle recently joined trumpeter Wynton Marsalis in a recording of baroque arias.

Thomas Green Bethune (1849–1909)
Pianist

Thomas "Blind Tom" Bethune was born blind and born a slave in Columbus, Georgia. He was also born a musical prodigy. His owner, James Bethune, allowed him access to his family's piano and realizing at once his musical and financial possibilities, arranged for his informal musical training. Young Tom quickly developed such skills that he could play whatever he heard; his training consisted mainly of having him listen to works to increase his repertoire.

"Blind Tom" began performing for the profit of his owner while still a slave and a child, and continued to tour the North and South during the Civil War. After the war, the Bethune family retained financial control over his performances through contracts. Tom performed in this country and in Europe. His repertoire consisted of the usual concert fair of serious classics by composers like Bach, Beethoven, and Chopin, fancy virtuosic pieces by composers such as Goltschalk and Liszt, improvised variations on contemporary popular ballads and arias, and his own light compositions, few of which survive today. He was said to have been able to play any one of seven thousand pieces on command. Tom retired in 1898.

vatory of Music, having received both a bachelor's and master's degree in music.

Battle made her Met debut in 1977 as the Shepherd in *Tannhauser* and has also been heard there as Sophie in *Werther* and Blondchen in *The Abduction from the Seraglio*. The 1980–1981 season included performances in *The Italian Girl in Algiers*, as well as debuts with the Zurich Opera and the Lyric Opera of Chicago. In 1982, she received critical praise for her Rosina in the Met's *Barber of Seville*.

In the 1987–1988 season, Battle returned to the Metropolitan Opera to sing the role of Zerbinetta in Strauss' *Ariadne auf Naxos*. She has since sung in major music festivals and with major orchestras, including the New York Philharmonic, Cleveland Orchestra, and Los Angeles Philharmonic.

Margaret Allison Bonds (1913–1972)
Composer, Pianist

Margaret Bonds grew up in an artistically and creatively active family in Chicago. Her mother, Estelle C. Bonds, an accomplished musician herself, invited many of the prominent musicians and artists of the time into her home. Margaret Bonds became good friends with the likes of composer Florence Price, poet Langston Hughes, singer Abbie Mitchell, and sculptor Richmond Barthe. She received her early piano lessons from her mother and composition lessons from Florence Price. While still in high school, she joined the National Association of Negro Musicians. She worked closely with such musicians as Price and Mitchell and played for dance rehearsals for Muriel Abbot.

Bonds continued her musical studies at Northwestern University in Evanston, Illinois, completing both a bachelor's and master's degree by age twenty-one. During the 1930s, she opened her own school for dance, music, and art in Chicago and frequently performed in solo recitals and with symphony orchestras. She moved to New York in 1989 to pursue her career and study further at the Juilliard School of Music. In the 1940s and 1950s, she performed as part of a piano duo with Gerald Cook. She soon left New York for Los Angeles where she taught piano, directed the Inner City Repertory Theatre, and wrote arrangements for the Los Angeles Jubilee Singers. Bonds' many compositions include songs, symphonies, musicals, ballets, a cantata and piano works.

Gwendolyn Bradley (1952–)
Singer

Soprano Gwendolyn Bradley was born in New York City but grew up in Bishopville, South Carolina. She was a finalist in the 1977 Metropolitan Opera National Council auditions and a graduate of the North Carolina School of the Arts. She has also attended both the Curtis Institute of Music and the Academy of Vocal Arts in Philadelphia and

has studied with Margaret Harshaw and Seth McCoy. Bradley made her Metropolitan Opera debut as the Nightingale in the Met premiere of Raval's "L'Enfant et les Sortileges" in February 1981. Since making her professional operatic debut in 1976 with the Lake George Opera Festival as Nanetta in *Falstaff*, she has been heard as Titania in *A Midsummer Night's Dream* with the Central City Opera, Lakme with Opera/South, and Aurelia in *Rumpelstiltskin* with the Opera Company of Philadelphia. Bradley has sung with the Philadelphia Orchestra, the Kansas City Philharmonic, and the Charleston Symphony. From 1980 to 1981 she appeared with the Los Angeles Philharmonic at the Hollywood Bowl and with the Seattle Symphony. In addition to the Metropolitan Opera she has performed with the opera companies of Philadelphia, Cleveland and Michigan.

Grace Ann Bumbry (1937–)
Singer

Mezzo-soprano Grace Bumbry is the first black performer to have sung at the Wagner Festival in Bayreuth, Germany, and one of the few singers who can boast of having been called to play a command performance at the White House. Bumbry sang at a formal state dinner opening Washington's official social season in 1962 as a guest of the Kennedys and the nation.

A native of St. Louis, Missouri, Bumbry, like many black singers, had her first exposure to music in a church choir, singing with her brothers and her parents at the Union Memorial Methodist Church in St. Louis. After studying voice locally, she won a nationwide talent contest in 1954 and went on, with scholarship aid, to study successively at Boston and Northwestern universities. At the latter school, she attended master classes in opera and lieder given by the famed singer and teacher Lotte Lehmann.

In 1959, Bumbry traveled to various European countries, performing in the operatic capitals of the world. On July 23, 1961, Wieland Wagner, grandson of Richard Wagner, shocked many traditionalists by selecting Bumbry to sing the role of Venus in *Tannhauser*, a role which conventionally calls for a figure of so-called Nordic beauty, usually a tall and voluptuous blond. Bumbry proceeded to give a performance which won acclamation from both the harshest and the kindest of critics, all of whom praised her both for her physical radiance and her brilliant singing.

In 1974, Bumbry performed with the Met in *Cavalleria Rusticana*. She has since appeared successfully with various opera companies as Dalilah, Lady Macbeth, Medea, and other great dramatic roles, which have become her specialty.

On December 6, 1981, Bumbry participated in a benefit concert at Carnegie Hall for Artists to End Hunger; and on January 31, 1982, she shared the stage with Shirley Verrett at Carnegie Hall to pay tribute to Marian Anderson on her eightieth birthday.

In the 1987–1988 season Grace Bumbry returned to the San Francisco Opera as Abigaille in *Nabucco* and starred as Lady Macbeth in a new production of *Macbeth* in Los Angeles. She celebrated her twenty-fifth anniversary at the Royal Opera, Covent Garden with a series of performances of *Tosca* and appeared at the Vienna State Opera in the same role. Bumbry returned to Barcelona for La Gioconda and was also heard in *Cavalleria Rusticana* and *Don Carlos* at the Hamburg State Opera. She has also appeared as Amneris in *Aida* at the Arena di Verona.

Henry Thacker "Harry" Burleigh (1866–1949)
Arranger, Composer, Singer

Harry Burleigh was born with talent, but was also born into poverty. He was unable to receive any formal musical training until he was an adult. At the age of twenty-six, he moved from his home in Erie, Pennsylvania to New York City, where he won a scholarship to the National Conservatory of Music. After graduation, he pursued a very successful singing career that included concertizing throughout the United States and Europe. He was soloist at St. George's Protestant Episcopal Church in New York for fifty-three years, and at Temple Emanu-El for twenty-five.

As a composer and arranger, Burleigh was the first to arrange spirituals in the style of art songs, and was the first African-American composer to receive critical acclaim for his art songs. As a performer, he established the tradition of concluding recitals with a group of spirituals. His art song compositions also included settings of poetry by Robert Burns and Langston Hughes, and he composed several pieces for violin and piano. He was a member of the American Society of Composers, Authors, and Publishers (ASCAP), and sat on its Board of Directors. He received an honorary master's degree from Atlanta University in 1918, and an honorary doctorate in 1920 from Howard University.

Frances Elaine Cole (1937–1983)
Violinist, Harpsichordist, Music Critic

Frances Cole began her musical life as a violinist. She studied at the Cleveland Institute of Music and at Miami University of Ohio, where she was concert master of the orchestra. She studied further in New York City privately and at Columbia University

Teacher's College, receiving her doctorate in 1966. During these years she played violin for the National Orchestral Association.

In the mid-1960s, as she was finishing her doctorate at Columbia, she discovered her interest in the harpsichord; she began studying the instrument at the Landowska Center in Connecticut. In 1967, she became resident harpsichordist with the Gallery Players in Provincetown, Massachusetts, started appearing on national television shows, and began appearing publicly in concerts and recitals throughout the United States and Europe.

While Cole concertized as a serious classical artist, she did not limit herself by any means. She was as well known for her humor and innovation as for her elegant musical interpretations. In 1976, for example, at an outdoor concert at Lincoln Center, she arrived dressed as Anna Magalena Bach in a horse drawn carriage. She also played jazz with a bassist and percussionist, and sang in lounges and supper clubs under the name of Elaine Frances. In 1979, she began appearing on CBS's "Sunday Morning" as performer and music critic. Cole also served as assistant professor of music at Queens College and the Westminister Choir College, and gave workshops at many colleges and universities.

Samuel Coleridge-Taylor

Samuel Coleridge-Taylor (1875–1912)
Composer

Coleridge-Taylor was one of England's most celebrated composers at the turn of the century.

Born to a doctor from Sierra Leone and a British mother, he showed musical gifts at age five and ten years later entered the Royal College of Music in London. There he studied with Sir Charles Wood and Sir Charles Villiers Stanford. Fame was his with the premiere of *Hiawatha's Wedding Feast*.

The composer was very warmly received in this country. James Weldon Johnson and Booker T. Washington were among his friends, and he was President Theodore Roosevelt's guest at the White House. In 1901, the Coleridge-Taylor Society was organized in Washington, DC specifically to study and perform his music.

Will Marion Cook (1869–1944)
Violinist, Composer, Conductor

Will Marion Cook wrote and directed in both popular and classical venues. He was well educated in classical genres—he entered Oberlin Conservatory when he was fifteen to study violin, studied further in Berlin, Germany between 1887 and 1889, and attended the National Conservatory of Music in New York.

In 1890, he shifted his energies from performing to conducting. He directed an orchestra in Washington, DC in 1890, and performed at the Chicago World's Fair in 1893. In 1898, he became active in writing and directing black musical comedies in New York, producing the first such show to play in a major theater for a wide audience. He organized choral societies and promoted all-black concerts. He directed the New York Syncopated Orchestra, which traveled Europe, and taught and sponsored many young and talented black musicians. In addition to his musicals, he wrote art songs, choral works, instrumental pieces, and operas.

Roque Cordero (1917–   )
Composer, Educator

Roque Cordero is respected as one of Latin America's most creative talents because of his abilities as a violinist, a conductor, and a composer who incorporates popular Panamanian forms into concert music.

Born in Panama, his interests developed from popular songwriting to classical music at the age of seventeen. Four years later he was appointed director of the Orquesta Sinfonica de la Union Musical in Panama, and he later joined the Orquesta Sinfonica de Panama as violist. In 1943, he began studying abroad. He was engaged by the University of Minnesota as Artistic Director of the Institute of Latin-American Studies, and after completing his course of study, was awarded a Guggenheim Fellowship. Dr. Cordero is presently music editor for the publishing company of Peer International Corporation and is professor of music at Illinois State University.

Philip Creech (1950–   )
Singer

Philip Creech is a native of Hempstead, New York and a graduate of Northwestern University. Creech performed with Margaret Hillis' Chicago Symphony Chorus from 1973 to 1975 and frequently appeared as tenor soloist. Since 1976 he has sung with the Chicago Symphony, the Boston Symphony, the New York Philharmonic, and the Cincinnati Symphony. Creech made his debut at the Salzburg Festival in 1979 singing in the Berlioz *Requiem*. He made his Metropolitan Opera debut in September 1979 as Beppe in the season's premiere of Leoncavallo's *Pagliacci*, and was heard later that season as Edmondo in the premiere and subsequent live overseas telecast of the new production of Puccini's *Manon Lescaut*. Creech has also appeared at the Met as Tonio in *Pagliacci*.

Creech made his recording debut in Stravinsky's *Les Noces*, with the Chicago Symphony on RCA Red Seal's *Music from Raviniar* series. He has recently recorded *Carmina Burana* with James Levine and the Chicago Symphony, which was released on the DGG label and became a best-seller and a Grammy Award winner. Creech is also recognized as an accomplished recitalist and has sung well over one-hundred recitals throughout the United States.

James Anderson DePreist (1936–   )
Conductor

Born in Philadelphia on November 21, 1936, James Anderson DePreist studied piano and percussion from the age of ten, but did not decide on a musical career until he reached his early twenties. After graduating from high school, he entered the Wharton School of the University of Pennsylvania as

James DePreist

a prelaw student, receiving a bachelor of science in 1958 and a master of arts degree in 1961. DePreist also studied music history, the theory of harmony, and orchestration at the Philadelphia Conservatory of Music, and composition with the distinguished American composer Vincent Persichetti.

In 1962, the United States State Department sponsored a cultural exchange tour of the Near and the Far East, engaging DePreist as an American specialist in music. During this tour, DePreist was stricken with polio, paralyzed in both legs, and flown home for intensive therapy. Within six months he had fought his way back to the point where he could walk with the aid of crutches and braces. Courage, determination, and talent carried him to the semifinals of the 1963 Dmitri Mitropoulos International Music Competition for Conductors.

After another overseas tour as conductor in residence in Thailand, DePreist returned to the United States, appearing with the Minneapolis International Symphony Orchestra, the New York Philharmonic, and the Philadelphia Orchestra.

In 1964, he recorded what is perhaps his most satisfying triumph, capturing first prize in the Mitropoulos International Competition. Another highlight of his career occurred on June 28, 1965 when he conducted Marian Anderson's farewell concert at Philadelphia's Robin Hood Dell.

Currently DePreist is the music director of the Oregon Symphony. He is one of a select and talented circle of American-born and trained conductors who have appeared with the nation's five premier orchestras—New York, Boston, Philadelphia, Cleveland, and Chicago. He has also been guest conductor in most of the capitals of Europe and the United States.

Chevalier de Saint-Georges (1739–1799)
Composer

Chevalier de Saint-Georges is considered to be the first man of African ancestry to have made a major impression on European music.

Born on the Caribbean island of Guadeloupe to an African slave mother and a French father, he displayed early talent on the violin. He studied with Francois Gossec, whom he succeeded as concertmaster of the celebrated Concert des Amateurs in 1769. His musical output was enormous, including several operas, symphonies concertantes, a dozen string quartets, violin concertos, and other instrumental and vocal works.

Dean Dixon (1915–1976)
Conductor

Dixon was born in Manhattan on January 10, 1915, and graduated from DeWitt Clinton High School in 1932. Exposed to classical music by his parents, (as a small boy he was regularly taken to Carnegie Hall) Dixon formed his own amateur orchestra at the Harlem YMCA while he was still in high school. On the basis of a successful violin audition, he was admitted to the Juilliard School where he received his bachelor's degree in 1936; three years later he acquired his master's from Columbia.

The Dean Dixon Symphony Society, which he had formed in 1932, began to receive financial support from the Harlem community in 1937, and in 1941 at the request of Eleanor Roosevelt, Dixon gave a concert at the Heckscher Theater. He was later signed by the musical director of NBC radio to conduct the network's summer symphony in two concerts. Two months after the NBC concerts, he made his debut with the New York Philharmonic. Dean

Dean Dixon

Dixon was the first black and, at twenty-six, the youngest musician ever to conduct the New York Philharmonic Orchestra.

Lucille Dixon (Robertson) (1923–)
Bassist

Lucille Dixon began playing bass in high school and was soon studying with the New York Philharmonic's principal bassist, Fred Zimmermen. After high school, she was the second of two black women to play in the WPA-sponsored National Youth Administration Orchestra. While this group normally served as a hiring house for major United States orchestras, Dixon realized she, as a black female, would not be hired by a symphony orchestra.

When the NYA orchestra folded, she turned to jazz for a living. She played for two years with the Earl Hines Band, and in 1946, formed a band of her own. However, she continued her classical pursuits. Dixon's affiliations include National Symphony of Panama, Westchester Philharmonic, Ridgefield Symphony, and Scranton Symphony, and the Symphony of the New World, for which she served as manager from 1972 to 1976.

Carl Rossini Ditton (1886–1962)
Pianist, Singer, Composer

Carl Ditton received his first piano lesson from his father, who was a professional musician. He continued study at the University of Pennsylvania, receiving a bachelor's degree in 1909. Following graduation, he went on to become the first black pianist to make a cross-country concert tour. With the aid of an E. Azalia Hackley Scholarship, he furthered his piano studies in Munich.

During the 1920s, he began to study voice, and made his concert debut in Philadelphia in 1926. He later studied voice at Juilliard, where he received an artists diploma in 1930. That year he also received the Harmon Award for composition; his compositions include primarily art songs and arrangements of spirituals.

Mattiwilda Dobbs (1925–   )
Singer

One of the world's most gifted coloratura sopranos is Mattiwilda Dobbs. Now residing in Sweden, where she is a national favorite, Miss Dobbs has gained international fame.

Born in Atlanta, Georgia on July 11, 1925, Mattiwilda Dobbs graduated from Spelman College in 1946 as class valedictorian, having majored in voice training. After studying Spanish at Columbia, where she received

her master's degree, she went on to Paris for two years on a Whitney Fellowship.

In October 1950, competing against hundreds of singers from four continents, she won the International Music Competition held at Geneva. She made her professional debut in Paris in 1953, and then became the first black to sing a principal role at La Scala in Milan. On March 8, 1954, she made her Town Hall debut in New York in the one-act opera *Ariadne auf Naxos* and received a rousing ovation. One year later she repeated the success with her first concert recital on the same stage.

Considered one of the world's most gifted coloratura sopranos, Dobbs has made numerous recordings, including *The Pearl Fishers* and *Zaidde* and has toured the world with great success.

Rudolph Dunbar (1917–1988)
Composer, Clarinetist

Born in British Guiana, Rudolph Dunbar received his musical education at the Institute of Musical Art in New York, as well as in Paris and Leipzig. He made his debut with the NBC Symphony Orchestra in New York City and conducted in Great Britain and throughout the United States. In addition to being a musical conductor, Dunbar was also a clarinetist. He is the author of *A Treatise on Clarinet Playing* and is known best for the composition *Dance of the 20th Century*.

Robert Todd Duncan (1903–   )
Singer, Actor

Although thinking of himself primarily as a teacher, Todd Duncan has made notable contributions to the world of theater and concert.

Duncan was born into a well-to-do family in Danville, Kentucky on February 12, 1903.

He graduated from Butler University in Indianapolis in 1925 and began a teaching career—first at a junior high school, and then in Louisville at the Municipal College for Negroes.

In 1934, he appeared in New York in a single performance of an all-black version of the opera *Cavalleria Rusticana*. On the strength of this alone, he was auditioned less than a year later by George Gershwin and received the role of Porgy in *Porgy and Bess*. He was such a success that he repeated his performance in the role in the 1938 and 1942 revivals of the play.

In 1940, he was a featured performer on Broadway in *Cabin in the Sky*. When the play closed, he headed for Hollywood to appear in the movie *Syncopation*.

His concert repertoire includes German lieder and French and Italian songs. Duncan retired in 1965 after singing at President Lyndon B. Johnson's inauguration. Only once has he broken his retirement and that was in 1972 to sing the title role of *Job* at Washington's Kennedy Center. Duncan currently teaches voice in his home in Washington, DC.

Simon Lamont Estes (1938–   )
Singer

Bass-baritone Simon Lamont Estes was the first black man to sing at the Bayreuth Festival, appearing in the title role of a new production of *Der Fliegende Hollander*, a portrayal he repeated there in three subsequent seasons. A native of Centerville, Iowa, Estes attended the University of Iowa and received a full scholarship to Juilliard, studying under Sergius Kagan and Christopher West. He won the Munich International Vocal Competition in 1965 and was the silver medalist in the Tchaikovsky Competition in 1966.

Estes made his operatic debut as Ramfis in *Aida* at the Deutsche Opera Berlin and since then has appeared in most of the world's major opera houses, including La Scala, the Hamburg State Opera, the Bavarian State Opera of Munich, the Vienna State Opera, the Lyric Opera of Chicago, the San Francisco Opera, and the Zurich Opera. He made his debut at the Metropolitan Opera in 1982, foregoing the honor of singing the national anthem on baseball's opening day—the day of his Met debut.

Estes has appeared as soloist with most of the world's leading symphony orchestras. He has also performed recitals and orchestral engagements in numerous European cities, including Paris, Zurich, Brussels, Munich, Bonn, Madrid, and Bordeaux. His North American highlights include appearances with the Chicago Symphony Orchestra conducted by Sir George Solti, and the Montreal Symphony conducted by Charles Dutoit.

In addition to having recorded *Der Fliegende Hollander* Estes has recorded Handel's *Messiah*, the Faure *Requiem*, Beethoven's Symphony No. 9, numerous spirituals, and highlights from *Porgy and Bess*.

Louis Moreau Gottschalk (1829–1869)
Composer, Pianist

Born in New Orleans, Louis Gottschalk was a violin prodigy at six years of age and later became a brilliant concert pianist. He was already something of a European matinee idol when he first appeared in New York, on February 10, 1853 and his romantic compositions enjoyed a wide vogue.

Although Gottschalk went to Paris when he was thirteen to study with Halle, Stamaty, and Maleden, much of his music reflected the Creole environment of his early childhood. One of his best-known compositions,

Louis Moreau Gottschalk

Bernstein's *West Side Story*. This success was followed by a performance with the New York Philharmonic in Mahler's Symphony No. 4.

Considered one of America's best coloratura sopranos, Grist has sung at most of the world's great opera houses, including La Scala, Vienna State, Britain's Royal Opera, and the Metropolitan Opera.

When Dr. Herbert Graf, the former stage director of the Met, left in 1960 to become director of the Zurich Opera, he persuaded many operatic talents, including Grist, to accompany him there. While in Europe, Grist was asked by Stravinsky to sing under his direction in *Le Rossignol*.

In addition to a career in performance, Grist has taught voice at Indiana University and the Hochschule fur Musik in Germany.

La Bambould, is based on the sights and sounds of New Orleans' Congo Square. His autobiographical book, *Notes of a Pianist*, provides an interesting description of his background and method of composition. Louis Moreau Gottschalk was, perhaps, the first black composer born in the United States to achieve international renown. Chopin praised his debut at the Salle Pleyel in April 1844, and Berlioz, with whom he studied, applauded his "sovereign power."

Reri Grist (1932–   )
Singer

Born in New York City, soprano Reri Grist, received her bachelor's degree in music in 1954 from Queens College. Grist first came to national attention when she performed the role of Consuela in Leonard

Reri Grist

Emma Azalia Hackley
(1867–1922)
Singer, Educator,
Choral Director

Emma Azalia Hackley did as much to promote African-American musicians as she did their traditional music. She received her own musical training while growing up in Detroit, Michigan, where she studied voice and piano and began giving local recitals at an early age. She attended the University of Denver, where she received her bachelor's degree in music in 1900. In 1905, she traveled to Paris where she continued her studies.

Hackley concertized extensively during the early years of the new century, but gradually turned to developing and supporting the careers of other talented young black artists. Through recitals, concerts, lecture/demonstrations, she raised funds for scholarships; in 1908 she established an ongoing scholarship to promote and fund study abroad. She sponsored debut recitals for young performers and helped many find good college-level teaching positions—many of the artists she supported and promoted went on to become successful musical leaders in their own right.

Hackley founded and directed the Vocal Normal Institute in Chicago between 1912 and 1916. In the last years of her life, she organized large community concerts promoting the importance of black folk music, raising the level of public interest and pride in African-American musical heritage. So much was her contribution that twenty years after her death, the National Association of Negro Musicians established the Hackley Collection of the Detroit Public Library for the preservation of materials relating to black musicians.

Helen Eugenia Hagen (1891–1964)
Pianist, Composer

Helen Hagen was born into a musical family—her mother played piano, and her father sang baritone. After receiving her initial musical education from her mother and the public school system in New Haven, Connecticut, in 1912 she became the first black pianist to earn a bachelor's of music degree from Yale University. She was also the first African-American to win Yale's Sanford Fellowship, which permitted her to study in Europe. She earned a diploma in 1914 from the Schola Cantorum, and later received a master's degree from Columbia University Teacher's College in New York.

Between 1914 and 1918, Hagen toured in the United States; her repertoire included many of her own piano compositions. In 1918, she toured Europe entertaining World War I service men; in 1919, she became the first black musician to teach in Chicago's downtown district; and in 1921, she became the first black pianist to give a solo recital in a major New York concert Hall when she performed at Town Hall. During the 1930s she taught at Tennessee State A&M College and served as dean of music at Bishop College in Marshal, Texas. In 1935, she established the Helen Hagen Music Studio in New York City.

Dorothy Antoinette Handy (Miller)
(1930–)
Flutist

Dorothy Antoinette Handy began to study music as a young child under the direction of her mother, who taught her violin and piano. She went on to study at Spelman College in Atlanta, at the New England Conservatory of Music (B.M. 1952), at Northwestern University in Illinois (M.M. 1953), and the National Conservatory in Paris (Artist's Diploma 1955).

Handy has worked with many orchestras, including the Chicago Civic Orchestra (1952–1953), the International Orchestra of Paris (1954–1955), Musica Viva Orchestra of Geneva (1955), Symphony of the Air on NBC (1956), The Orchestra of America in New York (1960–1962), the Symphony of the New World (1968–1971), and the Richmond (Virginia) Symphony (1966–1976). She is a founding member of the Trio Pro Viva which, among other activities, commissions and performs works by African-American composers.

Handy also toured widely as a concert artist, played for films and television, and has been a lecturer, consultant, project director, and radio commentator. She has taught at Florida A&M University, Tuskegee Institute, Jackson State College, and Virginia State College. She has written numerous articles for professional journals, and three books: *Black Music: Opinions and Reviews* (1974), *Black Women in American Bands and Orchestras* (1981), and *The International Sweethearts of Rhythm* (1983).

Margaret Rosezarion Harris (1943–   )
Pianist, Conductor, Composer

Margaret Harris began life as a child prodigy—she gave her first concert at age three, began touring nationally when she was four, and played with the Chicago Symphony when she was ten. She studied piano and conducting at the Curtis Institute and the Juilliard School of Music, receiving her bachelor's degree in 1964 and her master's in 1965.

Harris's conducting career has encompassed both symphony orchestras and Broadway shows. Her Broadway credits include *Hair* (1970–1972), *Two Gentlemen of*

Verona (1972–1974), *Raisin* (1974–1976), *Guys and Dolls* (1980), and *Amen Corner* (1983–1984). She has conducted major symphony orchestras in Chicago, Minneapolis, Detroit, San Diego, St. Louis, and Los Angeles—often in these concerts she both performed and conducted her own piano concertos. She was a founding member of Opera Ebony and has served as its music director. Her compositions include two piano concerti, four musical production scores, two ballets, themes for television shows, as well as choral and instrumental works.

Hazel Harrison (1883–1969)
Pianist

Hazel Harrison was one of the leading pianists of her day. As a child she studied with Victor Heinz, who arranged for her to study in Berlin for several years beginning in 1904. She studied with Ferruccio Busoni, gave recitals, and performed with the Berlin Philharmonic. Upon returning to the United States, she won an award that allowed her to return to Berlin between 1910 and 1914.

When she returned again to the States, she taught in Chicago and toured throughout the United States. In 1931 Harrison began teaching college—she taught at the Tuskegee Institute in Alabama (1931–1943), Howard University in Washington, DC. (1934–1959), and Alabama State A&M College at Montgomery (1959–1964). She continued to concertize frequently until retirement.

Roland Hayes (1887–1977)
Singer

Roland Hayes was born to former slave parents in Curryville, Georgia on June 3,

1887. His father, a tenant-farmer, died when Hayes was twelve. Determined that her seven children would not share her illiteracy, Hayes' mother sent them to Chattanooga, Tennessee, where they set up a rotating system whereby one brother worked while the others attended school. Hayes was employed in a machine shop, but when his turn came to go to school he passed it up, continuing to supply the family income while he studied at night.

In 1917, Hayes became the first black to give a recital in Boston's Symphony Hall. Three years later he traveled to London and gave a royal command performance, followed by other successes throughout Europe. His tenor voice was used to good advantage in programs blended from Negro spirituals, folk songs, operatic arias, and German lieder.

Hayes gave a well-received farewell concert at Carnegie Hall in New York on his seventy-fifth birthday in 1962. During his career, Hayes received many awards and citations including eight honorary degrees and the NAACP's Spingarn Medal for the most outstanding achievement among blacks. Hayes died in Boston on January 1, 1977 at the age of eighty-nine. The success of Roland Hayes in the concert field played a great part in broadening the opportunities later afforded to such singers as Paul Robeson and Marian Anderson.

Barbara Hendricks (1948–   )
Singer

Barbara Hendricks was born in Stephens, Arkansas. She graduated from the University of Nebraska with a bachelor of science degree in chemistry and mathematics, then attended the Juilliard School of music and received a bachelor of music degree in voice. Hendricks made her debut in 1974 with the San Francisco Spring Opera. She has since performed with major opera companies and festivals throughout the United States and Europe, including the Boston Opera, St. Paul Opera, the Deutsche Opera in Berlin, the Nederlandse Operastichting, the Aix Provence Festival, and the Glyndebourne Festival Opera. She has performed with numerous symphony orchestras, and has appeared in a film version of *La Boheme*.

Gail Hightower (1946–   )
Bassoonist

Gail Hightower displayed great musical promise as a child. She attended the High School of Performing Arts in New York City. Scholarships from the New Amsterdam Musical Association and the Rockefeller Foundation, and grants from the National Endowment for the Arts allowed her to attend the Manhattan School of Music from which she reveived her bachelor's degree in music and her master's in 1969.

She made her debut as a recitalist at Carnegie Hall in 1979, and in 1980, she was named the NAACP Outstanding Woman in the Arts. Hightower has performed with many symphony orchestras including the Symphony of the New World (1968–1978) and the Brooklyn Philharmonic (1979–1981; 1985). Her professional affiliations have included the Great Neck Symphony, Festival Orchestra in Siena, Italy, North Carolina School of the Arts Festival Orchestra, Urban Philharmonic (New York City and Washington DC) Harlem Philharmonic, and the instrumental ensemble of the Dance Theater of Harlem. She currently teaches at the Aaron Copland School of Music at the Queens College of City University of New York.

Ann Stevens Hobson (1943–)
Harpist

Ann Hobson, one of the first African-American women to hold a permanent position in a major national symphony orchestra, began studying piano with her mother at an early age. She took up the harp in high school so she would be playing an instrument on which her mother could not tell what she was doing wrong. Early in high school she tried to attend a summer program at the Maine Harp Colony, but was rejected on the basis of her race. Several years later she tried again and was accepted. While at the colony, she met Harpist Alice Chalifoux of the Cleveland Symphony Orchestra and transferred from the Philadelphia Musical Academy to the Cleveland Institute of Music to study with Chalifoux.

In 1966, the first harpist of the National Symphony Orchestra broke a finger; the orchestra's manager called Chalifoux, who recommended Hobson. Hobson played with the group for three seasons, before joining the Boston Symphony Orchestra, with whom she has played ever since. Hobson's other activities have included performing with the Boston Symphony chamber players, the New England Harp Trio, and solo appearances with orchestras throughout the country. She has taught at the Philadelphia Musical Academy and the New England Conservatory and has conducted many clinics and workshops, always encouraging other young harpists.

Ben Holt (1956–1990)
Singer

Born in Washington, DC, baritone Ben Holt attended the Oberlin Conservatory of Music and was a scholarship student at the Juilliard School of Music, where he worked with Sixten Ehrling, Tito Gobbi, and Manuel Rosenthal. He studied in Luciano Pavarotti's master classes and coached extensively with renowned pianist and coach Martin Isepp. While at the San Francisco Opera's Merola Program in master classes of Elisabeth Schwarzkopf, he was honored with an invitation to study privately at her studio in Zurich.

Holt made his Metropolitan Opera debut during the 1985–1986 season and in 1988 made his debut with the New York City Opera in the title role of *Malcolm X* by Anthony Davis. In addition, he sang *Porgy and Bess* with the Calgary Opera in Canada, and starred in *Le Nozze di Figaro* with the Cincinnati Opera. Holt was the winner of many competitions and awards, including the Joy of Singing Competition, Oratorio Society of New York, Independent Black Opera Singers, Washington International and D'Angelo Young Artists Competition.

Eva Jessye (1895–1992)
Choral Conductor, Composer

Eva Jessye noted by *Ebony* magazine to be the "first black woman to receive international distinction as a choral director," was also the first black woman to succeed as a professional choral conductor. She began her formal training at Western University in Kansas and Langston University in Oklahoma. She taught in public schools in Oklahoma, at Morgan State College in Baltimore, Maryland, and Claflin College in Orangeburg, South Carolina.

In the 1920s Jessye went to New York City. She sang with musical shows and began organizing choirs. By 1926 she had established the Eva Jessye Choir as a successful professional venture. The group toured widely in this country and in Europe and performed with conductors such as Ormandy, Stokowski, and Mitropoulous. In

1934, she directed the choir for Virgil Thompson and Gertrude Stein's opera *Four Saints in Three Acts;* in 1935 she served as choral director for Gershwin's *Porgy and Bess.* As a composer, Jessye chose to work mainly in the spiritual tradition, and produced many choral arrangements. Her works include the oratorios *Paradise Lost and Regained, The Life of Christ in Negro Spirituals,* and *The Chronicle of Job.*

John Rosamond Johnson (1873–1954)
Composer

J. Rosamond Johnson, brother to writer and lyricist James Weldon Johnson, was born in Jacksonville, Florida. He received his musical training at the New England Conservatory and, for a time, studied under composer Samuel Coleridge-Taylor.

In 1899, Johnson, eager to pursue a career in show business, teamed up with lyricist and vaudeville entertainer Bob Cole. Together, with lyrics supplied by his brother James, Johnson and Cole wrote numerous songs, including "Under the Bamboo Tree," "Congo Love Songs," "My Castle on the Nile," and "Lift Every Voice and Sing".

Johnson and Cole also wrote, directed, and produced several musicals, including *The Shoo-fly Regiment* in 1907 and *The Red Moon* in 1910.

In addition to songwriting, Johnson edited several collections of Negro spirituals.

Elayne Jones (1928–   )
Timpanist

Elayne Jones began studying piano with her mother when she was six years old. When she enrolled in New York City's High School of the Performing Arts, she found all the piano positions in the orchestra taken so she was forced to switch to a new instrument. She told *The New York Times,* "I was small and the only thing I could handle were the drums, which were small. I took a liking to them."

Jones has played with the orchestras of the New York City Opera (1949–1961), the New York City Ballet (1949–1952), the Brooklyn Philharmonic (1969–1972), the Westchester Philharmonic (1969–1972), and the American Symphony Orchestra (1962–1972). In 1972, conductor Seiji Ozawa invited her to join the San Francisco Symphony, and she became the first black female to hold a principal chair in a major symphony orchestra. When she was refused tenure in 1974, and again in 1975, she filed a suit that lasted over a year. Despite her exemplary professional record, and despite the support of friends, colleagues, and the San Francisco public, she lost her battle.

In 1965, Jones provided the impetus for the founding of the Symphony of the New World. As she explained to *The New York Times* (5–2–65), when the conductor Benjamin Steinberg had money for one concert, "I suggest that he should make it have more purpose than playing one concert. He agreed that we would try to organize an orchestra of some caliber, mostly of Negroes with some white musicians." The orchestra played for eleven years, and during part of that time she also served as its president.

In addition to her symphonic work, Jones holds an extensive resume of free lance work that includes Broadway shows, films, and television. She has taught at the Metropolitan Music School, the Bronx Community College of the City University of New York, the Westchester Conservatory, and the San Francisco Conservatory. She has also traveled widely giving lecture demonstration.

Scott Joplin (1868–1917)
Pianist, Composer

Coming from a musical family, Scott Joplin received much encouragement to study music. His father bought him a piano, and Joplin studied classical piano with a local German music teacher. When he left home, however, he could only find musical work in bars, brothels, and the like. In 1894, he settled in Sedalia, Missouri to teach piano and study theory and composition at George R. Smith College for Negroes. In 1899 he published "The Maple Leaf Rag" which was enormously successful; his piano rags appealed greatly to the public, and within a few years he had achieved great financial success with his ragtime compositions.

Joplin also composed larger works in the same style. He completed a ballet in 1899, his first opera in 1908 (the score of which

is now lost), and his second opera, *Treemonisha*. He was determined to produce this opera and see it performed, but had no luck. He personally financed the publication of the vocal score and produced a non-staged version of the opera for critics, but New York audiences were not ready for an opera about blacks by a black composer, and no one would back a full production. After the "Ragtime Renaissance" of the early 1970s, Joplin's opera was given a world premiere in Atlanta, Georgia, and has been performed elsewhere many times including a masterful performance, video, and audio recording by the Houston Grand Opera Company.

Scott Joplin

Ulysses Kay (1917–   )
Composer, Educator

Ulysses Kay was born in Tucson, Arizona. He attended the University of Arizona, where he received a bachelor's degree in music. He later went on to attend the Eastman School of Music at the University of Rochester, where he reveived a master's degree in music. Kay also studied with Paul Hindemith at Yale and Otto Luening at Columbia. He spent the years between 1942 and 1945 in the Navy, where he played with the bands, and from 1949 to 1952 in Rome studying music as a Fulbright fellow. Kay has taught at Boston University, the University of California, Los Angeles, and is currently professor of Music at Lehman College in New York.

Although his uncle was Joseph "King" Oliver, the legendary cornet player, Kay believes that jazz is a much more limited medium than symphonic music. His works for voice, chamber groups, and orchestra include *Choral Triptych*, *Six Dances* (for string orchestra), *Fantasy Variations* (for orchestra), *Sinfonia in E*, and *The Boor* (an

Ulysses Kay

opera). He has performed and recorded throughout the United States and Europe.

Tania Justina Leon (1944–   )
Composer, Conductor

Tania Leon was born, raised, and educated in Havana, Cuba. She studied piano and composition at the Carlos Alfredo Peyrellado Conservatory, receiving a bachelor's degree in 1963, and a master's in 1964. She won the Young Composer's Prize from the National Council of Arts in Havana in 1966. She moved to the United States in 1967, and in 1968, she joined the Dance Theater of Harlem as its music director and resident composer.

Leon received her introduction to conducting when the Dance Theatre attended the Spoletto Festival in the late 1960s; the director of the Dance Theatre, Arthur Mitchell, and the director of the festival, Gian-Carlo Menotti, encouraged her to conduct the festival orchestra instead of using recorded music for the dancers. When she returned to the States, she studied conducting at the Juilliard School of Music, the Berkshire Music Center at Tanglewood, and New York University, from which she received a bachelor's of science and a bachelor's of arts in 1971, and a master's of science degree in 1973. She has conducted such orchestras as Genoa Symphony Orchestra, the BBC Symphony Orchestra, and the Halle Orchestra; in 1978 she was appointed Music Director and Conductor of the Brooklyn Philharmonic.

Leon's compositions bring together the rich and varied elements of her cultural heritage as an African, Cuban, and American. She has written many ballets, orchestra works, chamber pieces, and vocal works. She has taught composition at Brooklyn College, has served as the resident composer for the Lincoln Center Institute, and was the artistic director of the Composer's Forum in New York.

Henry Lewis (1932–   )
Conductor, Bassist

Henry Lewis was born in Los Angeles, California and attended the University of Southern California. Between 1955 and 1957, Lewis, while stationed in Germany, directed the Seventh Army Symphony Orchestra. He made his debut as a conductor in 1972 with the New York Philharmonic and became the first black to conduct the Metropolitan Opera Orchestra. He is the founder of the Los Angeles Chamber Orchestra and the Black Academy of Arts and Letter, and has since served as guest conductor for numerous orchestras.

Dorothy Leigh Maynor (1910–   )
Singer

Born in Norfolk, Virginia, Dorothy Leigh Mayner (she changed the spelling of her last name when she became a singer) was raised in an atmosphere of music and singing. She originally intended to become a home economics teacher and, with this in mind, entered Hampton Institute at the age of fourteen. She received her bachelor's degree in 1933. She was heard by the director of the Westminster Choir, who made it possible for her to receive a scholarship at Westminster Choir College in Princeton, New Jersey.

In 1935, she received her bachelor's degree in music and left for New York to study voice. Singing at the Berkshire Music Festival in 1939, she was heard by Boston Symphony Orchestra conductor, Serge Koussevitzky. Maynor was acclaimed by critics as one of America's leading singers. She has since performed with the country's major orchestras, including the New York Orchestra, and the Los Angeles Symphony Orchestra.

In 1965, Maynor organized the Harlem School of the Arts in the St. James Presbyterian Church, which was pastored by her husband, the Reverend Shelby A. Rooks. In 1971, Maynor received a doctor of humane letters from Oberlin. She was elected to the Metropolitan Opera's board of directors in 1975, becoming the first black to serve on the organization's board.

Robert McFerrin (1921–   )
Singer, Educator

Born in Marianna, Arkansas, baritone Robert McFerrin received his musical training at the Chicago Musical College, obtaining a bachelor's degree. He sang the title role in *Rigoletto* with the New England Opera Company in 1950 and was a baritone soloist in the Lewisohn Stadium Summer Concert Series in 1954. McFerrin made his Metropolitan Opera debut with the role of Amonasro in *Aida* in 1955.

McFerrin has served as a guest professor of voice at Sibelius Academy, Finland, and Roosevelt University in Chicago. He has also served as a member of the voice faculty at Nelson School of Fine Arts in Nelson, British Columbia, Canada.

Lena Johnson McLin (1928–   )
Composer, Conductor, Educator

Lena McLin's musical life began in the Greater Mt. Calvary Baptist Church in Atlanta, where her father was minister, and her mother was music director. She received her first training in classical music from her mother, and learned traditional spirituals from her grandmother, and her M.A. from the American Conservatory in 1954. She has also studied at Roosevelt University in Chicago State College. She taught high school music and director church choirs in Chicago for several decades, and helped to establish new music programs in the curriculum. She has conducted many workshops and clinics at colleges and university around the country; in 1972, she won the Teacher of the Year award in Chicago. In the early 1960s, she started the McLin Opera Company to give promising young artists a performing venue.

McLin's compositions are primarily sacred pieces which combine spiritual traditions with classical musical styles. As a choir director, she wrote much music for her Sunday services. Her music also incorporates popular and rock idioms, and she served as the advisor on Rock Music for the Music Educators National Conference. Her compositions include cantatas, masses, spiritual arrangements, operas, works for piano, orchestras, and electronic music.

Leona Mitchell

Leona Mitchell (1949–)
Singer

Soprano Leona Mitchell is a native of Enid, Oklahoma, and a graduate of Oklahoma University. Mitchell has been heard with the San Francisco Opera, the Washington Opera Society, the Houston Opera, and at the Gran Teatro del Liceo in Barcelona. Her orchestral appearances have included concerts with the Cleveland Orchestra, the London Symphony, and the New Jersey Symphony.

During the summer of 1980 she sang Bess in the Cleveland Orchestra Blossom Festival production of *Porgy and Bess* and performed the same role in their subsequent recording of the work. Mitchell made her Metropolitan Opera debut as Micaela in *Carmen* in 1975 and since has been heard there as Lauretta in *Gianni Schicci*, Pamina in

The Magic Flute, and Madame Lidoine in *Dialogues of the Carmelites*.

Dorothy Rudd Moore (1940–)
Composer, Singer

Dorothy Rudd Moore studied music theory and composition at Howard University, graduating magna cum laude in 1963. She studied with Nadia Boulenger at the Conservatoire de Musique in France, and at Columbia University in New York. She has taught at the Harlem School of Arts, New York University, and Bronx Community College, and has taught piano and voice privately. Her compositions have been performed throughout the United States, including at such eminent places as Cargnegie Hall, Town Hall, Tuly Hall, and Philharmonic Hall. She has written symphonies, songs, chamber pieces, and an opera. The *New York Times* has called hers "a gifted and creative mind at work." *Opera News* reported that in her opera *Frederick Douglass* "Moore displays rare ability to wed musical and dramatic motion, graceful lyric inventiveness, (and) a full command of the orchestral palette."

Kermit Moore (1929–)
Cellist, Composer, Conductor

Kermit Moore's original musical identity was as a cellist. He studied cello at the Cleveland Institute of Music (B.M. 1951), at New York University (M.A. 1952), and at the Paris Conservatory (Artists Diploma, 1956). He has performed with orchestras throughout the world, including the Orchestra de la Suisse Romande, the Concertgebouw of Amsterdam, the National Radio Symphony of Paris, and the Belgian National Orchestra. He played his debut recital at the New York Town Hall in 1949, and has since given recitals in almost every major city in the world, including Paris, Brussels, Vienna, Cologne, Hamburg, Munich, Geneva, Basel, Amsterdam, Tokyo, Seoul, New York, Boston, Chicago, and San Francisco.

In 1965, Moore co-founded the Symphony of the New World in New York; he not only performed as cellist with the group, but conducted occasionally as well. He has also served as guest conductor with, among other groups, the Detroit Symphony Orchestra, the Brooklyn Philharmonic, the Festival Orchestra at the United Nations, the Berkeley (California) Symphony, the Dance Theatre of Harlem, and Opera Ebony. Moore is a member of ASCAP, and was co-founder of the Society of Black Composers. His works include solo music for cello, a cello concerto, a timpani concerto, songs, arias, and various pieces for chamber ensemble.

Undine Smith Moore (1904–1989)
Composer, Educator

Undine Smith Moore was one of the most influential music educators of the twentieth century, as is evident by her numerous awards and honors. She received honorary doctorates from Virginia State University in 1972, and from Indiana University in 1976. The Mayor of New York City, John Lindsay, presented her with a Certificate of Appreciation, she received the Seventh Annual Humanitarian Award from Fisk University in 1973, she won the National Association of Negro Musicians Award in 1975, and in that same year Mayor Remmis Arnold of Petersburg, Virginia, proclaimed April 13th as Undine Moore Day.

Moore received her B.A. and B.M. degrees from Fisk University in Nashville, and an M.A. and professional diploma from Columbia University's Teachers College in New York. She also studied at the Juilliard School of Music, the Manhattan School of Music, and the Eastman School of Music in Rochester, New York. She taught at Virginia State

College in Petersburg from 1927–1972, where she co-founded and directed the Black Music Center. She also served as visiting professor at numerous other schools, including Carleton College in Northfield, Minnesota; St. Benedict College in St. Joseph, Minnesota, St. Johns University in Collegeville, Minnesota, and Virginia Union University in Richmond.

As a composer, Moore wrote works for a variety of ensembles. Many of her works are for chorus, and she has also written for solo voice, piano, organ, flute, and clarinet. Her works have received much recognition, and her *Afro-American Suite*, commissioned by Antoinette Handy's Trio Pro Viva, has been performed widely. Her cantata *Scenes from the Life of a Martyr: To the Memory of Martin Luther King* received a nomination for a Pulitzer Prize.

Michael Morgan (1957–)
Conductor

Born in Washington DC, Michael Morgan attended the Oberlin College Conservatory of Music. He pursued additional studies at the Vienna master classes of Witold Rowicki and the Berkshire Music Center at Tanglewood, where he was a conducting fellow and student of Seiji Ozawa and Gunther Schuller. Michael Morgan appeared with the New York Philharmonic in September of 1986 in the Leonard Bernstein Young American Conductors concerts. From 1980 to 1987, he was Exxon/Arts Endowment assistant conductor of the Chicago Symphony Orchestra, where he is now affiliate artist conductor. Previously, he was apprentice conductor of the Buffalo Philharmonic under music director Julius Rudel. Morgan has appeared as a guest conductor with many of our nation's major orchestras. He made his New York City Opera debut conducting multiple performances of *La Traviata* in New

York, Wolftrap, and Taiwan. In Europe, Morgan has led performances of the Vienna State Opera, the Deutsche Staatsoper in East Berlin, the Vienna Symphony Orchestra, Warsaw Philharmonic Orchestra, and Danish Radio Orchestra.

The many awards Morgan has earned include first prizes in the 1980 Hans Swarowsky International Conductors Competition (Vienna), the Gino Marrinuzzi International Conductors Competition (San Remo, Italy) and the Baltimore Symphony Young Conductors Competition.

Jessye Norman (1945–)
Singer

Soprano Jessye Norman was born in Augusta, Georgia to a musical family. Her mother, a school teacher and amateur pianist, provided the family with piano lessons. At the age of sixteen, Norman went to Philadelphia to compete for the Marian Anderson Scholarship, but failed to win. Nevertheless, she later was granted a full four-year scholarship to Howard University, once the director of the music department heard her sing.

Norman graduated with honors from Howard in 1967 and went on to study at the Peabody Conservatory in Baltimore, Maryland and the University of Michigan, where she received a master's degree in 1968.

In 1968, Norman entered the Bavarian Radio Corporation's International Music Competition, receiving first prize. In 1969, she made her debut with the Deutsch Opera in Berlin as Elisabeth in Wagner's *Tannhauser*, and in 1970 she made her Italian opera debut. Appearing at La Scala in Milan, Wolf Trap in Virginia, the Tangle-

Jessye Norman

wood Music Festival, and at the Royal Opera House in Covent Garden, England, Norman has performed with some of the world's leading orchestras.

Following a temporary leave from opera in the mid-1970s, Norman returned to the stage in 1980 in Strauss' *Ariadne auf Naxos*. She has since made numerous concert appearances, has made numerous recordings, including Berg's *Lulu Suite*, Berlioz' *Les nuits d'ete* and *Romeo and Juliette*, Bizet's *Carmen*, Mahler's *Kindertotenlieder*, and a recent album entitled *Lucky To Be Me*.

Norman has received numerous awards for her work, including several Grammy awards, an Outstanding Musician of the Year Award, and several honorary degrees from American universities. She is also a member of the Royal Academy of Music.

Coleridge-Taylor Perkinson (1932–   )
Composer

Coleridge-Taylor Perkinson has been a figure in explorative musical movements in both Hollywood and New York.

Born in New York, Perkinson took graduate and postgraduate degrees from the Manhattan School of Music (1953, 1954), before going on to study at the Berkshire Music Center, the Mozarteum, and the Netherland Radio Union Hilversum. Becoming first composer-in-residence for the Negro Ensemble Company, he wrote the music for many plays, including Peter Weiss's *Song of the Lusitanian Bogey*, Ray McIver's *God Is a (Guess What?)*, and Errol Hill's *Man Better Man*. In 1965, when the Symphony of the New World was organized in New York, Perkinson was named associate conductor. His concert pieces include *Concerto for Violin and Orchestra* (1954) and *Attitudes* (1964), written for black opera star George Shirley. Perkinson has also composed music for tele-

vision and radio programs, the documentary film *Cross-roads Africa*, and ballet ensembles.

Julia Perry (1924–1979)
Composer, Conductor

Julia Perry was born in Lexington, Kentucky, and raised in Akron, Ohio. She studied violin, piano, and voice as a child. In 1942, she enrolled at the Westminister Choir College in Princeton, New Jersey, studying violin, piano, voice, conducting, and composition. Even before graduating, she began publishing her compositions—*Carillon Heigh-Ho* was published in 1947. After receiving her master's from Westminister in 1948, she went on to attend Juiliard School of Music. In 1950, her cantata *Ruth* was premiered in New York.

Between 1951 and 1959 she lived in Europe. After studying with composer Luigi Dallapiccola at the Berkshire Music Center, she won a Guggenheim Fellowship to continue study with him in Florence and to study with Nadia Boulanger in Paris. Throughout the United States and Europe her work received acclaim. In 1954, her one act opera *The Cask of Amontillado* was produced at Columbia University.

After her return to the States in 1959, she continued to compose. She taught at a number of universities, including Florida A&M University in Tallahassee and the Atlanta Colleges Center. In 1955, she received the Boulanger Grand Prix Award, and in 1964 she won the American Academy and National Institute of Arts and Letters Award. In 1969, she received Honorable Mention in the ASCAP Awards. Perry's compositions include *Stabat Mater* for contralto and strings (1951), *Pastoral* for flute and strings (1959), *Homunchulus* for soprano and percussion (1960), and the operas *The Bottle*, *The Cask of Amontillado*, and *The Selfish Giant*.

Evelyn La Rue Pittman (1910–)
Choral Director, Composer

While a senior at Spelman College in Atlanta studying African-American history, Evelyn Pittman committed herself to teaching black history through music. Her first work, a musical play, was produced at Spelman in 1933. During the years she taught in the public schools in Oklahoma City (1935 to 1956), she also conducted weekly broadcasts on a local radio station with her own professional group, The Evelyn Pittman Choir; she directed a 350-voice choir sponsored by the YWCA, and directed orchestras, choirs, and operettas in the schools. She also began composing songs about black leaders, and published a collection of songs, *Rich Heritage*, in 1944.

In 1948, she went to Juilliard to study composition, and then earned a master's degree from Oklahoma University in 1954. Between 1956 and 1958, she studied composition with Nadia Boulanger in Paris, and completed her first opera, *Cousin Esther*. It received its first performance in Paris in 1957 and in the next few years was performed in Europe and in the United States with rave reviews. She returned to public-school teaching in 1958 in New York State and continued to compose. After the assassination of Martin Luther King, Jr. in 1968, she wrote the opera *Freedom Child* in his memory and honor; when she retired, she dedicated herself to directing a touring company of *Freedom Child*. Her other compositions include choral arrangements of Spirituals, and a stage work titled *Jim Noble*.

Karl Hampton Porter (1939–)
Bassonist, Conductor, Educator

Karl Hampton Porter was born in Pittsburgh, Pennsylvania. While in high school, he learned to play bassoon and saxophone.

He received his musical training at Carnegie-Mellon University, the Peabody Conservatory and the Juilliard School of Music where he studied bassoon and conducting.

Porter has organized several musical groups throughout the New York area including the Harlem Youth Symphony, the Harlem Philharmonic Orchestra, the New Breed Brass Ensemble, the Harlem String Quartet, and the Harlem Woodwind Quintet. He has served as conductor of the Baltimore Symphony, the Massapequa Symphony, the Park West Symphony, and has served as musical director of numerous productions. Porter has taught at New York City Technical College, and has served as chairman of the Fine Arts Lecture Series at the College.

Florence Price (1888–1953)
Composer, Pianist

Florence Price was born in Little Rock, Arkansas and grew up in Chicago. She studied music first with her mother, a talented soprano and concert pianist. In 1902 she enrolled in the New England Conservatory of Music in Boston, majoring in piano and organ. After graduating in 1907, she returned to Little Rock as a music educator, performer, and composer. Her works, especially her songs, began to receive some notice. In 1927, due to racial tensions, she moved to Chicago and pursued further musical education. In the early 1920s Price's composition began to receive notice. She won the Rodman Wanamaker Foundation Award for a piano sonata and her *Symphony in E Minor;* the Chicago Symphony Orchestra premiered this work in 1933 at the Chicago World's Fair. She also presented a program of her pieces at the fair, and the Women's Symphony orchestra of Chicago also performed some of her works. In 1934, she appeared as soloist in her *Concerto in D Minor* in the Chicago Musical College and in

Pittsburgh. That same year, she conducted a performance of her *Concerto in F Minor* with pianist/composer Margaret Bonds as the soloist.

Her fame grew steadily. In 1940, she performed her *Concerto in One Movement* with the WPA Symphony Orchestra in Detroit, which played her *Symphony No. 3 in C Minor* in the same program. Faculty members of the Music School of the University of Illinois, and the Forum String Quartet of Chicago, performed some of her chamber music. The British Conductor Sir John Barbirolli commissioned her to write a suite for strings, which he presented in Manchester England. Marian Anderson sang her *Songs to the Dark Virgin* in her second American concert tour to rave reviews. In addition to her larger orchestral and chamber works, she wrote many art songs, spiritual arrangements, choral pieces, and piano, organ, and violin works.

Leontyne Price (1927–)
Singer

Born Mary Violet Leontyne Price, in Laurel, Mississippi, Price was encouraged by her parents, who were amateur musicians, to sing and play the piano at an early age. In 1949, she received her bachelor's degree from the College of Education and Industrial Arts (now Central State College) in Wilberforce, Ohio, where she had studied music education in hopes of becoming a music teacher.

Price received a scholarship to study at the Julliard School of Music in New York

Leontyne Price

City. While appearing in a student production of Verdi's *Falstaff*, she was noticed by the composer and music critic, Virgil Thomson, and cast in her first professional role in a revival of his opera *Four Saints In Three Acts*.

Between 1952 and 1954, Price performed the role of Bess in a revival of Gershwin's *Porgy and Bess*. It was during this production that she met and married her co-star, baritone William C. Warfield. The two, however, divorced in 1973, following years of separation.

In 1954, Price made her debut at New York's Town Hall. From there she went on to appear in Puccini's *Tosca*, in 1955, Mozart's *The Magic Flute*, in 1956, and Poulenc's *Dialogues of the Carmelites*. Between 1958 and 1960, she appeared at Verona, Vienna, Covent Garden, and La Scala. Price had become one of the world's leading sopranos.

On January 27, 1961, Price made her debut with the Metropolitan Opera in Verdi's *Il Trovatore*, where she received a standing ovation. She has since appeared in numerous Met productions, including Puccini's *The Girl of the Golden West*, and the world premiere of Samuel Barber's *Antony and Cleopatra*, in 1966.

Price has made numerous appearances at the White House, and has performed at two presidential inaugurations.

On April 20, 1982, Price opened the convention of the Daughters of the American Revolution in Constitution Hall with a concert honoring Marian Anderson. It was in 1939 that Anderson was barred from appearing in Constitution Hall by the DAR, prompting Eleanor Roosevelt to resign in anger from the organization. In September 1981, Price opened the 1981–1982 concert series at Rutgers University in New Brunswick, New Jersey, which marked her first New Jersey appearance after fifteen years. In 1977, she was awarded the San Francisco Opera medal in honor of the twentieth anniversary of her debut with the company.

Kay George Roberts (1950–)
Violinist, Conductor

Kay Roberts began her professional musical career as a violinist when she joined the Nashville Symphony during her last year in high school; she continued to play with the group until she graduated from Fisk University in 1972. In 1971, she represented the Nashville Symphony in Arthur Fiedler's World Symphony Orchestra. She received her M.M. in 1975, and her D.M.A. in 1986. She has guest conducted for many orchestras, including the Bangkok Symphony in Thailand, the Nashville Symphony Orchestra, the Mystic Valley Chamber Orchestra, and the Greater Dallas Symphony Orchestra. She became the music director of the New Hampshire Philharmonic in 1982, and the Music Director of the Cape Ann Symphony Orchestra in 1986. She has been teaching at the College of Music at the University of Lowell since 1978.

Paul Robeson (1898–1976)
Singer, Actor

Born in Princeton, New Jersey on April 9, 1898, Paul Robeson was the son of a runaway slave who put himself through Lincoln University and later became a Presbyterian minister. Robeson entered Rutgers College (now Rutgers University) on a scholarship, and won a total of twelve letters in track, football, baseball, and basketball. In addition to his athletic exploits, his academic ability gained him Phi Beta Kappa honors in his junior year.

Paul Robeson

ity than his artistic career. In 1950, for instance, his passport was revoked after refusing to sign an affidavit as to whether or not he had ever belonged to the Communist Party. Eight years later, the United States Supreme Court ruled that the refusal to sign such an affidavit was not valid grounds for denial of a passport. Robeson subsequently settled in London, making a number of trips to the continent (and to the Soviet Union as well) before returning to the United States in 1963.

Robeson played an active role in civil and human rights issues. He was a co-founder of the Council on African Affairs, and a member of the Joint Anti-Fascist Refugee Committee, and the Committee to Aid China. Robeson died January 23, 1976 in Philadelphia, Pennsylvania.

In 1923, Robeson received a law degree from Columbia University, financing his schooling by playing professional football. While at Columbia, Robeson was seen by Eugene O'Neill in an amateur play. After making his professional debut in *Taboo* (1922), Robeson appeared in O'Neill's *All God's Chillun Got Wings* and *Emperor Jones*. Called upon to whistle in the latter play, Robeson sang instead, and his voice met with instant acclaim. In 1925, he made his concert debut with a highly successful program of all-African-American music. He went on to such stage successes as *Show Boat*, *Porgy*, and *Othello*.

A world traveler in the Soviet Union, Asia, and Europe, Robeson spoke several languages, including Chinese, Russian, Gaelic, and Spanish. Robeson's political affiliations at times tended to attract even more public-

Philippa Schuyler (1932–1969)
Composer, Pianist

Born on August 21, 1932 in New York City, Philippa Schuyler was already playing the piano at the age of two and began composing a year later. By the time she was eight, she had some fifty compositions to her credit. Her published works include *Six Little Pieces* and *Eight Little Pieces*.

At the age of twelve, her first symphonic composition, *Manhattan Nocturne*, was performed at Carnegie Hall, and the following year her scherzo, *Rumpelstiltskin*, was performed by the Dean Dixon Youth Orchestra, the Boston Pops, the New Haven Symphony Orchestra, and the New York Philharmonic.

In 1953, Schuyler made her debut at Town Hall in New York as a pianist. She went on to travel to some fifty countries on good will concert tours sponsored by the United States State Department.

Philippa Schuyler was considered to be one of America's most outstanding musical prodigies. Remembered as a mature concert pianist, she died tragically at the height of her career.

George Shirley (1934–)
Singer

George Shirley was born April 18, 1934 in Indianapolis, and moved to Detroit in 1940. There he began giving vocal recitals in churches and decided on a musical career after playing baritone horn in a community band. In 1955, he graduated from Wayne State University in Detroit with a bachelor's degree in musical education.

After his discharge from the Army in 1959, he began serious vocal studies with Themy S. Georgi. In June of that year he made his

Philippa Schuyler, c.1966.

Philippa Schuyler at age eight.

operatic debut as Eisenstein in Strauss's *Die Fledermaus*, performing with the Turnau Players at Woodstock. A year later he won the American Opera Auditions, whereupon he journeyed to Milan, Italy, making his opera debut there in Puccini's *La Boheme*.

In 1961, his career was given tremendous impetus by his victory in the Metropolitan Opera auditions. In 1963, he made his debut at Carnegie Hall with the Friends of French Opera, singing opposite Rita Gorr in Massenet's *La Navarraise*.

Since then, he has sung with several of the Met's leading divas, including Renata Tebaldi in *Simon Boccanegra* and Birgit Nilsson in *Salome*. In 1974, he sang the title role in Mozart's *Idomeneo* at the Glyndeburne Festival, and he has remained a favorite at the Met over the years.

William Grant Still

William Grant Still (1895–1978)
Composer, Conductor

William Grant Still was born in Woodville, Mississippi. Since both of his parents were musicians and his father was the town's bandmaster, he received his early musical training at home.

Intending to study medicine, Still enrolled at Wilberforce College, but left before graduating. Still began to seriously consider a career in music. After working with various jazz musicians, including W.C. Handy and Paul Whiteman, Still enrolled at Oberlin College Conservatory of Music.

Still became the first African-American composer to have a large-scale work performed by a major American orchestra, when the Rochester Philharmonic Orchestra performed his *Afro-American Symphony*, in 1931. In 1936 Still became the first African American to conduct a major American orchestra, when he conducted the Los Angeles Philharmonic in a program of his work. He was also the first African-American composer to have an opera performed by a major opera company, when the New York City Opera performed his *Troubled Island* in 1949.

Still was awarded the Harmon Award in 1928 for his contribution to black culture. He was the winner of two Guggenheim Fellowships—one in 1944 and the other in 1961. In 1961, the National Federation of Music Clubs awarded him $1,500 for his composition *The Peaceful Land*. His major works include his composition *Song of A New Race*, the symphonic poem *Darker America*, the suites *Pages from Negro History* and *The American Scene*, and numerous songs and arrangements of spirituals.

Howard Swanson (1909–1978)
Composer

Howard Swanson was born in Atlanta and raised in Cleveland, where he studied at the Institute of Music. He was taught composition by Herbert Elwell. In 1938, he won a Rosenwald Fellowship to study with Nadia Boulanger in Paris. Returning to the United States, he devoted himself to composition, and in 1950, won wide acclaim, as well as serious attention, as an American composer when his *Short Symphony*, written in 1948, was performed by the New York Philharmonic with Dmitri Mitropoulos conducting. In 1952, this symphony won the New York Critics' Award. One of Swanson's well-known works is the song "The Negro Speaks of Rivers," based on a poem by Langston Hughes, which Marian Anderson has sung in recital.

Swanson died in 1978. In 1979, at the St. James Presbyterian Church in New York City a concert was given by the Triad Chorale as a memorial to him and the composer William Grant Still.

Shirley Verrett (1933–)
Singer

Born to musical family in New Orleans, Shirley Verrett moved to California at the age of five, but had no formal voice training during her childhood—largely because her father felt singing would involve his daughter in too precarious a career. Still, he offered his daughter the opportunity to sing in church choirs under his direction. She attended Ventura College, where she majored in business administration. By 1954, she was a prosperous real estate agent, but her longing for an artistic career had become so acute that she decided to take voice lessons in Los Angeles and train her sights on the concert stage anyway.

Shirley Verrett

After winning a television talent show in 1955, she enrolled at the Juilliard School on a scholarship, earning her diploma in voice some six years later. Her debut at New York's Town Hall in 1958 was not a sensational one. However, by 1962, at Spoleto, Italy she delivered an excellent *Carmen* and a year later, she performed at Lincoln Center in New York, where her recital was said to be "simply without flaws, simply a great event in the annals of American music-making."

By 1964, her *Carmen* had improved so dramatically that the New York *Herald Tribune* critic was able to claim it as "the finest" performance "seen or heard in New York" for the past generation. Other performances in such roles as Orfeo in Gluck's *Orfeo ed Euridice*, Ulrica in Verdi's *Un Ballo de Maschera*, and Leonora in Beethoven's *Fidelio* have been met with comparable acclaim.

In 1982, Verrett appeared with Grace Bumbry in a concert honoring Marian Anderson on her eightieth birthday. Her yearly recital tours take her to the major music centers throughout the country. During the 1986–1987 season the successes for Verrett included a series of operas staged especially for her by the Paris Opera; Rossini's *Mose*, Cherubini's *Medee*, and Gluck's *Iphigenie en Tauride* and *Alceste*. She made a triumphant return to the Metropolitan Opera in 1986 as Eboli in *Don Carlo* and also starred that year in a new production of *Macbeth* with the San Francisco Opera. In the 1987–1988 season, Verrett made her long awaited Chicago Lyric Opera debut as Lucena in *Il Trovatore*.

George Walker (1922–)
Pianist, Educator

Born in Washington, DC, George Walker studied at Oberlin, the Curtis Institute of Music, and at the Eastman School, where he completed his doctorate. His teachers included Rudolf Serkin, Giancarlo Menotti, and Robert Casadesus. Following his well-received Town Hall debut in 1945, Walker gained twenty seasons of experience touring the United States, Canada, and Europe.

Walker has served on the faculty of Smith College, Northhampton, Massachusetts, University of Colorado, University of Delaware, and the Peabody Institute of Johns Hopkins University, Baltimore, Maryland. He is currently professor of Music at Rutgers University.

William C. Warfield (1920–   )
Singer

Baritone William Warfield was born in West Helena, Arkansas, and later moved with his family to Rochester, New York, where he attended school. The son of a Baptist minister, he received early training in voice, organ, and piano and, in 1938, while a student at Washington Junior High School, won the vocal competition at the Music Educators National Convention in St. Louis.

He studied at the Eastman School of Music and the University of Rochester, receiving his bachelor's degree in 1942.

Warfield made his debut at New York's Town Hall on March 19, 1950. After his resounding New York debut in 1950, he made an unprecedented tour of Australia under the auspices of the Australian Broadcasting Commission. A year later he made his movie debut in *Show Boat*.

Warfield has appeared on several major television shows and starred in the NBC television version of *Green Pastures*. Between 1952 and 1959 he made five international tours under the auspices of the United States State Department. In 1966, he appeared in a revival of the Jerome Kern-Edna Ferber classic *Showboat*. His performances

William Warfield

as Porgy in the various revivals of *Porgy and Bess* have made him the best-known singer in this role. He was married to Leontyne Price, the brilliant opera star whom he met during a *Porgy and Bess* production.

Andre Watts (1946–   )
Pianist

One of America's most gifted young pianists, Andre Watts achieved a substantial degree of fame while playing under the baton of Leonard Bernstein of the New York Philharmonic.

Born in Nuremberg, Germany of a Hungarian mother and an American G.I. father, Andre Watts spent the first eight years of his life on Army posts in Europe before moving to Philadelphia. By the time he was nine, he was already performing as a soloist with the Philadelphia Orchestra.

At the age of seventeen, Watts appeared on television in one of Leonard Bernstein's Young People's Concerts and was a huge success. After graduating from Lincoln Preparatory School in Philadelphia, he enrolled at Baltimore's Peabody Conservatory of Music.

On one occasion, when Glenn Gould became ill just prior to a performance with the New York Philharmonic, Bernstein chose Watts as a last-minute replacement. At the conclusion of the concerto, Watts received a standing ovation not only from the audience but from the orchestra as well.

In June 1966, Watts made his debut in London, and a month later was the soloist for the two-day Philharmonic Stravinsky Festival at Lincoln Center.

Andre Watts

In the 1970s, Watts gave a concert in Teheran as part of the coronation festivities for the then Shah of Iran, and later, at a state dinner for Congo's President Mobutu, he was presented with the African republic's highest honor, the Order of the Zaire. Watts other rewards include the Lincoln Center Medallion in 1971 and the National Society of Arts and Letters Gold Medal in 1982.

Felix Fowler Weir (1884–1978)
Violinist

Felix Weir began studying violin when an uncle recognized his talent and encouraged him; he played his first public concert at age eleven. He attended the Chicago Musical College and the Conservatory in Leipzig, Germany. Between 1907 and 1914, he taught in public schools in Washington DC. In 1914, he began to perform again; he moved to New York, joined the New Amsterdam Musical Association, and played with the Clef-Club Orchestra. He formed a duo with cellist Leonard Jeter, and later a trio with pianist Olyve Jeter. In 1914, he formed the American String Quartet with cellist Jeter, violinist Joseph Lymos, and violinist Hall Johnson. In the 1920s, he formed another quartet with violinist Johnson, cellist Marion Cumbo, and violinist Arthur Boyd. During the 1920s and 1930s, he also played in the orchestras for Broadway musicals, and taught privately. In the 1930s, he returned to public school teaching in Washington, DC.

Clarence Cameron White (1880–1960)
Violinist, Composer

Clarence Cameron White achieved success as both a violinist and composer early in life. When he was only fifteen, he performed one of his own compositions in a recital he gave in Washington, DC, and when he was seventeen, he played some of his works in recital in Chicago. White studied violin and composition at Howard University in Washington, DC, the Oberlin Conservatory of Music in Ohio, and in London, Paris, and at Juilliard. Between 1900 and 1910, White taught in the public schools in Washington, and headed the string program at the newly established Washington Conservatory of Music (1903–1907). Between 1912 and 1923, he lived and taught in Boston and concertized widely. In the 1920s and early 1930s, he curtailed his touring and concentrated on teaching at the college level and composing. In 1931, he completed his opera, *Ouanga*. He returned to the concert circuit in the late 1930s. He composed a variety of works for violin, piano, voice, chorus, orchestra, organ, and chamber ensembles.

Olly W. Wilson (1937–)
Composer, Educator

Olly Wilson was born in St. Louis, Missouri. While in high school, his clarinet playing earned him a scholarship to his hometown's Washington University. In 1960, Wilson received a master of music degree, with honors, from the University of Illinois, and in 1964 he received a Ph.D. from the University of Iowa.

Wilson's best-known works include the *Sextet, Three Movements for Orchestra*, and *Cetus*. Wilson's style springs from his belief that an African-American composer's "reality" is different. He draws upon a wide spectrum of music not normally regarded as part of the Euro-American tradition.

22

Blues and Jazz

Blues and Jazz

Black Music in the Nineteenth Century ■ Early Recordings and Improvisation ■ The
Jazz Tradition

by Dan Morgenstern

*In a time span of less than a century, the
remarkable native American music called
jazz has risen from obscure origins to become
the most original form of musical expression
of our times—loved, admired and played
throughout the globe. Jazz has a long and rich
ancestry. Its roots go back to the arrival of the
first Africans on American soil and the encounter between native African and European musical traditions. Black music in
America took many forms, including work
songs, gospel and spirituals, and many and
varied kinds of music for dancing.*

■ BLACK MUSIC IN THE NINETEENTH
CENTURY

Ragtime and Blues

By the late nineteenth century, a dance
music called ragtime became very popular.
Its heavily syncopated rhythms and
sprightly melodies had a distinctly Afro-
American flavor. Its greatest exponent was
Scott Joplin (1868–1917) whose music was
rediscovered in the 1970s. About the same
time, a form of black American folk music

called the blues coalesced into a 12-bar pat-
tern that made it adaptable to popular song
writing. The blues has a unique harmonic
quality derived from a "flattening" of the
third and seventh notes of the tempered
scale, and while seemingly simple, lends itself to infinite variation. The blues had an
impact not only on jazz, but later on such
styles as rock and soul music, both of which
would be unthinkable without the blues element.

New Orleans Jazz

It was when ragtime (primarily an instrumental music) and blues (at first primarily a
vocal style) came together that jazz was
born, and though this process was taking
place in many parts of America, it was in
New Orleans that the basic language of jazz
was first spoken.

This was due not only to the rich musical
tradition of this port city (with its international climate), but also because social conditions in New Orleans, while certainly not
free from racist elements, were less restric-

tive and more open than in other large American cities of the time. Thus, there was much contact between musicians of varied ethnic background. Many histories of jazz mistakenly overemphasize the importance of the New Orleans red light district (called Storyville). While early jazz certainly was performed there, many other outlets for music-making existed. These included dances, parades, carnivals, and the traditional New Orleans funerals, for which a band would accompany the casket from church to cemetery with mournful strains, and then lead the march back to town with lively, peppy music including ragtime and early jazz.

Musicians from New Orleans began to tour the United States from about 1907 on, and had a big influence wherever they went. However, their intricate style of collective improvisation, in which each instrument in the band had its own specific role, was not so easily absorbed. It is another myth of jazz history that most of these early jazz players were a special breed of self-taught "naturals;" in fact, almost all of them had good basic musical training, and many could read music well.

■ EARLY RECORDINGS AND IMPROVISATION

Jazz developed almost simultaneously with the phonograph, and without dissemination on records, it is unlikely that jazz would have spread as quickly as it did. By studying recorded performances, musicians anywhere could learn at least the rudiments of jazz, a spontaneous music in which improvisation played a considerable role. "Improvisation" is a much misunderstood concept. It does not mean inventing music on the spot, without guidelines. It does mean adding one's own personal ideas to a common musical text, and taking liberties as long as they fit within a shared framework.

In addition, a jazz musician's personal style will be based on tonal qualities, a distinctive approach to rhythm and phrasing, and a vocabulary of melodic and thematic characteristics. Taken together, these ingredients are what makes it possible for a seasoned listener to almost immediately identify who is playing in a jazz performance, provided that the musician has developed his own personal style.

Ironically, the first New Orleans jazz to be recorded was performed by a white group, the Original Dixieland Jazz Band in 1917. By then, black musicians had already made records, but they were not in a jazz idiom. It would take some five more years before the best black New Orleans players got to make records. In the meanwhile, however, some of them had already visited Europe, notably the great clarinetist and soprano saxophonist Sidney Bechet (1897–1959), who has been called the first great jazz soloist. But it was a somewhat younger New Orleanian, Louis Armstrong (1901–1971), who would have the biggest impact on the future of jazz.

Armstrong, who was brought to Chicago (by then the center of jazz activity) in 1922 by his mentor and fellow trumpeter Joe "King" Oliver (1885–1938) and made his first records there, came to New York two years later to join the band of Fletcher Henderson (1897–1952). This was the first musically significant big band in jazz. While most New Orleans jazz bands used an instrumentation of trumpet, trombone, clarinet, piano, guitar (or banjo), bass (string or brass) and drums, the early big bands used three trumpets, one or two trombones, three reeds (saxophonists doubling clarinet), and the same rhythm section instruments.

They employed written scores (called arrangements), but gave the soloists freedom to "improvise" their contributions.

Armstrong's arrival was a revelation to the Henderson band. His first solos on its

Louis Armstrong in London, 1956.

Fletcher Henderson

records stand out like diamonds in a tin setting. What Louis brought to jazz was, first of all, his superior sense of rhythm that made other players sound stiff and clumsy in comparison. He discovered the rhythmic element called "swing" that sets jazz apart from other musics; a kind of rhythmic thrust that seems to float and soar. In addition, his sound on the trumpet was the biggest and most musically appealing yet heard, and he had exceptional range and powers of execution. Further, his gifts of melodic invention were so great that he can well be said to have laid the foundation for jazz as a medium for personal expression by an instrumental soloist.

One of his first Henderson colleagues to get the message was tenor saxophonist Coleman Hawkins (1904–1969), who soon created the first influential jazz style on his instrument. Also greatly affected was the band's chief arranger, Don Redman (1900–1964), who was the first to translate Louis' discoveries to big-band arranging. Many others followed suit, especially after Louis, now back in Chicago, began to make records with his own studio groups, the Hot Fives and Hot Sevens.

■ THE JAZZ TRADITION

The Twenties and Thirties

By the late 1920s, jazz had become a mainstay of American popular dance music and had spread to Europe as well. Black American musicians were touring worldwide, even in such exotic places as China and India, and wherever they went, their music left an imprint. Yet there was still quite a gap between jazz at its best and the more commercially acceptable versions of it. Not until the advent of the so-called "Swing Era" did unadulterated jazz reach a level of popular acceptance which, thus far, remains unmatched.

This was first of all due to the big bands, which had reached a new height of artistic maturity. This was in no small degree the result of the efforts of Duke Ellington (1899–1974), rightly called the greatest American composer. His unique band, for which he gradually created a perfect balance between written and improvised elements, not least due to such great soloists as Johnny Hodges (alto sax), Harry Carney (baritone sax), Barney Bigard (clarinet), Cootie Williams and Rex Stewart (trumpets), began a most important engagement at Harlem's famous Cotton Club in late 1927. Via appearances there, regular network radio broadcasts, and many recordings, Ellington's music was widely disseminated. His band visited Europe for the first time in 1933.

Other important work was done by Redman and by Benny Carter (b.1907), a brilliant multi-instrumentalist and arranger-composer. Fletcher Henderson himself had not previously arranged for his band, but began to do so in the early 1930s and soon became one of the best. Such efforts laid the foundation for the success of Benny Goodman (1909–1987), a white clarinetist and band leader, who commissioned the best black arrangers and also was the first white band leader to hire black musicians (pianist Teddy Wilson in early 1936; vibraphonist Lionel Hampton later that year).

By 1936, the Swing Era was under way. Black dance styles set at such places as Harlem's Savoy Ballroom swept the nation, and young people jitterbugged to the sounds of an astonishing number of excellent bands. Those led by Jimmy Lunceford (1902–1947) and Count Basie (1905–1985) stood out among the many. The big bands spawned a host of gifted young players and also brought into the limelight many giants with established jazz reputations, such as Armstrong, who led his own big bands from 1929 to 1947.

The Post War Period

World War II brought economic and social changes that affected the big bands. Gasoline rationing impaired the constant touring that was one of their mainstays. The singers, whose popularity was first established through their work with the bands, became stars in their own right. After the war, the advent of television wrought fundamental changes in the ways people entertained themselves. Among the chief victims of the new stay-at-home trend was ballroom dancing. The big bands went into rapid de-

Jazz greats, Ella Fitzgerald, Oscar Peterson (piano), Roy Eldridge (trumpet), and Max Roach (drums) 1952.

cline, and only a handful maintained themselves, among them Ellington and Basie.

Meanwhile, the music itself had also undergone fundamental changes. The new generation of players who had come to maturity by way of big-band experiences were eager to express themselves at greater length than most big-band work permitted, and they were also coming up with new and potentially radical musical ideas.

The most advanced soloists of the Swing Era, such as Roy Eldridge (trumpet), Lester Young (tenor sax), Art Tatum (piano) and Sid Catlett (drums) had been extending the rhythmic, harmonic and technical resources of their instruments. Two young geniuses, both doomed to early death by tuberculosis, guitarist Charlie Christian (1916–1942), featured with Benny Goodman, and bassist Jimmy Blanton (1918–1942), featured with Duke Ellington, revolutionized the language of their respective instruments.

Christian was among the many notable players who participated in jam sessions (informal musical get-together) at Minton's Playhouse, a night club in Harlem, in the early 1940s. Here, where pianist Thelonious Monk and drummer Kenny Clarke were in the regular house band, experimentation took place that fed into the new jazz mainstream and led to the advent of modern jazz in 1944–45.

Bebop

The chief creators of this new jazz language were trumpeter (and band leader-composer) Dizzy Gillespie and alto saxophonist-composer Charlie Parker, both of whom had put in time with leading big bands. While working together in the band of pianist Earl HinesHines, Earl "Fatha" (the father of modern jazz piano style) in

1943, they began to solidify their mutually compatible ideas. When they joined forces in a small group in 1945, on records and in person, bebop (as the new jazz style soon was called) came into first flowering.

Though bebop was solidly grounded in earlier jazz styles, it did not seem that way to the public, which often was unable to follow the intricate rhythmic and harmonic elaborations of the boppers. Furthermore, the bop musicians, unlike most of the jazz players who preceded them, were not interested in pleasing the public, but more concerned with creating music that fulfilled their own artistic ambitions. (Gillespie himself, however, was something of an exception, perhaps because his irrepressible sense of humor made him a natural entertainer).

A New Audience

In any case, the advent of bop which had its beginnings in the Swing Era, went hand in hand with a change in the audience for jazz. By the mid-1930s, small clubs catering to jazz connoisseurs had begun to spring up in most larger urban areas. The biggest and most famous concentration was in New York, in two blocks on West 52nd Street, which soon became known as "Swing Street." In such clubs, musicians could perform for knowledgeable listeners without making musical compromises; most of them were too small for dancing, so people came strictly to listen. By this time, also, many people all over the world had become seriously interested in jazz. Some studied and documented its origins and history, others collected, researched and classified jazz records. Publications like *Downbeat* and *Metronome*, which catered to musicians and serious fans, sprang up. These magazines

Ornette Coleman

(In this way, the foundation was laid for the advent of rock music, which filled the need for young people to have their own music to dance to at a time when jazz had largely abandoned them. Nevertheless, rock was resented by many jazz musicians and fans. Eventually, of course, rock itself spawned its own constituency of "serious" performers, commentators, and magazines).

Bebop was in turn succeeded by more radical new forms of jazz, though it has shown considerable staying power. In 1959, a young Texas-born alto saxophonist, Ornette Coleman, brought his adventurous quartet to New York, setting off a huge controversy with music that seemed to have abandoned most of the harmonic and structural principles of jazz as it had hitherto been known. In fact, Coleman's music was deeply rooted in the blues and in well-established improvisational jazz procedures and in time his music was accepted as part of the jazz tradition.

conducted polls and presented awards, as was also done, by 1944, by the prestigious *Esquire* magazine, which presented these awards at a huge all-star jazz concert on the stage of the Metropolitan Opera House in New York.

Jazz concerts had been a rarity in the 1920s. Then in 1938, Goodman staged one at Carnegie Hall, and from 1943, Duke Ellington gave an annual concert there. By the late 1940s, jazz concerts were regular events, among them the famous "Jazz at the Philharmonic" all-star tours. Thus, in many ways the stage was set for the acceptance, albeit in a limited way, of jazz as a music that no longer could be considered mere entertainment, or music primarily meant for dancing, but music having parity with "classical" music in its claim to serious artistic consideration.

The Varied Sounds of Jazz

By then, in the radical 1960s, so-called avant garde jazz was very much evidence, in many and varied forms. The trumpeter Miles Davis, who had worked with Charlie Parker and also led his own very influential groups (one of them gave birth to a style known as cool jazz), hired a then little-known tenor saxophonist, John Coltrane, in 1956. With Coltrane, who also worked with Thelonious Monk, Davis introduced a modal approach (based on scales rather than harmonies) to jazz improvisation in 1958. Coltrane soon formed his own group, which took modality much further and extended improvisation, both in length and intensity, to a point of near-ecstasy. The pianist Cecil Taylor, a virtuoso of the keyboard, further stretched the boundaries of jazz. Davis himself experimented with electronics and rock and soul rhythms. The bassist and composer Charles Mingus, deeply influenced by Ellington and Parker, found new and imaginative ways of combining written and improvised jazz. Tenor saxophonist Sonny Rollins, while remaining rooted in traditional harmonic ground, expanded solo improvisation dramatically. And by the end of the 1960s, Albert Ayler, a tenor saxophonist with roots in rhythm-and-blues music, brought another new and intensely personal voice to jazz.

When Coltrane died suddenly in 1967, jazz was at the height of its experimental, expansionist stage, much of it inspired by the social and political upheavals of the time. By then, the term "free jazz" had begun to replace "avant garde," and many young musicians were following in the footsteps of Coltrane and other standard-bearers of innovation. But within a few years of Coltrane's passing, the storm quieted. There was some more experimentation, which was still going on within jazz in the late 1980s. Yet, by the early 1970s, it had become clear that the period of rapid and sometimes almost overpowering changes in jazz had come to an end.

In its place came a period of what might be called "peaceful coexistence" of many kinds of jazz. A goodly number of young musicians have turned to the rich tradition of jazz for inspiration, among them the gifted trumpeter Wynton Marsalis (also an expert classical player) and several other remarkable musicians from New Orleans, among them Wynton's slightly older brother Branford (tenor and soprano saxophones), trumpeter Terence Blanshard, and alto saxophonist Donald Harrison. These young players reject both "fusion" with electronics and rock and the practices of "free jazz," and look to the bebop tradition and even to Armstrong and Ellington for inspiration.

John Coltrane

Another, even more direct way of dealing with the jazz tradition is the emergence in the late 1980s of the so-called "repertory jazz." This refers to the performance of big band compositions and arrangements. The most notable of these ensembles is the Lincoln Center Jazz Orchestra, with Wynton Marsalis as artistic director, which specializes in the music of Ellington, and the Smithsonian Jazz Masterpiece Ensemble, jointly directed by David Baker and Gunther Schuller, two master musicians with classical as well as jazz training.

The many gifted players who emerged from Chicago's 1960s Association for the Advancement of Creative Music pursued their various approaches with stirring results, in such groups as the Art Ensemble of Chicago, the World Saxophone Quartet, and Lester Bowie's Brass Fantasy.

Wycliffe Lincoln, Wynton Marsalis, and Wes Anderson at the JVC Jazz Festival, 1991.

No one can predict where jazz will go next. After a long and remarkable period of intense innovation, the music seems to have reached a point where it is taking stock of its past while looking to the future. Whatever that future may bring, one thing is certain: the story of jazz is one of the most remarkable chapters in the history of twentieth century artistic creativity, and names like Armstrong, Ellington and Parker are bound to loom large when that history is finally written.

Born in the crucible of slavery, jazz has become the universal song of freedom. (It's no coincidence that neither Hitler nor Stalin had any use for jazz and tried, unsuccessfully, to banish it.) Perhaps Thelonious Monk put it best when he said that "jazz and freedom go hand in hand."

■ BLUES AND JAZZ BANDLEADERS, COMPOSERS, INSTRUMENTALISTS, AND SINGERS

Muhal Richard Abrams (1930–)
Pianist, Composer, Bandleader

Born in Chicago, Abrams began his professional career in 1948, playing with many of the city's best musicians and bands. In 1961, he formed the Experimental Band, which soon became an informal academy for Chicago's most venturesome players. Under Abram's quiet but firm guidance, this grew into the Association for the Advancement of Creative Music (AACM). The AACM helped young musicians perform and promote their own music, which could not be presented through established venues.

The AACM attracted such musicians as Roscoe Mitchell, Joseph Jarman, Lester Bowie, Malachi Favors, and Don Moye, who would later achieve world-wide prominence as the Art Ensemble of Chicago, as well as other future leaders of avant garde jazz. Though he never so appointed himself, Abrams was the recognized leader and moral and spiritual force behind the AACM. In 1976, when his brood had come of age and flown the coop, Abrams moved to New York and finally began to get some of the national and international recognition he had so long deserved. In 1990, he was the first recipient of the prestigious Danish "Jazzpar" Award. His work as a pianist and composer spans the entire range of the black musical tradition.

Lilian "Lil" Hardin Armstrong (1898–1971)
Pianist, Singer, Composer

Lil Armstrong was born in Memphis in 1898. Lil was a classically trained musician who received her music education at Fisk University. Her family moved from Memphis to Chicago somewhere around 1914 or 1915. One of her first jobs was selling sheet music in Jones music store in Chicago. It is said that she met Jelly Roll Morton while working there and it was Morton who influenced her style of hitting the notes "real heavy." She worked with the New Orleans Creole Jazz Band, The New Orleans Rhythm Kings, and King Oliver's Creole Jazz Band, where she met her husband Louis Armstrong. Lil and Louie were married in 1924. She played and wrote music for many of Armstrong's Hot Five and Hot Seven concerts and recordings and helped Louie polish his raw brilliant talent. The Armstrongs were divorced in 1938. She also played in various bands and some combos of her own. Two of her songs "Bad Boy" and "Just For a Thrill"

became big hits in the 1960s. While playing at a tribute to Louis Armstrong at Chicago's Civic Center Plaza, Lilian Armstrong collapsed and died of a heart attack on July 7, 1971.

Louis Armstrong (1901–1971)
Trumpeter

Born in New Orleans at the turn of the century, Louis Armstrong was one of the most influential and durable of all jazz artists, and quite simply, one of the most famous people in the entire world.

On New Year's Eve in 1914, Armstrong was arrested in New Orleans for firing a pistol and sent to the Colored Waifs Home. It was there that he first learned to play the cornet. His skill increased with the experience he gained from playing in the Home's band. When he was finally released from the institution, he was already proficient enough with the instrument to begin playing for money.

Befriended by his idol, King Oliver, Armstrong quickly began to develop the jazz skills which he had, until then, been able to admire only from a distance. When Oliver left for Chicago in 1919, a place opened for Armstrong as a member of the Kid Ory band in New Orleans.

In 1922, Oliver asked Armstrong to join him in Chicago as second cornet with his Creole Jazz Band. The duets between "Dippermouth" (as Armstrong was called) and "Papa Joe" (Oliver's nickname) soon became the talk of the Chicago music world.

Two years later Armstrong joined the Fletcher Henderson band at the Roseland Ballroom in New York City. In 1925, he returned to Chicago to play with Erskine Tate, switching from cornet to trumpet, the instrument he played from then on. During the next four years he made a series of recordings which profoundly influenced the course of jazz.

In 1929, Armstrong returned to New York and there, in the revue "Hot Chocolates," scored his first triumph with a popular song (Fats Waller's "Ain't Misbehavin'"). This success was a turning point in his career. He now began to front big bands, playing and singing popular songs rather than blues or original instrumentals.

In 1932, Armstrong headlined the show at the London Palladium, where he acquired the nickname "Satchmo." From 1933 to 1935 he toured Europe, returning to the United States to film *Pennies from Heaven* with Bing Crosby. He continued to evolve from the status of musician to that of entertainer, and his singing soon became as important as his playing. In 1947, he formed a small group, which was an immediate success. He continued to work in this context, touring throughout the world.

Armstrong scored a tremendous success in 1964 with his recording of "Hello Dolly," which bounced the Beatles from the top spot on the Top 40 list, a great feat in the age of rock. Though his health began to decline, he kept up his heavy schedule of international touring, and when he died in his sleep at home in Corona, Queens, two days after his seventieth birthday, he had been preparing to resume work in spite of a serious heart attack suffered some three months before. "The music—it's my living and my life" was his motto.

Louis Armstrong's fame as an entertainer in the later stages of his extraordinary career sometimes made people forget that he remained a great musician to the end. More than any other artist, Louis Armstrong symbolized the magic of jazz, a music unimaginable without his contribution. "You can't play a note on the horn that Louis hasn't already played," said Miles Davis. "I mean even modern." And contemporary musicians like Wynton Marsalis echo that opinion.

In 1988, on the strength of its use in the film *Good Morning Vietnam*, Armstrong's recording of "What A Wonderful World" became a surprise hit, climbing to number eleven on the Billboard chart. In 1992, a Louis Armstrong Archive was established at Queens College in New York. It contains his personal papers, private recordings, memorabilia, instruments, etc.

William "Count" Basie (1904–1984)
Pianist, Bandleader

Count Basie is generally regarded as the leader of the best jazz band in the United States, and consequently, one of the major influences on jazz as a whole.

Count Basie

His musical career ranges from a boyhood spent watching the pit band at the local movie theater (he later learned the organ techniques of Fats Waller by crouching beside him in the Lincoln Theater in Harlem) to his dual triumphs in 1957 when his became the first American band to play a royal command performance for the Queen of England, and the first black jazz band ever to play at the Waldorf Astoria Hotel in New York City.

During the early 1920s, Basie toured in vaudeville. Stranded in Kansas City, he joined Walter Page's Blue Devils. (Jimmy Rushing was the singer.) After this band broke up, Basie joined Benny Moten, and in 1935 formed his own band at the Reno Club in Kansas City, where a local radio announcer soon dubbed him "Count."

At the urging of critic John Hammond, Basie brought his group to New York City in 1936. Within a year he had cut his first record and was well on his way to becoming an established presence in the jazz world.

The Basie trademark was his rhythm section, which featured Basie's own clean, spare piano style and outstanding soloists like Lester Young and Sweets Edison in the early years, and Lucky Thompson, J. J. Johnson, Clark Terry, and Benny Powell in the later period.

Except for the years 1950 and 1951 when he had a small group, Basie led a big band for almost 40 years. Immune to changing fashion, the Basie band completed numerous global tours and successful recording engagements without ever suffering an appreciable decline in its popularity. In 1974, on his seventieth birthday, the Count was honored at a "Royal Salute" party by virtually every big name in jazz.

Count Basie was again honored at Radio City Music Hall in New York City in 1982.

Among those honoring The Count were Dionne Warwick and Lena Horne.

Sidney Bechet (1897–1959)
Saxophonist, Clarinetist

Sidney Bechet was the first jazzman to achieve recognition on the soprano saxophone, and also one of the first to win acceptance in classical circles as a serious musician.

In 1919, Bechet played in England and on the Continent with Will Marion Cook's Southern Syncopated Orchestra. Even before this, his clarinet and soprano sax had been heard in the bands of King Oliver and Freddie Keppard in his native New Orleans.

During the early 1920s Bechet made a series of records with Clarence Williams' Blue Five, worked briefly with Duke Ellington (one of his great admirers), and then returned to Europe. He came back to the United States with Noble Sissle and expanded his career, making many records. In 1949, he moved to France where he enjoyed the greatest success of his career. He died there in 1959. After his death, a statue of Bechet was erected in Antibes.

Art Blakey (1919–1990)
Drummer, Bandleader

One of the greatest drummers in jazz, Art Blakey was also one of the music's foremost talent spotters. After early experience with Fletcher Henderson and Mary Lou Williams, he joined Billy Eckstine's band in 1944 and took part in the birth of bebop. After working with many of the greatest modern jazz musicians, he formed his own Jazz Messengers in 1954 with immediate success.

From then on until his death, Blakey hired and helped to stardom a vast number of gifted players, among them Horace Silver,

Lee Morgan, Freddie Hubbard, Benny Golson, Woody Shaw, Wayne Shorter and Wynton Marsalis, to name but a very few. Blakey had one of the most powerful beats in jazz and took part in some of the finest recordings of his time.

Jimmy Blanton (1918–1942)
Bassist

During his brief life, Jimmy Blanton changed the course of jazz history by originating a new way of playing the string bass. Playing the instrument as if it were a horn, he lifted it from rhythmic back-up to melodic focal point.

Born in St. Louis, Missouri, he played with Jeter Pillars and Fate Marable before joining Duke Ellington in 1939. Until this time the string bass rarely played anything but quarter notes in ensemble or solos, but Blanton began sliding into eighth- and sixteenth-note runs, introducing melodic and harmonic ideas that were totally new to the instrument. His skill put him in a different class from his predecessors; it made him the first true master of the bass and demonstrated the instrument's unsuspected potential as a solo vehicle.

Blanton died of tuberculosis.

Buddy Bolden (1868–1931)
Cornetist

Buddy Bolden, a plasterer by trade, formed what may have been the first real jazz band in the 1890s in New Orleans. By the turn of the century, his cornet was so popular that he was often called upon to sit in with several bands on a single evening.

His cornet style was the starting point for a chain of musicians from King Oliver to Louis Armstrong to Dizzy Gillespie; put another way, from New Orleans to Chicago to New York. Because his career predates the recording of jazz, the only lasting memorial to his talent lies in the oral tradition which carries on his legend, and in the known successes of his descendants.

Bolden was committed to East Louisiana State Hospital in 1907, suffering from schizophrenia, and remained there until his death, never playing another note.

Clifford Brown (1930–1956)
Trumpeter, Composer, Bandleader

Clifford Brown's death at twenty-five in a car crash was one of jazz's great tragedies. Acclaimed as the greatest trumpet talent of his generation, Brown was on the brink of stardom as co-leader of the successful Clifford Brown-Max Roach Quintet (recently joined by Sonny Rollins); recording artist in his own right (his album with strings was very popular); and as a role model for aspiring jazz musicians (Brown had no vices, was raising a happy family, and was loved by all who knew him, not just for his music but also for his warm and gentle personality).

He studied music at the University of Maryland, but at twenty-one was injured, ironically, in a car accident that left him inactive for months. In 1952, he joined Chris Powell's R&B band (with which he made his first records), worked with the great composer-arranger Tadd Dameron, and toured Europe with Lionel Hampton's band. A year later, he teamed up with Max Roach and all seemed "go" until death struck, shocking the brilliant young trumpeter's friends and fans world-wide. Brown was also a gifted composer; tunes like "Joy Spring" and "Dahoud" are classics, as are Brown's recordings, which still influence young musicians more than thirty-seven years after his death.

Ray Brown (Raymond Matthews) (1926–)
Bassist

Ray Brown is perhaps the most versatile bass player in jazz today and is in demand around the world. He was born in Pittsburgh in 1926. In 1951, after having worked with Dizzy Gillespie and Charlie Parker, he joined Oscar Peterson's Trio—an association that lasted fifteen years. During this time, he and Peterson produced award-winning records and were in constant demand for concerts. Since leaving Peterson in 1966, Brown has joined forces with many famous artists in both live and recorded performances. He also works as a record producer and personal manager.

Benny Carter (1907–)
Saxophonist, Trumpeter, Composer, Bandleader

Bennett Lester Carter made his professional debut in 1923, and seventy years later still ranks at the top of jazz as an instrumentalist, composer-arranger and leader. In 1988, he toured Europe, visited Japan with his own band, performed in Brazil for the first time in his career, and recorded three albums. He continued at the same pace in 1993.

Admired and respected by generations of musicians, many of whom "went to school" in his bands (Sid Catlett, Miles Davis, J.J. Johnson, Max Roach and Teddy Wilson were some), Carter helped shape the language of big-band jazz. His scoring for saxophone sections was especially influential. On the alto saxophone, he and Johnny Hodges were the pacesetters before Charlie Parker and bebop. He has few peers as a trumpeter and has composed many standards.

Carter was the first black composer to break the color barrier in the Hollywood film studios. He scored many major films and TV shows ("M-Squad"). The subject of one of the best biographies of a jazz artist (*"Benny Carter: A Life in American Music"*), Carter received an honorary doctorate in music from Princeton University, where he taught, in 1974.

Ray Charles (1932–)
Singer, Pianist, Bandleader

Blinded at the age of six, Charles received his first musical training at a school for the blind in St. Augustine, Florida. Originally from Georgia, he left school at the age of fifteen to play local engagements. Two years later, he formed a trio which had some success in the Northwest. In 1954, he organized a seven-piece rhythm and blues group.

In 1957, his first LP was released, consisting of a potpourri of instrumentals drawn from pop, gospel, and modern jazz sources. His singing and piano playing found particular favor with a number of jazz artists who were drawing away from what they felt was a growing tendency for jazz to become overscored and underfelt. In Charles, they saw an artist who had restored both a sense of "soul" and instrumental "funkiness" to the jazz idiom. By the end of the 1960s, he had become one of the world's most popular performers and remains a star in the 1990s.

Charlie Christian (1916–1942)
Electric Guitarist

Charlie Christian did for the electric guitar what Jimmy Blanton did for the bass.

Christian joined Benny Goodman in 1939, and after only two years with the Goodman Sextet, achieved great fame as the first electric guitarist to play single-string solos. In his after-hour activities at such Harlem clubs as Minton's, he was an early contributor to the jazz revolution which would one day come to be called "Bop."

In 1941, he was hospitalized with tuberculosis, and died the following year. His recordings are still an inspiration to young guitarists.

Kenny Clarke (Liaqat Ali Salaam) (1914–1985)
Drummer

Kenny Clarke was one of the "founding fathers" of the Bop movement. Along with Dizzy Gillespie, and Thelonious Monk, Clarke made Minton's in Harlem the late-hour haunt for musicians in the 1940s.

A pioneer in the use of drums as a solo instrument and not just a background presence, he was one of the first musicians to move away from emphasis on the bass drum to a more flexible style in which he maintained a steady rhythm on the top cymbal while "dropping bombs" with surprise bass-drum punctuations.

From a musically-inclined Pittsburgh family, Clarke studied vibes, piano, and trombone as well as musical theory. His early professional experience was gained with Roy Eldridge and Edgar Hayes. (He traveled to Finland and Sweden with Hayes in 1937.)

In the early 1940s, he played with Teddy Hill and then moved into Minton's. Later he worked with Dizzy Gillespie, Coleman Hawkins, Tadd Dameron, and many others. In 1951, he toured with Billy Eckstine, and in the following year he helped organize the Modern Jazz Quartet, where he remained for the next three years. He moved to France in 1956 where he continued to work with a long list of visiting American talents, and co-led a fine "big band" with Belgian pianist and arranger Frency Boland from 1961 to 1972.

Ornette Coleman (1930–)
Saxophonist, Trumpeter, Violinist, Composer

Texas-born Ornette Coleman began his musical career in carnival and rhythm-and-blues bands. Fired by guitarist-singer Pee Wee Crayton for his unconventional style of playing, Coleman settled in Los Angeles, making his living as an elevator operator while studying music on his own. He began to compose and sat in at jam sessions, and made his first album in 1958. Encouraged by John Lewis, who recommended him for a scholarship to Gunther Schuller's Lennox School of Jazz in the summer of 1959, Coleman and his quartet (Don Cherry, pocket cornet; Charlie Haden, bass; Billy Higgins, drums) opened at the Five Spot in Manhattan, stirring up great debates among jazz musicians, critics and fans.

Coleman's music, while abandoning traditional rules of harmony and tonality, obviously wasn't the senseless noise that some heard it as. In fact, the music of the first Coleman quartet, which made many recordings, was very melodic, had a strong blues feeling, and sounds not at all startling. Eventually, Coleman was accepted by many of his peers. He continued to go his own way in music, creating a system he called "harmolodic," teaching himself to play trumpet and violin (the latter left-handed and amplified). In the seventies, he composed and performed a long work for symphony orchestra and alto sax, "The Skies of America," and in the 1980s, he formed Prime Time, a kind of jazz-fusion band with two electric guitars and two drummers. The original quartet was triumphantly reunited at the 1989 JVC Jazz Festival and also recorded again that year.

Though Coleman has influenced some players (Dewey Redman, Steve Coleman), his music remains a very personal means of expression; as such, it has much beauty and feeling to offer the open-minded listener.

John Coltrane (1926–1967)
Saxophonist, Bandleader

John Coltrane was the last great innovator in jazz to profoundly influence the course of the music. He played first clarinet, then alto saxophone in high school in his native North Carolina. After graduating, he moved to Philadelphia and continued to study music, winning several scholarships. After playing in a Navy band in Hawaii, he started his professional career with rhythm-and-blues bands, joining Dizzy Gillespie's big band (on alto) in 1949. When Dizzy broke up the band in 1951 and scaled down to a sextet, he had Coltrane switch to tenor sax and kept him with him. After stints with two great but very different alto saxophonists, Earl Bostic and Johnny Hodges, Coltrane was hired by Miles Davis in 1955. At first, some musicians and listeners didn't care for what they felt was Coltrane's "harsh" sound, but as the Davis Quintet became the most popular jazz group of its day, Coltrane was not only accepted but began to influence younger players. He briefly left Davis in 1957 to work with Thelonious Monk, an important relationship in developing what already was a highly original style. Back with Miles, he participated in the great *Kind Of Blue* record dates, and Miles' experiments with modal improvising set the stage for Coltrane's work as a leader.

In 1959, while still with Miles, he composed and recorded "Giant Steps," a piece so harmonically intricate and fast that it staggered most of his fellow saxophonists. With his own group, now including pianist McCoy Tyner, bassist Jimmy Garrison and drummer Elvin Jones, he recorded the song "My Favorite Things" from the musical and film *The Sound of Music*, in a performance that featured his soprano sax and lasted

John Coltrane

more than fifteen minutes, in 1960. This became such a hit with the jazz audience that it sustained Coltrane's popularity even when he began to experiment with very demanding music. The quartet became one of the most tightly knit groups in jazz history; the empathy between Coltrane and Elvin Jones was astonishing, and in their live performances, the four musicians would sometimes play for more than an hour, creating music so intense that some listeners likened it to a religious experience.

Coltrane was himself a deeply spiritual man. One of his masterpieces, the suite "A Love Supreme," was his offering to the Lord, and he wrote a poem to accompany the music. The quartet's live recordings at the Village Vanguard and Birdland also became instant classics, and Coltrane was regarded as the leading figure of the 1960s jazz avant garde, a position he himself did not seek, and which caused him (he was a very kind man who found it hard to say "no") to be surrounded, in the final stages of his life, by players who looked for exposure on his coat tails. The quartet broke up in 1966, and Coltrane searched for new roads of expression, never satisfied with his work at any given time in his career. His death at forty-one, of liver cancer, came as a shock to the jazz world. Since then, no comparably influential figure has come along, and Coltrane (or just "Trane," as he was known to many) has become a legend whose influence continues, though few have attempted to follow him into the uncharted realms of his final years, when he stretched both the physical and mental limits of what it was possible to do on a horn.

Miles Davis (1926–1991)
Trumpeter, Bandleader

Miles Davis played a major role in the transition from the hard, aggressive stance of Bop to the softer, more subtle side of jazz.

As a teenage musician in St. Louis in the early 1940s, Davis sat in with his idols Charlie Parker and Dizzy Gillespie when they passed through town with the Billy Eckstine Band.

In 1945, his well-to-do dentist father sent him to the Juilliard School of Music in New York. Within a short time, Davis was working the 52nd Street clubs with Parker and Coleman Hawkins, and touring with the bands of Billy Eckstine and Benny Carter.

In 1949, Davis formed a nine-piece band, including Lee Konitz, Gerry Mulligan, John Lewis, and Max Roach. The group was short lived, but its recordings had great impact on musicians and defined cool jazz.

Success came in 1956, the year after Davis had formed a quintet with John Coltrane featured on tenor sax, and the year in which he made his first record with arranger Gil Evans, "Miles Ahead." This was followed by two other collaborations with Evans, "Porgy and Bess" and "Sketches Of Spain," both landmarks in jazz. In 1958, came *Kind Of Blue*, an album by a new sextet, still with Coltrane, but with Cannonball Adderley added on alto sax and Bill Evans on piano. This album established modal improvisation in jazz and set the stage for Coltrane's explorations on his own.

Davis continued to introduce new ideas and give exposure to new talent. By 1964, he had Wayne Shorter on saxophones, Herbie Hancock on piano, Ron Carter on bass and the sensational eighteen-year-old Tony Williams on drums. This was a group that introduced new ideas, mostly in the realm of rhythmic and harmonic freedom. However, in 1968 Davis got restless again, attracted by the possibilities of electronic instruments. Hancock, Chick Corea, Joe Zawinul and Keith Jarrett were among the keyboard players who contributed to the new stage of Miles, starting with the album *Bitches Brew*.

Some of his many fans, and quite a few musicians, did not care for this new Miles, but characteristically, he couldn't have cared less. Going his own way, he gradually moved further away from jazz into contemporary black pop music, or rather, an unclassifiable and frequently changing music that appealed to a young audience not much interested in jazz. In the late 1970s, Miles became a cult figure, and his famous reserve (he had long been known for not acknowledging applause, walking off the stand when he wasn't playing, and being a difficult interview subject) was replaced by a new open manner that included smiling, waving to the audience and even shaking hands with those nearest the stage, and giving frequent and amiable interviews.

But those who saw Miles as a jazz star lost to pop didn't listen to his trumpet. No matter

Miles Davis

what the setting, it always spoke the language of jazz, creating beautiful sounds and melodies.

Eric Dolphy (1928–1964)
Alto Saxophonist, Clarinetist, Flutist

Eric Dolphy is greatly admired by musicians. Although his linear derivations were from Charlie Parker, his attack on alto sax and bass clarinet had a fierce bite that sprang from earlier jazz. His mastery of the bass clarinet has never been equaled.

Born in Los Angeles, his first recognition came with the Chico Hamilton quintet of 1958 to 1959. In 1960, he joined Charles Mingus in New York, and in 1961 he played many club dates with trumpeter Booker Little before joining John Coltrane for some historic tours, concerts, and recordings. Dolphy also played in a group with trumpeter Freddie Hubbard and recorded with Ornette Coleman. In 1964, while on tour again with Mingus, he decided to stay in Europe, where he recorded with Dutch, Scandinavian, and German rhythm sections. He died suddenly in Berlin of a heart attack possibly brought on by diabetes.

Dolphy was the winner of *Down Beat* magazine's New Star award for alto, flute, and miscellaneous instruments in 1961, and was elected to that magazine's Hall of Fame in 1965. His legacy includes many recordings for Prestige, Blue Note, Impulse, and smaller companies, both as leader and sideman.

Charles Mingus said of Dolphy that he had the "great capacity to talk in his music . . . he knew the level of language which very few musicians get down to."

Roy "Little Jazz" Eldridge (1911–1989)
Drummer, Trumpeter, Singer

Born in Pittsburgh, Roy Eldridge played his first "job" at the age of seven on drums. When he was fifteen and had switched to trumpet, he ran away from home with a carnival band. After playing with some of the best bands in the midwest, he arrived in New York in 1931, impressing the locals with his speed and range and finding jobs with good bands. But it wasn't until 1935 with Teddy Hill, that he could be heard on records. By the next year, he was the star of Fletcher Henderson's band, and in 1937, he put together his own group and made some records that stood other trumpeters on their ears. One of them was young Dizzy Gillespie, who had been listening to Roy on the radio since 1935 and tried his best to copy him. By 1938, Roy was setting the pace for swing trumpeters, playing higher and faster than even Louis Armstrong had dared anyone to do, and making musical sense as well. The fact that he was also a good singer didn't hurt.

In 1941, Roy, now known in the world of music as "Little Jazz," took up an offer from drummer Gene Krupa to join his big band, thus becoming the first black musician to be featured in a white band not just as a special attraction (like Teddy Wilson and Lionel Hampton with the Benny Goodman Quartet, though Hamp sometimes took over the drum chair in the Goodman band as well) but as a member of the band's section. Duetting with girl singer Anita O'Day, Roy scored

a smash hit for Krupa with "Let Me Off Uptown," while his instrumental feature "Rockin' Chair" was hailed as a jazz classic. Roy led his own big band for a while, but joined Artie Shaw, another white band, in 1944. A brief stint with his own big band followed, but small groups proved more viable. By 1949, Roy was a star of "Jazz At The Philharmonic," a touring concert group of famous players including, at that time, Charlie Parker, Lester Young and Buddy Rich. An offer to tour with a Benny Goodman small group brought him to Paris, where he stayed for a year and regained his confidence, a bit shaken by the advent of bebop and the trumpet innovations of his former disciple Gillespie. (Rivalry aside, the two always remained good friends and often recorded together.)

The 1950s and 1960s saw a long association with Coleman Hawkins; the two went together like ham and eggs. During this time Roy also backed Ella Fitzgerald and toured with JATP. A full decade, from 1970 on, found Little Jazz leading the house band at Jimmy Ryan's club in New York City, but a heart attack in 1980 put an end to his trumpet playing, though he still worked occasionally as a singer and gave lectures and workshops on jazz.

Roy Eldridge comprised, in his music and personality, the essence of jazz as a music that comes straight from, and goes straight to, the heart and soul.

Edward Kennedy "Duke" Ellington (1899–1975)
Bandleader, Composer, Pianist

Edward Kennedy Ellington, nicknamed Duke in his teens for his dapper dress style and courtly manners, was born into a middle-class family in Washington, D.C. After graduating from high school, he was offered an art scholarship at Pratt Institute in New York, but he already had a taste of band leading and preferred to stay with music. He had some success in his home town, mainly because he had the biggest band advertisement in the telephone book, but by 1923 he felt the urge to go to New York—where careers were made. He didn't succeed at first (he later said that he and his friends were so broke they had to split a hot dog three ways), but by 1924 he was leading his Washingtonians at a Broadway nightclub and making his first records. That early band was only five pieces, but it had grown to ten by the time the young pianist-composer opened at the Cotton Club, the most famous Harlem night spot.

Here the unique Ellington style evolved during a five-year stay. Unlike most other bands, Duke's played almost only his own music, though a few pop tunes were occasionally thrown in, and also unlike most other bands, Duke kept the same players with him once he'd decided that he liked what they could do. He had a great sense for their potential—almost like a great coach knows how to develop an athlete's skills—and some of Duke's bandsmen stayed with him for decades (none longer than baritone saxophonist Harry Carney, in the band from 1927 until the end). Many became stars in their own right (Johnny Hodges, alto sax; Cootie Williams, trumpet; Barney Bigard, clarinet) but somehow they always sounded better with Ellington, who knew just what to write for what he called their "tonal personalities." Ellington's scoring for the band was also strictly his own, and other arrangers found it hard to copy him.

By 1933, Ellington was ready for his first European tour; performing in London and Paris, the band, whose many recordings had prepared the way, was enthusiastically received. Back home, the band had already appeared in films and soon made more; they had long been well-exposed on radio and on records (Ellington was among the first musi-

cians to truly understand the importance of records, and the fact that making good ones required something different than playing in public). In 1935, deeply touched by the death of his mother, Ellington composed "Reminiscing in Tempo," his longest work to date, but most of his output was tailored to the time limit of a little over three minutes imposed by the 78 rpm technology.

The band reached a first peak in 1940, when almost all of the musicians had been aboard for many years, though the two exceptions, tenor Ben Webster and bassist Jimmy Blanton, who both joined in 1939, were of key importance to the music. So was a third newcomer, who didn't play in the band but quickly became essential to Ellington as an associate composer-arranger; this was Billy Strayhorn (1915–1967), who would spend the rest of his life with Duke and his men. A second peak was reached in 1956, when the band gave a tremendous performance at the Newport Jazz Festival, which fortunately was recorded; the album, highlighted by "Crescendo and Diminuendo In Blue," featuring twenty-seven choruses by tenorman Paul Gonsalves, became the best-selling Ellington record of all (and Duke made more records than any other jazz artist). It was Duke's success as a composer of popular songs that allowed him to keep the big band going through five decades; among them are "Solitude," "Mood Indigo," "Sophisticated Lady," "Satin Doll," and "Don't Get Around Much Any More." All began as instrumentals. Ellington's major longer works include "Black, Brown and Beige," "Harlem," "Such Sweet Thunder," and "Far East Suite," the last two in collaboration with Strayhorn.

Ellington and his astonishing creations have been an inspiration to generations of musicians, most recently to Wynton Marsalis, who both in his own composing and in his efforts to get Ellington's music per-

James Reese Europe

country. Following his return to the United States, Europe toured the country with his band. In 1919 he was stabbed to death by a member of his band while on tour.

Ella Fitzgerald (1918–   )
Singer

Ella Fitzgerald has emerged as the top female vocalist in virtually every poll conducted among jazz musicians and singers. No other vocalist has been so unanimously acclaimed. She is fondly known as "The First Lady of Song."

Discovered in 1934 by drummer-band leader Chick Webb at an amateur contest at Harlem's Apollo Theater in New York City, she cut her first side with Webb a year later. In 1938, she recorded "A Tisket, A Tasket," a novelty number which brought her commer-

formed live (as with the Lincoln Center Jazz Ensemble) has done much to keep the Ellington legacy in the forefront of American music. There can be no doubt that Duke Ellington (who was also a brilliant pianist) will stand as one of the greatest composers of the 20th century.

James Reese Europe (1881–1919)
Bandleader

James Resse Europe was born in Mobile, Alabama in 1881, but later moved to New York. In 1906 he organized the New Amsterdam Musical Association and in 1910 formed the Clef Club orchestra.

During World War I, Europe directed the 369th Infantry Regimental Band, which performed throughout France and was a major force in the development of jazz in that

Ella Fitzgerald

cial success and made her name widely known among the general public. Among musicians, however, her reputation rests on her singular ability to use her voice like an instrument, improvising effortlessly in a style filled with rhythmic subtleties.

For more than fifty years Ella Fitzgerald has been the leading jazz interpreter of popular song.

Tommy Flanagan (1930–   )
Pianist

Detroit-born Tommy Flanagan came to New York in the mid-1950s as part of the "Motor City" invasion of gifted jazzmen (fellow pianist Barry Harris; trumpeters Thad Jones and Donald Byrd; guitarist Kenny Burrell, etc.) and soon was much in demand for recordings and "live" dates with all the great names in modern jazz. A long stint as Ella Fitzgerald's accompanist and musical director (a role he also filled, much more briefly, with Tony Bennett) kept Flanagan out of the limelight, but since the mid-1970s, as leader of his own fine trios and recording prolifically in the United States, Europe and Japan, he has assumed his rightful place as one of the greatest living masters of jazz piano, his touch alone a thing of beauty.

Erroll Garner (1921–1977)
Pianist, Composer

A keyboard artist who played and composed by ear in the tradition of the founding fathers of jazz, Erroll Garner won the international acclaim of jazz lovers, music critics, and the general public. Strong and bouncy left-hand rhythms and beautiful melodies are the trademarks of his extremely enjoyable music. He was the best-selling jazz pianist in the world.

Born in Pittsburgh, Garner grew up in a musical family and began picking out piano melodies before he was three years old. He started taking piano lessons at six, but his first and only piano teacher gave up on him when she realized he was playing all his assignments by ear instead of learning to read notes. At seven, he began playing regularly on Pittsburgh radio station KDKA. He dropped out of high school to play with a dance band and first came to New York in 1939 as an accompanist for nightclub singer Ann Lewis. In 1946, he recorded "Laura," which sold a half million copies, and his fame began to grow. On March 27, 1950 he gave a solo recital at Cleveland's Music Hall, and in December a concert at New York's Town Hall. Gradually recitals and recording sessions took precedence over nightclub performances.

Garner's most famous composition, "Misty" was a big hit for Johnny Mathis and Sarah Vaughan. His unique piano style has often been copied but never equaled.

Dizzy Gillespie (1917–1993)
Trumpeter, Bandleader

Dizzy Gillespie and Charlie Parker were the co-founders of the most revolutionary movement in jazz during the 1940s—the phenomenon known as Bop. The role which each played in this revolution has been a subject of considerable debate. Billy Eckstine, whose band at one time included both Gillespie and Parker, defined Parker's role more as instrumentalist, and Gillespie's more as writer and arranger. Whatever their particular contributions were, however, it cannot be disputed that the sum total of their ideas brought about a change in jazz which continues to the present time.

Gillespie received his early musical training in his native South Carolina, and after

Dizzy Gillespie

moving to Philadelphia in 1935 and gaining more professional experience there, joined the Teddy Hill band where he replaced his early idol Roy "Little Jazz" Eldridge.

He toured Europe with Hill in 1939, and when he returned to New York to play with Cab Calloway, his bop experimentation was already beginning to develop and his career as arranger began. After working with Ella Fitzgerald, Benny Carter, Charlie Barnet, Earl Hines, and others, he joined Eckstine's band in 1944 and started his own jazz band the next year.

Gillespie toured Europe, the Middle East, and Latin America with big bands and quintets, subsidized by the United States State Department. He became a revered elder statesman of jazz.

Dexter Gordon (1923–1989)
Saxophonist, Bandleader

Born in Los Angeles, the son of a prominent physician whose patients included famous jazz musicians, Dexter Gordon joined Lionel Hampton's newly formed big band in 1940. He was with Louis Armstrong in 1944, and later that year joined the Billy Eckstine Band. After freelancing in New York, he returned home and in 1946 recorded a "tenor battle," "The Chase," with Wardell Gray, which became one of the biggest modern jazz hits. He then teamed up with Gray on and off until 1952, after which he temporarily disappeared from the jazz spotlight.

Gordon made a major comeback in the early 1960s with a series of much-acclaimed recordings. In 1962, he settled in Copenhagen, and the Danish capital became his

Dexter Gordon

forming his own group and winning many new fans. In 1986, he starred in the French feature film *Round Midnight*, in which his portrayal of a character based on Lester Young and Bud Powell won him an Oscar nomination as best actor. In 1988, he began work on an autobiography.

Dexter Gordon was the premier tenor saxophone stylist of bebop, but his strong, swinging music transcends categories. He greatly influenced the young John Coltrane.

Johnny Griffin (1928–)
Saxophonist

Johnny Griffin was born in Chicago and played with most of the prominent jazz personalities over the years. Among them have been Lionel Hampton, Art Blakey, Thelonious Monk, and Eddie Lockjaw Davis. Griffin, like many Chicago musicians, pre-

headquarters for the next fourteen years, though he made brief playing visits to his homeland. In 1977, he came home for good,

Lionel Hampton and his orchestra.

Herbie Hancock

ferred to stay and play in the Windy City, and much of his early development took place there. In December 1962, he moved to Europe and played all over the continent. He lived in Paris in the late 1960s and later moved to the Netherlands, where he owned a farm. In the late 1970s, Griffin moved back to the United States, celebrating the occasion with outstanding concerts and recordings with his friend Dexter Gordon.

Lionel Hampton (1909–   )
Vibraphonist, Pianist, Bandleader

Lionel Hampton was the first jazz musician to feature the vibes, an instrument which has since come to play a vital role in jazz. His first recorded effort on the instrument was in 1930 on "Memories of You," which featured Louis Armstrong, then fronting the Les Hite band in California.

Hampton later left Hite's band to form his own Los Angeles group. When Benny Goodman heard him in 1936, he used him on a record date with Teddy Wilson and Gene Krupa, and then persuaded him to join on a permanent basis.

Hampton played with the Goodman Quartet until 1940, the year he formed his own big orchestra. The following year, it scored its first big hit: "Flyin' Home."

Hampton has enjoyed great success since then, and continued to tour the world even after passing his eightieth birthday in 1989. Dozens of musicians who later became famous started in his band.

Herbie Hancock (1940–)
Keyboardist, Composer, Bandleader

Herbie Hancock was born in Chicago and has notably been associated with the piano, although he has also turned to electronics as a vehicle of communication in his music: electric guitar, electric bass, electric piano, echoplex, phase shifter, and synthesizer. From 1963 to 1968, he traveled and played with Miles Davis, establishing himself as a composer and instrumentalist of the first rank. While with Davis, Hancock recorded with numerous other groups and became firmly established as a major jazz figure. He has won many awards, including *Down beat* Jazzman of the Year in 1974 and *Cash Box* and *Playboy* Awards of the Year in 1974. Hancock has also written film scores and television specials.

William Christopher Handy (1873–1958)
Trumpeter, Composer, Bandleader

Although he began as a cornetist and bandleader in the 1890s, W.C. Handy's fame as the "Father of the Blues" rests almost entirely on his work as a composer.

After studying at Kentucky Musical College, Handy toured with an assortment of musical groups, becoming the bandmaster of the Mahara Minstrels in 1896.

In 1909, during a political campaign in Memphis, Handy wrote "Mr. Crump," a campaign song for E. H. "Boss" Crump. Three years later, the song was published as the "Memphis Blues."

In 1914, Handy published his most famous song, "St. Louis Blues," and that same year,

William Christopher Handy

also wrote "Yellow Dog Blues." Others which have become perennial favorites are "Joe Turner Blues" (1915), "Beale Street Blues" (1916); "Careless Love" (1921); and "Aunt Hagar's Blues" (1922).

In the 1920s, Handy became a music publisher in New York. Despite his failing sight, he remained active until his death in 1958. His songs extended beyond the world of jazz to find their way into the general field of popular music in many forms. Their popularity continues unabated today.

Coleman Hawkins (1904–1969)
Saxophonist

With the position occupied by the tenor saxophone in jazz today, it is difficult to imagine that until Coleman Hawkins came along, this instrument was not seriously considered as a suitable jazz vehicle. The full, rich tone which Hawkins brought to the tenor has helped make it one of the most vital instruments in the contemporary jazz ensemble.

When Hawkins took up the tenor at the age of nine, he had already had four years of training on piano and cello. He continued his studies at Washburn College in Topeka, Kansas and in 1922 toured with Mamie Smith's Jazz Hounds. In 1924, he began a ten-year stint with Fletcher Henderson's band.

Hawkins left Henderson in 1934 to tour England and the Continent, recording with Django Reinhardt, Benny Carter, and others. When he returned to the United States in 1939, he recorded his biggest hit, "Body and Soul," with his own band.

Unlike many of his contemporaries, Hawkins was open to the experimentation of the young musicians of the 1940s. In 1944, for example, he formed an all-star band for the first Bop record session, and he gave help and encouragement to Dizzy Gillespie, Charlie Parker, Thelonious Monk and others he admired.

With the advent of the "cool school," Hawkins lapsed into temporary decline, but the power of his style was recognized anew and he became a revered elder statesman of jazz.

Roy Haynes (1925–)
Drummer, Bandleader

Boston-born Roy Haynes is one of the originators and greatest exponents of modern jazz drumming. Turning pro in his late teens, he went on the road with Luis Russell's big band, then joined Lester Young's sextet, with which he established his reputation. Settling in New York, he worked with Charlie Parker and Dizzy Gillespie, then toured for several years in Sarah Vaughan's trio.

Other important associations include Stan Getz, Gary Burton, Thelonious Monk and John Coltrane, for whom he was first choice when Elvin Jones was unavailable. Haynes recorded prolifically with these and many others, also as leader of his own groups, known from the 1980s on as the "Hip Ensemble." Haynes is both a fantastic soloist and a great, creative ensemble drummer. His foot is undoubtedly the fastest ever, and his playing has an elegance that is reflected in his always stylish appearance—he was once chosen by *Esquire* magazine as one of America's 10 best-dressed men. Never out of date, Haynes in his sixties teamed up the such modernists as Pat Metheny and Chick Corea, and always picks young players for his group.

Fletcher Henderson (1897–1952)
Bandleader, Arranger, Piano

Born in Georgia, the son of an educator, Fletcher Henderson came to New York in 1920 to study chemistry, but took a job to earn some extra money as house pianist and musical director for Black Swan, the first black-owned and operated record company. Chemistry soon took a back seat, and in 1924 he was persuaded by some of his recording studio colleagues to audition with a band for a new club. They got the job, and soon graduated to the Roseland Ballroom on Broadway, where they resided for eight years, also touring and making hundreds of records.

The Henderson band was the first big band to play interesting jazz, and it became an incubator for some of the greatest stars of the day, among them Louis Armstrong, Coleman Hawkins and Benny Carter. It was the arranger and saxophonist Don Redman who shaped the band's early style. When he left in 1928, Carter and others, including Fletcher's younger brother Horace, also a

The Fletcher Henderson Orchestra, 1927.

pianist and arranger, took over. It was not until 1933 that Fletcher himself began to write full-time for his band, but he had such a talent for arranging that he soon became one of the architects of swing. Ironically, just as he hit his stride as a writer, his band fell on hard days, and for a brief while he gave it up and became a freelance arranger, contributing mightily to the library of the newly formed Benny Goodman Band.

Though he took up leading again soon, and had such greats as Ben Webster, Chu Berry and Roy Eldridge in his bands, he never again achieved the success of the 1920s.

music at Wayne State University in Detroit, where he played with visiting stars like Sonny Stitt and had his own first group in 1960. After military service, he came to New York where he co-led a band with trumpeter Kenny Dorham, then joined Horace Silver in 1964, and Herbie Hancock in 1969. Since the '70s, he has led his own groups and continued to develop an original and ultimately influential solo style.

Among his compositions, which other musicians like to play, are "Recordame," "Tetragon," and "Isotope." He won a Grammy Award in 1993 for his fine album of Billy Strayhorn compositions.

Joe Henderson (1937–)
Saxophonist, Composer

One of the foremost tenor stylists of the post-Coltrane era, Joe Henderson studied

Earl "Fatha" Hines (1903–1983)
Pianist, Bandleader

Except for increased technical proficiency, the piano style of Earl "Fatha" Hines has barely changed from what it was in the late 1920s.

Hailing from a Pittsburgh background musically rounded out by his trumpeter father and organist mother, Hines originally planned a concert career, but was soon caught up in the world of jazz. Forming his own trio while still in high school. he began to play in local clubs before moving on to Chicago in 1925.

While there, he made a brilliant series of records with Louis Armstrong's Hot Five, and soon became known as "the trumpet-style pianist." The intricacy of his style was well beyond that of his contemporaries, but served as a touchstone for a succeeding generation of pianists.

In 1928, Hines formed his own band at the Grand Terrace in Chicago. For the next twenty years, this band served as a proving ground for many great instrumentalists and innovators of the period (from Bud Johnson and Trummy Young in the early era to Dizzy Gillespie and Charlie Parker in the later years).

From 1948 to 1951, Hines worked again with Armstrong, then played a long engagement in San Francisco. In 1963, a New York recital revitalized his career, and he enjoyed great success in Europe, Japan, and at home until his death.

Milton J. "Milt" Hinton (1910–   )
Bass

Milt Hinton was born in Vicksburg, Mississippi and is considered one of the greatest of bass players. He has played with many top jazz artists, including Cab Calloway, Count Basie, Louis Armstrong, Teddy Wilson, and Benny Goodman. Hinton has appeared in concerts throughout the world and on numerous television shows, and has made more records than any other jazz musician. He is also an accomplished photographer and writer, whose autobiography, *Bass Lines*, appeared in 1988.

Billie Holiday (1915–1959)
Singer

Billie Holiday, dubbed "Lady Day" by Lester Young, was one of the greatest jazz singers of all time.

While still a young girl, she moved from her hometown of Baltimore to New York City, and in 1931 began her singing career in an assortment of Harlem night spots. In 1933, she cut her first sides with Benny Goodman, and from 1935 to 1939, established her reputation with a series of records made with Teddy Wilson. She also sang with the bands of Count Basie and Artie Shaw.

In such classic records as "Strange Fruit" and her own "God Bless the Child," she departed from popular material to score her greatest artistic triumphs, depicting the harsh reality of Southern lynchings and the personal alienation she had experienced.

Once addicted to drugs and alcohol, she had written in her 1956 autobiography, *Lady Sings the Blues*, "All dope can do for you is kill you—and kill you the long, slow, hard way." The subject of a feature film, several books, and videos, Billie Holiday is still a powerful force in music decades after her untimely death.

Howlin' Wolf (1910–1976)
Singer, Harmonica Player

Blues singer and harmonica player Howlin' Wolf was born Chester Arthur Burnett in West Point, Mississippi. He learned to play the harmonica from blues musician Sonny Boy Williamson and made his first recording in 1950; his baying style of singing won him the name Howlin' Wolf. His

Billie Holiday

best known recordings include, "Moanin' at Midnight," "Poor Boy," and "My Country Sugar Mama."

Jean-Baptiste "Illinois" Jacquet (1933–)
Saxophonist, Bandleader

Born in Louisiana and raised in Texas, the man who contributed to making the tenor sax the most popular jazz horn began as an altoist; it was Lionel Hampton who made him switch to tenor when he joined the vibist's new big band in 1942. Soon thereafter, Jacquet recorded his famous solo on "Flyin' Home" and made both his own and the Hampton band's name.

After stints with Cab Calloway and Count Basie, Jacquet joined the Jazz at the Philharmonic touring group in which he starred in tenor "battles" with Flip Phillips and others. He soon formed his own swinging little band, and became a mainstay in the international jazz circuit, a position he still occupied in the early 1990s. He formed a fine big band in the 1980s which has toured Europe and recorded; the European tour and other incidents in Jacquet's life as a musician are part of the documentary film *Texas Tenor*, premiered at the 1992 JVC Jazz Festival.

Jacquet was one of the first to "overblow" the tenor sax, reaching high harmonics that were dismissed by some as a circus stunt but really got to audiences; eventually, of course, such overblowing became part and parcel of the instrument's vocabulary, as in the later work of John Coltrane and the style of David Murray. But Jacquet is also a warm ballad player, and first of all, one of the swingingest of tenormen.

J. J. Johnson (1924–)
Trombonist, Bandleader

J.J. Johnson is the unchallenged master of the modern jazz trombone. He is the first musician to have adapted this instrument to the demanding techniques called for by the advent of Bop.

Early in his career, Johnson displayed such skill in performing high-speed and intricate solos that those who knew him only from records found it hard to believe that he was actually using a slide—and not a valve—trombone.

Johnson spent the 1940s with the bands of Benny Carter, Count Basie, and Dizzy Gillespie. During the those years, his trombone was as widely imitated as the trumpet and alto of Gillespie and Parker.

In the 1950s, Johnson retired for a time, only to return as partner of fellow trombonist Kai Winding's in the Jay and Kai Quintet. This group enjoyed great success.

Johnson's ability as a composer has been widely praised. In 1959, he performed several of his works with the Monterey Festival Orchestra. He has also composed for films and TV and has been active as a teacher.

James P. Johnson (1894–1955)
Pianist, Composer

James P. Johnson is less known than his most famous protege, Fats Waller, but he made a substantial contribution to the fields of jazz piano and popular show music.

Johnson was the master of the "stride piano," an instrumental style which derives its name from the strong, striding, left hand of the player. "Stride piano" came into its own during the 1920s, particularly in conjunction with the phenomenon known as the "rent party." Such a party was held for the purpose of raising rent money, and involved the payment of an admission fee which entitled a patron to food, drink, conviviality, and a stride piano session. Duke Ellington and Count Basie were among the many who sharpened their skills in the rent party training ground.

Johnson was also an early bridge between the worlds of jazz and Broadway. Numbered among his song hits are "If I Could Be With You," "Charleston," and "Runnin' Wild."

Elvin Jones (1927–)
Drummer, Bandleader

The youngest of the remarkable Jones Brothers (see Hank and Thad Jones) broke in with bands in Detroit (near his native Pontiac, Michigan), came to New York in the '50s, and worked with such notables as J.J. Johnson, Sonny Rollins and Donald Byrd before joining John Coltrane's quartet in 1960.

With this group—the most influential of its time—Elvin Jones astonished musicians and listeners with his awesome independence of limbs (he can keep four rhythms going at once), amazing drive (nothing seemed able to tire him out, no matter how fierce the tempo), and ability to respond within mini-seconds to Coltrane's furious flow of ideas.

Elvin Jones left Coltrane when the saxophonist added another drummer to his group (no doubt influenced by his new wife, the pianist Alice McLeod) and soon led his own groups, which almost always have featured fine saxophonists; in 1992, Coltrane's son Ravi joined him. One of jazz's master drummers, Elvin Jones integrated the drums with the front-line (melody) players to a further extent than anyone had done before, always maintaining the pulse.

Hank Jones (1918–   )
Pianist

The eldest of the three remarkable Jones Brothers (see Elvin and Thad Jones) was raised near Detroit, where he began his professional career. He came to New York in 1944 and worked and recorded with the great trumpeter and singer Hot Lips Page. His brilliant keyboard technique and skill as both soloist and accompanist soon found him in the company of such giants as Coleman Hawkins and Charlie Parker. He toured with Jazz at the Philharmonic and became Ella Fitzgerald's accompanist.

Settling into studio work in New York, Hank Jones became one of the most-recorded jazz musicians—he is to piano what Milt Hinton and George Duvivier were to the bass—in all sorts of contexts. From the 1970s on, happily, Hank Jones began to do more work in clubs and on tour and to record more as a soloist and trio leader, often billed as "The Great Jazz Trio," with various star bassists and drummers.

In the 1990s, Jones is still at the head of the pack when it comes to great jazz piano.

Thad Jones (1923–1986)
Cornetist, Composer, Arranger, Bandleader

The middle brother of the gifted Jones family (see Elvin and Hank Jones), in his early teens Thad played in a band led by brother Hank and in the early 1950s was in a band that included Elvin. Coming to New York in 1954, he was quickly discovered by Charles Mingus, who recorded him for his Debut label and hailed him as the greatest jazz trumpeter (but Thad always preferred the cornet) since Dizzy Gillespsie. Thad joined Count Basie's band that same year, staying for almost a decade. During this time he honed his writing skills, but wasn't heard as much in solo as Joe Newman and other section-mates whose styles were not as harmonically advanced as Thad's. However, he did solo on Basie's biggest instrumental hit, "April In Paris."

In New York in 1963, Thad Jones joined forces with the great drummer Mel Lewis to co-lead what began as a rehearsal band but soon became the most talked-about new big band in jazz. As the Thad Jones-Mel Lewis Jazz Orchestra, it gave new life to the language of big-band jazz as Thad Jones blossomed as a composer and arranger of music that was swinging but fresh. Perhaps his best-known composition, however, is the beautiful ballad "A Child Is Born." The band held together until 1979, when Thad Jones moved to Denmark and Mel took over, keeping much of Thad's "book" alive. Thad led his own bands in Scandinavia, then came home in 1985 to briefly take on leadership of the Count Basie Band, returning to Denmark in ill health six months prior to his death in August 1986.

B. B. King (1925–   )
Singer, Guitarist, Bandleader

B.B. King is one of the most successful artists in the history of the blues. B.B.'s career started when, as a boy of 14 in Indianola, Mississippi, he met a preacher who played the guitar. B.B. soon owned his own guitar, which he bought for eight dollars, paid out of meager wages he earned working in the cotton fields. From that time on, B.B. spent his spare time singing and playing the guitar with other budding musicians in the town, and listening to blues guitarists who came to Indianola clubs. In the early 1940s, he would travel to a nearby town where he would stand on street corners and play. Sometimes he'd come home with as much as twenty-five dollars.

After the war, B.B. hitchhiked to Memphis where a relative who was a musician got him a performing job at the 16th Street Grill. He was paid twelve dollars a night, five nights a week, and room and board. B.B. then found a spot on a newly opened radio station in Memphis called WDIA. He played ten minutes each afternoon, then became a disc jockey. The station named him "The Boy from Beale Street" and thereafter Riley B. King was known as "B.B."

B.B.'s first record was made in 1949 for RPM. He had a number one disc on the rhythm and blues charts in 1950 and has been known nationally ever since. A change of managers led to a new direction away from the "chitlin' circuit" and into prestigious "pop"-oriented clubs, colleges, and the fastgrowing field of pop festivals.

B.B. King

A series of personal appearances on major television shows sparked his popularity. In 1969, B.B. toured Europe, for the first of many times, starting with the Royal Albert Hall in London and continuing through England, France, Germany, Switzerland, Denmark, and Sweden. Returning to the United States, he joined a fourteen-city tour with the Rolling Stones. Twenty years later, he toured with the Stones again.

Rahsaan Roland Kirk (1936–1977)
Composer, Flutist, Saxophonist

At first called "gimmicky" by critics, Roland Kirk proved to be one of the most exciting jazz instrumentalists. His variety of instruments was matched only by the range of his improvisational styles, often switching in the middle of a number from a dissonant exploration to a tonal solo based on a conventional melody.

Born in Columbus, Ohio, Kirk was technically blind, having been able to see nothing but light from infancy. Educated at the Ohio State School for the Blind, he began picking up horns at the age of nine. At nineteen, while touring with Boyd Moore, he started experimenting with playing more than one instrument at a time. Finding obscure horns like the stritch and the manzello, he worked out a technique for playing three-part harmony through the use of false fingering.

In 1960, Ramsey Lewis helped Kirk get his first important recording date (with Argo Records). In 1961, he played with Charles Mingus' group, and later that year he went on the international circuit.

Among his many compositions are "Three for Dizzy"; "Hip Chops"; "The Business Ain't Nothin' but the Blues"; "From Bechet, Byas, & Fats"; and "Mystical Dreams."

John Lewis (1920–   )
Pianist, Composer, Bandleader

John Lewis has become an international force in the world of jazz as an arranger, conductor, composer, and instrumentalist.

Raised in a middle-class environment in Albuquerque, New Mexico, Lewis studied music and anthropology at the University of New Mexico until 1942. After three years in the Army, he went to New York City and soon became pianist and arranger with Dizzy Gillespie's band. Two years later at Carnegie Hall, Gillespie's band performed Lewis' first major work, "Toccata for Trumpet and Orchestra."

After a European tour with Gillespie, Lewis returned to the United States to play with Lester Young and Charlie Parker, and to arrange for Miles Davis. In 1952, after having finished his studies at the Manhattan School of Music, Lewis founded the group upon which a major part of his reputation rested: The Modern Jazz Quartet (MJQ). Though it briefly disbanded in 1974, the MJQ was still together in 1993.

Lewis has never confined his creativity to the MJQ but has assumed a variety of roles, ranging from conducting in Europe and Japan to serving as music director of the highly acclaimed Monterey Jazz Festival.

Abbey Lincoln (1940–   )
Singer

Born Anna Marie Wooldridge in Chicago, Lincoln graduated from Kalamazoo Central High School in Kalamazoo, Michigan and later studied music for a number of years in Hollywood under several prominent vocal and dramatic coaches.

She began her professional career in Jackson, Michigan in 1950. Since then she has performed in movies (*Nothing but a Man*), made many records (*Abbey Is Blue, Straight Ahead*), played prominent clubs, and appeared on nationwide television. More important, she has been hailed by many outstanding black jazz performers, including Coleman Hawkins, Benny Carter, and Charles Mingus, as a singer to be classed with the likes of Billie Holiday.

Melba Liston (1926–   )
Arranger, Trombonist

Melba Liston, who has played with the greatest names in jazz, is one of the very few female trombonists. Born in Kansas City, Missouri in 1926, Liston's family later moved to California. Her musical history began in 1937, in a youth band under the tutelage of Alma Hightower. Ms. Liston continued her trombone studies, in addition to music composition, throughout high school. She got work with the Los Angeles Lincoln Theater upon graduation. She met band leader Gerald Wilson on the night club circuit, and he introduced her to Dizzy Gillespie, Count Basie, Duke Ellington, Charlie Parker and many others. By the late 1940s, she was playing alongside John Coltrane and John Lewis in Dizzy's band, and later toured with Billie Holiday as her assistant musical director and arranger. When the Big Band era waned, Liston jumped off the music circuit and returned to California, where she passed a Board of Education examination and taught for four years. She was coaxed back into performing by Dizzy, and during the next twenty years, led an all-female jazz group, toured Europe with Quincy Jones, and did arrangements for Ellington, Basie, Dizzy and Diana Ross. In 1974, she went to Jamaica to explore reggae. When she returned to the United States in 1979, she formed Melba Liston and Company, in which she revived swing, bebop and contemporary compositions, many of which were her own. She is regarded as a brilliant and creative arranger and an exceptional trombonist by her peers.

Jimmy Lunceford (1902–1947)
Bandleader

"The Lunceford style"—although its originator himself never played an instrument while recording with his band (except flute in his recording of "Liza")—was one which influenced many band leaders and arrangers up to the 1950s. The Lunceford band reigned with those of Duke Ellington, Count Basie, and Benny Goodman as the leading and most influential of the big jazz orchestras in the 1930s.

A native of Fulton, Missouri, Lunceford received his B.A. at Fisk University and later studied at City College in New York. After having become proficient on all reed instruments, Lunceford began his career as a leader in Memphis in 1927. By 1934, he was an established presence in the field of jazz. During the next decade, the Lunceford band was known as the best-disciplined and most showmanly black jazz ensemble in the nation and featured a host of brilliant instrumentalists.

The Lunceford vogue faded after 1943, by which time the band was already experiencing charges in personnel. Lunceford died of a heart attack in 1947 while the band was on tour.

Branford Marsalis (1960–)
Saxophonist, Bandleader

Fourteen months older than his brother Wynton, Branford has gained equal fame, not least due to his wide exposure as band leader for the "Tonight" show, which started with Jay Leno's incumbency. Branford has also been seen beyond the jazz arena during his mid-1980s stint with Sting, and bit acting parts in several feature films.

Branford Marsalis is a very gifted player whose many recordings, including some as sideman with brother Wynton, show him to be a warm and consistently inventive soloist and an imaginative leader-organizer. Though he is more inclined to adapt himself to contemporary surroundings than Wynton, he is also solidly grounded in the jazz tradition.

Wynton Marsalis (1961–)
Trumpeter, Bandleader

Born into a musical family in New Orleans (his father, Ellis Marsalis, is a prominent pianist and teacher), Wynton Marsalis was well-schooled in both the jazz and classical traditions. At seventeen, he won an award at the prestigious Berkshire Music Center for his classical prowess; a year later, he left the Juilliard School of Music to join Art Blakey's Jazz Messengers.

After touring and recording in Japan and the United States with Herbie Hancock, he made his first LP in 1981, formed his own group, and toured extensively on his own. Soon he made a classical album, and in 1984 became the first instrumentalist to win simultaneous Grammy Awards as best jazz and classical soloist, with many other awards to follow. He also received a great deal of media coverage—more than any other serious young musician in recent memory.

A brilliant virtuoso of the trumpet with total command of any musical situation he chooses to place himself in, Marsalis has also made himself a potent spokesman for the highest musical standards in jazz, to which he is firmly and proudly committed. He has urged young musicians to acquaint themselves with the rich tradition of jazz and to avoid the pitfalls of "crossing over" to

Wynton Marsalis

pop, fusion and rock. His own adherence to these principles and his stature as a player has made his words effective. He has composed music for films and ballet and is a co-founder of the Lincoln Center Jazz Ensemble.

Carmen McRae (1922–   )
Singer, Pianist

Born in Brooklyn in 1922, McRae's natural talent on the keyboards won her numerous music scholarships. During her teen years, she carefully studied the vocal style of Billie Holiday and incorporated it into her own style. An early highlight came when Miss Holiday recorded one of McRae's compositions, "Dream of Life." After finishing her education, McRae moved to Washington, D.C. and worked as a government clerk by day and a nightclub pianist/singer by night. In the early 1940s, she moved to Chicago to work with Benny Carter, Mercer Ellington and Count Basie. By 1954, she had gained enough attention through her jazz and pop recordings to be dubbed a "new star" by *Downbeat* magazine. Since then, she has made many records, toured world-wide, and become one of jazz's most acclaimed singers.

Charles Mingus (1922–1979)
Bassist, Composer, Bandleader

Arizona-born Mingus grew up in the Watts area of Los Angeles. Starting on trombone and cello, he settled on the bass and studied with Red Callender, a noted jazz player, and Herman Rheinschagen, a classical musician. He also studied composition with Lloyd

Reese. Early in his professional career he worked with Barney Bigard in a band that included the veteran New Orleans trombonist Kid Ory, and toured briefly in Louis Armstrong's big band; he also led his own groups and recorded with them locally. After a stint in Lionel Hampton's band, which recorded his interesting composition "Mingus Fingus," he joined Red Norvo's trio, with which he came to New York in 1951.

Settling there, he worked with many leading players, including Dizzy Gillespie and Charlie Parker, and with Max Roach, he founded his own record label, Debut. He also formed his first of many so-called jazz workshops, in which new music, mostly written by himself, was rehearsed and performed. Mingus believed in spontaneity as well as discipline, and often interrupted public performances by his band if the playing didn't measure up. Some musicians refused to work with him after such public humilia-

Charles Mingus

tions, but there were some who thought so well of what he was trying to do that they stayed with him for years. Drummer Dannie Richmond was with Mingus from 1956 to 1970 and again from 1974 until the end; other longtime Mingusians include trombonist Kimmy Knepper, pianist Jaki Byard, and the saxophonists Eric Dolphy, Booker Ervin and John Handy in the earlier years; saxophonist Bobby Jones and trumpeter Jack Walrath, later on.

Mingus' music was as volatile as his temper, filled with ever-changing melodic ideas and textures and shifting, often accelerating, rhythmic patterns. He was influenced by Duke Ellington, Art Tatum and Charlie Parker, and his music often reflected psychological states and social issues—Mingus was a staunch fighter for civil rights, and wrote such protest pieces as "Fables of Faubus," "Meditations On Integration" and "Eat That Chicken." He was also steeped in the music of the Holiness Church ("Better Git It In Your Soul," "Wednesday Night Prayer Meeting") and in the whole range of the jazz tradition ("My Jelly Roll Soul," "Theme For Lester Young," "Gunslinging Bird," "Open Letter To Duke"). Himself a virtuoso bassist, he drove his sidemen to their utmost, often with vocal exhortations that became part of a Mingus performance. He composed for films and ballet and experimented with larger forms; his most ambitious work, an orchestral suite called "Epitaph," lasts more than two hours and was not performed in full until years after his death from amiotrophic lateral sclerosis, a disease with which he struggled valiantly—composing and directing (from a wheelchair) until almost the end. Though he was often in financial trouble and once was evicted from his home, he also received a Guggenheim fellowship in composition and was honored by President Carter at a White House jazz event in 1978.

At its best, Mingus' music—angry, humorous, always passionate—ranks with the greatest in jazz. He also wrote a strange but interesting autobiography, *Beneath the Underdog* (1971). A group, Mingus Dynasty, continued to perform his music into the 1990s, and in 1992, a Mingus Big Band performed weekly in New York City.

Thelonious Monk (1917–1982)
Pianist, Composer

Along with Charlie Parker and Dizzy Gillespie, Thelonious Monk was a vital member of the jazz revolution which took place in the early 1940s. Some musicians (among them Art Blakey) have said that Monk actually predated his more renowned contemporaries. Monk's unique piano style and his talent as a composer made him a leader in the development of modern jazz.

Thelonious Monk

Aside from brief work with the Lucky Millender Band, Coleman Hawkins, and Dizzy Gillespie, Monk generally was leader of his own small groups. He has been called the most important jazz composer since Ellington. Many of his compositions ("Round About Midnight," "Ruby My Dear") have become jazz standards.

Monk was unique as both an instrumentalist and composer, maintaining his own musical integrity and his melodic originality.

Thelonious Monk died in Englewood, New Jersey in 1982.

Ferdinand "Jelly Roll" Morton (1890–1941)
Composer, Pianist, Bandleader

New Orleans-born, Morton claimed (in 1938) that he had "invented" jazz in 1902. That was at the height of the Swing Era, and the few who remembered Morton paid little attention to his boast. However, it did sufficiently intrigue Alan Lomax, a folklorist at the Library of Congress, to lead to Morton's recording his life story, interspersed with fine piano playing, for Loma's archives. Morton was then living in Washington, D.C., managing an obscure night club. He had made his last commercial records in 1930.

But in the mid-1920s, Morton had made some wonderful records for Victor, the leading label of that day, under the name of Jelly Roll Morton and his Red Hot Peppers. Most were his own compositions, all were his arrangements, and they showed that he was a major talent, quite possibly the first real composer in jazz, if not the inventor of the music. The 1920s were the peak decade in Morton's up-and-down career. He was a much-in-demand pianist in his hometown while still in his teens, working in the Storyville "houses." Restless and ambitious, he hit the road, working in vaudeville, hustling pool, running gambling halls, occasionally playing piano, and traveling as far as Alaska and Mexico. He finally settled in Chicago in 1923, made his first records, worked for a music publisher, and let everybody know that he was the greatest.

In 1927 he moved to New York, still with a Victor contract but no longer doing as well, and when big band swing came to the fore, Jelly's career took a dive. But after the Library of Congress sessions, Victor was persuaded to record him again, and he was briefly back in the spotlight. Failing health and restlessness led him to drive to California, where he had a lady friend. But the trip made him ill, and he died in his 50th year, just before the revival of interest in traditional jazz, which would have given him the break he needed, got under way.

In 1992, a musical, *Jelly's Last Jam*, opened with great success on Broadway. It

Ferdinand "Jelly Roll" Morton

was loosely based on Morton's life and featured new arrangements of his music. If nothing else, it rekindled interest in that music, which, in the original recordings, still sounds almost as great as Jelly thought he was.

Muddy Waters (1915–1983)
Guitarist, Singer

Blues singer and guitarist, Muddy Waters was born Morganfield McKinley in Rolling Fork, Mississippi. He began playing guitar at the age of seventeen. He moved to Chicago at the age of twenty-eight, where in 1947 he began to record commercially. He was best known for such songs as "I'm Your Hoochie Coochie Man," "Got My Mojo Working," "Tiger in Your Tank," and "Manish Boy."

Theodore "Fats" Navarro (1923–1950)
Trumpeter

Fats Navarro was born in Key West, Florida. He started on trumpet at age thirteen, and also played tenor sax. Navarro was first heard nationally as a member of Andy Kirk's band from 1943 to 1944 when Dizzy Gillespie recommended him to Billy Eckstine, with whom he played for eighteen months. From 1947 to 1948 Fats played with Illinois Jacquet, Lionel Hampton, and Coleman Hawkins. He also worked with Tadd Dameron in 1948 to 1949. Navarro, a victim of drug addiction, was ranked with Dizzy Gillespie and Miles Davis as one of the greatest modern jazz trumpeters.

Joseph "King" Oliver (1885–1938)
Cornetist

Joe Oliver first earned the sobriquet "King" in 1917 after establishing himself as the best against the likes of Freddie Keppard, Manuel Perez, and a host of other cornetists who filled the nights with the first sounds of New Orleans jazz. Oliver soon teamed up with Kid Ory and organized what was to become the leading jazz band in New Orleans.

During the Storyville era, Oliver met and befriended Louis Armstrong. Lacking a son of his own, he became Armstrong's "unofficial father," sharing with him the musical knowledge which he had acquired over the years. In return, Armstrong treated him with great respect, referring to him as "Papa Joe."

With the closing of Storyville, Oliver left and Armstrong replaced him in Ory's band. By 1922, however, Oliver was in a position to summon Armstrong to Chicago to play in his Creole Jazz Band as second cornetist. In 1923, the Creole Jazz Band made the first important recordings by a black jazz group.

The work of Oliver and Armstrong put Chicago on the jazz map of the United States. However, changing tastes caused Oliver's music to decline in popularity and by the time he moved to New York in 1928, his best years were behind him.

From 1932, Oliver toured mainly in the South before ill health forced him to give up music. He died in Savannah, Georgia, where he worked in a poolroom from 1936 until his death in 1938.

Edward "Kid" Ory (1886–1973)
Trombonist, Bandleader

Kid Ory's musical career is in many ways emblematic of the story of jazz itself. They both reached a high point in New Orleans during the first two decades of this century. They both moved north during the 1920s, only to lapse into obscurity in the 1930s before being revived in the next two decades.

Ory was the best known of the so-called tailgate trombonists. He led his own bands

in New Orleans and Los Angeles until 1924, when he moved to Chicago to play with King Oliver, Jelly Roll Morton and others. In 1926, with Louis Armstrong, he recorded his famous composition "Muskrat Ramble."

He returned to the West Coast in 1929, and after playing for a time with local bands, retired to run a successful chicken ranch from 1930 to 1939. In the 1940s, he gradually returned to music with Barney Bigard, Bunk Johnson, and other New Orleans notables. He toured Europe successfully in 1956 and again in 1959, and spent his final years comfortably in Hawaii.

Charlie "Bird" Parker (1920–1955)
Saxophonist

The influence of Charlie Parker on the development of jazz has been felt not only in the realm of the alto saxophone, which he dominated, but on the whole spectrum of jazz ideas. The astounding innovations which he introduced melodically, harmonically, tonally, and rhythmically made it impossible for any jazz musician from the mid-1940s to the present time to develop without reflecting some of Parker's influence, with or without acknowledgment.

Parker left school at sixteen to become a professional musician in Kansas City, his hometown. Parker visited New York in 1939. Back in Kansas City, he joined pianist Jay McShann with whom he recorded his first sides. At this time Parker met Dizzy Gillespie, who was developing parallel ideas and who would become known as co-founder with Parker of the bop movement some four years later.

In the early 1940s, Parker played with the bands of Earl Hines, Cootie Williams and Andy Kirk, as well as the original Billy Eckstine band—the first big band formed expressly to feature the new jazz style in both solos and arrangements.

In 1945, Parker cut a series of remarkable sides with Gillespie that put Bebop on the map. Although Parker was revered by a host of younger musicians, his innovations, at first, met with a great deal of opposition from traditionalist jazz musicians and critics.

In 1946, Parker, addicted to heroin, suffered a breakdown and was confined to a state hospital in California. Six months later he was back recording with Erroll Garner. From this point until his death from a heart attack in 1955, he confined most of his activity to working with a quintet, but also recorded and toured with a string section, and visited Europe in 1949 and 1950. He made his final appearance in 1955 at Birdland, the club which had been named in his honor.

Oscar Peterson

Oscar Peterson (1925–)
Pianist

Oscar Peterson began classical study of the piano at the age of six in his native Canada, and in less than a decade, was playing regularly on a local radio show in Montreal.

In 1944, he became a featured soloist with Johnny Holmes, one of the top bands in Canada, and his reputation soon spread throughout the United States jazz world. He continued to resist offers from Jimmie Lunceford and others to tour the States, but in 1949 was persuaded by Norman Granz to come to New York City for a Carnegie Hall appearance. The following year he began to record and to tour the United States with Jazz at the Philharmonic.

His original group used bass (Ray Brown) and guitar (Barney Kessel, Herb Ellis), but when Ellis left in 1958, Peterson hired drummer Ed Thigpen to fill out the trio.

A phenomenal technician, Peterson has remained at the head of the jazz piano class though he cut back on his schedule of concerts and recordings by the late 1980s.

Oscar Pettiford (1922–1960)
Bassist

Oscar Pettiford was the leading bassist in the modern era of jazz. Building his own style on the foundation established by Jimmy Blanton, Pettiford achieved renown as the most technically capable and melodically inventive bassist in the jazz world of the late 1940s.

Pettiford was born on an American Indian reservation and raised in Minneapolis. Until he was nineteen, he toured with the family band (father and eleven children), and was well known in the Midwest. In 1943, Charlie

Barnet heard him in Minneapolis and hired him to team up with bassist Chubby Jackson.

Pettiford left Barnet later that year, and led his own group on 52nd Street and also played with Coleman Hawkins, Duke Ellington, and Woody Herman.

Pettiford's fame grew during the 1950s through his recordings and his tours of Europe and the Orient. In 1958, he settled permanently in Europe, where he continued to work until his death in Copenhagen in 1960.

Bud Powell (1924–1966)
Pianist, Composer

Along with Charlie Parker and Dizzy Gillespie, with whom he often worked, and Thelonious Monk, an early supporter, Earl "Bud" Powell was one of the founding fathers of modern jazz. A piano prodigy, he had his first big-time job with trumpeter Cootie Williams' big band in 1943, and became involved in the "birth of bebop" at Minton's Playhouse in Harlem and on 52nd Street.

The first to transfer the melodic, harmonic and rhythmic innovations of bop to the piano keyboard, he set the style for modern jazz piano, though he was greatly influenced by Art Tatum as well. Although he suffered recurrently from mental instability from his early twenties until the end of his life, Powell was capable of long stretches of musical brilliance. He lived in Paris from 1959 to 1964, frequently working with his old friend Kenny Clarke. More than 5,000 people attended his funeral in Harlem. One of Powell's finest compositions and performances is the ironically titled "Un Poco Loco," but there was nothing crazy about his hugely influential playing.

Ma Rainey (1886–1939)
Singer

Ma Rainey, the "Mother of the Blues," who enveloped the 1920s with her powerful, message-oriented blues songs, is remembered as a genuine jazz pioneer. Born Gertrude Pridgett in Columbus, Georgia, Rainey gave her first public performance as a twelve-year-old at the local Springer Opera House. At age eighteen, she married singer/dancer William "Pa" Rainey and the duo embarked on a long entertainment career. Around 1912, Rainey introduced a teen-aged Bessie Smith into her act, a move which was later seen as having a major impact on the blues/jazz singing styles. Ten years later, Rainey was recording with Fletcher Henderson, Louis Armstrong, and Coleman Hawkins and racking up the biggest record sales at the time for Paramount Records. She stopped recording in 1928, but continued to

"Ma" Rainey

1094

tour the South for a few more years. She retired 1935, and until her death four years later, managed the two theaters she owned in Georgia. Her eloquent and communicative voice lives on in the more than one hundred recordings she made in her lifetime, singing of the many facets of black experience.

Dewey Redman (1931–   )
Saxophonist

Dewey Redman has spent most of his life in search of a greater knowledge of his instrument, the tenor saxophone, constantly reevaluating his relationship to his music.

Born in Ft. Worth, Texas, he started playing the clarinet when he was twelve, taking private lessons briefly for six months before he turned to self-instruction. At fifteen, he got a job with an eight-piece band that performed in church as the minister passed the collection plate.

At Prairie View A&M College, Dewey teamed up with a piano and bass player to work in local clubs, found a spot in the Prairie View "swing" band, and graduated in 1953 with a degree in industrial arts and a grasp on a new instrument he had worked on in college, the saxophone.

After a stint in the Army, Dewey obtained a masters degree in Education at North Texas State University and taught school and directed school bands in west and south Texas.

In 1959, he moved to Los Angeles, where he found the music scene to be very cliquish, and then to San Francisco, where he remained for seven years, studying music, working out his own theories on chord progressions, improvisation and technique. In 1967, Dewey went to New York City, and fell in with Ornette Coleman, who brought him

into his group with Dave Izenson on bass and Denardo Coleman on drums.

By 1973, Dewey was dividing his playing time between solo efforts, gigs with Ornette Coleman and Keith Jarrett, and the composition of *Peace Suite*, dedicated to the late Ralph Bunche. Later he co-founded the group Old and New Dreams. His son, Joshua, emerged as one of the finest young tenor saxophonists of the early 1990s.

Don Redman (1900–1964)
Saxophonist, Composer

The first composer-arranger of consequence in the history of jazz, Don Redman was known in the 1920s as a brilliant instrumentalist on several kinds of saxophones. He also made many records with Bessie Smith, Louis Armstrong, and other top-ranking jazz artists.

Born in Piedmont, West Virginia, in 1900, Redman was a child prodigy who played trumpet at the age of three, joined a band at six, and later studied harmony, theory, and composition at the Boston and Detroit conservatories. In 1924, he joined Fletcher Henderson's band as lead saxophonist and staff arranger, and in 1928 became leader of McKinney's Cotton Pickers.

During most of the 1930s, Redman led his own band, regarded as one of the leading black orchestras of the day, and the first to play a sponsored radio series. He also wrote for many other prominent bands, black and white.

In 1951, Redman became musical director for Pearl Bailey. From 1954 to 1955, he appeared in a small acting role in *House of Flowers* on Broadway. He continued to arrange and record until his death in 1964.

Maxwell "Max" Roach (1925–   )
Percussionist, Composer

Brooklyn-born Max Roach was one of the key figures in the development of modern jazz. He was in the first group to play bebop on 52nd Street in New York, led by Dizzy Gillespie from 1943 to 1944, and later worked with Charlie Parker's finest group from 1947 to 1948. In 1954, he joined the brilliant young trumpeter Clifford Brown as co-leader of the Clifford Brown-Max Roach Quintet. After Brown's untimely death in a car crash, Roach began to lead his own groups of various sizes and instrumentation (including interesting work with solo and choral voices, an all percussion band, and a jazz quartet combined with a string quartet). His many compositions include *We Insist-Freedom Now*—a suite written with his wife at the time, singer Abbey Lincoln—was one of the first jazz works with a strong and direct political and social thrust.

A phenomenally gifted musician with a matchless percussion technique, Roach developed the drum solo to new heights of structural refinement; he has been an influence on every drummer to come along since the 1940s. A professor of music at the University of Massachusetts since 1972, Roach in 1988 became the first jazz artist to receive a MacArthur Fellowship, the most prestigious (and lucrative) award in the world of arts and letters. His daughter, Maxine, is a violinist, and they have worked and recorded together.

Sonny Rollins (1929–   )
Saxophonist, Bandleader

Born and raised in New York City, Theodore Walter Rollins made his recording debut at nineteen, in such fast company as J.J. Johnson and Bud Powell. Distinctively personal from the start, his style developed

Sonny Rollins

through work with Thelonious Monk, Powell, Art Blakey and Miles Davis. In 1955, he joined the Clifford Brown-Max Roach Quintet. In 1959, he took two years off from active playing, studying and practicing. When he reappeared at the helm of his own quartet in 1961, he surprised even those who already knew the quality of his work with the power and conviction of his playing.

Since then, though briefly overshadowed by John Coltrane, Rollins has been the unchallenged master of modern jazz tenor saxophone, with a sound and style totally his own. He often draws on his West Indian heritage for melodic and rhythmic inspiration and is one of the undisputed masters of extended improvisation, often playing all by himself as his group "lays out" in amazement—a feeling shared by his listeners.

Jimmy Rushing (1903–1972)
Singer

The song "Mister Five by Five," written in tribute to him, is an apt physical description of Jimmy Rushing, who was one of the greatest male jazz and blues singers.

Rushing played piano and violin as a boy, but entered music professionally as a singer in the after-hours world of California in 1925. After that, Rushing was linked with leading bands and musicians: Walter Page from 1927 to 1928; Benny Moten in 1929; and from 1936 to 1949 as a mainstay of the famed Count Basie Band.

Rushing formed his own small group when he left Basie and in the ensuing years worked most often as a "single." Following the rediscovery of the blues in the mid-1950s, Rushing regained widespread popularity.

His nightclub and festival engagements were always successful, and his world tours, on his own and also with Benny Goodman, earned him critical acclaim and commercial success. His style has endured across four decades of jazz largely due to its great warmth, a sure, firm melodic line, and a swinging use of rhythm. Late in life, he appeared in a featured acting role in Gordon Parks' film *The Learning Tree*.

Bessie Smith (1894–1937)
Singer

They called her "The Empress Of the Blues," and she had no peers. Her magnificent voice, sense of the dramatic, clarity of diction (you never missed a word of what she sang) and incomparable time and phrasing set her apart from the competition and made her appeal as much to jazz lovers as to lovers of the blues. Her first record, "Down Hearted Blues," sold more than a million copies, in 1923, when only Caruso and Paul Whiteman were racking up those kind of figures.

By then, Bessie Smith had been singing professionally for some fifteen years, but records by black singers had only been made since 1920, and only by much less earthy voices. She already had a big following and had appeared in big shows, so the timing was right—not least for Columbia Records, whom she pulled out of the red. Before long, she was backed by the best jazz players, including Louis Armstrong, and by 1925 starred in her own touring show, which traveled in its own private Pullman car. By 1927, she was the highest paid black artist in the world, and in 1929 she made a short film, *St. Louis Blues*, that captures for posterity some of her magnetism as a stage performer. But tastes in music were changing rapidly, and though Bessie Smith added popular songs to her repertory (she'd always

Bessie Smith

done some of those) and moved with the times, the Depression nearly killed the business for jazz and blues records, and in 1931, Columbia dropped her and she was soon touring as a "single."

John Hammond brought her back to the studios in 1933. Her records were wonderful, her singing as powerful and swinging as ever, but they didn't sell and turned out to be her last. She still found plenty of work on the traveling circuit, but the money was not what it used to be. On the road early one morning in Mississippi, she was fatally injured in a collision. For years, it was held as a fact that she died because a white hospital refused to treat her, but this wasn't so. The hospital in which her nearly severed right arm was amputated was black, but she had lost too much blood to survive. She was only forty-two. Had she lived, her star would surely have risen once more.

In 1968, Columbia reissued all of her records and did so again on CD in the 1990s. She would have been pleased with the response.

Billy Strayhorn (1915–1967)
Composer, Arranger, Pianist

Born in Dayton and raised in Pittsburgh, Strayhorn early on showed an unusually sophisticated gift for songwriting (music and lyrics); while still in his teens, he wrote "Lushlife," and this was one of the songs he showed Duke Ellington in 1938, backstage during a visit by the band. A year or so later, the young man, who also was a gifted pianist, joined the Ellington entourage in New York. Duke first thought of him as a lyricist (something he was always looking for) but soon found out that Strayhorn had a knack for arranging.

Before long the two had established a working relationship that remains unique in the history of music—a collaboration so close that they were often themselves unsure of who had written what of a given composition. However, each man did also continue to work on his own, and among the many Strayhorn-signed contributions to Ellingtonia are such standouts as "Take the A Train," "Passion Flower," "Chelsea Bridge," "Rain Check," and "Blood Count,"— the latter written in the hospital as Strayhorn was dying of cancer.

Self-effacing and modest to a fault, Strayhorn stayed out of the limelight. But musicians and serious Ellington fans knew just how much he contributed to the band's work during his lifetime within its ranks.

Art Tatum (1909–1956)
Pianist

He was a wizard of the keyboard. Nobody, not even the greatest classical virtuosi, surpassed his technique, but what made Art Tatum, nearly blind from birth, so very special was the musical imagination brought to life by his exceptional facility. Harmonically, he matched the boppers in sophistication— young Charlie Parker took a job as dishwasher in a club where Tatum worked so he could hear him every night. Rhythmically, he also anticipated modern jazz developments and could play rings around anyone, regardless of their instrument.

Though he enjoyed a full career, mostly as a soloist but also as leader of a trio (with electric guitar and bass, patterned on Nat King Cole's), and recorded quite prolifically, Tatum was born and died a bit too soon to benefit from the acceptance that came to jazz as a concert hall music. The concert hall, in which he rarely had the chance to perform, was Tatum's ideal medium. As it was, what he loved best was to play "after hours" for the edification of fellow musicians and perhaps in a challenge to some newcomer on the piano, whom he would cut down to size. When there were no rivals around, Tatum would challenge himself, setting seemingly impossible tempos or picking tunes with the toughest "changes."

There was no one like Art Tatum, and there never will be. His records remain to keep generations of piano players from gaining too high an opinion of their own skills.

Billy Taylor (1921–   )
Pianist, Composer, Educator

Few musicians have done more for the cause of jazz than Dr. Billy Taylor, who has been in the forefront of getting proper respect and recognition for African-American music since the 1950s, when he began to contribute articles to major magazines like *Esquire* and appeared on what was then known as "educational" television. He was by then already well established as a pianist on the New York scene, having arrived in the Big Apple shortly after graduating from Virginia State College in 1942. He became a regular on "Swing Street," later was the house pianist at Birdland, and started leading his own trios in 1951.

Taylor earned a doctorate in music education from the University of Massachusetts in 1975; his dissertation was later published as "Jazz Piano: History and Development," and became the text for a course offered on National Public Radio. Dr. Taylor led an eleven-piece band for TV's "David Frost Show," from 1969 to 1972, was founder-director of the program "Jazz Alive" on NPR, and has been a regular on CBS-TV's "Sunday Morning" since 1981. He has served on more boards and panels than one can mention here, but notably served on the prestigious National Council on the Arts.

Cecil Taylor (1929–   )
Pianist, Composer

Cecil Taylor, Ornette Coleman and John Coltrane—each completely different from the other—are the leading figures of avant garde jazz (later known as "free jazz," a perhaps more fitting term). Of these, Taylor is the farthest removed from the blues and swing roots of the music called jazz. He is a music unto himself—a fantastic virtuoso of the piano, with staggering energy and endurance and astonishing improvisatory abilities.

He attended New England Conservatory but says he learned more from listening to Ellington; another early influence was Bud Powell. He made his first recording (with Steve Lacy on soprano sax) in 1956; the following year he appeared at the Newport Jazz Festival and was also recorded there. Settling in New York City (he was born on Long Island) Taylor often struggled with lack of work and acceptance but continued to go his own musical way, and making interesting if infrequent recordings. In the mid-1960s, he experimented with larger frameworks for his playing, recording with the Jazz Composers Orchestra and in the early 1970s, he briefly taught at various universities. Meanwhile, he had gained a following in Europe and Japan, and in the 1980s there was more frequent work and a spate of recordings, including some brilliant solo efforts. He also teamed for concerts with Mary Lou Williams and with Max Roach. In 1988, he was featured in a month-long festival of concerts and workshops in Berlin; some of the results were issued in a lavish eleven-CD boxed set. In that decade, Taylor, always fascinated by dance (which he sometimes included in his performances), teamed with the famous ballet star Mikhail Baryshnikov in concert. In 1992, Taylor received a MacArthur Fellowship—one of the greatest awards an artist can receive.

McCoy Tyner (1938–   )
Pianist, Composer, Bandleader

The Philadelphia-born pianist came to fame when he joined John Coltrane's quartet in 1960. Prior to that, his most important job was with the Art Farmer-Benny Golson Jazztet. During his five years with Coltrane, Tyner developed a unique two-handed, densely harmonic style and became one of the most widely admired and imitated pianists in jazz.

As leader of his own groups of various sizes—from trios to a unique big band—Tyner has continued to develop as a musician of great originality and integrity.

Sarah Vaughan (1924–1990)
Singer

Her voice was of such beauty, range and power, her ear so sure, her musicality so rare that Sarah Vaughan could have become an operatic star, had she wanted to. Fortunately, she went the way of jazz and brought joy to the world since starting to sing professionally in 1943.

She had already sung in church in her native Newark and accompanied the choir on the piano (she played it well, one reason why she was so surefooted harmonically) and tried a few pop songs at high school parties when, on a dare, she entered the Wednesday night amateur contest at Harlem's famed Apollo Theater. As in a fairy tale, Billy Eckstine happened to be backstage. He ran out front as soon as he heard that voice, and recommended the young woman to his boss, band leader Earl Hines, who came, heard, and hired—of course she won the contest, which meant a week's work at the Apollo. In the Hines band of the time were Charlie Parker and Dizzy Gillespie. They and Sarah all left Hines when Eckstine decided to start his own band. By 1945, she'd made her first records under her own name. She also was the only singer to record with Bird and Dizzy together.

A year later, she started her solo career. Though she had some big pop hits during her long and rich career, she never strayed from jazz for long. Incredibly, as she got older, she got better, losing none of her amazing top range and adding to the bottom while her mastery of interpretation also grew. Her fans called her "the Divine One."

Thomas "Fats" Waller (1904–1943)
Composer, Pianist, Singer, Bandleader

Weighing in at over three hundred pounds and standing more than six feet tall, Tom Waller, a preacher's son (born in Greenwich Village in New York City), came by his nickname naturally. Big as he was, he was, as one of his many good friends said, "all music." His father wanted him to follow in his footsteps, but Fats liked the good times that came with playing the piano well, which he did almost from the start. At fifteen, he turned pro, backing singers in Harlem clubs and playing piano for silent movies. Wherever he went, people loved him, and he loved to spread joy. Few pianists, then or now, can match his terrific beat. He was also a master of the stride piano style. He also loved to play Bach, especially on the organ, which he was the first to make into a jazz instrument. In Paris in 1932, the world-famous Marcel Dupre invited Fats to play the organ at Notre Dame.

A talent for writing songs soon became evident. His first and biggest hit was "Ain't Misbehavin," from 1929; others include "Honeysuckle Rose," "Blue Turning Gray Over You," and "The Jitterbug Waltz." He also wrote "London Suite" for solo piano.

Fats was great on that new medium of the 1920s—the radio. He had an instant line of patter to go along with his great piano and

Thomas "Fats" Waller

Dinah Washington (1924–1963)
Singer

Dinah Washington's style defies categorization, but is seen as laying the groundwork for numerous rhythm and blues and jazz artists. Like many black singers, Washington got her start singing gospel; in her case, at St. Luke's Baptist Church on Chicago's South Side. She toured churches with her mother, playing the piano and singing solos, until another opportunity beckoned, an amateur talent contest at Chicago's Regal Theater. Her triumphant performance there led to performances at local nightclubs, and in 1943, the nineteen year-old singer successfully auditioned for a slot in Lionel Hampton's band. She was soon discovered by composer and critic, Leonard Feather, and together Ms. Washington and Mr. Feather created several chart toppers, including "Baby Get Lost," "Salty Papa Blues," "Evil Gal Blues," and "Homeward Bound." She gained legendary status with "What A Difference A Day Makes" and "Unforgettable." Washington proved to be such a versatile artist that she was acclaimed—and mourned when she died at age thirty-nine—by blues, jazz, gospel, pop, and rhythm and blues audiences alike. Aretha Franklin dedicated one of her early albums to Ms. Washington, labelling it simply "Unforgettable."

carefree singing. He also made it to Hollywood. But his true medium was records. With his fine little group and occasional big band, he cut more than five hundred sides between 1934 and his untimely death at thirty-nine in 1943. He came across on records, and no matter how trite the tune, he turned it into a jazz gem. What killed Fats in his prime was his huge appetite (he was capable of consuming two whole chickens at one sitting, or polishing off two fullsize steak dinners) and drinking. Ironically, his first complete Broadway musical (he'd written songs for many others) was becoming a hit as he started off for home from California, where he had just finished filming *Stormy Weather*. He never arrived because pneumonia took him on a bitter cold December night just as the Superchief pulled into Kansas City.

Ben Webster (1909–1973)
Saxophonist

Born in Kansas City, Kansas or Missouri, Ben Webster was at first a pianist, but switched to saxophone in his late teens. He worked with the family band led by Lester Young's father and with many other midwestern bands, and came to New York in 1931 with Benny Moten (whose pianist was Count Basie). After gaining a name among musicians as one of the most gifted disciples of Coleman Hawkins, he made many records and toured with many prominent bands (Fletcher Henderson, Cab Calloway, Teddy Wilson).

But it was when he joined Duke Ellington in 1939 that Webster really blossomed and soon became an influence in his own right. When he left Duke in 1943, he mainly led his own small groups, recorded prolifically, and also became one of the first black musicians to join a network radio musical staff. In 1964, he left on what had been planned as his first brief visit to Europe, but he never returned home. Settling in Copenhagen, he spent the final decade of his life as a revered and beloved elder statesman of jazz. During this period, his always masterful ballad playing ripened to full maturity, and his sound, ranging from a whisper to a gruff roar, became one of the unsurpassed landmarks of classic jazz.

Mary Lou Williams (1910–1981)
Pianist, Composer, Arranger

Most women who have achieved fame in jazz have been singers, from Bessie Smith to Betty Carter. A singular exception to this rule was Mary Lou Williams, dubbed the "First Lady of Jazz."

Brought up in Pittsburgh, Atlanta-born Mary Elfrieda Scruggs had already performed in public at the age of six and was a pro by thirteen. Three years later she married saxophonist John Williams, with whom she made her record debut. When he joined Andy Kirk's band she took over the group. Soon, however, she was writing arrangements for Kirk, and in 1931, she became the band's pianist and musical director.

Though she also wrote for Benny Goodman and other bands, she stayed with Kirk until 1942, helping to make the band one of the swing era's best. Settling in New York, she led her own groups (sometimes all fe-

male) and began to compose longer works, including the "Zodiac Suite," performed at Town Hall in 1946. A champion of modern jazz, she gave advice and counsel to such rising stars as Dizzy Gillespie and Thelonious Monk. Miss Williams lived in England and France from 1952 to 1954. Back at home, she retired from music for some three years, but was coaxed out by Gillespie. Resuming her career, she toured widely, wrote several religious works including a Jazz Mass performed at St. Patrick's Cathedral, and in 1977 became artist-in-residence and teacher of jazz history and performance at Duke University, a position she held until her death. As pianist, composer and arranger, Mary Lou Williams ranks with the very best.

Teddy Wilson (1912–1986)
Pianist, Bandleader

Theodore Wilson's father taught English and his mother was head librarian at Tuskegee Institute. He turned to music as a career while studying printing in Detroit in 1928, was befriended by the great Art Tatum, played in Louis Armstrong's big band, and was brought to New York by Benny Carter in 1933.

Two years later, he began to make a series of records—which became classics—often with Billie Holiday and always with the greatest musicians of the time. Meanwhile, he was becoming famous as the first black jazzman to be featured with a white band, playing with the Benny Goodman Trio and Quartet. His marvelously clear, harmonically impeccable piano style was a big influence on the pianists of the swing era. His own big band, formed in 1939 was excellent but not a commercial success. From 1940 on, he mostly led small groups or appeared as a soloist, touring world-wide and making hundreds of records. Though seriously ill, he continued to perform until a week before his death. Two of his three sons are professional musicians.

Lester "Prez" Young (1909–1959)
Saxophonist

It was Lester Young who gave Billie Holiday the name "Lady Day" when both were with Count Basie, and it was Lady Day in turn who christened Lester Young "President" (later shortened to "Prez").

Young spent his youth on the carnival circuit in the Midwest with his musical family, choosing to concentrate on the tenor saxophone, only one of the many instruments he was able to play.

When Young took over Coleman Hawkin's chair in Fletcher Henderson's orchestra, he was criticized for not having the same style as his predecessor. As a result of this, he returned to Kansas City to play with Andy Kirk, and then with Count Basie from 1936 to 1940. During the Basie years, Young surpassed Hawkins as the vital influence on the tenor. Hardly a tenor man from the middle 1940s through the 1950s achieved prominence without building on the foundations laid by Lester Young.

Young suffered a complete breakdown in 1955 but made a comeback the next year. He died within hours of returning from a long engagement in Paris.

Bibliography

Bibliography

Compiled by Donald Franklin Joyce

Included in this selected bibliography are titles which were published between 1990 and 1992, reviewed favorably in the reviewing media, and judged to be significant contributions to the study of black history and culture in the United States and in Africa. The titles are arranged under two major divisions: "Africana" and "African Americana." Within these two divisions titles are arranged alphabetically by author under categories indicative of their subject matter. A list of the names, addresses and telephone numbers of all publishers included follows the bibliography.

■ AFRICANA

Agriculture

Barnett, Tony, and Abbas Abdelkarim. *Sudan: The Gezira Scheme and Agricultural Transition.* London: Frank Cass, 1991.

Freeman, Donald B. *A City of Farmers: Informal Urban Agriculture in the Open Spaces of Nairobi, Kenya.* Montreal: McGill-Queen's University Press, 1991.

Gyllstrom, Bjorn. *State Administrative Rural Change: Agricultural Cooperatives in Rural Kenya.* New York: Routledge, 1991.

Kidane, Mengisteab. *Ethiopia: Failure of Land Reform and Agricultural Crisis.* Westport, CT: Greenwood Press, 1990.

Apartheid

Burman, Sandra, and Pamela Reynolds, eds. *Growing Up In a Divided Society.* With forewords by Archbishop Desmond Tutu and Robert Coles. Evanston, IL: Northwestern University Press, 1992.

Cohen, Robin, Yvonne G. Muthien, and Abebe Zegeye, eds. *Repression and Resistance: Inside Accounts of Apartheid.* London; New York: Hans Zell Publishers, 1990.

Davis, R. Hunt, ed. *Apartheid Unravels.* Gainesville, FL: University of Florida Presses, 1991.

Dumor, E.K. *Ghana, OAU and Southern Africa: An African Response to Apartheid.* Accra: Ghana University Press, 1991.

Ellis, Stephen. *Comrades Against Apartheid: The ANC and the South African Communist Party in Exile.* London: James Currey/Indiana University Press, 1992.

Ellman, Stephen. *In a Time of Trouble: Law and Liberty in South Africa's State of Emergency.* New York: Oxford University Press, 1992.

Giliomee, Herman, and Laurence Schlemmer. *From Apartheid to Nation-Building.* Capetown, S.A.: Oxford University Press, 1990.

Grundy, Kenneth. *South Africa: Domestic Crisis and Global Challenge.* Boulder, CO: Westview Press, 1991.

Heard, Anthony Hazlett. *The Cape of Storms: A Personal History of the Crisis in South Africa.* Fayetteville: University of Arkansas Press, 1990.

Holland, Heidi. *The Struggle: A History of the African National Congress.* New York: Braziller, 1990.

Hull, Richard W. *American Enterprise in South Africa: Historical Dimensions of Engagement and Disengagement.* New York: New York University Press, 1990.

Human Rights Watch. *The Killings of South Africa: The Role of the Security Forces and the Response of the State.* New York: Human Rights Watch, 1991.

Johns, Sheridan, and R. Hunt Davis, eds. *Mandela, Tambo and the African National Congress: The Struggle Against Apartheid, 1948-1990: A Documentary Survey.* New York: Oxford University Press, 1991.

Kalley, Jacqueline A. *South Africa's Road to Change, 1987–1990.* Westport, CT: Greenwood Press, 1991.

Lemon, Anthony, ed. *Homes Apart: South Africa's Segregated Cities.* Bloomington: Indiana University Press, 1991.

Maasdorp, Gavin, and Alan Whiteside, eds. *Towards a Post-Apartheid Future: Political and Economic Relations in South Africa.* New York: St. Martin's Press, 1992.

Mallaby, Sebastian. *After Apartheid: The Future of South Africa.* New York: Times Books, 1992.

Moss, Rose. *Shouting at the Crocodile: Popo Molefe, Patrick Lekota, and the Freeing of South Africa.* Boston: Beacon Press, 1990. (Dist. by Farrar, Strauss, Giroux)

Price, Robert M. *The Apartheid State in Crisis: Political Transformation in South Africa, 1975–1990.* New York: Oxford University Press, 1991.

Shepherd, George W., ed. *Effective Sanctions on South Africa: The Cutting Edge of Economic Intervention.* Westport, CT: Greenwood Press, 1991.

Sparks, Allister. *The Mind of South Africa.* New York: Knopf, 1990.

Spink, Kathryn. *Black Sash: The Beginning of a Bridge in South Africa.* With a foreword by Archbishop Desmond Tutu. London: Methuen, 1991.

Art

Courtney-Clarke, Margaret. *African Canvas: The Art of West African Women.* New York: Rizzoli, 1990.

Okediji, Mayo, ed. *Principles of "Traditional" African Art.* Ile Ife: Bard Book, 1992 (Dist. by Avon).

Smithsonian Institution. Libraries. National Museum of African Art Branch. *Catalog of the Library of the National Museum of African Art Branch of the Smithsonian Library.* Boston: G.K. Hall, 1991.

Vogel, Susan. *Africa Explores: Twentieth Century African Art.* New York: The Center for African Art, 1991.

Williams College Museum of Art. *Assuming the Guise: African Masks Considered and Reconsidered.* Williamstown, MA: Williams College Museum of Art, 1991.

Williamson, Sue. *Resistance Art in South Africa.* New York: St. Martin's Press, 1990.

Autobiography and Biography

Appiah, Joseph. *Joe Appiah: The Autobiography of an African Patriot.* New York: Praeger, 1990.

Bunche, Ralph Johnson. *An African American in South Africa: The Travel Notes of Ralph J. Bunche, 28 September 1937–1 January 1938*. Edited by Roger R. Edgar. Athens: Ohio University Press, 1992.

Gastrow, Shelagh, ed., *Who's Who in South African Politics*. 3rd ed., London: Hans Zell Publishers, 1990.

Glickman, Harvey, ed., *Political Leaders of Contemporary Africa South of the Sahara: A Biographical Dictionary*. Westport, CT: Greenwood Press, 1992.

Harris, Eddy L. *Native Stranger: A Black American's Journey into the Heart of Africa*. New York: Simon & Schuster, 1992.

Isert, Paul Erdmann. *Letters on West Africa: Paul Erdmann Isert's Journey to Guinea and the Caribbean Islands in Columbia (1788)*. Translated by Selena Axelrod Winsnes. New York: Oxford University Press, 1992.

Lockot, Hans Wilhelm. *The Mission: The Life, Reign and Character of Haile Selassie I*. New York: St. Martin's Press, 1990.

Mashinini, Emma. *Strikes Have Followed Me All My Life: A South African Autobiography*. New York: Routledge, 1991.

Meer, Fatima. *Higher Than Hope: The Authorized Biography of Nelson Mandela*. New York: Harper & Row, 1990.

Mendelsohn, Richard. *Sammy Marks: the Uncrowned King of the Transvaal*. Athens: Ohio University Press, 1991.

Modisan, Blake. *Blame Me on History*. New York: Simon & Schuster, 1990.

Nkrumah, Kwame. *Kwame Nkrumah: The Conakry Years: His Life and Letters*. Compiled by June Milne. New York: Zed Books, 1991. (Dist. by Humanities Press)

Rake, Alan. *Who's Who in Africa: Leaders for the 1990s*. Metuchen, NJ: Scarecrow, 1992.

Rodney, Walter. *Walter Rodney Speaks: The Making of an African Intellectual*. With introduction by Robert Hill. Foreword by Howard Dodson. Trenton, NJ: Africa World Press, 1990.

Vaillant, Janet G. *Black, French and African: A Life of Leopold Sedar Senghor*. Cambridge: Harvard University Press, 1990.

Vigne, Randolph, ed. *A Gesture of Belonging: Letters from Bessie Head, 1965–1979*. Portsmouth, NH: Heinemann, 1991.

Wiseman, John A. *Political Leaders in Black Africa: A Biographical Dictionary of the Major Politicians Since Independence*. Brookfield, VT: Gower Publishing Co., 1991.

Economics

Blumenfield, Jesmond. *Economic Interdependence in Southern Africa: From Conflict to Cooperation*. New York: Printer/St. Martin's Press, 1991.

Chole, Eschetu, ed. *Food Crisis in Africa: Policy and Management Issues*. New Delhi: Vikas Publishing House, 1990. (Dist. by Advent House)

Claessen, Henri J.M., and Pieter van de Velde, eds. *Early State Economies*. New Brunswick, NJ: Transaction Publishers, 1991.

Cock, Jacklyn, ed. *Going Green: People, Politics and the Environment in South Africa*. New York: Oxford University Press, 1991.

Crockcroft, Laurence. *Africa's Way: A Journey from the Past*. UK: Tauris, 1990. (Dist. by St. Martin's Press)

Crush, Jonathan, Alan Jeeves, and Donald Yudelman *Africa's Labor Empire: A History of Black Migrancy to the Gold Mines*. Boulder, CO: Westview Press/D. Philip, 1991.

Edington, J.A.S. *Rubber in West Africa*. Anaheim, CA: Collings, 1991.

Henige, David, and T.C. McCaskie, eds. *West African Economic and Social History: Studies in Memory of Marion Johnson*. Madison: African Studies Program, University of Wisconsin, 1990.

Hodd, Michael. *The Economies of Africa: Geography, Population, History, Stability, Performance, Forecasts*. Boston: G. K. Hall, 1991.

Mahjoub, Azzam, ed. *Adjustment or Delinking? The African Experience.* London: Zed Press, 1990. (Dist. by Humanities Press)

Martin, Matthew. *The Crumbling Facade of African Debt Negotiations: No Winners.* New York: St. Martin's Press, 1991.

Mingst, Karen A. *Politics and the African Development Bank.* Lexington: University of Kentucky Press, 1990.

Nyango'oro, Julius, and Timothy Shaw, eds. *Beyond Structural Adjustment in Africa: The Political Economy of Sustainable and Democratic Development.* New York: Praeger, 1992.

Okolo, Julius Emeka, and Stephen Wright, eds. *West African Regional Cooperation and Development.* Boulder, CO: Westview Press, 1990.

Peckett, James, and Hans Singer, eds. *Towards Economic Recovery in Sub-Saharan Africa: Essays in Honor of Robert Gardner.* New York: Routledge, 1991.

Pradervand, Pierre. *Listening to Africa: Developing Africa from the Grassroots.* New York: Praeger, 1990.

Pryor, Frederic L. *The Political Economy of Poverty, Equity and Growth: Malawi and Madagascar.* New York: Oxford University for the World Bank, 1990.

Rau, Bill. *From Feast to Famine: Official Cures and Grassroots Remedies to Africa's Food Crisis.* New York: Zed Books, 1991 (Dist. by Humanities Press).

Riddell, Roger C. *Manufacturing Africa: Performance and Prospects of Seven Countries in Sub-Saharan Africa.* Portsmouth, NH: Heinemann, 1990.

Sarhof, Joseph A. *Hydropower Development in West Africa: A Study in Resource Development.* New York: P. Lang, 1990.

Siddle, David, and Ken Swindell. *Rural Change in Tropical Africa: From Colonies to Nation-States.* Cambridge, MA: Basil Blackwell, 1990.

Stewart, Frances, ed. *Alternative Development Strategies in Sub-Saharan Africa.* New York: St. Martin's Press, 1992.

Education

King, Kenneth, ed., *Botswana: Education, Culture and Politics.* Edinburgh: University of Edinburgh Press, 1990.

Mungazi, Dickson A. *Colonial Education for Africana: George Starks in Zimbabwe.* Westport, CT: Praeger, 1991.

Njobe, M.W. *Education for Liberation.* Johannesburg: Skotaville, 1990.

Okeem, E.O., ed. *Education in Africa: Search for Realistic Alternatives.* London: Institute for African Alternatives, 1990.

Okunor, Shiame. *Politics, Misunderstandings, Misconceptions: The History of Colonial Universities.* New York: P. Lang, 1991.

Folklore and Folk Culture

Berry, Jack, comp. and trans. *West African Folktales.* Edited with introduction by Richard Spears. Evanston, IL: Northwestern University Press, 1991.

Gunner, Liz, and Mafika Gwala, eds. and trans., *Musho!: Zulu Popular Praises.* East Lansing: Michigan State University Press, 1991.

McDermott, Gerald. *Zomo the Rabbit: A Trickster Tale from West Africa.* San Diego: Harcourt Brace Jovanovich, 1992.

Mohindra, Kamlesh. *Folk Tales of West Africa.* New Delhi: Sterling Pubs., 1991. (Dist. by APT Books)

Njoku, John E. Eberegbulaum. *The Igbos of Nigeria: Ancient Rites, Changes and Survival.* Lewiston, NY: Edwin Mellen Press, 1990.

Schipper, Mineke. *Source of All Evil: African Proverbs and Sayings on Women.* Chicago: Ivan R. Dee, 1991.

Smith, Alexander McCall. *Children of Wax: African Folk Tales.* New York: Interlink Books, 1991.

Ugorji, Okechukwu K. *The Adventures of Torti: Tales from West Africa.* Trenton, NJ: Africa World Press, 1991.

General Reference

Asante, Molafi Keto *The Book of African Names.* Trenton, NJ: Africa World Press, 1991.

Blackhurst, Hector, comp. *Africa Bibliography 1989.* Manchester, UK: Manchester University Press, 1991. (Dist. by St. Martin's Press, Inc.)

Fredland, Richard. *A Guide to African International Organizations.* New York: Hans Sell Publishers, 1991.

Morrison, Donald George, Robert Cameron Mitchell, and John Naber Paden. *Black Africa: A Comparative Handbook.* 2nd ed., New York: Paragon House/Irvington, 1990.

Moss, Joyce, and George Wilson. *Peoples of the World: Africans South of the Sahara.* Detroit: Gale Research Inc., 1991.

Sarfoh, Joseph A. *Energy in the Development of West Africa: A Selected Annotated Bibliography.* New York: Greenwood Press, 1991.

Thurston, Anne. *Guide to Archives and Manuscripts Relating to Kenya and East Africa in the United Kingdom.* New York: Hans Zell Publishers, 1991.

Zell, Hans M. *The African Studies Companion: A Resources Guide and Directory.* Providence, NJ: Hans Zell Publishers, 1990.

Government and Politics

Bowman, Larry W. *Mauritius: Democracy and Development in the Indian Ocean.* Boulder, CO: Westview Press, 1991.

Charlick, Robert B. *Niger: Personal Rule and Survival in the Sahel.* Boulder, CO: Westview Press, 1991.

Clingman, Stephen, ed. *Regions and Repertoires: Topics in South African Politics and Culture.* Johannesburg: Raven Press, 1991. (Dist. by Ohio University Press.)

Clough, Marshall S. *Fighting Two Sides: Kenyan Chiefs and Politicians, 1918–1940.* Niwot, CO: University Press of Colorado, 1990.

Cowell, Alan. *Killing the Wizards: Wars of Power and Freedom from Zaire to South Africa.* New York: Simon & Schuster, 1992.

Deng, Frances M., and I. William Zartman, eds. *Conflict Resolution in Africa.* Washington: Brookings Institution, 1991.

Forrest, Joshua B. *Guinea-Bissau: Power, Conflict and Renewal in a West African Nation.* Boulder, CO: Westview Press, 1992.

Gambari, I.A. *Political and Comparative Dimensions of Regional Integration: The Case of ECOWAS.* New York: The Humanities Press, 1991.

Hanlon, Joseph. *Mozambique: Who Calls the Shots.* Bloomington: Indiana University Press, 1991.

Hansen, Holger Bernt, ed. *Changing Uganda: The Dilemmas of Structural Adjustment and Revolutionary Change.* Athens: Ohio University Press, 1991.

Henze, Paul B. *The Horn of Africa: From War to Peace.* New York: St. Martin's Press, 1991.

Herbst, Jeffrey. *State Politics in Zimbabwe.* Berkeley: University of California, 1990.

Hughes, Arnold, ed. *The Gambia: Studies in Society and Politics.* Birmingham, UK: University of Birmingham, Centre for African Studies, 1991.

Ingham, Kenneth. *Politics in Modern Africa: The Uneven Tribal Dimension.* New York: Routledge, 1990.

Johnson, Willard R. *West African Governments and Volunteer Development Organizations: Priorities for Partnerships.* Lanham, MD: University Press of America, 1990.

Khalid, Mansour. *The Government They Deserve: The Role of the Elite in Sudan's Political Evolution.* New York: Kegan Paul International, 1990.

Kriger, Norma J. *Zimbabwe's Guerrilla War: Peasant Voices*. New York: Cambridge University Press, 1991.

Machobane, L.B.B.J. *Government and Change in Lesotho, 1800–1966: A Study of Political Institutions*. New York: Macmillan, 1990.

Moss, Glenn, and Ingrid Obery, eds. and comps. *South Africa Contemporary Analysis*. London: Hans Zell Publishers, 1990.

Nyang'oro, Julius E., and Timothy M. Shaw, eds. *Beyond Structural Adjustment in Africa: The Political Economy of Sustainable and Democratic Development*. New York: Praeger, 1992.

O'Brien, Donal B. Cruise, John Dunn, and Richard Rathbone, eds. *Contemporary West African States*. New York: Cambridge University Press, 1990.

Ogunsanwo, Alaba. *The Transformation of Nigeria: Scenarios and Metaphors*. Lagos: University of Lagos Press, 1991.

Reyna, Stephen P. *Wars Without End: The Political Economy of a Precolonial African State*. Hanover, NH: University Press of New England, 1990.

Riley, Eileen. *Major Political Events in South Africa, 1948–1990*. New York: Facts on File, 1991.

Schlosser, Dirk Berg, and Rainer Siegler. *Political Stability and Development: A Comparative Analysis of Kenya, Tanzania and Uganda*. Boulder, CO: Lynne Rienner, 1990.

Sklar, Richard L., and C. S. Whitaker. *African Politics and Problems in Development*. Boulder, CO: Lynne Rienner, 1991.

Tareke, Gebru. *Ethiopia, Power and Protest: Peasant Revolts in the Twentieth Century*. New York: Cambridge University Press, 1991.

Vines, Alex. *Renamo: Terrorism in Mozambique*. Bloomington: Indiana University Press, 1991.

Wunsch, James S., and Dele Olowu, eds. *The Failure of the Centralized State: Institutions and Self-Governance in Africa*. Boulder, CO: Westview Press, 1990.

Wylie, Diana. *A Little God: The Twilight of Patriarchy in a Southern Africa Chiefdom*. Hanover, NH: University Press of New England, 1990.

Health

Baron, Vida C. *African Power: Secrets of the Ancient Ibo Tribe*. San Diego, Barez Publishing Co., 1992.

Falala, Toyin, ed. *The Political Economy of Health in Africa*. Athens: Ohio University for International Studies/Ohio University Press, 1992.

King, Richard D. *African Origin of Biological Psychiatry*. Germantown, TN: Seymour-Smith, Inc., 1990.

Turner, Edith L.B., et al. *Experiencing Ritual: A New Interpretation of African Healing*. Philadelphia: University of Pennsylvania Press, 1992.

Williams, A. Olufemi. *AIDS: An African Perspective*. Boca Rotan, FL: CRC Press, 1992.

Wolff, James, et. al. *Beyond Clinic Walls, Case Studies in Community-Based Distribution*. West Hartford, CT: Kumarian Press, 1990.

History

Ayittey, George B.N. *Indigenous African Institutions*. Ardsley-on-Hudson, NY: Transnational Publishers, 1991.

Banbera, Tayiru. *A State of Intrigue: The Epic of Bamana Segu According to Tayiru Banbera*. Edited by David Conrad; transcribed and translated with the assistance of Soumaila Diakit'e. Oxford, UK: Oxford University Press, 1990.

Cammack, Diana. *The Rand at War, 1899–1902: The Witwatersrand and the Anglo-Boer War*. Berkeley: University of California Press, 1990.

Collelo, Thomas. *Angola: A Country Study* 3rd ed., Washington, DC: Government Printing Office, 1991.

Collins, Robert O. *Western African History.* New York: W. Wiener, 1990.

Crais, Clifton C. *White Supremacy and Black Resistance in Pre-Industrial South Africa: The Making of the Colonial Order in the Eastern Cape, 1770–1865.* Cambridge, UK: Cambridge University Press, 1992.

Digre, Brian. *Imperialism's New Clothes: The Repartition of Tropical Africa, 1914–1919.* New York: P. Lang, 1990.

Diop, Cheikh Anta. *Civilization or Barbarism: An Authentic Anthropology.* Translated by Yaa-Lengi Meema Ngemi; edited by Harold J. Salemson and Marjolijn de Jager. Brooklyn: Lawrence Hill Books, 1991.

Echenberg, Myron J. *Colonial Conscripts: The Tirailleurs S'en'egalais in French West Africa, 1857–1960.* Portsmouth, NH: Heinemann, 1991.

Friedman, Kajsa Ekholm. *Catastrophe and Creation: The Transformation of an African Culture.* Philadelphia: Hardwood Academic Publishers, 1991.

Gann, L.H., and Pete Duignan. *Hope for Africa.* Stanford, CA: Stanford University Press, 1991.

Gordon, April, ed. *Understanding Contemporary Africa.* Boulder, CO: Lynne Reinner Publishers, 1992.

Hair, P.E.H. *Black Africa in Time Perspective: Four Talks on Wide Historical Themes.* Liverpool, UK: Liverpool University Press, 1990. (Dist. by University of Pennsylvania Press).

Hair, P.E.H. *English Seamen and Traders in Guinea, 1553–1565: The New Evidence of their Wills.* Lewiston, NY: E. Mellen Press, 1992.

Hansen, Emmanuel. *Ghana Under Rawlings: Early Years.* Lagos: Malthouse Press, 1991.

Hassen, Mohammed. *The Oromo of Ethiopia: A History.* New York: Cambridge University Press, 1990.

Hudson, Peter. *Two Rivers: In the Footsteps of Mungo Park.* London: Chapmans Publishers, 1991.

Human Rights Watch. *Evil Days: Thirty Years of War and Famine in Ethiopia.* New York: Human Rights Watch, 1990.

Ki-Zerbo, J., ed.*UNESCO General History of Africa, Vol. 1: Methodology and African Prehistory.* Berkeley: University of California Press, 1990.

Lamphear, John. *The Scattering Time: Turkans Responses to Colonial Time.* New York: Oxford University Press, 1992.

Law, Robin. *The Slave Coast of West Africa, 1550–1750: The Impact of the Atlantic Slave Trade on African Society.* New York: Oxford University Press, 1991.

Manning, Patrick. *Slavery and African Life: Occidental, Oriental and African Slave Trades.* New York: Cambridge University Press, 1990.

Metaferia, Getchew. *The Ethiopian Revolution of 1974 and the Exodus of Ethiopia's Trained Human Resources.* Lewiston, NY: Edwin Mellen Press, 1991.

Mokhtar, G., ed. *UNESCO General History of Africa, Vol. II: Ancient History of Africa.* Berkeley: University of California Press, 1990.

Mooncraft, Paul L. *African Nemesis: War and Revolution in Southern Africa (1945–2010).* Riverside, NJ: Pergamon Press, 1990.

Morton, Fred. *Children of Ham: Freed Slaves and Fugitive Slaves on the Kenya Coast, 1873–1907.* Boulder, CO: Westview, 1990.

Mostert, Noel. *Frontiers: The Epic of South Africa's Creation and the Tragedy of the Xhosa People.* New York: Knopf, 1992.

Munford, Clarence J. *The Black Ordeal of Slavery and Slave Trading in the French West Indies, 1625–1715.* Lewiston, NY: Edwin Mellen Press, 1991.

Nasson, Bill. *Abraham Esau's War: A Black South African War in the Cape, 1899–1902.* New York: Cambridge University Press, 1991.

Obasanjo, Olusegun, and Hans d'Orville, eds. *The Impact of Europe in 1992 on West Africa.* New York: C. Russak, 1990.

Ochieng, William, ed. *Themes in Kenyan History.* Nairobi: Heinmann Kenya, 1990.

Ogot, B.A., ed. *Africa from the Sixteenth to the Eighteenth Century.* Berkeley: University of California Press, 1992.

Remmer, Douglas, ed. *Africa Thirty Years Ago.* Portsmouth, NH: Heinemann, 1991.

Shillington, Kevin. *History of Africa.* New York: St. Martin's Press, 1990.

Solow, Barbara L., ed. *Slavery and the Rise of the Atlantic System.* Cambridge, UK; New York: Cambridge University Press, 1991.

Stauton, Irene, comp. and ed. *Mothers of the Revolution: The War Experiences of Thirty Zimbabwean Women.* Bloomington: Indiana University Press, 1991.

Stedman, Stephen John. *Peacemaking in the Civil War: International Mediation in Zimbabwe, 1974–1980.* Boulder, CO: Lynne Rienner, 1991.

Temperley, Howard. *White Dreams, Black Africa: The Anti-Slavery Expedition to the River Niger, 1841–42.* New Haven: Yale University Press, 1991.

Thompson, Leonard. *A History of South Africa.* New Haven: Yale University Press, 1990.

Wyse, Akintola J.G., and H.C. Bankhole-Bight. *Politics in Colonial Sierra Leone, 1919–1958.* New York:Cambridge University Press, 1991.

Yarak, Larry W. *Asante and the Dutch, 1744–1873.* New York: Oxford University Press, 1990.

Young, John. *They Fell Like Stones: Battles and Casualties of the Zulu War, 1879.* Novato, CA: Presidio Press, 1991.

International Relations

Kent, John. *The Internationalization of Colonialism: Britain, France and Black Africa.* New York: Oxford University Press, 1992.

Russell, Sharon Stanton, Karen Jacobsen, and William Deane Stanley. *International Migration and Development in Sub-Sahara Africa.* Washington, DC: The World Bank, 1991.

Thompson, Joseph E. *American Policy and African Famine: The Nigeria-Biafra War, 1966–1970.* New York: Greenwood Press, 1970.

Winros, Gareth M. *The Foreign Policy of GDR in Africa.* Cambridge, UK: Cambridge University Press, 1991.

Language and Literature

Abraham, Cecils ed. *The Tragic Life: Bessie Head and Literature in South Africa.* Trenton, NJ: Africa World Press, 1990.

Achebe, Chinua. *Hopes and Impediments: Selected Essays.* New York: Doubleday, 1990.

Bjornson, Richard. *The African Quest for Freedom and Identity: Cameroonian Writing and the National Experience.* Bloomington: Indiana University Press, 1991.

Dram'e, Kandioura. *The Novel as Transformation Myth: A Study of the Novels of Mongo Beti and Ngugi wa Thiongo.* Syracuse, NY: Syracuse University, 1990.

Dunton, Chris. *Make Man Talk True: Nigerian Drama in English Since 1970.* New York: Hans Zell Publishers, 1992.

Elimimian, Isaac Iraber. *Theme and Style in African Poetry.* Lewiston, NY: E. Mellen, 1991.

February, V.A. *Mind Your Colour: The Coloured Stereotype in South African Literature.* London and New York: Kegan Paul International, 1991. (Dist. by Routledge, Chapman & Hall, Inc.).

Gikandi, Simon. *Reading Chinua Achebe: Language and Ideology in Fiction.* Portsmouth, NH: Heinemann, 1991.

Gunner, Liz, ed., and trans. *Musho!: Zulu Popular Praises.* East Lansing: Michigan State University Press, 1991.

Hale, Thomas A. *Scribe, Griot and Novelist: Narrative Interpreters of the Songhay Empire Followed by the Epic of Askia Mohammed Recounted,* Gainesville, FL: University of Florida Press/Center for African Studies, 1990.

Harrow, Kenneth, ed., *Faces of Islam in African Literature*. Portsmouth, NH: Heinemann, 1991.

Harrow, Kenneth, Jonathan Ngate, and Clarissa Zimra, eds. *Crisscrossing Boundaries in African Literatures, 1986*. Washington, DC: Three Continents Press/African Literature Association, 1991.

Ikonne, Chidi, Emelia Oko, and Peter Onwudinjo, eds. *African Literature and African Historical Experience*. New York: Heinemann, 1991.

Innes, Catherine Lynette. *Chinua Achebe*. New York: Cambridge University Press, 1990.

Innes, Catherine Lynette. *The Devil's Own Mirror: The Irishman and the African Modern Literature*. Washington, DC: Three Continents Press, 1990.

James, Adeola, ed., *In Their Own Voices: African Women Writers Talk*. Portsmouth, NH: Heinemann, 1990.

Jones, Eldred Durosimi, ed. *The Question of Language in African Literature Today: Borrowing and Carrying: A Review*. Trenton, NJ: Africa World Press, 1991.

Julien, Eileen. *African Novels and the Question of Orality*. Bloomington: Indiana University Press, 1992.

Lazarus, Neil. *Resistance in Postcolonial African Fiction*. New Haven, CT: Yale University Press, 1991.

Lindfors, Bernth. *Popular Literature in Africa*. Trenton, NJ: Africa World Press, 1991.

Liyong, Taban Lo. *Another Last Word*. New York: Heinemann, 1990.

Miller, Christopher L. *Theories of Africans: Franco-Phone Literature and Anthropology in Africa*. Chicago: University of Chicago Press, 1990.

Mortimer, Mildred. *Journey Through the French African Novel*. Portsmouth, NH: Heinemann, 1990.

Nethersole, Reingard, ed. *Emerging Literature*. New York: P. Lang, 1990.

Ngara, Emmanuel. *Ideology and Form in African Poetry: Implications for Communication*. Portsmouth, NH: Heinemann, 1990.

Obiechina, Emmanuel N. *Language and Theme: Essays on African Literature*. Washington, DC: Howard University Press, 1990.

Orisawayi, Dele, et. al., eds. *Literature and Black Aesthetics*. New York: Heinemann, 1990.

Owomoyela, Onjekan. *Visions and Revisions: Essays on African Literatures and Criticisms*. New York: P. Lang, 1991.

Research in African Literatures: Critical Theory and African Literature. Bloomington: Indiana University Press, 1990.

Research in African Literature: Dictatorship and Oppression. Bloomington: Indiana University Press, 1990.

Roscoe, Adrian A., and Hangson Msika. *The Quiet Chameleon: Modern Poetry from Central Africa*. New York: Hans Zell Publishers, 1992.

Scheub, Harold. *The African Storyteller: Stories from African Oral Traditions*. Dubuque, IA: Kendell/Hunt, 1991.

Schipper, Mineke. *Beyond the Boundaries: Text and Context in African Literature*. Chicago: Ivan R. Dee, 1990.

Sicherman, Carol. *Ngugi wa Thiong: A Source Book on Kenyan Literature and Resistance*. New York: Hans Zell Publishers, 1990.

Soyinka, Wole. *Myth, Literature, and the African World*. New York: Cambridge University Press, 1990.

Trump, Martin, ed. *Rendering Things Visible: Essays on South African Literary Culture*. Athens: Ohio University Press, 1991.

Wilentz, Gay Alden. *Binding Cultures: Black Women Writers in Africa and the Diaspora*. Bloomington: Indiana University Press, 1992.

Wylie, Hal, Dennis Brutus, and Juris Silenieks, eds. *African Literature, 1988: New Masks*. Washington, DC: Three Continents Press/The African Literature Association, 1990.

Law, Law Enforcement, Civil and Human Rights

Ahire, Philip Terdo. *Imperial Policing: The Emergence and Role of the Police in Nigeria, 1860–1960.* Philadelphia: Open University Press, 1991.

Bazille, Susan, ed. *Putting Women on the Agenda.* Johannesburg, S.A.: Raven Press, 1991. (Dist. by Ohio University Press).

Braham, Peter, ed. *Racism and Antiracism: Inequalities in Opportunities and Policies.* Philadelphia: Sage/Open University Press, 1992.

Hansson, Desiree, and Dirk van Zyl Smit, eds. *Toward Justice? Crime and State Control in South Africa.* New York: Oxford University Press, 1990.

Mann, Kristin, ed. *Law in Colonial Africa.* Portsmouth, NH: Heinemann, 1991.

Shepherd, George W., and Mark O.G. Anikpo, eds. *Emerging Human Rights: The African Political Economy Concept.* Westport, CT: Greenwood Press, 1990.

Media

Faringer, Gunilla L. *Press Freedom in Africa.* Westport, CT: Praeger, 1991.

Harden, Blaine. *Africa: Dispatches from a Fragile Continent.* London: Harper Collins, 1990.

Hawk, Beverly G., ed. *Africa's Media Image.* New York: Praeger, 1992.

Sturges, Paul, and Richard Neill. *The Quiet Struggle: Libraries and Information for Africa.* New York: Mansell, 1990.

Music

Arom, Simha. *African Polyphony and Polyrhythm: Musical Structure and Methodology.* Translated by Martin Thom and Barbara Tucker. New York: Cambridge University Press, 1991.

Bender, Wolfgang. *Sweet Mother: Modern African Music.* Translated by Wolfgang Freis. Chicago: University of Chicago Press, 1991.

Collins, John. *West African Pop Roots.* Philadelphia: Temple University Press, 1992.

Gray, John. *African Music: A Bibliographic Guide to the Traditional Popular Art and Liturgical Music of Sub-Saharan Africa.* Westport, CT: Greenwood Press, 1991.

Lems-Dworkin, Carol. *African Music: A Pan-African Annotated Bibliography.* New York: Hans Zell Publishers, 1991.

Stewart, Gary. *Breakout: Profiles in African Rhythm.* Chicago: University of Chicago Press, 1992.

Waterman, Christopher Alan. *Juju: A Social History and Ethnography of an African Popular Music.* Chicago: University of Chicago Press, 1990.

Pan-Africanism

Agyeman, Opoku. *Nkrumah's Ghana and East Africa: Pan-Africanism and African Interstate Relations.* Cranbury, NJ: Fairleigh Dickinson University Press, 1992.

Clarke, John H. *Africans at the Crossroads: Notes for an African World Revolution.* Trenton, NJ: Africa World Press, 1992.

Staniland, Martin. *American Intellectuals and African Nationalists, 1950–1970.* New Haven: Yale University Press, 1991.

Performing Arts

Diawara, Manthia. *African Cinema: Politics and Culture.* Bloomington: Indiana University Press, 1992.

Erlman, Veit. *African Stars: Studies in Black South African Performance.* Chicago: University of Chicago Press, 1991.

Lee, Jacques K. *Sega: The Mauritius Folk Dance.* London: Nautilus Publishing Co., 1990.

Orkin, Martin. *Drama and the South African State.* Manchester, UK: Manchester University Press, 1991. (Dist. by St. Martin's Press)

Religion and Philosophy

Dankwa, Nano O., III. *Christianity and African Traditional Beliefs.* Edited by John W. Branch. New York: Power of the World Publishing Co., 1990.

Felder, Cain Hope, ed. *Stony the Road We Trod: African American Biblical Interpretation.* Minneapolis: Fortress Press, 1991.

Gbadegesin, Segun. *African Philosophy: Traditional Yoruba Philosophy and Contemporary African Realities.* New York: Lang, 1991.

Gifford, Paul. *The New Crusaders: Christianity and the New Right in Southern Africa.* London: Pluto, 1991.

Gray, Richard. *Black Christians and White Missionaries.* New Haven: Yale University Press, 1991.

Oldfield, J.R. *Alexander Crummell (1819–1898) and the Creation of an African-American Church in Africa.* Lewiston, NY: Edwin Mellin Press, 1990.

Olupona, Jacob K. *African Traditional Religions in Contemporary Society.* New York: Paragon, 1991.

Oruka, H. O. *Trends in Contemporary African Philosophy.* Nairobi, Kenya: Shirikon Publishers, 1990.

Peek, Philip M., ed. *African Divination Systems: Ways of Knowing.* Bloomington: Indiana University Press, 1991.

Prozesky, Martin, ed. *Christianity Amidst Apartheid.* New York: London, Macmillan, 1990.

Soyinka, Wole. *The Credo of Being and Nothingness.* Ibadan: Spectrum Books, 1990.

Vanderaa, Larry A. *A Survey of Christian Reformed World Missions and Churches in West Africa.* Grand Rapids, MI: Christian Reformed World Missions, 1991.

Sociology and Psychology

Barnes, James Franklin. *Gabon: Beyond the Colonial Legacy.* Boulder, CO: Westview Press, 1992.

Bell, Leland V. *Mental and Social Disorder in Sub-Saharan Africa: The Case of Sierra Leone, 1787–1990.* Westport, CT: Greenwood Press, 1991.

Carr-Hill, Roy A. *Social Conditions in Sub-Saharan Africa.* London; New York: Macmillan, 1991.

Cleaver, Tessa, and Marion Wallace. *Namibia: Women in War.* Foreword by Glenys Kinnock. Atlantic Highlands, NJ: Zed Books, 1990.

Cobley, Alan Gregord. *Class and Consciousness: The Black Petty Bourgeoisie in South Africa, 1924–1950.* Westport, CT: Greenwood Press, 1990.

Coles, Catherine, and Beverly Mack, eds. *Hausa Women in the Twentieth Century.* Madison: University of Wisconsin Press, 1991.

Gordon, Robert J. *The Bushman Myth: The Making of a Namibian Underclass.* Boulder, CO: Westview Press, 1992.

Hill, Martin J.D., ed. *The Harambee Movement in Kenya: Self-Help Development and Education Among the Kamba of Chat District.* Atlantic Highlands, NJ: Athlone Press, 1991.

Kilbride, Philip Leroy. *Changing Family Life in East Africa: Women and Children at Risk,* Philadelphia: Pennsylvania State University Press, 1990.

Mohammad, Duri, ed., *Social Development in Africa: Strategies, Policies and Programmes After the Lagos Plan.* Providence, NJ: H. Zell Publishers, 1991.

Moran, Mary. *Civilized Women: Gender and Prestige in Southeastern Liberia.* Ithaca, NY: Cornell University Press, 1991.

Nsamenang, A. Bame. *Human Development in Cultural Conflict.* Foreword by Michael Lamb. Newbury Park, CA: Sage Publications, 1992.

Ominde, S. H., ed. *Kenya' s Population Growth and Development to the Year 2000.* Columbus: Ohio University Press, 1990.

Reynolds, Pamela. *Dance Cat: Child Labour in the Zambezi Valley.* London: Hans Zell Books, 1991.

Riseman, Paul. *First Find Your Child A Good Mother: The Construction of Self in Two African Communities.* New Brunswick, NJ: Rutgers University Press, 1992.

Robertson, Struan. *The Cold Choice: Pictures of a South African Reality.* Grand Rapids, MI: Wm. B. Erdmans Publishing Co., 1992.

■ AFRICAN AMERICANA

Art, Architecture, and Photography

Bearden, Romare. *Memory and Metaphor: The Art of Romare Bearden, 1940–1987.* New York: Studio Museum of Harlem/Oxford University Press, 1991.

Durham, Michael S. *Powerful Days: The Civil Rights Photography of Charles Moore.* Introduction by Andrew Young. New York: Stewart, Tabori & Chang, 1991.

Easter, Eric, D. Michael Cheers, and Dudley M. Brooks, eds. *Songs of My People: African Americans: A Self-Portrait.* Introduction by Gordon Parks. Essays by Sylvester Monroe. Boston: Little, Brown, 1992.

McElroy, Guy C. *Facing History: The Black Image in American Art, 1710–1940.* Edited by Christopher C. French. Washington, DC: Bedford Arts/Corcoran Gallery, 1990.

Powell, Richard J. *Homecoming: The Art and Life of William H. Johnson.* New York: National Museum of American Art/Rizzoli, 1991.

Rozelle, Robert V., et. al. eds. *Black Art: Ancestral Legacy: The African-American Impulse in African-American Art.* New York: Abrams, 1990.

Thomison, Dennis, comp. *The Black Artist in America: An Index to Reproductions.* Metuchen, NJ: Scarecrow Press, 1991.

Travis, Jack, ed. *African-American Architects in Current Practice.* New York: Princeton Architecture Press, 1991.

Autobiography and Biography

Baker, Donald P. *Wilder: Hold Fast to Dreams: A Biography of L. Douglas Wilder.* Cabin John, MD: Seven Locks, 1990.

Baldwin, Lewis V. *There Is a Balm in Gilead: The Cultural Roots of Martin Luther King, Jr.* Minneapolis: Fortress Press, 1991.

Bigelow, Barbara Carlisle, ed. *Contemporary Black Biography.* Detroit: Gale Research Inc., 1992.

Bjarkman, Peter C. *Ernie Banks.* Introduction by Jim Murray. New York: Chelsea House, 1992.

Brown, Drew T., III. *You Gotta Believe!: Education + Hard Work − Drugs = The American Dream.* New York: Morrow, 1991.

Brown, James, and Bruce Tucker. *James Brown: The Godfather of Soul.* New York: Thunder's Mouth Press, 1990.

Buchmann-Moller, Frank. *You Just Fight for Your Life: The Story of Lester Young.* New York: Praeger, 1990.

Campbell, James. *Talking at the Gate: A Life of James Baldwin.* New York: Viking, 1991.

Carson, Clayborne. *Malcolm X; The FBI File.* Introduction by Spike Lee. Edited by David Gallen. New York: Carroll & Graf Publishers, Inc., 1991.

Carson, Clayborne, ed. *The Papers of Martin Luther King, Jr.* Berkeley: University of California Press, 1991.

Chilton, John. *The Song of the Hawk: The Life and Recordings of Coleman Hawkins.* New York: St. Martin's Press, 1990.

Davis, Benjamin O., Jr. *Benjamin O. Davis, Jr., American: An Autobiography.* Washington, DC: Smithsonian Institution, 1991.

Davis, Miles, and Quincy Troupe. *Miles, The Autobiography.* New York: Simon & Schuster, 1990.

Deane, Bill. *Bob Gibson.* Introduction by Jim Murray. New York: Chelsea House, 1992.

Dees, Morris. *A Season for Justice: The Life and Times of Civil Rights Lawyer Morris Dees.* New York: Scribner, 1991.

Faser, Jane. *Walter White.* New York: Chelsea House, 1991.

Goldman, Roger, and David Gallen. *Thurgood Marshall: Justice for All.* New York: Carroll & Graf, 1992.

Hamilton, Charles V. *Adam Clayton Powell, Jr.: The Political Biography of an American Dilemma.* New York: Atheneum, 1991.

Hawkins, Walter L. *African American Biographies: Profiles of 558 Current Men and Women.* Jefferson, NC: McFarland & Co., 1992.

Hayes, Bob. *Run, Bullet, Run.* New York: Harper Collins, 1990.

Kranz, Rachel C. *The Biographical Dictionary of Black Americans.* New York: Facts on File, 1992.

Kremer, Gary R. *James Milton Turner and the Promise of America: The Public Life of a Post-Civil War Black Leader.* Columbia: University of Missouri Press, 1991.

Levi, Darrell E. *Michael Manley: The Making of a Leader.* Athens: University of Georgia Press, 1990.

McFeely, William S. *Frederick Douglass.* New York: Norton, 1990.

Mosby, Dewey F., and Darrel Sewell. *Henry Ossawa Tanner.* New York: Rizzoli, 1991.

Naughton, Jim. *Taking to the Air: The Rise of Michael Jordan.* New York: Warner Books, 1992.

Pallister, Janis L. *Aime Cesaire.* New York: Twayne, 1991.

Perry, Bruce. *Malcolm: The Life of a Man Who Changed Black America.* Barrytown, NY: Station Hill, 1991.

Pfieffer, Paula F. *A. Philip Randolph, Pioneer of the Civil Rights Movement.* Baton Rouge: Louisiana State University Press, 1990.

Phelps, J. Alfred. *Chappie: America's First Black Four-Star General.* Novato, CA: Presidio Press, 1991.

Phelps, Shirelle, ed. *Who's Who Among Black Americans, 1993–94.* 7th ed., William C. Matney, Jr., Consulting Editor. Detroit: Gale Research Inc., 1993.

Pickens, William. *Bursting Bonds: Enlarged edition (of) The Heir of Slaves: The Autobiography of a "New Negro".* Edited by William L. Andrews. Bloomington: Indiana University Press, 1991.

Rattenbury, Ken. *Duke Ellington, Jazz Composer.* New Haven: Yale University Press, 1991.

Rivlin, Benjamin, ed. *Ralph Bunche, The Man and His Times.* Foreword by Donald F. Henry. New York: Holmes & Meier, 1990.

Rose, Cynthia. *Living in America: The Soul Saga of James Brown.* London: Serpent Tale, 1990 (Dist. by Consortium Book Sales Distribution.)

Rout, Kathleen. *Eldridge Cleaver.* Boston: Twayne/G.K. Hall, 1991.

Schwartzman, Myron. *Romare Bearden: His Life and Art.* New York: Abrams, 1990.

Shapiro, Leonard. *Big Man on Campus: John Thompson and the Georgetown Hoyas.* New York: Holt, 1991.

Shapiro, Miles. *Bill Russell.* Introductory essay by Coretta Scott King. New York: Chelsea House, 1991.

Sifford, Charlie. *Just Let Me Play: The Story of Charlie Sifford: The First Black PGA Golfer.* Latham, NY: British American Publishers, 1992.

Smith, Eric Ledell. *Bert Williams: A Biography of the Pioneer Black Comedian.* Jefferson, NC: McFarland, 1992.

Stewart, James Brewer. *William Lloyd Garrison and the Challenge of Emancipation.* Arlington Heights, IL: Harlan Davidson, 1992.

Strode, Woody, and Sam Young. *Goal Dust: An Autobiography*. Lantham, MD: Madison Books, 1990.

Tucker, Ken. *Ellington: The Early Years*. Champaign: University of Illinois Press, 1991.

Urban, Wayne J. *Black Scholar: Horace Mann Bond, 1904–1972*. Athens: University of Georgia Press, 1992.

Vache, Warren W. *Crazy Fingers: Claude Hopkins' Life in Jazz*. Washington, DC: Smithsonian Institution Press, 1992.

Watts, Jill. *God, Harlem U.S.A.: The Father Divine Story*. Berkeley: University of California Press, 1992.

Weland, Gerald. *Of Vision and Valor: General O. O. Howard, A Biography*. Canton, OH: Daring Publishing Group, 1991.

Wells, Dicky. *The Night People: The Jazz Life of Dicky Wells*. As told to Stanley Dance. rev. ed., Washington, DC: Smithsonian Institution Press, 1991.

Wills, Maury, and Mike Celizic. *On the Run: The Never Dull and Often Shocking Life of Maury Wills*. New York: Carroll & Graf, 1991.

Black Nationalism and Pan-Africanism in the United States

Crosby, Edward W., and Linus A. Hoskins, eds. *Africa for the Africans: Selected Speeches of Marcus Mosiah Garvey; Malcolm X; and Nelson Kolihlahla Mandela*. Kent, OH: The Institute for African American Affairs, Department of Pan-African Studies, Kent State University, 1991.

Crummell, Alexander. *Destiny and Race: Selected Writings, 1840–1898*. Edited with introduction by Wilson J. Moses. Amherst: University of Massachusetts Press, 1992.

Drake, St. Clair. *Black Folks Here and There: An Essay in History and Anthropology*. 2 vols. Los Angeles: University of California, Los Angeles, Center for Afro-American Studies, 1991.

Harris, Robert, et. al. *Carlos Cooks: And Black Nationalism from Garvey to Malcolm*. Dover, MA: Majority Press, 1992.

Jacques, Geoffrey. *The African-American Movement Today*. New York: Watts, 1992.

Lemelle, Sid. *Pan-Africanism for Beginners*. New York: Writers and Readers Publishing, Inc., 1992.

Lewis, Rupert, ed. *Garvey: His Work and Impact*. Trenton, NJ: Africa World Press, 1991.

Martin, Tony, comp. and ed. *African Fundamentalism: A Literary and Cultural Anthropology of Garvey's Harlem Renaissance*. Dover, MA: Majority Press, 1991.

Moses, Wilson J. *Alexander Crummell: A Study of Civilization and Discontent*. Amherst: University of Massachusetts Press, 1992.

Civil Rights, Law, and Civil Protests

Administrative History of the Civil Rights Division of the Department of Justice During the Johnson Administration. 2 vols., New York: Garland Publishing Co., 1991.

Aguirre, Adalberto, Jr., and David V. Baker. *Race, Racism and the Death Penalty in the United States*. Barrien Springs, MI: Vande Vere Publishers, 1992.

Belknap, Michal. *Racial Violence and Law Enforcement in the South*. New York: Garland Publishing Co., 1991.

Belknap, Michal. *Securing the Enactment of Civil Rights Legislation, 1965–1968*. New York: Garland Publishing Co., 1991.

Belknap, Michal. *Urban Race Riots*. New York: Garland Publishing Co., 1991.

Belknap, Michal. *Voting Rights*. New York: Garland Publishing Co., 1991.

Belz, Herman. *Equality Transformed: A Quarter-Century of Affirmative Action*. New Brunswick, NJ: Transaction, 1991.

Blumberg, Rhoda L. *Civil Rights, the Freedom Struggle.* rev. ed., Boston: Twayne G.K. Hall, 1991.

Bolick, Clint. *Unfinished Business: A Civil Rights Strategy for America's Third Century.* San Francisco: Research Institute of Public Policy, 1990.

Cagin, Seth, and Philip Dray. *We Are Not Afraid: The Story of Goodman, Schwerner and Chaney and the Civil Rights Campaign for Mississippi.* New York: Bantam Books, 1991.

Capeci, Dominic, and Martha Wilkerson. *Layered Violence: the Detroit Rioters of 1943.* Jackson: University Press of Mississippi, 1991.

Carson, Clayborne, et. al. eds. *"The Eyes on the Prize" Civil Rights Reader: Documents, Speeches, and Firsthand Accounts from the Black Freedom Struggle, 1954–1990.* New York: Viking, 1991.

Cashman, Sean Dennis. *African-Americans and the Quest for Civil Rights, 1900–1990.* New York: New York University Press, 1991.

Cashmore, Ellis, and Eugene McLaughlin, eds. *Out of Order?: Policing Black People.* New York: Routledge, 1991.

Cone, James H. *Martin and Malcolm and America: A Dream or a Nightmare.* New York: Orbis Books, 1991.

Cook, Anthony. *Law, Race and Social Theory.* Boston: New England School of Law, 1991.

Detefsen, Robert R. *Civil Rights Under Reagan.* San Francisco: ICS Press, 1991.

Encyclopedia of African American Civil Rights: From Emancipation to the Present. Westport, CT: Greenwood Press, 1992.

Epstein, Richard Allen. *Forbidden Grounds: The Case Against Employment Discrimination Laws.* Cambridge: Harvard University Press, 1992.

Ezorsky, Gertrude. *Racism and Justice: The Case for Affirmative Action.* Ithaca, NY: Cornell University Press, 1991.

Fendrich, James Max. *Ideal Citizens: The Legacy of the Civil Rights Movement.* Albany: State University of New York Press, 1993.

Finkelman, Paul, ed. *African Americans and the Law.* New York: Garland Publishing Co., 1991 (*Race, Law and American History, 1700–1900. The African American Experience.*)

Finkelman, Paul, ed. *African-Americans and the Legal Profession in Historical Perspective.* New York: Garland Publishing Co., 1991 (*Race, Law, and American History, 1700–1990. The African American Experience,* vol. 10).

Finkelman, Paul, ed. *African-Americans and the Right to Vote.* Edited by Paul Finkelman. New York: Garland Publishing Co., 1992. (*Race, Law, and American History, 1700–1900. The African-American Experience,* vol. 6).

Finkelman, Paul, ed. *Lynching, Racial Violence, and Law.* New York: Garland Publishing Co., 1992. (*Race, Law, and American History, 1700–1990. The African-American Experience,* vol. 9.)

Finkelman, Paul, ed. *Race and Criminal Justice.* New York: Garland Publishing Co., 1992. (*Race, Law, and American History, 1700–1900. The American Experience,* vol. 8.)

Finkelman, Paul, ed. *Race and Law Before Emancipation.* New York: Garland Publishing Co., 1992. (*Race, Law and American History, 1700–1990. The African American Experience,* vol. 2.)

Finkelman, Paul, ed. *The Era of Integration and Civil Rights, 1930–1990.* New York: Garland Publishing Co., 1992. (*Race, Law, and American History, 1700–1990. The African American Experience,* vol. 5).

Fiscus, Ronald Jerry. *The Constitutional Logic of Affirmative Action.* Edited by Stephen Wasby. Durham, NC: Duke University Press, 1992.

Fisher, Sethard. *From Margin to Mainstream: The Social Progress of Black Americans.* 2nd ed., Savage, MD: Rowman & Littlefield, 1992.

Goings, Kenneth W. *The NAACP Comes of Age: The Defeat of Judge Parker.* Bloomington: Indiana University Press, 1990.

Goldwin, Robert A. *Why Blacks, Women and Jews Are Not Mentioned in the Constitution, and Other Unorthodox Views.* Washington, DC: American Enterprise Institute, 1990.

Graetz, Robert S. *Montgomery, A White Preachers Memoir.* Minneapolis: Fortress Press, 1991.

Grafman, Bernard, ed. *Controversies in Minority Voting: The Voting Rights Act in Perspective.* Washington, DC: Brookings Institute, 1992.

Graham, Hugh Davis. *The Civil Rights Era: Race, Gender and National Policy, 1960–1972.* New York: Oxford University Press, 1990.

Hampton, Henry, and Steve Fayer, comps. *Voices of Freedom: An Oral History of the Civil Rights Movement from the 1950s Through the 1980s.* New York: Bantam Books, 1990.

Harding, Vincent. *Hope and History: Why We Must Share the Story of the Movement.* Maryknoll, NY: Orbis Books, 1990.

Harris, Jacqueline. *A History of the NAACP.* New York: Watts, 1992.

Jackson, James E. *The Bold Bad '60s: Pushing the Point for Equality Down South and Out Yonder.* New York: International Publishers, 1992.

James, Hunter. *They Didn't Put That on the Huntley-Brinkley Report!: A Vagabound Reporter Encounters the New South.* Athens: University of Georgia, 1993.

Justice Department Briefs in Crucial Civil Rights Cases. 2 vols., New York: Garland, 1991.

Kapur, Sudarshan. *Raising Up a Prophet: The African-American Encounter with Gandhi.* Boston: Beacon, 1992.

King, Richard. *Civil Rights and the Idea of Freedom.* New York: Oxford University Press, 1992.

Kull, Andrew. *The Color-Blind Constitution.* Cambridge: Harvard University Press, 1992.

Levy, Peter B., ed. *Dictionary History of the Modern Civil Rights Movement.* New York: Greenwood Press, 1992.

Levy, Peter B., ed. *Let Freedom Ring: A Documentary History of the Modern Civil Rights Movement.* New York: Praeger, 1992.

Lyon, Danny. *Memories of the Civil Rights Movement.* Text and photographs by Danny Lyon; foreword by Julian Bond. Chapel Hill: University of North Carolina Press, 1992.

Meier, August, et. al. eds. *Black Protest in the Sixties.* New York: M. Wiener, 1991.

Meier, August. *A White Scholar and the Black Community, 1945–1965: Essays and Reflections.* Afterword by John H. Bracey, Jr. Amherst: University of Massachusetts Press, 1992.

Mills, Nicolaus. *Like a Holy Crusade: Mississippi, 1964—The Turning of the Civil Rights Movement in America.* Chicago: I.R. Dee, 1992.

Nieli, Russell, ed. *Racial Preference and Racial Justice: The New Affirmative Action Controversy.* Washington, DC: Ethics and Public Policy Center, 1991 (Dist. by National Book Network.)

Nieman, Donald G. *Promises to Keep: African Americans and the Constitutional Order, 1776 to the Present.* New York: Oxford University Press, 1991.

O'Reilly, Kenneth. *Racial Matters: The FBI's Secret File on Black America, 1960–1972.* New York: Free Press, 1991.

Powledge, Fred. *Free At Last?: The Civil Rights Movement and the People Who Made It.* Boston: Little, Brown, 1990.

Reed, Merl E. *Seedtime for the Modern Civil Rights Movement: The President's Committee on Fair Employment Practice, 1941–1946.* Baton Rouge: Louisiana State University Press, 1991.

Robinson, Amelia Boynton. *Bridge Across Jordan.* rev. ed., Washington, DC: Schiller Institute, 1991.

Robinson, Armistead L., and Patricia Sullivan, eds. *New Directions in Civil Rights Studies.*

Charlottesville: University Press of Virginia, 1991.

Sigelman, Lee, and Susan Welch. *Black Americans' Views of Racial Inequality: The Dream Deferred*. New York: Cambridge University Press, 1991.

Sikora, Frank. *Until Justice Rolls Down: The Birmingham Church Bombing Case*. Tuscaloosa: University of Alabama Press, 1991.

Stern, Mark. *Calculating Visions: Kennedy, Johnson and Civil Rights*. New Brunswick, NJ: Rutgers University Press, 1992.

Swift, Jeanne, ed. *Dream and Reality: The Modern Black Struggle for Freedom and Equality*. New York: Greenwood Press, 1991.

Thomas, Clarence. *Clarence Thomas: Confronting the Future: Selections from the Senate Confirmation Hearing and Prior Speeches*. Washington, DC: Regnery Gateway, 1992.

Urofsky, Melvin I. *A Conflict of Rights: The Supreme Court and Affirmative Action*. New York: Scribners, 1991.

Watson, Denton L. *Lion in the Lobby: Clarence Mitchell, Jr.'s Struggle for the Passage of Civil Rights Laws*. New York: Morrow, 1990.

Wright, Roberta Hughes. *The Birth of the Montgomery Bus Boycott*. Southfield, MI: Charro Book Co., 1991.

Economics, Entrepreneurship, and Labor

Broadnax, Derek. *The Black Entrepreneurs Guide to Million Dollar Business Opportunities*. Austin, TX: Black Entrepreneurs Press, 1990.

Broadnax, Derek. *The Black Entrepreneurs Guide to Money Sources: How to Get Your Share*. Austin, TX: Black Entrepreneurs Press, 1990.

Butler, John Sibley. *Entrepreneurship and Self-Help Among Black Americans: A Reconsideration of Race and Economics*. Albany: State University of New York Press, 1991.

Dewart, Janet, ed. *The State of Black America, 1991*. New York: National Urban League, 1991.

Duncan, Mike. *Reach Your Goals In Spite of the Old Boy Network: A Guide for African American Employees*. Edgewood, MD: M.E. Duncan and Co., 1990.

Grant, Nancy L. *TVA and Black Americans: Planning for the Status Quo*. Philadelphia: Temple University Press, 1990.

Green, Shelley, and Paul Pryde. *Black Entrepreneurship in America*. Brunswick, NJ: Transactions Publishers, 1990.

Greenberg, Jonathan D. *Staking a Claim: Jake Simmons and the Making of an African-American Oil Dynasty*. New York: Atheneum, 1991.

Reed, Wornie, ed. *Social, Political and Economic Issues in Black America*. Amherst: University of Massachusetts, William Monroe Trotter Institute, 1990.

Rosen, George H. *Black Money*. Chelsea, MI: Scarborough House, 1990.

Education

Allen, Walter R., Edgar Epps, and Nesha Z. Haniff, eds. *College in Black and White: African American Students in Predominately White and Historically Black Public Universities*. Albany: State University of New York Press, 1991.

Altbach, Philip G., and Kofi Lomotey, eds. *The Racial Crisis in American Higher Education*. Albany: State University of New York Press, 1991.

Bowman, J. Wilson. *America's Black Colleges*. South Pasadena, CA: Sandcastle Publishing Co., 1992.

Fife, Brian L. *Desegregation in American Schools: Comparative Intervention Strategies*. New York: Praeger, 1992.

Finkelman, Paul, ed. *The Struggle for Equal Education*. New York: Garland Publishing Co., 1992. (*Race, Law, and American History, 1700–1990. African-American Experience*, vol. 7.)

Formisano, Ronald P. *Boston Against Busing: Race, Class, and Ethnicity in the 1960s and 1970s.* Chapel Hill: University of North Carolina Press, 1991.

Harmon, Marylen E. *The Infusion of African and African American Studies into the Curriculum.* Roanoke, VA: Absolute Writings Ltd., 1991.

Irvine, Jacqueline Jordan. *Black Students and School Failure: Policies, Practices, and Prescriptions.* Westport, CT: Greenwood Press, 1990.

Lomotey, Kofi, ed. *Going to School: The African-American Experience.* Albany: State University of New York Press, 1990.

Lusane, Clarence. *The Struggle for Equal Education.* New York: F. Watts, 1992.

Margo, Robert A. *Race and Schooling in the South, 1880–1950.* Chicago: University of Chicago Press, 1991.

National Afro-American Museum and Cultural Center. *From Victory to Freedom: The African American Experience: Curriculum Guide, Secondary School Course of Study.* Wilberforce, OH: National Afro-American Museum and Cultural Center, 1991.

Neufeldt, Harvey G., and Leo McGee, eds. *Education of the African American Adult: An Historical Overview.* Westport, CT: Greenwood, 1990.

Pratt, Robert A. *The Color of Their Skin: Education and Race in Richmond, Virginia, 1954–89.* Charlottesville: University of Virginia Press, 1992.

Sachar, Emily. *Shut Up and Let the Lady Teach: A Teacher's Year in a Public School.* New York: Poseidon Press, 1991.

Thompkins, Susie Powers. *Cotton-Patch Schoolhouse.* Tuscaloosa: University of Alabama Press, 1992.

Willie, Charles V., Antoine M. Garibaldi, and Wornie L. Reed, eds. *The Education of African*

Americans. Westport, CT: Auburn House/Greenwood Publishing Group, 1991.

Folklore and Folk Culture

Abrahams, Roger D. *Singing the Master: The Emergence of African American Culture in the Plantation South.* New York: Pantheon Books, 1992.

Hall, Gwendolyn Midlo. *Africans in Colonial Louisiana: The Development of Afro-Creole Culture.* Baton Rouge: Louisiana State University Press, 1992.

Hazzard-Gordon, Katrina. *Jookin': The Rise of Social Dance Formation in African-American Culture.* Philadelphia: Temple University Press, 1990.

Hill, James L., ed. *Studies in African and African American Culture.* New York: P. Lang, 1990.

Holloway, Joseph E., ed. *Africanisms in American Culture.* Bloomington: Indiana University Press, 1990.

Njeri, Itabari. *Every Good-Bye Ain't Gone: Family Portraits and Personal Escapades.* New York: Times Books, 1990.

Roberts, John W. *From Trickster to Badman: The Black Folk Hero in Slavery and Freedom.* Philadelphia: University of Pennsylvania Press, 1990.

Spalding, Henry D., comp. and ed. *Encyclopedia of Black Folklore and Humor.* Introduction by J. Mason Brewer. Middle Village, NY: Jonathan David Publishers, 1990.

Sundquist, Eric J. *The Hammers of Creation: Folk Culture in Modern African-American Culture.* Athens: University of Georgia Press, 1992.

Twining, Mary A., and Keith E. Baird, eds. *Sea Island Roots: African Presence in Carolina and Georgia.* Trenton, NJ: Africa World Press, 1991.

General Reference

Asante, Molefi K. *The Historical and Cultural Atlas of African Americans.* New York: Macmillan, 1991.

The Black Resource Guide, 1990–1991 Edition. Washington, DC: Black Resource Guide, Inc., 1991.

Bogle, Donald, ed. *Black Arts Annual, 1988/89.* New York: Garland, 1990.

Donovan, Richard X. *Black Scientists of America.* Portland, OR: National Book Co., 1990.

Fitzpatrick, Sandra, and Maria Godwin. *The Guide to Black Washington: Places and Events of Historical and Cultural Significance in the Nation's Capital.* New York: Hippocrene, 1990.

Furtaw, Julia C., ed. *Black American Information Directory.* 2nd ed., Detroit: Gale Research Inc., 1992.

Hancock, Sybil. *Famous Firsts of Black Americans.* Gretna, LA: Pelican Publishing Co., 1991.

Horton, Carrell Peterson, and Jessie Carney Smith, comps. and eds. *Statistical Record of Black America.* 2nd ed., Detroit: Gale Research Inc., 1991.

Smithsonian Institution. *African and African American Resources at the Smithsonian.* Washington, DC: Smithsonian Institution, 1991.

Southern, Eileen, and Josephine Wright, comps. *African American Traditions in Song, Sermon, Tale, and Dance, 1600s–1920: An Annotated Bibliography of Literature, Collections, and Artworks.* Westport, CT: Greenwood Press, 1990.

Thum, Marcella. *Hippocrene U.S.A. Guide to Black America: A Directory of Historic and Cultural Sites Relating to Black America.* New York: Hippocrene Books, 1992.

Health

Bailey, A. Peter. *The Harlem Hospital Story: 100 Years of Struggle Against Illness.* Richmond, VA: Native Sun Publishers, 1991.

Bailey, Eric J. *Urban African American Health Care.* Lantham, MD: University Press of America, 1991.

The Black Women's Health Book: Speaking for Ourselves. Seattle: Seal Press, 1990.

Duh, Samuel V. *Blacks and AIDS: Genetic or Environmental Causes.* Newbury Park, CA: Sage Publications, 1991.

Health of Black Americans from Post Reconstruction to Integration, 1871–1960: An Annotated Bibliography of Contemporary Sources. Westport, CT: Greenwood Press, 1990.

McBride, David. *From TB to AIDS: Epidemics Among Urban Blacks Since 1900.* Albany: State University of New York Press, 1991.

National Black Health Leadership Directory, 1990–91. Washington, DC: NRW Associates, 1991.

History

The African American Experience: A History. Sharon Harley, Stephen Middleton, and Charlotte Stokes, Consultants. Englewood Cliffs, NJ: Prentice-Hall, 1992.

America, Richard, ed. *The Wealth of Races: The Present Value of Benefits from Past Injustices.* Westport, CT: Greenwood Press, 1991.

Anderson, Eric, and Alfred Moss, Jr., eds. *The Facts of Reconstruction: Essays in Honor of John Hope Franklin.* Baton Rouge: Louisiana State University Press, 1991.

Andrews, George Reid. *Blacks and Whites in Sao Paulo Brazil, 1888–1988.* Madison: University of Wisconsin Press, 1992.

Aptheker, Herbert. *Anti-Racism in U.S. History: The First Hundred Years.* New York: Greenwood Press, 1992.

Aptheker, Herbert. *To Be Free: Pioneering Studies in Afro-American History.* Introduction by John Hope Franklin. New York: Citadel Press, 1991.

Bailey, Richard. *Neither Carpetbaggers Nor Scalawags: Black Officeholders During the Re-*

construction in Alabama. Montgomery, AL: R. Bailey Publishers, 1991.

Beeth, Howard, and Cary E. Wintz, eds. *Black Dixie: Afro-Texan History and Culture in Houston.* College Station, TX: Texas A&M University Press, 1992.

Berlin, Irs, and Philip D. Morgan, eds. *The Slaves' Economy: Independent Production by Slaves in the Americas.* London: F. Cass, 1991.

Berlin, Irs, et. al., eds. *Slaves No More: Three Essays on Emancipation and the Civil War.* New York: Cambridge University Press, 1992.

The Black Abolitionist Papers, Vol. 3: The United States, 1830–1846. Chapel Hill: University of North Carolina Press, 1991.

Boney, F.N., Richard L. Hume, and Rafia Zafar. *God Made Man, Man Made the Slave.* Macon, GA: Mercer University Press, 1990.

Bryan, Patrick. *The Jamaican People, 1880–1902: Race and Social Control.* New York: Macmillan, 1991.

Bush, Barbara. *Slave Women in Caribbean Society, 1650–1838.* Bloomington: University of Indiana Press, 1990.

Campbell, Randolph B. *An Empire for Slavery: The Peculiar Institution in Texas, 1821–1865.* Baton Rouge: Louisiana State University Press, 1991.

Cantor, George. *Historic Landmarks of Black America.* Detroit: Gale Research Inc., 1991.

Cohen, William. *At Freedom Edge: Black Mobility at the Southern Quest for Racial Control, 1861–1915.* Baton Rouge: Louisiana State University Press, 1991.

Cornelius, Janet Duitsman. *"When I Can Read My Title Clear": Literacy, Slavery, and Religion in the Antebellum South.* Columbia: University of South Carolina Press, 1991.

Counter, S. Allen. *North Pole Legacy: Black, White and Eskimo.* Amherst: University of Massachusetts Press, 1991.

Crouch, Berry A. *The Freedmen's Bureau and Black Texans.* Austin: University of Texas Press, 1992.

Davis, Lenwood G. *A Travel Guide to Black Historical Sites and Landmarks in North Carolina.* Winston-Salem, NC: Bandit Books, 1991.

Deromantizing Black History: Critical Essays and Reappraisals. Knoxville: University of Tennessee Press, 1991.

Dillon, Merton L. *Slavery Attacked: Southern Slaves and Their Allies, 1619–1865.* Baton Rouge: Louisiana State University Press, 1990.

Downey, Dennis B., and Raymond M. Hyser. *No Crooked Death: Coatsville, Pennsylvania, and the Lynching of Zachariah Walker.* Champaign: University of Illinois Press, 1991.

Drago, Edmund L., ed. *Broke by the War: Letters of a Slave Trader.* Columbia: University of South Carolina Press, 1991.

Dykstra, Robert. *Bright Radical Star: Black Freedom and White Supremacy on the Hawkeye Frontier.* Cambridge: Harvard University Press, 1993.

Fede, Andrew. *People Without Rights: An Interpretation of the Fundamentals of the Law of Slavery in the U.S. South.* New York: Garland Publishing Co., 1992.

Ferguson, Leland G. *Uncommon Ground: Archaeology and Early African America, 1650–1800.* Washington, DC: Smithsonian Institution Press, 1992.

Finkelman, Paul, ed. *The Age of Jim Crow: Segregation from the End of Reconstruction to the Great Depression.* New York: Garland Publishing Co., 1992. (*Race, Law, and American History, 1760–1990. The African American Experience,* vol. 4.)

Finkelman, Paul, ed. *Emancipation and Reconstruction.* New York: Garland Publishing Co., 1992. (*Race, Law and American History, 1700–1990. The African American Experience,* vol. 3.)

Franklin, Vincent P. *Black Self-Determinism: A Cultural History of African-American Resistance.* 2nd ed., Brooklyn, NY: Lawrence Hill Books, 1992.

Frey, Sylvia. *Water from the Rock: Black Resistance in a Revolutionary Age.* Princeton, NJ: Princeton University Press, 1992.

Gatewood, Willard B. *Aristocrats of Color: The Black Elite, 1880–1920.* Bloomington: Indiana University Press, 1990.

Genovese, Eugene D. *The Slaveholders' Dilemma: Freedom and Progress in Southern Conservative Thought, 1820–1860.* Columbia: University of South Carolina Press, 1992.

Greenberg, Cheryl Lynn. *"Or Does It Explode?": Black Harlem in the Great Depression.* New York: Oxford University Press, 1991.

Hamilton, Kenneth Marvin. *Black Towns and Profit, Promotion and Development in the Trans-Appalachian West, 1877–1915.* Champaign: University of Illinois Press, 1991.

Harley, Sharon. *The African American Experience: A History.* Englewood Cliffs, NJ: Globe, 1992.

Harris, Richard S. *Politics & Prejudice: A History of Chester, Pennsylvania Negroes.* Apache Junction, AZ: Relmo Pubs., 1991.

Harrison, Alfredteen, ed. *Black Exodus: The Great Migration from the American South.* Oxford: University Press of Mississippi, 1991.

Henry, Paget, and Paul Buhle, eds. *C.L.R. James' Caribbean.* Durham, NC: Duke University Press, 1992.

Hornsby, Jr., Alton. *Chronology of African-American History: Significant Events and People from 1619 to the Present.* Detroit: Gale Research Inc., 1991.

Horton, James Oliver. *Free People of Color: Inside the African American Community.* Washington, DC: Smithsonian Institution, 1993.

Inikoroi, Joseph E., and Stanley L. Engerman, eds. *The Atlantic Slave Trade: Effects on Economic Societies, and Peoples in Africa, the Americas and Europe.* Durham, NC: Duke University Press, 1992.

Jackson, Terrance. *Putting It All Together: World Conquest, Global Genocide and African Liberation.* Bronx, NY: AKASA, 1991.

Jones, Howard. *The Red Diary: A Chronological History of Black Americans in Houston and Some Neighboring Harris County Communities-122 Years Later.* Austin, TX: Nortex Press, 1992.

Jones, Norrece T. *Born a Child of Freedom, Yet A Slave: Mechanisms of Control and Strategies of Resistance in Antebellum South Carolina.* Middletown, CT: Wesleyan University Press, 1990.

Jordan, Winthrop. *Tumult and Silence at Second Creek: An Inquiry into a Civil War Slave Conspiracy.* Baton Rouge: Louisiana State University Press, 1993.

Katz, William Loren. *Breaking the Chains: African American Slave Resistance.* New York: Atheneum, 1990.

Lane, Roger. *William Dorsey's Philadelphia and Ours: On the Origins and Future Prospects of Urban Black America.* New York: Oxford University Press, 1991.

Lesko, Kathleen M., ed. *Black Georgetown Remembered: A History of Its Black Community from the Founding of "The Town of George" in 1751 to the Present Day.* Washington, DC: Georgetown University Press, 1991.

Malone, Ann Patton. *Sweet Chariot: Slave Family and Household Structure in Nineteenth Century Louisiana.* Chapel Hill: University of North Carolina Press, 1992.

McLaurin, Melton A. *Celia, a Slave.* Athens: University of Georgia Press, 1991.

McMillen, Sally Gregory. *Southern Women: Black and White in the Old South.* Arlington Heights, IL: Harlan Davidson, 1992.

Meillassaux, Claude. *The Anthropology of Slavery: The Womb of Iron and Gold.* Translated by

Alide Dasnois. Chicago: University of Chicago Press, 1991.

Meyer, Mary K. *Free Blacks in Hartford, Somerset, and Talbort Counties, Maryland.* Mt. Airy, MD: Pipe Creek Publications, 1991.

Middleton, Stephen. *The Black Laws in the Old Northwest: A Documentary History.* New York: Greenwood Press, 1992.

Munford, Clarence J. *The Black Ordeal of Slavery and Slave Trading in the French West Indies, 1625–1715.* Lewiston, ME: Edwin Mellen, 1991.

Nash, Gary B. *Freedom by Degrees: Emancipation in Pennsylvania and Its Aftermath.* New York: Oxford University Press, 1991.

Nash, Gary B. *Race and Revolution.* Madison, WI: Madison House, 1990.

Oakes, James. *Slavery and Freedom: An Interpretation of the Old South.* New York: Knopf, 1990.

Pearson, Edward. *Slave Work and Culture in Town and Country.* Williamsburg, VA: Institute of Early American History and Culture, 1991.

Perdue, Charles L., ed. *Weevils in the Wheat: Interviews with Virginia Ex-Slaves.* Charlottesville: University Press of Virginia, 1992.

Reidy, Joseph. *From Slavery to Agrarian Capitalism in the Cotton Plantation South: Central Georgia, 1800–1880.* Chapel Hill: University of North Carolina Press, 1992.

Richardson, Bonham C. *The Caribbean in the Wide World, 1492–1922.* New York: Cambridge University Press, 1992.

Richter, William L. *Overreached on All Sides: The Freedmen's Bureau Administrators in Texas, 1865–1868.* College Station: Texas A&M University Press, 1991.

Schwartz, Stuart B. *Slaves, Peasants, and Rebels: Reconsidering Brazilian Slavery.* Champaign: University of Illinois Press, 1992.

Schweninger, Loren. *Black Property Owners in the South, 1790–1915.* Champaign: University of Illinois Press, 1990.

Slaughter, Thomas P. *Bloody Dawn: The Christiana Riot and Racial Violence in Antebellum North.* New York: Oxford University Press, 1991.

Solow, Barbara L., ed. *Slavery and the Rise of the Atlantic System.* New York: Cambridge University Press/W.E.B. DuBois Institute for Afro-American Research, 1991.

Stanisland, Martin. *American Intellectuals and African Nationalists; 1955–1970.* New Haven, CT: Yale University Press, 1991.

Stevenson, Lisbeth Gant. *African-American History: Heroes in Hardship.* Cambridge, MA: Cambridgeport Press, 1992.

Stone, Albert E. *The Return of Nat Turner: History, Literature, and Cultural Politics in Sixties America.* Athens: University of Georgia, 1992.

Stone, Frank Andrews. *African American Connecticut: African Origins, New England Roots.* Storrs, CT: Isaac N. Thut World Education Center, 1991.

Terry, Ted. *American Black History: Reference Manual.* Tulsa, OK: Myles Publishing Co., 1991.

Thomas, Richard W. *Life for Us: Building Black Community in Detroit, 1915–1945.* Bloomington: Indiana University Press, 1992.

Thornton, John. *Africa and Africans in the Making of the Atlantic World, 1400–1680.* New York: Cambridge University Press, 1992.

White, Shane. *Somewhat More Independent: The End of Slavery in New York City 1770–1870.* Athens: University of Georgia Press, 1991.

Williams, Jacob C. *Lillie: Black Life in Martins Ferry, Ohio During the 1920s and 1930s.* Ann Arbor, MI: Braun-Brumfield, 1991.

Williams, Lee E. *Post-War Riots in America, 1919 and 1946: How the Pressures of War Exacerbated American Urban Tensions to the Breaking Points.* Lewiston, NY: E. Mellen, 1991.

Language, Literature, and Drama

Babb, Valerie Melissa. *Ernest Gaines.* Boston: Twayne/G.K. Hall, 1991.

Bailey, Guy, Natalie Maynor, and Patricia Cukor-Avila, eds. *The Emergence of Black English: Text and Commentary*. Philadelphia: J. Benjamins Publishing Co., 1991.

Baker, Houston A., and Patricia Redmond, eds. *Afro-American Literary Study in the 1990s*. Chicago: University of Chicago Press, 1990.

Baraka, Imamu Amiri. *The Leroi Jones/Amiri Baraka Reader*. Edited William J. Harris. New York: Thunder's Mouth Press, 1991.

Barksdale, Richard K. *Praisesong of Survival: Lectures and Essays, 1957–1989*. Introduction by R. Baxter Miller. Urbana: University of Illinois, 1992.

Bassett, John E. *Harlem in Review: Critical Reactions to Black American Writers, 1917–1939*. Selinsgrove, PA: Susquehanna University Press, 1992.

Benitoz-Rojo, Antonio. *The Repeating Island: The Caribbean and the Postmodern Perspective*. Durham, NC: Duke University Press, 1992.

Blackshire-Belay, Carol Aisha, ed. *Language and Literature in the African American Imagination*. Westport, CT: Greenwood Press, 1992.

Bloom, Harold, ed. *Bigger Thomas*. New York: Chelsea House, 1990.

Brown, Stewart, ed. *The Art of Derek Walcott*. UK: Seren Books, 1992. (Dist. by Dufour Editions, Inc.)

Busby, Mark. *Ralph Ellison*. Boston: Twayne/G.K. Hall, 1991.

Butler, Robert. *Native Son: The Emergence of a New Black Hero*. Boston: Twayne/G.K. Hall, 1991.

Cartey, Wilfred. *Whispers from the Caribbean: I Going Away, I Going Home*. Los Angeles: University of California, Los Angeles, Center for Afro-American Studies, 1991.

DeJongh, James. *Vicious Modernism: Black Harlem and the Literary Imagination*. New York: Cambridge University Press, 1990.

Dieke, Ikenna. *The Primordial Image: African, Afro-American, and Caribbean Mythopoetic Text*. New York: P. Lang, 1991.

Draper, James P., ed. *Black Literature Criticism: Excerpts from Criticism of the Most Significant Works of Black Authors over the Past 200 Years*. 3 vols., Detroit: Gale Research Inc., 1992.

Edwards, Walter F., and Donald Winford, eds. *Verb Phrase Patterns in Black English and Creole*. Detroit: Wayne State University Press, 1991.

Fabre, Michel. *Richard Wright: Books and Writers*. Oxford: University Press of Mississippi, 1990.

Gates, Henry Louis, Jr. *Loose Canons: Notes on the Culture Wars*. New York: Oxford University Press, 1992.

Hamalian, Leo, and James V. Hatch, eds. *The Roots of African American Drama: An Anthology of Early Plays, 1858–1938*. Detroit: Wayne State University Press, 1991.

Hord, Fred L. *Reconstructing Memory: Black Literary Criticism*. Chicago: Third World Press, 1991.

Johnson, Dianne. *Telling Tales: The Pedagogy and Power of African American Literature for Youth*. New York: Greenwood Press, 1990.

Jones, Gayl. *Liberating Voices: Oral Tradition in African American Literature*. Cambridge, MA: Harvard University Press, 1991.

Joseph, Margaret Paul. *Caliban in Exile: The Outsider in Caribbean Fiction*. New York: Greenwood Press, 1992.

Kinnamon, Kenneth, ed. *New Essays on Native Son*. New York: Cambridge University Press, 1990.

Metzger, Linda, Hal May, Deborah A. Straub, and Susan M. Trosky, eds. *Black Writers*. Detroit: Gale Research Inc., 1989.

Mikolyzk, Thomas A. comp. *Langston Hughes: A Bio-Bibliography*. Westport, CT: Greenwood Press, 1990.

Miller, R. Baxter. *The Art and Imagination of Langston Hughes.* Lexington: University of Kentucky Press, 1990.

Morrison, Toni. *Playing in the Dark: Whiteness and the Literary Imagination.* Cambridge, MA: Harvard University Press, 1992.

Newby, James Edwards. *Black Authors: A Selected Annotated Bibliography.* New York: Garland, 1990.

Ntire, Daphne Williams, ed., and comp. *Roots and Blossoms; African American Plays for Today.* Troy, MI: Bedford Publishers, 1991.

Peterson, Bernard L. *Early Black American Playwrights and Dramatic Writers: A Biographical Dictionary and Catalog of Plays, Films and Broadcasting Scripts.* Westport, CT: Greenwood Press, 1990.

Rajiv, Sudhi. *Forms of Black Consciousness.* New York: Advent Books, 1992.

Rollock, Barbara. *Black Authors and Illustrators of Children's Books: A Biographical Dictionary.* 2nd ed., New York: Garland, 1992.

Smith, Valerie. *Self-Discovery and Authority in Afro-American Narrative.* Cambridge, MA; Harvard University Press, 1991.

Stepto, Robert B. *From Behind the Veil: A Study of Afro-American Narrative.* 2nd ed., Urbana: University of Illinois Press, 1991.

Thurman, Wallace. *Infants of the Spring.* With foreword by Amritjit Singh. Boston: Northeastern University Press, 1992.

Toomer, Jean. *Essentials.* Edited by Rudolph P. Bird. Athens: University of Georgia Press, 1991.

Washington, Mary Helen, ed. *Memory of Kin: Stories About Family by Black Writers.* New York: Doubleday, 1991.

Wilson, August. *Two Trains Running.* New York: Dutton, 1992.

Media, Publishing, and Book Collecting

Chester, Thomas Morris. *Thomas Morris Chester, Black Civil War Correspondent: His Dispatches from the Virginia Front.* With Biographical Essay and Notes by R.J.M. Blackett. New York: DeCapo Press, 1991.

Dates, Jannette L., and William Barlow. *Split Image: African Americans in the Mass Media.* Washington, DC: Howard University Press, 1990.

Hill, George. *Black Women in Television: An Illustrated History and Bibliography.* New York: Garland Publishing Co., 1990.

Joyce, Donald Franklin. *Black Book Publishers in the United States: A Historical Dictionary of the Press, 1817–1990.* Westport, CT: Greenwood Press, 1991.

Schuyler, George S. *Black Empire: George S. Schuyler Writing As Samuel I. Brooks.* Edited by Robert A. Hill and R. Kent Rasmussen. Boston: Northeastern University, 1991.

Silk, Catherine, and John Silk. *Racism and Anti-Racism in American Popular Culture: Portrayals of African-Americans in Fiction and Film.* Manchester, UK: Manchester University Press, 1990. (Dist. by St. Martin's Press)

Sinnette, Elinor Des Verney, W. Paul Coates, and Thomas C. Battle, eds. *Black Bibliophiles and Collectors: Preservers of Black History.* Washington, DC: Howard University Press, 1990.

Military Participation

Collum, Danny Duncan, ed. *African Americans in the Spanish Civil War: "This Ain't Ethiopia, but It'll Do".* New York: G.K. Hall, 1992.

Cox, Clinton. *Undying Glory: The Story of the Massachusetts 54th Regiment.* New York: Scholastic, Inc., 1991.

Donaldson, Gary. *The History of African-Americans in the Military: Double V.* Malabar, FL: Krieger Publishing Co., 1991.

Gooding, James Henry. *On the Altar of Freedom: A Black Soldier's Civil War Letters from the Front.* Edited by Virginia Matzke Adams. Amherst: University of Massachusetts Press, 1991.

Johnson, Charles. *African American Soldiers in the National Guard: Recruitment and Deploy-*

ment During Peacetime and War. New York: Greenwood Press, 1992.

Redkey, Edwin S., ed. *A Grand Army of Black Men: Letters from African-American Soldiers in the Union Army.* New York: Cambridge University Press, 1992.

Music

Allen, Ray. *Singing in the Spirit: African-American Sacred Quartets in New York City.* Philadelphia: University of Pennsylvania Press, 1991.

Boggs, Vernon W. *Salsiology: Afro-Cuban Music and the Evolution of Salsa in New York City.* Westport, CT: Greenwood Press, 1992.

Booth, Stanley. *Rhythm Oil: A Journey Through the Music of the American South.* New York: Pantheon, 1991.

Cantor, Louis. *Wheelin' on Beale.* Foreword by B.B. King. New York: Pharos, 1992.

Costello, Mark, and David Foster Wallace. *Signifying Rappers: Rap and Race in the Urban Present.* New York: Ecco Press, 1990.

Donovan, Richard X. *Black Musicians of America.* Portland, OR: National Book Co., 1991.

Finn, Julio. *The Bluesman: The Musical Heritage of Black Men and Women in the Americas.* New York: Interlink Books, 1991.

Floyd, Samuel A., ed. *Black Music in the Harlem Renaissance: A Collection of Essays.* Westport, CT: Greenwood Press, 1990.

Friedwall, Will. *Jazz Singing: America's Great Voices from Bessie Smith to Bebop and Beyond.* New York: Scribner's, 1990.

Harris, Michael W. *The Rise of Gospel Blues: The Music of Thomas Andrew Dorsey in the Urban Church.* New York: Oxford University Press, 1992.

Horne, Aaron, comp. *Keyboard Music of Black Composers: A Bibliography.* Westport, CT: Greenwood Press, 1992.

Horne, Aaron, comp. *String Music of Black Composers: A Bibliography.* Westport, CT: Greenwood Press, 1991.

Horne, Aaron. comp. *Woodwind Music of Black Composers* Westport, CT: Greenwood Press, 1990.

Jackson, John A. *Big Beat Heat: Alan Freed and the Early Years of Rock & Roll.* New York: Schirmer/Macmillan, 1991.

Merrill, Hugh. *The Blues Route.* New York: Morrow, 1990.

Morgan, Thomas L. *From Cakewalk to Concert Hall: An Illustrated History of African American Popular Music from 1895 to 1930.* Washington, DC: Elliott & Clark Publishers, 1992.

Morton, David C. and Charles K. Wolfe. *DeFord Bailey: A Black Star in Early Country Music.* Knoxville: University of Tennessee Press, 1991.

Peretti, Burton W. *The Creation of Jazz: Music, Race and Culture in Urban America.* Urbana: University of Illinois Press, 1992.

Perry, Frank. *Afro-American Vocal Music: A Select Guide to Fifteen Composers.* Berrien Springs, MD: Vande Verde Publishers, 1991.

Porter, Lewis, ed. *A Lester Young Reader.* Washington, DC: Smithsonian Institution Press, 1991.

Price, Sammy. *What Do They Want: A Jazz Autobiography.* Edited by Caroline Richmond. Chronological discography compiled by Bob Weir. Urbana: University of Illinois Press, 1990.

Roach, Hildred. *Black American Music Past and Present: Pan-African Composers.* 2nd ed., Malabar, FL: Kruger, 1992.

Rosenthal, David H. *Hard Bop: Jazz and Black Music, 1955–1965.* New York: Oxford University Press, 1992.

Scott, Frank. *The Down Home Guide to the Blues.* Pennington, NJ: A Capella Books, 1990.

Spencer, Jon Michael, ed. *The Emergency Black and the Emergence of Rap.* Durham: Duke University Press, 1991.

Spencer, Jon Michael, ed. *Sacred Music of the Secular City: From Blues to Rap*. Durham: Duke University Press, 1992.

Story, Rosalyn. *And So I Sing: African American Divas of Opera and Concert*. New York: Warner Books, 1990.

Tate, Greg. *Flyboy in the Buttermilk: Essays on Contemporary America*. New York: Simon and Schuster, 1992.

Turner, Patricia. *Dictionary of Afro-American Performers: 78 RPM and Cylinder Recordings of Opera, Choral Music and Song, ca. 1900–1949*. New York: Garland, 1990.

Walker-Hill, Helen. *Piano-Music by Black Women Composers: A Catalogue of Solo and Ensemble Works*. New York: Greenwood Press, 1992.

Wright, Josephine, and Samuel A. Floyd, Jr., eds. *New Perspectives on Music: Essays in Honor of Eileen Southern*. Warren, MI: Harmonie Park Press, 1992.

Performing Arts

Adamczke, Alice J. *Black Dance: An Annotated Bibliography*. New York: Garland Publishing Co., 1990.

Ely, Melvin Patrick. *The Adventures of Amos 'n' Andy: A Social History of an American Phenomenon*. New York: Free Press, 1991.

Gray, John, comp. *Black Theatre and Performance: A PanAfrican Bibliography*. Westport, CT: Greenwood Press, 1990.

Gray, John, comp. *Blacks in Film and Television: A Pan-African Bibliography of Films, Filmmakers, and Performers*. Westport, CT: Greenwood Press, 1990.

Hansberry, Lorraine. *A Raisin in the Sun: The Unfilmed Original Screenplay*. Edited by Robert Nemiroff. Foreword by Jewell Gres. Afterword by Spike Lee. New York: Dutton, 1992.

Hughes, Langston, and Zora Neale Hurston. *Mule Bone: A Comedy of Negro Life*. Edited by George

H. Bass and Henry L. Gates. New York: Harper Collins, 1991.

Jhally, Sut, and Justin Lewis. *Enlightened Racism: The Cosby Show, Audiences, and the Myth of the American Dream*. Boulder, CO: Westview Press, 1992.

Jones, G. William. *Black Cinema Treasurey: Lost and Found*. Denton, TX: University of North Texas Press, 1991.

Klotman, Phyllis Rauch, ed. *Screenplays of the African American Experience*. Bloomington: Indiana University Press, 1991.

Mapp, Edward. *Directory of Blacks in the Performing Arts*. 2nd ed., Metuchen, NJ: Scarecrow Press, 1990.

Politics

Barker, Lucius J., ed. *Ethnic Politics and Civil Liberties*. New Brunswick, NJ: Transaction Books, 1992.

Clavel, Pierre, and Wim Wiewel, eds. *Harold Washington and the Neighborhoods: Progressive City Government in Chicago, 1983–1987*. New Brunswick, NJ: Rutgers University Press, 1991.

Gomes, Ralph C., and Linda Faye Williams eds. *From Exclusion to Inclusion: The Long Struggle for African American Political Power*. Westport, CT: Greenwood Press, 1992.

Henry, Charles P. *Culture and African American Politics*. Bloomington: Indiana University Press, 1990.

Henry, Charles P. *Jesse Jackson: The Search for Common Ground*. Oakland, CA: Black Scholar Press, 1990.

Jennings, James. *The Politics of Black Empowerment: The Transformation of Black Activism in Urban America*. Detroit: Wayne State University Press, 1992.

Joint Center for Political and Economic Studies. *Black Elected Officials: A National Roster*. Washington, DC: Joint Center for Political and Economic Studies Press, 19–.

Kimball, Penn. *Keep Hope Alive: Super Tuesday and Jesse Jackson's 1988 Campaign for the Presidency.* Washington, DC: Joint Center for Political and Economic Studies, 1992.

Lawson, Steven. *Running for Freedom: Civil Rights and Black Politics in America Since 1941.* Philadelphia: Temple University Press, 1990.

Marable, Manning. *The Crisis of Color and Democracy: Essays on Race, Class and Power.* Monroe, ME: Common Courage Press, 1992.

McCartney, John T. *Black Power Ideologies: An Essay in African American Political Thought.* Philadelphia: Temple University Press, 1992.

Natanson, Nicholas. *The Black Image in the New Deal: The Politics of FSA.* Knoxville: University of Tennessee Press, 1992.

Orfield, Gar, and Carole Ashkinaze. *The Closing Door: Conservative Policy and Black Opportunity.* Chicago: University of Chicago Press, 1991.

Parker, Frank R. *Black Votes Count: Political Empowerment in Mississippi After 1965.* Chapel Hill: University of North Carolina Press, 1990.

Rees, Matthew. *From the Deck to the Sea: Blacks and the Republican Party.* Wakefield, NH: Longwood Press, 1991.

Rivlin, Gar. *Fire on the Prairie: Chicago's Harold Washington and the Politics of Race.* New York: Holt, 1992.

Van DeBurg, William L. *New Day in Babylon: The Black Power Movement and American Culture.* Chicago: University of Chicago Press, 1992.

Race Relations

Brady, Paul L. *A Certain Blindness: A Black Family's Quest for the Promise of America.* Atlanta: ALP Publishers, 1990.

Brooks, Roy L. *Rethinking the American Race Problem.* Berkeley: University of California, 1991.

Collier, Peter, ed. *Second Thoughts About Race in America.* Lanham, MD: Madison Books, 1991.

Crouch, Stanley. *Notes of a Hanging Judge: Essays and Reviews.* New York: Oxford University Press, 1990.

Davis, F. James. *Who Is Black: One Nation's Definition.* University Park: Pennsylvania State University Press, 1991.

DeSantis, John. *For the Color of His Skin: The Murder of Yusuf Hawkins and the Trial of Bensonhurst.* Introduction by Alan M. Dershowitz. New York: Pharos Books, 1991.

Essed, Philomena. *Understanding Racism: An Interdisciplinary Theory.* Newbury Park, CA: Sage, 1991.

Hacker, Andrew. *Two Nations: Black and White, Separate, Hostile, Unequal.* New York: Scribner's, 1992.

Horowitz, Irving Louis. *Daydreams and Nightmares: Reflections on a Harlem Childhood.* Jackson: University Press of Mississippi, 1990.

Hynes, Charles J., and Bob Drury. *Incident at Howard Beach: The Case for Murder.* New York: Putnam, 1990.

Leiman, Melvin M. *Racism in the U.S.A.: History and Political Economy.* Concord, MA: Paul & Co., 1992.

Lewis, Earl. *In Their own Interests: Race, Class, and Power in Twentieth-Century Nolf, Virginia.* Berkeley: University of California Press, 1991.

McFadden, Robert, et. al. *Outrage: The Story Behind the Tawana Brawley Hoax.* New York: Bantam, 1990.

Pemberton, Gayle. *The Hottest Water in Chicago: One Family, Race, Time and American Culture.* Winchester, MA: Faber & Faber, 1992.

Perlmutter, Philip. *Divided We Fall: A History of Ethnic, Religious, and Racial Prejudice in America.* Ames: Iowa State University Press, 1992.

Rasberry, William. *Looking Backward at Us.* Jackson: University Press of Mississippi, 1991.

Salzman, Jack, ed. *Bridges and Boundaries: African Americans and American Jews.* New York: Braziller, 1992.

Steele, Shelby. *The Contest of Our Character: A New Vision of Race in America.* New York: St. Martin's Press, 1990.

Stepan, Nancy Leys. *The Hour of Eugenics: Race, Gender, and Nation.* Ithaca, NY: Cornell University Press, 1991.

Terkel, Studs. *Race: How Blacks and Whites Think and Feel About the American Obsession.* New York: New Press/Norton, 1992.

Welch, Susan, and Lee Sigelman. *Black America's Views of Racial Equality: The Dream Deferred.* New York: Cambridge University Press, 1991.

Zegeye, Abebe, ed. *Exploitation and Exclusion: Race and Class in Contemporary U.S. Society.* London: Hans Zell Publishers, 1991.

Zweigenhaft, Richard L., and G. William Domhoff. *Blacks in the White Establishment: A Study of Race and Class in America.* New Haven, CT: Yale University Press, 1991.

Religion and Philosophy

Baer, Hans, and Merrill Singer. *African-American Religion in the Twentieth Century: Varieties of Protest and Accommodation.* Knoxville: University of Tennessee, 1992.

Davis, Lenwood G. *Daddy Grace: An Annotated Bibliography.* New York: Greenwood Press, 1992.

Dvorak, Katherine L. *An African-American Exodus: the Segregation of Southern Churches.* With preface by Jerald C. Brauer. Brooklyn, NY: Carlson Publishing Co., 1991.

Harris, Leonard, ed. *The Philosophy of Alain Locke.* Philadelphia: Temple University Press, 1990.

Haynes, Lemuel. *Black Preacher to White America: the Collected Writings of Lemuel Haynes, 1774–1833.* Edited by Richard Newman. New York: Carlson Publishing Co., 1990.

Hopkins, Dwight N., and George C.L. Cummings, eds. *Cut Loose Your Stammering Tongue: Black Theology in the Slave Narratives.* Maryknoll, NY: Orbis Books, 1991.

Howard, Victor B. *Conscience and Slavery: the Evangelistic Calvinistic Domestic Missions, 1837–1861.* Kent, OH: Kent State University Press, 1990.

Irvin, Dona L. *The Unsung Heart of Black America: A Middle-Class Church at Midcentury.* Columbia: University of Missouri Press, 1992.

Jacobs, Claude F., and Andrew J. Kaslow. *The Spiritual Churches of New Orleans: Origins, Beliefs and Rituals of an African-American Religion.* Knoxville: University of Tennessee Press, 1991.

Johnson, John L. *Black Biblical Heritage.* Nashville: Winston-Derek Publishers, 1990.

Lincoln, C. Eric, and Lawrence H. Mamiya. *The Black Church in the American Experience.* Durham, NC: Duke University Press, 1990.

Martin, Sandy D. *Black Baptists and African Missions: the Origins of a Movement, 1880–1915.* Macon, GA: Mercer University Press, 1990.

Ochs, Stephen J. *Desegregating the Altar: The Josephites and the Struggle for Black Priests, 1871–1960.* Baton Rouge: Louisiana State University Press, 1990.

Payne, Wardell J., ed. *Directory of African American Religious Bodies: A Compendium by the Howard University School of Divinity.* Prepared under the auspices of the Research Center on Black Religious Bodies, Howard University School of Divinity. Washington, DC: Howard University Press, 1991.

Seymour, Robert E. *Whites Only: A Pastor's Retrospective on Signs of a New South.* Valley Forge, PA: Judson Press, 1991.

Spencer, Jon Michael. *Black Hymnody: A Hymnological History of the African-American Church.* Knoxville: University of Tennessee Press, 1992.

Spencer, Jon Michael. *Protest and Praise: Sacred Music of Black Religion.* Minneapolis: Augsburg Fortress Publishers, 1990.

Walker, Theodore, Jr. *Empower the People: Social Ethics for the African-American Church.* Maryknoll, NY: Orbis Books, 1991.

Walker, Wyatt Tee. *Spirits That Dwell in Deep Woods III: The Prayer and Praise Hymns of the Black Religious Experience.* New York: Martin Luther King Press, 1991.

Wood, Forrest G. *The Arrogance of Faith: Christianity and Race in America from the Colonial Era to the Twentieth Century.* New York: Knopf, 1990.

Sociology and Psychology

Andersen, Margaret L. *Race, Class and Gender: An Anthology.* Belmont, CA: Wadsworth Publishing Co., 1992.

Anderson, Elijah. *Streetwise: Race, Class and Social Change in an Urban Community.* Chicago: University of Chicago Press, 1990.

Baer, Hans, and Yvonne Jones, eds. *African Americans in the South: Issues of Race, Class and Gender.* Athens: University of Georgia Press, 1992.

Benjamin, Lois. *The Black Elite: Facing the Color Line in the Twentieth Century.* Chicago: Nelson-Hall, 1991.

Billingsley, Andrew. *Climbing Jacob's Ladder: The Future of the African-American Family.* New York: Simon and Schuster, 1991.

Blackwell, James Edward. *The Black Community: Diversity and Unity.* 3rd ed., New York: Harper Collins, 1991.

Bowser, Benjamin, ed. *Black Male Adolescents: Parenting and Education in Community Context.* Latham, MD: University Press of America, 1991.

Consortium for Research on Black Adolescence Staff and Patricia Bell-Scott. *Black Adolescence: Current Issues and Annotated Bibliography.* Boston: G.K. Hall, 1990.

Edelman, Marian Wright. *The Measure of Our Success: A Letter to My Children and Yours.* Boston: Beacon Press, 1992.

Hay, Fred J. *African-American Community Studies from North America. A Classified, Annotated Bibliography.* New York: Garland, 1991.

Hopson, Darlene, and Derek Hopson. *Different and Wonderful: Raising Black Children in a Race Conscious Society.* New York: Simon and Schuster, 1992.

Jones, Howard, and Wanda Jones. *Heritage and Hope: The Legacy and Future of the Black Family in America.* Wheaton, IL: Victor Books, 1992.

Kunjufu, Jawanza. *Countering the Conspiracy to Destroy Black Boys.* Chicago: African American Images, 1990.

Leigh, Wilhelmina A., ed. *The Housing Status of Black Americans.* New Brunswick, NJ: Transaction Books, 1992.

Lemann, Nicholas. *The Promised Land: The Great Black Migration and How It Changed America.* New York: Knopf, 1991.

Platat, Anthony M. *E. Franklin Frazier Reconsidered.* New Brunswick, NJ: Rutgers University Press, 1991.

Trotter, Joe William, ed. *The Great Migration in Historical Perspective: New Dimensions of Race, Class and Gender.* Bloomington: Indiana University Press, 1991.

Sports

Cooper, Michael L. *Playing America's Game: The Story of Negro League Baseball.* New York: Lodestar Books, 1993.

Page, James A. *Black Olympian Medalists.* Englewood, CO: Libraries Unlimited, 1991.

Women

Alexander, Adele Logan. *Free Women of Color in Rural Georgia, 1789–1879.* Fayetteville: University of Arkansas Press, 1991.

Baker, Houston A. *Working of the Spirit: The Poetics of Afro-American Women's Writings.* Chicago: University of Chicago Press, 1991.

The Black Women Oral History Project. *Guide to the Transcripts.* Edited by Ruth E. Hill. Westport, CT: Meckler, 1991.

Braxton, Joanne M. *Black Women Writing Autobiography: A Tradition Within a Tradition.* Philadelphia: Temple University Press, 1990.

Braxton, Joanne M., and Andree Nicola McLaughlin, eds. *Wild Women in the Whirlwind: Afro-American Culture and the Contemporary Literary Renaissance.* New Brunswick, NJ: Rutgers University Press, 1990.

Brown, Karen McCarthy. *Mama Lola: A Voodoo Priestess in Brooklyn.* Berkeley, University of California Press, 1991.

Brown-Guillory, Elizabeth, ed., and comp. *Wines in the Wilderness: Plays by African American Women from the Harlem Renaissance to the Present.* Westport, CT: Greenwood Press, 1990.

Bundles, A'Lelia Perry. *Madam C. J. Walker.* New York: Chelsea House, 1991.

Busby, Margaret, ed. *Daughters of Africa: An International Anthology of Words and Writings by Women of African Descent; From the Ancient World to Present.* New York: Pantheon, 1992.

Butler-Evans, Elliott. *Race, Gender, and Desire: Narrative Strategies in the Fiction of Toni Cade Bambara, Toni Morrison, and Alice Walker.* Philadelphia: Temple University Press, 1990.

Caraway, Nancie. *Segregated Sisterhood: Racism and the Politics of American Feminism.* Knoxville: University of Tennessee Press, 1991.

Celsi, Teresa N. *Rosa Parks and the Montgomery Bus Boycott.* Brookfield, CT: Millbrook Press, 1991.

Crawford, Vicki L., Jacqueline Anne Reese, and Barbara Woods, eds. *Women in the Civil Rights Movement: Trailblazers and Torchbears, 1941–1965.* Brooklyn, NY: Carlson Publishing Co., 1990. (*Black Women in United States History*, vol. 16.)

Davis, Michael D. *Black American Women in Olympic Track and Field: A Complete Illustrated Reference.* Jefferson, NC: McFarland, 1992.

Gates, Henry Louis, Jr. *Reading Black, Reading Feminist.* New York: Meridan, 1991.

Glassman, Steve, and Kathryn Lee Seidel, eds. *Zora in Florida.* Gainesville: University Presses of Florida, 1991.

Guy-Sheftall, Beverly. *Daughters of Sorrow: Attitudes Toward Black Women.* New York: Carlson Publishing Co., 1990. (*Black Women in United States History*, vol. 11.)

Harris, Trudier. *Fiction and Folklore: The Novels of Toni Morrison.* Knoxville: University of Tennessee Press, 1991.

Hine, Darlene Clark, ed. *Black Women in American History, From Colonial Times Through the Nineteenth Century.* Brooklyn, NY: Carlson Publishing Co., 1990.

Hooks, Bell. *Black Looks: Race and Representation.* Boston: South End Press, 1992.

Ihle, Elizabeth L., ed. *Black Women in Higher Education: An Anthology of Essays, Studies and Documents.* New York: Garland Publishing Co., 1992.

Jackson, Carlton. *Hattie: The Life of Hattie McDaniel.* Lantham, MD: Madison Books, 1990.

Jones, Adrienne Lash. *Jane Edna Hunter: A Case Study of Black Leadership.* Brooklyn, NY: Carlson Publishing Co., 1990. (*Black Women in United States History*, vol. 12)

Jones, Beverly Washington. *Quest for Equality: The Life and Writing of Mary Eliza Church Terrell, 1863–1954.* Brooklyn, NY: Carlson Publishing Co., 1990. (*Black Women in United States History*, vol. 13.)

Kent, George E. *A Life of Gwendolyn Brooks.* Lexington: University of Kentucky Press, 1990.

King, Joyce Elaine, and Carolyn Ann Mitchell. *Black Mothers to Sons: Juxtaposing African American Literature and the Social Practice.* New York: Peter Lang, 1990.

Kubitschek, Missy Dehn. *Claiming the Heritage: African-American Women Novelists and History*. Oxford: University Press of Mississippi, 1991.

Mabalia, Dorethea Drummond, *Toni Morrison's Developing Class Consciousness*. Cranbury, NJ: Susquehanna University Press/Associated University Presses, 1991.

Morton, Patricia. *Disfigured Images: The Historical Assault on Afro-American Women*. Westport, CT: Greenwood Press, 1991.

Nathiri, N.Y., ed. *Zora! Zora Neale Hurston: A Woman and Her Community*. Orlando, FL: Sentinel Books, 1991.

Neverdon-Morton, Cynthia. *Afro-American Women of the South and the Advancement of the Race, 1895–1925*. Knoxville: University of Tennessee Press, 1990.

Otfinoski, Steven. *Marian Wright Edelman—Defender of Children's Rights*. New York: Rosen Publishing Group, 1991.

Reckley, Ralph. *Twentieth Century Black Women in Print: Essays*. Acton, MA: Copley Publishers, 1991.

Roses, Lorraine Elena, and Ruth Elizabeth Randolph. *Harlem Renaissance and Beyond: Literary Biographies of 100 Black Women Writers, 1900–1945*. Boston: G.K. Hall, 1990.

Salem, Dorothy. *To Better Our World: Black Women in Organized Reform*. Brooklyn, NY: Carlson Publishing Co., 1990. (*Black Women in United States History*, vol. 14.)

Samuels, Wilfred D., and Clenora Hudson-Weems. *Toni Morrison*. Boston: G.K. Hall, 1990.

Scott, Kesho Yvonne. *The Habit of Surviving: Black Women's Strategies for Life*. New Brunswick, NJ: Rutgers University Press, 1991.

Smith, Jesse Carney, ed. *Notable Black American Women*. Detroit: Gale Research Inc., 1991.

Smith, Rita Webb, and Tony Chapelle. *The Woman Who Took Back Her Streets: One Woman Fights the Drug Wars and Rebuilds Her Community*. Far Hill, NJ: New Horizon, 1991.

Thompson, Mildred I. *Ida B. Wells-Barnett: An Exploratory Study of An American Black Woman, 1893–1930*. Brooklyn, NY: Carlson Publishing Co., 1990. (*Black Women in United States History*, vol. 15)

Walker, Melissa. *Down From the Mountaintop: Black Women's Novels in the Wake of the Civil Rights Movement, 1966–1989*. New Haven, CT: Yale University Press, 1991.

Walker, Robbie Jean, ed. *The Rhetoric of Struggle: Public Addresses by African American Women*. New York: Garland Publishing Co., 1992.

Werner, Craig. *Black American Women Novelists: An Annotated Bibliography*. Englewood Cliffs, NJ: Salem Press, 1990.

Williams, Constance Willard. *Black Teenage Mothers: Pregnancy and Child Rearing from Their Perspective*. Lexington, MA: Lexington Books, 1991.

Woody, Bette. *Black Women in the Workplace: Impacts of Structural Change in the Economy*. Westport, CT: Greenwood Press, 1992.

Yee, Shirley J. *Black Women Abolitionists: A Study in Activism, 1828–1860*. Knoxville: University of Tennessee Press, 1992.

■ NAMES AND ADDRESSES OF PUBLISHERS OF BOOKS WHICH APPEAR IN THIS BIBLIOGRAPHY

A

A cappella Books, PO Box 380, Pennington, NJ 08534, Tel.: (609)737-6525.

ABC-Clio, Inc., PO Box 1911, Santa Barbara, CA 93116-1911, Tel.: (800)422-2546.

Harry N. Abrams, Inc., 100 5th Ave., New York, NY 10011, Tel.: (800)345-1359.

AKASA Press, 2440-10 Hunter Ave., Ste. lOG, Bronx, NY 10475, Tel.: (212)671-9639.

Bibliography

Advent Books, Inc., 141 E. 44th St., Ste. 511, New York, NY 10017, Tel.: (212)697-0887.

Africa World Press, PO Box 1892, Trenton, NJ 08607, Tel.: (609)771-1666.

African Studies Association, Emory University, Credit Union Bldg., Atlanta, GA 30322, Tel.: (404)329-6410.

Algonquin Books, PO Box 2225, Chapel Hill, NC 27515, Tel.: (919)933-0108.

American Enterprise Institute for Public Policy Research, 1150 17th St. NW, Washington, DC 20036, Tel.: (202)862-5800.

Apt Books, Inc., 141 E. 44th St., Ste. 511, New York, NY 10017, Tel.: (212)697-0887.

Associated University Presses, 440 Forsgate Dr., Cranbury, NJ 08512, Tel.: (609)655-4770.

Atheneum, c/o MacMillan Publishing Co., 866 3rd Ave., New York, NY 10022, Tel.: (800)257-5755.

B

Backwards & Backwards Press, 7561 Pearl Rd., Cleveland, OH 44130, Tel.: (216)243-5335.

Richard Bailey, Box 1264, Montgomery, AL 36102, Tel.: (205)271-6565.

Bandit Books, Inc., PO Box 11721, Winston-Salem, NC 27106, Tel.: (919)785-7414.

Bantam Books, 666 5th Ave., New York, NY 10103, Tel.: (212)765-6500.

Barez Publishing Co., 8690 Aero Dr., Ste. M-332, San Diego, CA 92123-1734, Tel.: (800)247-5900.

Beacon Press, 25 Beacon St., Boston, MA 02108, Tel.: (617)742-2110.

Bedford Arts/Corcoran Gallery of Art, 301 Brannon St., Ste. 410, San Francisco, CA 94107, Tel.: (415)882-7870.

Bedford Publishers, Inc., 779 Kirts, Troy, MI 48084, Tel.: (313)362-0369.

John Benjamins North America, Inc., 821 Bethlehem Pike, Philadelphia, PA 19118, Tel.: (215)836-1200.

Black Entrepreneurs Press, 4502 S. Congress Ave., Ste. 254, Austin, TX 78744, Tel.: (512)444-9962.

The Black Resources Guide, Inc., 501 Oneida Pl. NW, Washington, DC 20011, Tel.: (202)291-4373.

George Braziller, Inc., 60 Madison Ave., Ste. 1001, New York, NY 10010, Tel.: (212)889-0909.

British American Publishing Ltd., 19 British American Blvd., Latham, NY 12148, Tel.: (518)786-6000.

C

Calyx Books, PO Box B, Corvalis, OR 97339, Tel.: (503)753-9384.

Cambridge University Press, 40 W. 20th St., New York, NY 10011, Tel.: (212)924-3900.

Cambridgeport Press, 15 Chalk St., Cambridge, MA 02139, Tel.: (617)497-4437.

Carlson Publishing Co., 52 Remsen St., Brooklyn, NY 11201, Tel.: (718)875-7460.

Carol Publishing Group, 600 Madison Ave., New York, NY 10022, Tel.: (212)486-2200.

Carroll & Graf Publishers, Inc., 260 5th Ave., New York, NY 10001, Tel.: (212)889-8772.

The Center for African-Art, 560 Broadway, Ste. 206, New York, NY 10012-3945, Tel.: (212)966-1313.

Charro Books Co., Inc., 29777 Telegraph Rd., No. 2500, Southfield, MI 48034, Tel.: (313)356-0950.

Chelsea House Publishers, 95 Madison Ave., New York, NY 10011, Tel.: (212)683-4400.

Christian Reformed World Missions, 2850 Kalamazoo SE, Grand Rapids, MI 49560.

Citadel Press, c/o Carol Publishing Group, 600 Madison Ave., New York, NY 10022, Tel.: (212)486-2220.

Adam Randolph Collings, Inc., PO Box 8658, Anaheim, CA 92812, Tel.: (714)534-7976.

Common Courage Press, Box 702, Jackson Rd. and Rte. 19, Monroe, ME 04951, Tel.: (207)525-0900.

Consortium Book Sales & Distribution, 287 E. 6th St., Ste. 365, St. Paul, MN 55101, Tel.: (612)221-9035.

Copley Publishing Group, 138 Great Rd., Acton, MA 01720, Tel.: (508)263-9090.

Cornell University Press, 124 Roberts Pl., PO Box 250, Ithaca, NY 14851, Tel.: (607)257-7000.

CRC Press, Inc., 2000 Corporate Blvd. NW, Boca Raton, FL 33431, Tel.: (407)994-0555.

D

Daring Publishing Group, 913 Tuscarawas St. W., Canton, OH 44702, Tel.: (216)454-7519.

Ivan R. Dee, Inc., 1332 N. Halsted St., Chicago, IL 60622, Tel.: (312)787-6262.

Doubleday, 666 5th Ave., New York, NY 10103, Tel.: (800)223-6834.

Dufour Editions, Inc., PO Box 449, Chester Springs, PA 19425-0449, Tel.: (215)458-5005.

Duke University Press, PO Box 6697, College Sta., Durham, NC 27108, Tel.: (919)684-2173.

E

ECA Associates, PO Box 15004, Great Bridge Sta., Chesapeake, VA 23320, Tel.: (804)547-5542.

William B. Eerdmans Publishing Co., 255 Jefferson Ave. SE, Grand Rapids, MI 49503, Tel.: (800)253-7521.

F

Faber & Faber, Inc., 50 Cross St., Winchester, MA 01890, Tel.: (617)721-1427.

Facts on File, Inc., 460 Park Ave. S., New York, NY 10016, Tel.: (212)683-2214.

Fairleigh Dickinson University Press, 440 Forsgate Dr., Cranbury, NJ 08512, Tel.: (609)655-4770.

Farrar, Straus & Giroux, Inc., 19 Union Sq. W., New York, NY 10003, Tel.: (800)631-8571.

Augsburg Fortress, Publishers, 426 S. 5th St., PO Box 1209, Minneapolis, MN 55440, Tel.: (800)848-2738.

Free Press, 866 3rd Ave., New York, NY 10022, Tel.: (212)702-3130.

G

Gale Research Inc., 835 Penobscot Bldg., Detroit, MI 48226-4094, Tel.: (800)877-4253.

Garland Publishing, Inc., 717 5th Ave., New York, NY 10016, Tel.: (212)751-7447.

Georgetown University Press, Intercultural Center, Rm. 111, Washington, DC 20057, Tel.: (202)687-6063.

Gower Publishing Co., Old Post Rd., Brookfield, VT 05036, Tel.: (802)276-3162.

Greenwood Publishing Group, Inc., 88 Post Rd. W., PO Box 5007, Westport, CT 06881, Tel.: (203)226-3571.

Grove Weidenfeld, 841 Broadway, 4th Fl., New York, NY 10003-4793, Tel.: (212)614-7850.

Guilford Publications, Inc., 72 Spring St., New York, NY 10012, Tel.: (212)431-9800.

H

G.K. Hall & Co., Inc., 70 Lincoln St.1, Boston, MA 02111, Tel.: (617)423-3990.

Harlan Davidson, Inc., 110 N. Arlington Heights Rd., Arlington Heights, IL 60004, Tel.: (708)253-9720.

Harmonie Park Press, 23630 Pinewood, Warren, MI 48091, Tel.: (313)755-3080.

Harmony Books, c/o Crown Publishers, Inc., 201 E. 50th St., New York, NY 10022, Tel.: (212)572-6120.

HarperCollins Inc., 10 E. 53rd St., New York, NY 10022, Tel.: (800)331-3761.

Harvard University Press, 79 Garden St., Cambridge, MA 02138, Tel.: (617)495-2600.

Heinemann Educational Books, Inc., 361 Hanover St., Portsmouth, NH 03801-3912, Tel.: (603)431-7894.

Hemisphere Publishing Corp., 1900 Frost Rd., Ste. 101, Bristol, PA 19007, Tel.: (215)785-5000.

Hippocrene Books, Inc., 171 Madison Ave., New York, NY 10016, Tel.: (212)685-4371.

Holmes & Meier Publishers, Inc., 30 Irving Pl., New York, NY 10003, Tel.: (212)254-4100.

Holt, Rinehart & Winston, Inc., 6277 Sea Harbor Dr., Orlando, FL 32887, Tel.: (407)345-2500.

Hoover Institute Press, Stanford University, Stanford, CA 94305-6010, Tel.: (415)723-3373.

Howard University Press, 2900 Van Ness St. NW, Washington, DC 20008, Tel.: (202)806-8450.

Human Rights Watch, 485 5th Ave., New York, NY 10017-6104, Tel.: (212)972-8400.

Humanities Press International, Inc., 165 1st Ave., Atlantic Highlands, NJ 07716-1289, Tel.: (908)872-1441.

I

ICS Press, 243 Kearny St., San Francisco, CA 94108, Tel.: (415)981-5353.

Independent Publishers Group, 814 N. Franklin St., Chicago, Il 60610, Tel.: (312)337-0747.

Indiana University Press, 601 N. Morton St., Bloomington, IN 47404-3797, Tel.; (812)855-4203.

Institute of Early American History and Culture, PO Box 220, Williamsburg, VA 23187, Tel.: (804)221-1110.

Interlink Publishing Group, Inc., 99 7th Ave., Brooklyn, NY 11215, Tel.: (718)797-4292.

International Publishers Co., Inc., 239 W. 23rd St., New York, NY 10011, Tel.: (212)366-9816.

International Specialized Book Services, 5602 NE Hassalo St., Portland, OR 97213-3640, Tel.: (503)287-3093.

Ivy Books, 201 E. 50th St., New York, NY 10022, Tel.: (212)572-2573.

J

Joint Center for Political and Economic Studies, Inc., 1301 Pennsylvania Ave. NW, Ste. 400, Washington, DC 20041-1797, Tel.: (202)626-3500.

Jonathan David Publishers, Inc., 68-22 Eleat Ave., Middle Village, NY 11379, Tel.: (718)456-8611.

Judson Press, PO Box 851, Valley Forge, PA 19482-0851, Tel.: (800)331-1053.

Just Us Books, Inc., 301 Main St., Ste. 22-24, Orange, NJ 07050, Tel.: (800)762-7701.

K

Kendell/Hunt Publishing Co., 2460 Kerper Blvd., Dubuque, IA 52001, Tel.: (319)588-1451.

Kent State University Press, 101 Franklin Hall, Kent, OH 44242, Tel.: (800)666-2211.

Kluwer Academic Publishers, 101 Philip Dr., Assinippi Park, Norwell, MA 02061, Tel.: (617)871-6600.

Alfred A. Knopf, Inc., 201 E. 50th St., New York, NY 10022, Tel.: (212)572-2103.

Krieger Publishing Co., Inc., PO Box 9542, Melborne, FL 32902, Tel.: (407)724-9542.

Kumarian Press, Inc., 630 Oakwood Ave., Ste. 119, West Hartford, CT 06110-1505, Tel.: (203)953-0214.

L

Lexington Books, 125 Spring St., Lexington, MA 02173, Tel.: (617)862-6650.

Little, Brown & Co., Inc., 34 Beacon St., Boston, MA 02108, Tel.: (800)343-9204.

Louisiana State University Press, Highland Rd., Baton Rouge, LA 70893, Tel.: (504)388-6294.

Lynne Rienner Publishers, Inc., 1800 30th St., Ste. 314, Boulder, CO 80301, Tel.: (303)444-6684.

M

McFarland & Co., Inc., Publishers, Box 611, Jefferson, NC 28640, Tel.: (919)246-4460.

MacMillan Publishing Co., 866 3rd Ave., New York, NY 10022, Tel.: (800)257-6509.

Madison Books, 4720 Boston Way, Lantham, MD 20706, Tel.: (800)462-6420.

Madison House Publishers, Inc., PO Box 3100, Madison, WI 53704, Tel.: (608)244-6210.

Majority Press, PO Box 538, Dover, MA 02030, Tel.: (617)828-8450.

Martin Luther King Press, 132 W. 116th St., New York, NY 10026, Tel.: (212)866-0301.

Meckler Corp., 11 Ferry Ln. W., Westport, CT 06880, Tel.: (203)226-6967.

Edwin Mellen Press, PO Box 450, Lewiston, NY 14092, Tel.: (716)754-2266.

Mercer University Press, 1400 Coleman Ave., Macon, GA 31207, Tel.: (912)752-2880.

Michigan State University Press, 1405 S. Harrison Rd., East Lansing, MI 48824, Tel.: (517)355-9543.

Millbrook Press, Inc., Old New Milford Rd., Brookfield, CT 06804, Tel.: (203)740-2220.

Myles Publishing Co., 436 E. Ute St., Tulsa, OK 74106, Tel.: (918)663-7701.

N

NRW Associates Directory, 1315 Hamlin St. NE, Washington, DC 20017, Tel.: (202)635-4808.

National Academy Press, 2101 Constitution Ave. NW, Washington, DC 20418, Tel.: (800)624-6242.

National Afro-American Museum and Cultural Center, PO Box 578, Wilberforce, OH 45384, Tel.: (513)376-4944.

National Book Co., PO Box 8795, Portland, OR 97207-8795, Tel.: (503)228-6345.

National Book Network, 4720 Boston Way, Lanham, MD 20706-4310, Tel.: (301)459-8696.

National Urban League, Inc., 500 E. 62nd St., New York, NY 10021, Tel.: (212)310-9000.

Native Sun Publishers, Inc., PO Box 13394, Richmond, VA 23225, Tel.: (804)233-8249.

New York University Press, 70 Washington Sq. S., New York, NY 10012, Tel.: (212)998-2575.

Northeastern University Press, 360 Huntington Ave., 272 Huntington Plaza, Boston, MA 02115, Tel.: (617)437-5480.

Northwestern University Press, 625 Colfax St., Evanston, IL 60201, Tel.: (708)491-5315.

W.W. Norton & Co., Inc., 500 5th Ave., New York, NY 10110, Tel.: (212)354-5500.

O

Ohio University Press, 220 Scott Quadrangle, Athens, OH 45701, Tel.: (614)593-1155.

Open University Press, c/o Taylor & Francis, Inc., 79 Madison Ave., Ste. 1106, New York, NY 10016, Tel.: (212)725-1999.

Orbis Books, Fathers & Brothers of Maryknoll, Walsh Bldg., Maryknoll, NY 10545, Tel.: (800)258-5838.

Oxford University Press, Inc., 200 Madison Ave., New York, NY 10016, Tel.: (800)334-4349.

P

Pacific Research Institute for Public Policy, 177 Post St., Ste. 500, San Francisco, CA 94108, Tel.: (415)989-0833.

Pantheon Books, Inc., 201 E. 50th St., New York, NY 10022, Tel.: (212)872-8238.

Paragon House Publishers, 90 5th Ave., New York, NY 10011, Tel.: (212)620-2820.

Pathfinder Press, 410 West St., New York, NY 10014, Tel.: (212)741-0690.

Paul & Co. Publishers, Consortium, Inc., PO Box 442, Concord, MA 01742, Tel.: (508)369-3049.

Pelican Publishing Co., Inc., 1101 Monroe St., Gretna, LA 70053, Tel.: (800)843-4558.

Pennsylvania State University Press, 820 N. University Dr., Ste. C, University Park, PA 16802, Tel.: (814)865-1327.

Pergamon Press, Inc., Front & Braun Sts., Riverside, NJ 08075-1197, Tel.: (609)461-6500.

Peter Lang Publishing, Inc., 62 W. 45th St., New York, NY 10036, Tel.: (212)302-6740.

Pharos Books, 200 Park Ave., New York, NY 10166, Tel.: (212)692-3830.

Power of the Word Publishing Co., 176-03 Jamaica Ave., Jamaica, NY 11432, Tel.: (718)949-1987.

Praeger Publishers, c/o Greenwood Press Publishing Group, Inc., 88 Post Rd., W., Box 5007, Westport, CT 06881, Tel.: (203)226-3571.

Presidio Press, 31 Pamaron Way, Novato, CA 94949, Tel.: (415)883-1373.

Princeton Architectural Press, 37 E. 7th Ave., New York, NY 10003, Tel.: (800)458-1131.

Princeton University Press, 41 William St., Princeton, NJ 08540, Tel.: (800)777-4726.

Putnam Publishing Group, 200 Madison Ave., New York, NY 10016, Tel.: (800)631-8571.

R

Raintree Steck-Vaughn Publications, 11 Prospect St., Madison, NJ 07940, Tel.: (800)531-5015.

Regnery Gateway, Inc., 1130 17th Ave. NW, Ste. 600, Washington, DC 20036, Tel.: (202)457-0978.

Rizzoli International Publications, Inc., 300 Park Ave. S., New York, NY 10010, Tel.: (800)462-2387.

Rosen Publishing Group, Inc., 29 E. 21st St., New York, NY 10010, Tel.: (212)777-3017.

Routledge, Chapman & Hall, Inc., 29 W. 35th St., New York, NY 10001-2291, Tel.: (212)244-3336.

Rowman & Littlefield, Publishers, Inc., 4720 Boston Way, Lanham, MD 20706, Tel.: (301)459-3366.

Russell Sage Foundation, 112 E. 64th St., New York, NY 10021, Tel.: (415)931-6000.

Rutgers University Press, 109 Church St., New Brunswick, NJ 08901, Tel.: (201)932-7764.

S

Sage Publications, Inc., 2455 Teller Rd., Newbury Park, CA 91320, Tel.: (805)499-0721.

St. Martin's Press, Inc., 175 5th Ave., New York, NY 10010, Tel.: (800)325-5525.

Salem Press, Inc., PO Box 1097, Englewood Cliffs, NJ 07632, Tel.: (201)871-3700

Sandcastle Publishing Co., PO Box 3070, South Pasadena, CA 91031-6070, Tel.: (213)255-3616.

K.G. Saur, 121 Chanlon Rd., New Providence, NJ 07974, Tel.: (908)665-2828.

Scarborough House, PO Box 459, Chelsea, MI 48118, Tel.: (313)475-1210.

Scarecrow Press, Inc., 52 Liberty St., Box 4167, Metuchen, NY 08840, Tel.: (800)537-7107.

Schiller Institute, Inc., PO Box 66082, Washington, DC 20005, Tel.: (202)628-0272.

Scholastic, Inc., 730 Broadway, New York, NY 10003, Tel.: (212)505-3000.

Charles Scribner's Sons, c/o MacMillan Publishing Co., 866 3rd Ave., New York, NY 10022, Tel.: (212)702-2000.

Seal Press-Feminist, 3131 Western Ave., No. 410, Seattle, WA 98121-1028, Tel.: (206)283-7844.

Seven Locks Press, PO Box 27, Cabin John, MD 20818, Tel.: (800)537-9359.

Seymour-Smith, Inc., PO Box 381063, Germantown, TN 38138-1063, Tel.: (901)754-4418.

Simon & Schuster, Inc., 1230 Avenue of Americas, New York, NY 10020, Tel.: (212)698-7000.

Smithsonian Institution Press, 470 L'Enfant Plaza, Ste. 7100, Washington, DC 20560, Tel.: (202)287-3748.

South Asia Books, PO Box 502, Columbia, MO 75205, Tel.: (314)474-0116.

South End Press, 116 St. Botolph St., Boston, MA 02115, Tel.: (617)266-0629.

State University of New York Press, State University Plaza, Albany, NY 12246-0001, Tel.: (800)666-2211.

Station Hill Press, Station Hill Rd., Barrytown, NY 12507, Tel.: (914)758-5840.

Steward, Tabori & Chang Publishers, 575 Broadway, New York, NY 10012, Tel.: (212)941-2929.

Summit Books, 1230 Avenue of the Americas, New York, NY 10020, Tel.: (212)698-7501.

Syracuse University Foreign & Comparative Studies Program, 321 Sims Hall, Syracuse, NY 13244, Tel.: (315)443-4667.

T

Temple University Press, 1601 N. Broad St., University Services Bldg., Rm. 305, Philadelphia, PA 19122, Tel.: (800)447-1656.

Texas A&M University Press, Drawer C, College Stat., TX 77843, Tel.: (800)826-8911.

Third World Press, 7524 S. Cottage Grove Ave., PO Box 730, Chicago, IL 60619, Tel.: (312)651-0700.

Three Continents Press, 1901 Pennsylvania Ave. NW, Ste. 407, Washington, DC 20006, Tel.: (202)223-2554.

Thunder's Mouth Press, 54 Greene St., Ste. 45, New York, NY 10013, Tel.: (212)226-0277.

I.N. Thut World Education Center, University of Connecticut, School of Education, Box U-93, Storrs, CT 06269-2093, Tel.: (203)486-4812.

Times Books, c/o Random House, Inc., 201 E. 50th St., New York, NY 10022, Tel.: (800)726-0600.

Times Change Press, PO Box 1380, Ojai, CA 93023, Tel.: (800)488-8595.

Transaction Publishers, Rutgers University, New Brunswick, NJ 08903, Tel.: (201)932-2280.

Transnational Publishers, Inc., PO Box 7282, Ardsley-on-Hudson, NY 10503, Tel.: (914)693-0089.

Turman Publishing Co., 1319 Dexter Ave. N., Ste. 30, Seattle, WA 98119, Tel.: (206)282-6900.

Twayne, c/o G.K. Hall, 70 Lincoln St., Boston, MA 02111, Tel.: (617)423-3990.

Tycooly Publishing USA, PO Box 2178, Riverton, NJ 08077, Tel.: (509)486-1755.

U

University of Alabama Press, PO Box 870380, Tuscaloosa, AL 35487-0380, Tel.: (205)348-5180.

University of Arkansas Press, 201 Ozark St., Fayetteville, AR 72701, Tel.: (509)575-5647.

University of California, Los Angeles, Center for Afro-American Studies, 160 Haines Hall, 405 Hilgard Ave., Los Angeles, CA 90024-1545, Tel.: (213)825-3528.

University of California Press, 2120 Berkeley Way, Berkeley, CA 94720, Tel.: (415)642-4247.

University of Chicago Press, 5801 S. Ellis Ave., Chicago, IL 60637, Tel.: (800)621-2736.

University of Illinois Press, 54 E. Gregory Dr., Champaign, IL 61820, Tel.: (217)333-0950.

University of Massachusetts, William Monroe Trotter Institute for the Study of Black Culture, Harbor Campus, Boston, MA 02125, Tel.: (617)287-5880.

University of North Carolina Press, PO Box 2288, Chapel Hill, NC 27515-2288, Tel.: (800)848-6224.

University of North Texas Press, PO Box 13856, Denton, TX 76203, Tel.: (817)565-2142.

University of Pennsylvania Press, 418 Service Dr., Philadelphia, PA 19104-6097, Tel.: (215)898-6261.

University of South Carolina Press, 1716 College St., Columbia, SC 29208, Tel.: (803)777-5243.

University of Tennessee Press, 293 Communications Bldg., Knoxville, TN 37996-0325, Tel.; (615)974-3321.

University Press of America, Inc., 4720 Boston Way, Lanham, MD 20706, Tel.: (301)459-3366.

University Press of Kentucky, 663 S. Limestone St., Lexington, KY 40508-4008, Tel.: (606)257-2951.

University Press of Mississippi, 3825 Ridgewood Rd., Jackson, MS 39211, Tel.: (601)982-6205.

University Press of New England, 17 1/2 Lebanon St., Hanover, NH 03755, Tel.: (603)646-3340.

University Press of Virginia, PO Box 3608, University Sta., Charlottesville, VA 22903, Tel.: (804)924-3468.

University Presses of Florida, 15 NW 15th St., Gainesville, FL 32611, Tel.: (904)392-1351.

University Publications of America, 4520 E. West Hwy., Ste. 600, Bethesda, MD 20814-3319, Tel.: (301)657-3200.

Urban Research Press, Inc., 840 E. 87th St., Chicago, IL 60619, Tel.: (312)994-7200.

V

Vande Vere Publishing, Ltd., 8744 College Ave., Berrien Springs, MI 49103, Tel.: (616)473-1510.

Vantage Press, Inc., 516 W. 34th St., New York, NY 10001, Tel.: (212)736-1767.

Victor Books, 1825 Wheaton Ave., Wheaton, IL 60187, Tel.: (800)323-9409.

Virago Press, c/o Trafalgar Square, PO Box 257, North Comfort, VT 05053, Tel.: (800)423-4525.

W

Wadsworth Publishing Co., 10 Davis Dr., Belmont, CA 94002, Tel.: (415)595-2350.

Warner Books, Inc., 666 5th Ave., New York, NY 10103, Tel.: (800)733-3000.

Franklin Watts, Inc., 387 Park Ave., New York, NY 10016, Tel.: (212)686-7070.

Wayne State University Press, 5959 Woodward Ave., Detroit, MI 48202, Tel.: (313)577-4601.

Wesleyan University Press, c/o University Press of New England, 17 1/2 Lebanon St., Hanover, NH 03755, Tel.: (603)646-3340.

Westview Press, 5500 Central Ave., Boulder, CO 80301-2847, Tel.: (303)444-3541.

Wiener, Moshe, 854 Newburg Ave., N., Woodmere, NY 11581.

Winston-Derek Publishers, Inc., PO Box 90883, Nashville, TN 37209, Tel.: (800)826-1888.

Y

Yale University Press, 92A Yale Sta., New Haven, CT 06520, Tel.: (203)432-0825.

Z

Hans Zell (UK), c/o K.G. Saur, 121 Chanlon Rd., New Providence, NJ 07974, Tel.: (908)665-2828.

Picture and Text Credits

Picture and Text Credits

Pictures

Cover: Colin Powell: AP/Wide World Photos; Three men: S.B. Burns M.D. and the Burns Archive; Firefighter: UPI/Bettmann.

Chronology: p. 4: The Bettmann Archive; p. 5: Library of Congress; p. 6: Library of Congress; p. 7: Library of Congress; p. 8: Library of Congress; p. 9: New York Public Library; p. 11: Library of Congress; p. 12: Archive Photos; p. 17: Library of Congress; p. 18: Library of Congress; p. 19: Library of Congress; p. 20: Library of Congress; p. 22: The Bettmann Archive; p. 23: Library of Congress; p. 24: Library of Congress; p. 25: National Archives; p. 26: Library of Congress; p. 28: Library of Congress; p. 30: National Archives; p. 32: AP/Wide World Photos; p. 33: UPI/Bettmann; p. 34: Library of Congress; p. 35: UPI/Bettmann; p. 37: Library of Congress; p. 38: Library of Congress; p. 40: AP/Wide World Photos; p. 41: Library of Congress; p. 42: UPI/Bettmann; p. 43: AP/Wide World Photos; p. 45: UPI/Bettmann; p. 46: UPI/Bettmann; p. 46: Library of Congress; p. 47: National Archives; p. 48: UPI/Bettmann; p. 49: UPI/Bettmann; p. 50: UPI/Bettmann; p. 51: UPI/Bettmann; p. 54: UPI/Bettmann; p. 55: AP/Wide World Photos; p. 57: AP/Wide World Photos; p. 58: AP/Wide World Photos; p. 59: UPI/Bettmann; p. 63: AP/Wide World Photos; p. 67: AP/Wide World Photos; p. 70: AP/Wide World Photos; p. 73: AP/Wide World Photos; p. 74: UPI/Bettmann; p. 77: UPI/Bettmann; p. 77: AP/Wide World Photos; p. 78: AP/Wide World Photos; p. 82: AP/Wide World Photos; p. 90: AP/Wide World Photos; p. 93: AP/Wide World Photos; p. 96: UPI/Bettmann; p. 97: UPI/Bettmann; p. 98: UPI/Bettmann; p. 99: AP/Wide World Photos; p. 100: AP/Wide World Photos.

African-American Firsts: p. 106: Library of Congress; p. 110: United States Army; p. 111: AP/Wide World Photos; p. 112: AP/Wide World Photos; p. 114: AP/Wide World Photos; p. 116: AP/Wide World Photos; p. 117: National Association for the Advancement of Colored People; p. 118: AP/Wide World Photos; p. 119: AP/Wide World Photos; p. 120: UPI/Bettmann; p. 120: AP/Wide World Photos; p. 121: AP/Wide World Photos.

Significant Documents in African-American History: p. 131: Library of Congress; p. 134: Library of Congress; p. 137: Library of Congress; p. 141: Library of Congress; p. 145: Library of Congress; p. 147: The Bettmann Archive; p. 148: AP/Wide World Photos; p. 155: Library of Congress; p. 165: AP/Wide World Photos; p. 171: AP/Wide World Photos; p. 177: Consulate General of Jamaica; p. 182: Library of Congress; p. 187: AP/Wide World Photos; p. 188: Eisenhower Library; p. 193: National Broadcasting Corporation; p. 197: UPI/Bettmann; p. 203: Tex Harris, *Amsterdam News*; p. 207: UPI/Bettmann.

African-American Landmarks: p. 215: AP/Wide World Photos; p. 216: AP/Wide World Photos; p. 220: AP/Wide World Photos; p. 221: National Park Service; p. 225: UPI/Bettmann; p. 232: AP/Wide World Photos; p. 231: Burton Historical Collection, Detroit Public Library; p. 239: AP/Wide World Photos; p. 242: AP/Wide World Photos; p. 244: AP/Wide World Photos; p. 253: Denver Public Library; p. 254: Schomburg Center for Research in Black Culture, New York Public Library; p. 258: UPI/Bettmann; p. 259: AP/Wide World Photos.

Africa and the Western Hemisphere: p. 263: United Nations; p. 265: National Museum of African Art; p. 270: United Nations; p. 270: National Museum of African Art; p. 271: National Museum of African Art; p. 274: United Nations; p. 276: United Nations; p. 278: United Nations; p. 280: United Nations; p. 281: United Nations; p. 282: United Nations; p. 283: United Nations; p. 287: United Nations; p. 289: National Museum of African Art; p. 290: National Museum of African Art; p. 292: United Nations; p. 294: United Nations; p. 295: National Museum of African Art; p. 296: National Museum of African Art; p. 300: United Nations; p. 301: United Nations; p. 302: United Nations; p. 304: United Nations; p. 306: United Nations; p. 307: National Museum of African Art; p. 308: National Museum of African Art; p. 310: National Museum of African Art; p. 313: Bahama News Bureau; p. 317: United Nations; p. 319: United Nations; p. 320: Judy Gurovitz, The Clement-Petrolik Co.; p. 321: United Nations; p. 322: Jamaica Tourist Board; p. 323: United Nations; p. 324: United Nations.

Africans in America: 1600–1900: p. 334: New York Public Library; p. 335 Library of Congress; p. 336 Library of Congress; p. 337: Library of Congress; p. 338: Library of Congress; p. 341: Library of Congress; p. 342: Library of Congress; p. 343: New York Historical Society; p. 343: Library of Congress; p. 346: Library of Congress; p. 347: National Portrait Gallery; p. 348: Library of Congress; p. 350: Library of Congress; p. 353: The Bettmann Archive; p. 354: Library of Congress; p. 355: Library of Congress; p. 356: Library of Congress; p. 357: New York Public Library; p. 358: AP/Wide World Photos; p. 360: New York Public Library; p. 362: Archive Photos; p. 362: Library of Congress.

Civil Rights: p. 370: Library of Congress; p. 371: Schomburg Center for Research in Black Culture, New York Public Library; p. 371: UPI/Bettmann; p. 372: AP/Wide World Photos; p. 373: AP/Wide World Photos; p. 374: AP/Wide World Photos; p. 374: Library of Congress; p. 376: UPI/Bettmann; p. 377: AP/Wide World Photos; p. 379: AP/Wide World Photos; p. 380: AP/Wide World Photos; p. 381: UPI/Bettmann; p. 383: AP/Wide World Photos; p. 384: AP/Wide World Photos; p. 387: AP/Wide World Photos; p. 388: UPI/Bettmann; p. 389: AP/Wide World Photos;p. 390: Library of Congress; p. 391: *Amsterdam News*; p. 392: UPI/Bettmann; p. 394: AP/Wide World Photos; p. 396: Library of Congress.

Black Nationalism: p. 406: Library of Congress; p. 408: The Bettmann Archive; p. 409: Archive Photos; p. 411: Library of Congress; p. 412: Library of Congress;p. 414: AP/Wide World Photos; p. 417: UPI/Bettmann; p. 418: Archive Photos; p. 418: Library of Congress.

National Organizations: p. 424: The Bettmann Archive; p. 425: National Association for the Advancement of Colored People; p. 426: Library of Congress; p. 427: AP/Wide World Photos; p. 428: Library of Congress; p. 429: Ace Creative Photos; p. 430: AP/Wide World Photos; p. 431: AP/Wide World Photos; p. 432: AP/Wide World Photos; p. 433: UPI/Bettmann; p. 434: AP/Wide World Photos; p. 435: AP/Wide World Photos; p. 437: Library of Congress; p. 438: UPI/Bettmann; p. 438: AP/Wide World Photos; p. 440: AP/Wide World Photos; p. 441: AP/Wide World Photos; p. 442: AP/Wide World Photos; p. 443: UPI/Bettmann; p. 444: A. Philip Randolph Institute; p. 445: AP/Wide World Photos; p. 446: UPI/Bettmann; p. 447: Bill Sparow, *Encore*; p. 448: National Urban League.

Law: p. 502: New York Public Library; p. 507: UPI/Bettmann; p. 508: AP/Wide World Photos; p. 509: AP/Wide World Photos; p. 515: Library of Congress; p. 516: Library of Congress; p. 517: AP/Wide World Photos; p. 517: UPI/Bettmann; p. 522: National Association for the Advancement of Colored People; p. 523: UPI/Bettmann; p. 525: UPI/Bettmann; p. 533: UPI/Bettmann; p. 524: Library of Congress; p. 536: AP/Wide World Photos; p. 537: AP/Wide World Photos;

p. 539: AP/Wide World Photos; p. 544: UPI/Bettmann; p. 549: AP/Wide World Photos; p. 550: UPI/Bettmann; p. 551: AP/Wide World Photos; p. 552: AP/Wide World Photos; p. 553: AP/Wide World Photos; p. 554: AP/Wide World Photos; p. 555: AP/Wide World Photos; p. 556: UPI/Bettmann; p. 557: UPI/Bettmann; p. 559: AP/Wide World Photos.

Politics: p. 563: UPI/Bettmann; p. 567: UPI/Bettmann; p. 568: UPI/Bettmann; p. 569: AP/Wide World Photos; p. 570: AP/Wide World Photos; p. 571: UPI/Bettmann; p. 573: AP/Wide World Photos; p. 574: UPI/Bettmann; p. 575: United States Senate Historical Office; p. 577: AP/Wide World Photos; p. 578: AP/Wide World Photos; p. 579: AP/Wide World Photos; p. 580: AP/Wide World Photos; p. 581: AP/Wide World Photos; p. 582: AP/Wide World Photos; p. 583: AP/Wide World Photos; p. 584: Archive Photos; p. 585: AP/Wide World Photos; p. 586: UPI/Bettmann; p. 587: AP/Wide World Photos; p. 588: AP/Wide World Photos; p. 590: AP/Wide World Photos; p. 592: AP/Wide World Photos; p. 593: AP/Wide World Photos; p. 594: UPI/Bettmann; p. 597: AP/Wide World Photos; p. 598: AP/Wide World Photos; p. 601: United States Senate Historical Office; p. 602: United Nations; p. 603: AP/Wide World Photos; p. 604: Library of Congress; p. 605: AP/Wide World Photos; p. 606: AP/Wide World Photos; p. 607: AP/Wide World Photos; p. 609: AP/Wide World Photos; p. 610: AP/Wide World Photos.

Population: p. 618: Kenneth Estell; p. 619: Kenneth Estell; p. 620: S.B. Burns and the Burns Archive; p. 621: Library of Congress; p. 621: National Archives; p. 626: Kenneth Estell; p. 627: Kenneth Estell.

Employment and Income: p. 644: UPI/Bettmann; p. 647: Sue Steller; p. 649: Kenneth Estell; p. 653: UPI/Bettmann; p. 654: National Aeronautics and Space Administration; p. 655: Sue Steller; p. 656: Kenneth Estell.

Entrepreneurship: p. 668: Library of Congress; p. 670: Walker Collection of A'Lelia Perry Bundles; p. 672: Andy Roy; p. 674: AP/Wide World Photos; p. 675: Kenneth Estell; p. 676: AP/Wide World Photos; p. 677: Superb Manufacturing,

Inc.; p. 678: AP/Wide World Photos; p. 679: AP/Wide World Photos; p. 680: UPI/Bettmann; p. 681: AP/Wide World Photos; p. 683: Fisk University Library.

The Family: p. 694: Faustine Jones-Wilson; p. 694: Library of Congress; p. 695: Brain V. Jones; p. 696: Brain V. Jones; p. 700: Brain V. Jones; p. 702: Kenneth Estell; p. 703: Kenneth Estell; p. 709: Kenneth Estell; p. 710: Edwin L. Wilson, Sr.

Education: p. 724: Library of Congress; p. 725: Schomburg Center for Research in Black Culture, New York Public Library; p. 726: Library of Congress; p. 726: South Carolina Historical Society; p. 727: Library of Congress; p. 443: Library of Congress; p. 727: The Bettmann Archive; p. 728: The Bettmann Archive; p. 729: Library of Congress; p. 730: AP/Wide World Photos; p. 729: AP/Wide World Photos; p. 731: UPI/Bettmann; p. 733: UPI/Bettmann; p. 735: AP/Wide World Photos; p. 736: Bruce Griffin; p. 737: Beverly Hardy; p. 730: Molefi Kete Asante; p. 739: Surlock Photographers; p. 741: AP/Wide World Photos; p. 742: AP/Wide World Photos; p. 743: AP/Wide World Photos; p. 744: AP/Wide World Photos; p. 746: John F. Kennedy Library; p. 748: AP/Wide World Photos; p. 749: AP/Wide World Photos; p. 750: AP/Wide World Photos.

Religion: p. 774: New York Public Library; p. 776: Archive Photos; p. 777: SB. Burns and the Burns Archive; p. 779: Archive Photos; p. 780: AP/Wide World Photos; p. 782: AP/Wide World Photos; p. 783: AP/Wide World Photos; p. 784: AP/Wide World Photos; p. 786: AP/Wide World Photos; p. 787: *New York Daily News*; p789]791: AP/Wide World Photos; p. 790: UPI/Bettmann; p. 791: AP/Wide World Photos; p. 795: AP/Wide World Photos; p. 797: AP/Wide World Photos; p. 797: New York Public Library; p. 798: UPI/Bettmann; p. 800: UPI/Bettmann; p. 802: AP/Wide World Photos; p. 802: The Bettmann Archive; p. 804: AP/Wide World Photos; p. 807: AP/Wide World Photos.

Literature: p. 813: Schomburg Center for Research in Black Culture, New York Public Library; p. 814: AP/Wide World Photos; p. 816: AP/Wide World Photos; p. 817: AP/Wide World Photos; p. 818: AP/Wide World Photos; p. 821: UPI/Bettmann; p. 823: AP/Wide World Photos; p. 828: AP/Wide World Photos; p. 830: UPI/Bettmann; p. 833: AP/Wide World Photos; p. 834: Springer/Bettmann Film Archive; p. 835: AP/Wide World Photos; p. 839: AP/Wide World Photos; p. 840: AP/Wide World Photos; p. 841: AP/Wide World Photos; p. 842: AP/Wide World Photos; p. 843: New York Historical Society; p. 844: AP/Wide World Photos; p. 845: AP/Wide World Photos; p. 846: AP/Wide World Photos.

The Media: p. 856: AP/Wide World Photos; p. 858: AP/Wide World Photos; p. 859: AP/Wide World Photos; p. 861: American Broadcasting Company; p. 862: AP/Wide World Photos; p. 864: AP/Wide World Photos; p. 865: Tony Brown Productions, Inc.; p. 866: Black Entertainment Television; p. 867: AP/Wide World Photos; p. 869: AP/Wide World Photos; p. 870: Turner Broadcasting System Management; p. 871: Black Enterprise Magazine; p. 872: AP/Wide World Photos; p. 874: UPI/Bettmann; p. 875: Associated Publishers; p. 876: AP/Wide World Photos; p. 877: Washington Post; p. 878: AP/Wide World Photos; p. 880: AP/Wide World Photos; p. 881: AP/Wide World Photos; p. 882: AP/Wide World Photos; p. 883: AP/Wide World Photos.

Performing Arts: p. 941: Library of Congress; p. 944: AP/Wide World Photos; p. 946: AP/Wide World Photos; p. 947: AP/Wide World Photos; p. 948: Ron Scherl; p. 950: AP/Wide World Photos; p. 951: WABC-TV, New York; p. 952: AP/Wide World Photos; p. 953: New York City Ballet; p. 954: UPI/Bettmann; p. 955: AP/Wide World Photos; p. 957: AP/Wide World Photos; p. 958: AP/Wide World Photos; p. 959: AP/Wide World Photos; p. 962: AP/Wide World Photos; p. 963: AP/Wide World Photos; p. 965: AP/Wide World Photos; p. 966: AP/Wide World Photos; p. 967: AP/Wide World Photos; p. 969: AP/Wide World Photos; p. 971: AP/Wide World Photos; p. 972: AP/Wide World Photos; p. 973: AP/Wide World Photos; p. 974: AP/Wide World Photos; p. 975: AP/Wide World Photos; p. 976: Tri-Star Pictures; p. 979: Matha Swope Associates; p. 980: UPI/Bettmann; p. 980: AP/Wide World Photos; p. 981: AP/Wide World Photos; p. 982: AP/Wide World Photos; p. 982: Archive Photos; p. 983: Island Pictures; p. 984: UPI/Bettmann;

p. 985: Archive Photos; p. 990: AP/Wide World Photos; p. 991: AP/Wide World Photos; p. 993: Archive Photos; p. 994: AP/Wide World Photos; p. 995: AP/Wide World Photos; p. 997: AP/Wide World Photos; p. 998: Archive Photos; p. 999: AP/Wide World Photos; p. 1000: UPI/Bettmann; p. 1000: AP/Wide World Photos; p. 1001: AP/Wide World Photos; p. 1003: Darlene Hammond/Archive Photos.

Classical Music: p. 1008: Schomburg Center for Research in Black Culture, New York Public Library; p. 1009: Schomburg Center for Research in Black Culture, New York Public Library; p. 1010: AP/Wide World Photos; p. 1011: AP/Wide World Photos; p. 1012: AP/Wide World Photos; p. 1014: AP/Wide World Photos; p. 1015: Hurok Attractions; p. 1017: AP/Wide World Photos; p. 1020: The Bettmann Archive; p. 1022: AP/Wide World Photos; p. 1027: AP/Wide World Photos; p. 1033: The Bettmann Archive; p. 1034: Archive Photos; p. 1036: UPI/Bettmann; p. 1038: AP/Wide World Photos; p. 1041: AP/Wide World Photos; p. 1043: AP/Wide World Photos; p. 1044: AP/Wide World Photos; p. 1045: Archive Photos; p. 1046: AP/Wide World Photos.

Jazz Music: p. 1055: AP/Wide World Photos; p. 1055: The Bettmann Archive; p. 1057: UPI/Bettmann; p. 1059: AP/Wide World Photos; p. 1060: *Downbeat*; p. 1061: AP/Wide World Photos; p. 1063: AP/Wide World Photos; p. 1068: Shaw Artists Corporation; p. 1070: William Morris; p. 1073: National Archives; p. 1073: AP/Wide World Photos; p. 1075: AP/Wide World Photos; p. 1076: AP/Wide World Photos; p. 1076: S.B. Burns and The Burns Archive; p. 1077: AP/Wide World Photos; p. 1078: Springer/Bettmann Film Archive; p. 1080: The Bettmann Archive; p. 1082: Columbia Records; p. 1085: Ron Rogers; p. 1088: AP/Wide World Photos; p. 1089: UPI/Bettmann; p. 1090: AP/Wide World Photos; p. 1091: The Bettmann Archive; p. 1093: AP/Wide World Photos; p. 1094: AP/Wide World Photos; p. 1096: AP/Wide World Photos; p. 1101: UPI/Bettmann.

Popular Music: p. 1108: AP/Wide World Photos; p. 1109: Archive Photos; p. 1112: AP/Wide World Photos; p. 1113: AP/Wide World Photos; p. 1114: AP/Wide World Photos; p. 1116: AP/Wide World Photos; p. 1119: AP/Wide World

Photos; p. 1121: Archive Photos; p. 1122: AP/Wide World Photos; p. 1123: AP/Wide World Photos; p. 1124: AP/Wide World Photos; p. 1126: AP/Wide World Photos; p. 1127: AP/Wide World Photos; p. 1130: AP/Wide World Photos; p. .1133: AP/Wide World Photos; p. 1134: AP/Wide World Photos; p. 1135: Archive Photos; p. 1137: AP/Wide World Photos; p. 1138: AP/Wide World Photos; p. 1141: AP/Wide World Photos; p. 1142: AP/Wide World Photos; p. 1144: UPI/Bettmann; p. 1146: AP/Wide World Photos; p. 1147: AP/Wide World Photos; p. 1149: AP/Wide World Photos; p. 1151: AP/Wide World Photos.

Fine and Applied Arts: p. 1157: National Museum of American Art/Art Resource; p. 1161: Galbreath Photo Service; p. 1162: Whitney Museum of American Art; p. 1165: Whitney Museum of American Art; p. 1167: Fairchild Publications; p. 1169: AP/Wide World Photos; p. 1171: Art Resource; p. 1173: AP/Wide World Photos; p. 1174: AP/Wide World Photos; p. 1177 AP/Wide World Photos; p. 1183: National Museum of American Art/Art Resource; p. 1185: Whitney Museum of American Art; p. 1186: UPI/Bettmann; p. 1189: UPI/Bettmann; p. 1190: UPI/Bettmann; p. 1191: AP/Wide World Photos; p. 1195: National Museum of American Art/Art Resource; p. 1197: UPI/Bettmann; p. 1198: National Museum of American Art/Art Resource; p. 1199: AP/Wide World Photos; p. 1201: General Motors, Public Relations; p. 1202: AP/Wide World Photos; p. 1205: United Nations.

Science and Medicine: p. 1224: The Bettmann Archive; p. 1224: AP/Wide World Photos; p. 1225: AP/Wide World Photos; p. 1227: The Bettmann Archive; p. 1229: AP/Wide World Photos; p. 1230: Library of Congress; p. 1233: The Granger Collection, New York; p. 1235: UPI/Bettmann; p. 1236: AP/Wide World Photos; p. 1236: AP/Wide World Photos; p. 1237: Library of Congress; p. 1239: AP/Wide World Photos; p. 1240: AP/Wide World Photos; p. 1241: AP/Wide World Photos; p. 1242: The Bettmann Archive.

Sports: p. 1254: UPI/Bettmann; p. 1255: UPI/Bettmann; p. 1257: AP/Wide World Photos; p. 1258: AP/Wide World Photos; p. 1259: AP/Wide World Photos; p. 1260: AP/Wide World Photos; p. 1261: AP/Wide World Photos; p. 1262: AP/Wide World Photos; p. 1263: AP/Wide World Photos; p. 1265: Carl Nesfield; p. 1266: AP/Wide World Photos; p. 1266: Archive Photos; p. 1268: AP/Wide World Photos; p. 1269: AP/Wide World Photos; p. 1270: AP/Wide World Photos; p. 1273: UPI/Bettmann; p. 1274: AP/Wide World Photos; p. 1275: AP/Wide World Photos; p. 1276: National Broadcasting Co.; p. 1276: UPI/Bettmann; p. 1277: AP/Wide World Photos; p. 1278: AP/Wide World Photos; p. 1279: AP/Wide World Photos; p. 1280: AP/Wide World Photos; p. 1281: UPI/Bettmann; p. 1284: AP/Wide World Photos; p. 1286: AP/Wide World Photos; p. 1288: AP/Wide World Photos; p. 1289: AP/Wide World Photos; p. 1290: AP/Wide World Photos; p. 1291: AP/Wide World Photos; p. 1299: AP/Wide World Photos; p. 1300: AP/Wide World Photos.

Military: p. 1304: AP/Wide World Photos; p. 1304: Library of Congress; p. 1305: Library of Congress; p. 1306: AP/Wide World Photos; p. 1307: National Archives; p. 1308: Library of Congress; p. 1310: National Archives; p. 1312: National Archives; p. 1314: United States Army; p. 1316: United States Air Force; p. 1319: United States Army; p. 1323: United States Army; p. 1324: United States Marine Corps; p. 1325: AP/Wide World Photos; p. 1325: United States Marine Corps; p. 1326: United States Navy; p. 1328: United States Air Force: p. 1328: United States Army; p. 1329: National Archives; p. 1331: AP/Wide World Photos; p. 1332: AP/Wide World Photos; p. 1332: United States Navy; p. 1333: UPI/Bettmann; p. 1334: AP/Wide World Photos.

Text

Significant Documents in African-American History: "Lift Every Voice and Sing," p. 176: Used by permission of Edward B. Marks Music Company. "I Have a Dream," pp. 192–95: Reprinted by arrangement with The Heirs to the Estate of Martin Luther King, Jr., c/o Joan Daves Agency as agent for the proprietor; copyright 1963 by Martin Luther King, Jr., copyright renewed 1991 by Coretta Scott King.

Picture and Text Credits

Law: "African-American Federal Judges," p. 510–11: courtesy of NAACP Legal Defense and Educational Fund, Inc.

Entrepreneurship: "Largest Black Companies," pp. 684–89: The Earl G. Graves Publishing co., Inc., 130 Fifth Ave., New York, NY 10011. Copyright June 1993. All rights reserved.

Index

Index

Harper, Frances Ellen Watkins   251, 811
Harper v. Virginia State Board of Elections   52
Harpers Ferry National Historic Park   258
Harpers Ferry, West Virginia   20, 248, 352
Harris, Barbara C.   120, 796
Harris, Leon   866
Harris, Margaret Rosezarion   1013, 1029
Harris, Patricia Roberts   69, 118, 589
Harris, Rupert H.   1124
Harris-Stowe State University   753
Harris, Wynonie   1110
Harrison, Donald   1060
Harrison, Hazel   1029, 1125
Harrison Museum of African American Culture   1220
Harrison, Richard B.   944, 975
Hartford Inquirer   858, 892
Hartigan, Linda Roscoe   1165
Harvey and the Moonglows   1127
Hastie, William H.   34, 109, 113, 548
Hastings, Alcee L.   86, 98, 566
Hatch-Billops Collection, Inc.   1214
Hatch-Billops Studio   1207
Hatcher, Richard B.   66, 68, 79
Hatchett, Joseph W.   548
Hathaway, Donny   1126
Hausa   290, 294, 295
Hawaii Attorney General's Office   398
Hawkins, Coleman   1055, 1078, 1079
Hawkins, June   944
Hawkins v. Board of Control   39, 524
Hawkins, Yusuf K.   89
Hayden, Palmer   1159, 1204
Hayden, Robert E.   814, 832
Hayer, Talmadge   50
Hayes, Elvin   1256
Hayes, Issac   1129
Hayes, Marcella A.   118
Hayes, Roland   1029
Haynes, George Edmond   426
Haynes, Lemuel   105, 248, 339, 359
Haynes, Roy   1079
Hayward, Dubose   252
Hayward, William   1311
Hazel   854

Hazelwood School District v. United States   528
Health   704, 1360, 1373
Healy, James Augustine   107, 796
Healy, Patrick F.   26
Hearns, Thomas   1260
The Heart of a Woman   817, 835
Heart of Atlanta v. United States   536
Heart-Shape in the Dust   832
Height, Bob   942
Height, Dorothy I.   437
Helen Hagen Music Studio   1028
Henderson, Cassandra   866
Henderson, Fletcher   1054, 1056, 1062, 1064, 1079
Henderson, Gordon   1168
Henderson, Joe   1080
Henderson, Julia L.   854
Henderson, Ricky   1255
Henderson v. United States   38
Hendricks, Barbara   1030
Hendrix, James Marshall   1130
Hendrix, Jimi   1111, 1116, 1130, 1139
Hendrix, Johnny Allen   1130
Henrik-Clark, John   736
Henry, Herbert   945
Henry, Ragan A.   872
Henson, Josiah   14, 231, 350, 359
Henson, Matthew Alexander   27, 29, 231, 245, 1233
Herald Dispatch   889
The Herald   894
Herero   294
Heritage Press   885
Hermenway, James   1008
The Hermit Woman   836
Herndon Home   1210
A Hero Ain't Nothing but a Sandwich   824
Herrings, James V.   1159
Herskovits, Melville   410
Hewlet, James   940
Hickman, Fred   866
Higginbotham, Jr., A. Leon   116, 550
Hightower, Gail   1030
The Highway QCs   1124
Hill, Abram   945

Index

Principal of Ethnology: The Origin of Races and Color 414

Professor Griff 1143

Program for Research on Black Americans 762

The Progressive-American 505

Progressive National Baptist Convention 780

Progressive National Baptist Convention, Inc. 791

Progressive National Baptists 782

Project Equality 491

Project Magazines, Inc. 858

Prosser, Gabriel 12, 361, 407

Protestant Episcopal Church 784

Provident Hospital and Training School 228, 1242

Pryor, Richard 954, 991

psychology 1365, 1383

public accommodations 504, 532

Public Enemy 1117, 1143

The Public Post 902

Public Works Employment Act 673

Public Works Employment Act of 1977 517, 543

publishing 1378

Puerto Rico 325

Purlie 950

Purlie Victorious 950

Purviance, Florence 1160

Purvis, William 1224

Puryear, Martin 1193

PUSH-EXCEL 386, 430

Pygmies 273, 280, 309

Q

Quakers 6, 8, 9, 15, 335, 337, 338, 346, 723

Quality Education for Minorities Network 491

Quality Education for Minorities Project 90

The Quality of Hurt: The Autobiography of Chester Himes 833

Quarles, Norma 862, 866, 876

Queen Latifah 1117, 1143

Queen of Sheba 281

Queen's Head Tavern 245

Quicksand 836

Quitman, Cleo 949

Qwaqwa 303

R

Rabah 277

Rabbi Matthew 787

The Rabbit Foot Minstrels 1136

Race and History: Selected Essay 744

Race Contacts and Inter-Racial Relations 745

Race, Fear and Housing in a Typical American Community 854

race records 1109

race relations 1381

Race Relations Abstract 739

Race Relations Institute 762

racial intermarriage 538, 700

racism 1008

Rackley, Alex 61, 446

radio 859, 866

ragtime 961, 1033, 1053, 1054, 1107

Rainbow Commission for Fairness in Athletics 1256

Rainbow Jordan 824

Rainey, Gertrude "Ma" 942, 1094

Rainey, Joseph H. 107, 252, 599

Rainey, William "Pa" 1094

Raisin 832, 950

Raisin in the Sun 945, 950

The Rally 822

Ramirez, Blandina Cardenas 79

Randall, Dudley 876

Randolph, Asa Philip 32, 372, 394, 427, 444, 1315, 1322

Randolph, Virginia 256

Rang Tang 943

Rangel, Charles 600

Rankin, John 249

Ransom, Reverend 779

rap music 1107, 1116, 1117

A Rap on Race 819

Rashad, Phylicia 992

Raspberry, William J. 877

Rastafarians 792

The Ravens 1110

Ravitch, Diane 736

X

Y